# JUDICIAL POLITICS AND
# URBAN REVOLT IN
# SEVENTEENTH-CENTURY FRANCE

# JUDICIAL POLITICS AND URBAN REVOLT IN SEVENTEENTH-CENTURY FRANCE

## The Parlement of Aix, 1629-1659

SHARON KETTERING

PRINCETON UNIVERSITY PRESS

PRINCETON, NEW JERSEY

Copyright © 1978 by Princeton University Press
Published by Princeton University Press, Princeton, New Jersey
In the United Kingdom: Princeton University Press, Guildford, Surrey

All Rights Reserved

Library of Congress Cataloging in Publication Data will
be found on the last printed page of this book

Publication of this book has been aided by a grant from
The Andrew W. Mellon Foundation

This book has been composed in Linotype Times Roman

Printed in the United States of America
by Princeton University Press, Princeton, New Jersey

*For My Father*

# CONTENTS

## Contents

# LIST OF ILLUSTRATIONS

# LIST OF ABBREVIATIONS

| | |
|---|---|
| A.A.E. | Archives des Affaires Etrangères, Paris |
| ADBR, Aix, Marseille | Archives Départementales, Bouches du Rhône |
| A.C., Aix | Archives Communales, Aix |
| A.N. | Archives Nationales, Paris |
| *Annales: ESC* | *Annales: Economies, Sociétés, Civilisations,* a journal published quarterly by Librairie Armand Colin, Paris |
| B.M. | British Museum, London |
| B. Apt | Bibliothèque Municipale, Apt |
| B. Inguimbertine | Bibliothèque Inguimbertine, Carpentras |
| B. Marseille | Bibliothèque Municipale, Marseille |
| B. Mazarine | Bibliothèque Mazarine, Paris |
| B. Méjanes | Bibliothèque Méjanes, Aix |
| B.N. | Bibliothèque Nationale, Paris |
| Delib. Parl. | "Délibérations du Parlement de Provence," B. Méjanes Mss. 951–954 (1629–1659) |
| EDB | *Les Bouches-du-Rhône, encyclopédie départementale,* ed. Paul Masson, 17 vols.; Paris, 1913–1937 |
| M. Arbaud | Musée d'Arbaud, Aix |

Orthography is a problem in studying seventeenth-century France. Not only does the spelling differ from modern usage, but so do accents, capitalization, and punctuation; all were a matter of great personal freedom. Modern rules have been followed, and quotations have been translated into modern English with an attempt to retain some of the flavor of seventeenth-century French. Names have been spelled as they were by their owners according to holograph signatures, and for this reason some individuals appear under their family names, some under their titles, some with or without a partitive.

# ACKNOWLEDGMENTS

The author wishes to thank Orest Ranum, Richard Bonney, Philip Dawson, and A. Lloyd Moote for reading all or part of the manuscript and making helpful suggestions. Peter Berger, William Beik, Margaret Silsby, and Frances Phipps offered encouragement and advice at critical moments. The author is indebted for help to the staffs of the libraries and archives where she has worked, in particular to Florence Chu of the Stanford University Interlibrary Loan, Augustin Roux and Charles Foucquart of the Aix departmental archives, and Madame Déniau-Treppo of the Aix municipal archives. Mary Costabile and Elaine Brasted cheerfully typed the manuscript, and Karen Wood did the illustrations. Grants from Stanford University, the French government, and the National Endowment for the Humanities permitted research trips to France. The author owes special thanks to Lewis Spitz, who first directed her toward history, and to her parents for their encouragement.

JUDICIAL POLITICS AND
URBAN REVOLT IN
SEVENTEENTH-CENTURY FRANCE

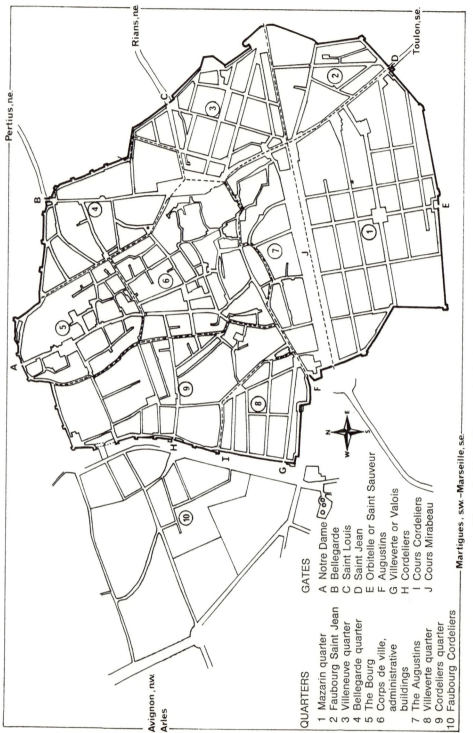

QUARTERS

1 Mazarin quarter
2 Faubourg Saint Jean
3 Villeneuve quarter
4 Bellegarde quarter
5 The Bourg
6 Corps de ville,
   administrative
   buildings
7 The Augustins
8 Villeverte quarter
9 Cordeliers quarter
10 Faubourg Cordeliers

GATES

A Notre Dame
B Bellegarde
C Saint Louis
D Saint Jean
E Orbitelle or Saint Sauveur
F Augustins
G Villeverte or Valois
H Cordeliers
I Cours Cordeliers
J Cours Mirabeau

Pertius, ne.

Rians, ne.

Toulon, se.

Avignon, nw.
Arles

Martigues, sw.—Marseille, se.

Figure 1. Aix-en-Provence in the late seventeenth century

# INTRODUCTION

Reaching the crest of a low hill, a seventeenth-century visitor to Aix-en-Provence saw a cluster of terra-cotta buildings with tile roofs nestled in a shallow valley. The Midi sun was hot; the road was dry and dusty; the air was filled with the pungent smell of pine. Riding through the open fields and gardens of the suburbs, he followed the city walls until he reached the southeastern Saint Jean gate, where strangers customarily entered. The walls are gone today, and rows of slender, dark-green cypress trees mark the entrance to the town. Once inside, he may have followed the narrow, cobblestoned streets toward the domed palace of justice and the spire of the cathedral. Near the top of a winding street of mansions, opposite the cathedral, stood the hôtel Maynier d'Oppède. Its carriage entrance of carved wooden doors led to a small paved courtyard where visitors were greeted, and a large tree-lined courtyard where their carriages waited. The Forbin-Mayniers, barons d'Oppède, lived here for nearly two centuries and four were first presidents of the Parlement. The hôtel itself was the scene of revolts in 1630, 1649, and 1659. Appropriately, it now houses the archives where an historian begins his efforts to understand the parlementaires of Aix and their revolts.

An angry crowd stormed the hôtel on September 19, 1630, looking for fugitive royal commissioner Dreux d'Aubray and the Parlement's first president, Vincent-Anne de Forbin-Maynier d'Oppède. Both men eluded the crowd and fled Aix. The first president died five months later from a stroke at Avignon. On January 20, 1649, a group of parlementaires used the hôtel as a headquarters for revolt. Erecting barricades on surrounding streets, brandishing swords and pistols, they marched in their red judicial robes to occupy the town hall and courthouse, imprisoning the governor and sending his troops from Aix. A leader of the second revolt was Henri de Forbin-Maynier d'Oppède, whose father had been first president of the Parlement in 1630. Ten years later, on February 14, 1659, another mob stormed the hôtel looking for Henri himself, now first president and acting intendant. An angry crowd also occupied the courthouse. With typical courage, Oppède scat-

3

tered the men in the streets and pushed his way through a crowd of angry Aixois in the courthouse to attend a session of the Parlement. By late afternoon, the crowd was threatening to throw him from a window; he was saved by the archbishop of Aix. A crowd attempting to storm and sack his hôtel on the next day were stopped by his servants firing from the windows.

A small town in the Midi, Aix drowsed in the heat of the Provençal sun, its inhabitants following a placid routine adjusted to the sun, the church bells, and the seasons. Yet, three times in the early seventeenth century revolts exploded within its quiet streets, shattering the calm. There were several hundred urban and rural uprisings scattered across France in the years from 1620 to 1660, the greatest number in the west and the south.[1] The protests culminated in the Fronde, a national aggregation of revolts from 1648 to 1653.

The parlementaires of Aix encouraged and made use of revolts that at first glance seemed popular and spontaneous. They were aided by relatives, friends, and clients—nobles, gentlemen, municipal and provincial officials, magistrates of the Cour des Comptes and the seneschal court of Aix. The 1630 revolt at Aix had the most popular support, the 1649 revolt the least. Roland Mousnier has described this type of pseudo-popular protest led by members of the provincial ruling elite.[2] Uprisings in the provincial capital were serious because they disrupted the provincial government. But local revolts in the seventeenth century needed to unite several

---

[1] See Boris Porchnev, *Les soulèvements populaires en France de 1623 à 1648* (Paris, 1963); or Y.-M. Bercé, *Histoire des Croquants: Etude des soulèvements populaires au XVII<sup>e</sup> siècle dans le sud-ouest de la France*, 2 vols. (Paris, 1974).

[2] Roland Mousnier is one of the most prolific and best known of contemporary French historians. His seminal study, *La vénalité des offices sous Henri IV et Louis XIII*, first appeared at Rouen in 1945. His classic rebuttal of the Porchnev thesis is entitled "Recherches sur les soulèvements populaires en France avant la Fronde," *Revue d'histoire moderne et contemporaine*, 5 (1958), 81–113. Another rebuttal appears in *Lettres et mémoires adressés au chancelier Séguier (1633-1649)*, 2 vols. (Paris, 1964), I, 187–192. A good summary of the Porchnev-Mousnier controversy is provided by J.H.M. Salmon, "Venality of Office and Popular Sedition in Seventeenth Century France," *Past and Present*, 37 (1967), 26–47. A succinct summary in English of Mousnier's views can be found in "The Fronde," *Preconditions of Revolution in Early Modern Europe*, ed. Robert Forster and Jack Greene (Baltimore, 1970), pp. 131–159.

4

social groups, including an elite, and paralyze a major city or region before they frightened the Paris government. When rebel parlementaires, with their potential of establishing an alternate government, forged an uneasy temporary union with ordinary Aixois, they frightened the crown.

Members of a provincial high court, the parlementaires were dedicated by profession to the maintenance of law and order. Yet they rebelled, and our purpose here is to discover why. In 1624, Richelieu became the chief minister of Louis XIII, launching a hidden war against the Habsburgs, which became open in 1635 and continued until 1659. The underlying causes of the revolts were the crown's relentless taxation to finance its long-term Habsburg war, which alienated the popular classes, and its clumsy attempts to centralize the provincial administration, which angered the privileged classes. Richelieu and Mazarin conducted a national offensive against uncooperative local authorities. In Provence, their offensive was directed against the sovereign courts of the Parlement and Cour des Comptes, provincial Estates and General Assemblies, procureurs du pays, governors, and municipal governments. Eight traditional privileges of these institutions were suspended or seriously weakened by agents of the crown. The parlementaires rebelled to protect their authority and privileges from attack by the crown.

The basic source for the customary constitution of Provence was the will of the last count of Provence, Charles III of Anjou, who left the county to King Louis XI of France on December 10, 1481, with the stipulation "not only to embrace, cherish, and receive the said Provence and adjacent lands . . . but to conserve it and maintain it in its parts, conventions, privileges, liberties, franchises, statutes, charters, exemptions, and prerogatives, as well as in its usages, manners, styles, and customs."[3] The king of France, in inheriting the county, accepted the will's condition that he recognize existing privileges and liberties. His representative, Palamède de Forbin, first president of the Aix Chambre des Comptes and later governor, convoked the Estates of Provence on January 15, 1482, to secure approval for the new count-king. As evidence

[3] ADBR, Marseille, B 704; text partially reprinted by Félix Tavernier, *Marseille et la Provence sous la royauté, 1481–1789* (Marseille, n.d.), pp. 14–15. Also see Gustave Arnaud d'Agnel, *Politique des rois de France en Provence*, 2 vols. (Paris, 1914), II, 61–64, 68–94, 126–130.

5

of the king's good will, Forbin presented a cahier of fifty-three articles defining the traditional liberties and privileges of Provence. The first six articles of the cahier promised observance of Provençal privileges, judgment *in situ* of all civil and criminal cases, resident royal officials, and provincial autonomy under a royal lieutenant. These articles were read aloud to the Estates and greeted with such enthusiasm that the other, less agreeable, forty-seven articles were approved without a reading. Each king, thereafter, in ratifying the union of Provence with the throne of France, promised to recognize its traditional privileges.[4]

Although the cahier of 1482 was the basic source in law for the customary constitution of Provence, its definition in fact depended upon the interpretation of local institutions, in particular provincial law courts and law codes, and the crown's recognition in royal legislation registered by the Parlement.[5] The customary constitution was vague and ill-defined. It served as a convenient rallying cry for the parlementaires, who never clarified its substance. Historians of Provence have agreed that the customary constitution included at least five traditional privileges: the king of France reigning in Provence as its count and signing himself as such in legislation, regularly observed since it was only a matter of protocol; the registration of legislation by the Conseil éminent, ancestor of the Parlement; the city of Aix recognized as the administrative capital; the consent of the provincial Estates for taxation; and its member communities serving as the tax-collecting agents.[6] This list should include four other privileges: the observance of customary procedures in municipal elections; the exemption of Aix, Arles, Marseille, and Tarascon from troop billeting; the approval of the procureurs du pays, interim executive authority of the provincial

<hr />

[4] ADBR, Marseille, B 19, fol. 162 ff.; C 2053, fol. 2; Edouard Baratier, ed., *Documents de l'histoire de la Provence* (Toulouse, 1971), pp. 148–153; and ed., *Histoire de la Provence* (Toulouse, 1969), pp. 219–221.

[5] See Jacques Mourgues, *Les statuts et coutumes du pays de Provence* (Aix, 1642); Jean Bomy, *Statuts et coutumes du pays de Provence* (Aix, 1620); and J. Tholosan, *Privilèges, franchises et immunités concédés par les rois et comtes de Provence à la ville d'Aix* (Aix, 1620).

[6] Raoul Busquet, EDB, III, 281–282; Charles de Ribbe, *Pascalis: Etude sur la fin de la Constitution provençale, 1781–1790* (Paris, 1854), pp. 37–45; Pierre-Albert Robert, *Les remontrances et arrêtés du Parlement de Provence au XVIIIᵉ siècle, 1715–1790* (Paris, 1912), pp. 363–382.

Estates, for troop billeting and payment; and the Parlement's Grand'Chambre acting as governor in the absence of the governor and the lieutenant general.

Royal attacks on Provençal privileges took many forms. The crown forced the Parlement's registration of unwanted edicts in 1641 and 1648. It ignored the Parlement's right to register or remonstrate on edicts in 1638 and 1657 by ordering enforcement without registration. The company's first president became acting intendant of justice in 1657 without royal letters of commission; the Parlement refused to register such letters. The Grand'Chambre of the Parlement permanently lost its right to act as governor to the first president-intendant in 1657. The crown attacked the position of Aix as the administrative capital in 1631 and 1659, with threats to transfer its judicial courts. An abortive attempt in 1629 to suspend the right of the provincial Estates to collect the taille was followed by the crown's refusal to convene the Estates after 1639 and its replacement by the General Assembly of the Communities. The governors attempted taxation by ordinance without approval of the Estates, General Assemblies, or their interim executive authority, the procureurs du pays, in 1625, 1628, 1633–1634, and 1658. In the name of the crown, the governors suspended elections and appointed members of the Aix municipal government in fourteen of twenty-nine municipal elections from 1631 to 1659. Municipal elections were also regularly suspended at Arles, Marseille, Tarascon, Draguignan, Toulon, Brignoles, Grasse, and other Provençal communities. Ordinances of the governors assigning troop billets in Provence were issued without the *attache* or approval of the procureurs du pays in 1629, 1637, 1648–1649, and 1658. As punishment for disobedience, royal troops were billeted on Aix in 1631, 1649, 1652, and 1658. By 1661, at least eight traditional privileges had been repeatedly ignored and suspended by the crown.

The Aix parlementaires led three protests against the crown within three decades; they organized into an opposition party; they were implicated in two murders; large numbers were cited in disciplinary legislation; their struggles with the crown were intense enough to paralyze the court's operation from 1641 to 1649, when they incited a temporarily successful revolt. But the classic explanation that the parlementaires were defending the customary con-

7

stitution and privileges of Provence does not explain the length, intensity, or tenacity of their resistance.[7]

Only four of the ten parlements in France rebelled in 1648 and 1649. Their protests were later expanded by an unruly provincial nobility into a civil war that lasted until 1653. The Fronde has always been a difficult event to grasp in its entirety because of its shifting casts of characters and scenes, its paradoxical nature and complexity. Historians have engaged in a controversy on its causes and significance for more than a century.[8] The Parlement of Aix rebelled on January 20, 1649, and this revolt—the apogee of the parlementaires' power and influence—presented a serious challenge to royal authority. The progress of bureaucratic centralization in Provence was blocked by the peace treaty ending the revolt, and the crown temporarily abandoned its offensive against the parlementaires' authority and privileges. Six months later, the revolt escalated into the Provençal Fronde, during which factions of the provincial nobility fought for and against the governor and Mazarin's government. Only a small group of parlementaires participated in the Provençal Fronde, and the Parlement as an institution joined the crown and Mazarin after a year's hesitation. Mazarin resumed the offensive in his program of bureaucratic centralization in 1655. He used the 1659 revolt at Aix as a pretext to destroy the Parlement's opposition, ending serious protest

[7] An example of the classic constitutional interpretation of the parlementaires' role in the revolts is offered by Raoul Busquet, EDB III, 371: "After the troubles at the beginning of the reign of Louis XIII, in which Provence was not involved, the royal government, served by a minister of formidable energies, became essentially authoritarian and tended to destroy what remained of provincial liberties. The *Etats* [Estates] appeared as weak and uncertain defenders of the 'Constitution.' Armed with the right of *enregistrement*, the Parlement, therefore, filled the function of register to the undertakings of the central government and became of primary significance, not as the usurper of the direction of provincial affairs, but as the guardian of the privileges of the province." This view has been shared by Charles-François Bouche, *Essai sur l'histoire de Provence* (Marseille, 1785); Prosper Cabasse, *Essais historiques sur le Parlement de Provence*, 3 vols. (Paris, 1826); and Paul Gaffaret, "La Fronde en Provence," *Revue historique*, 2 (1876), 60–103 and 5 (1877), 20–67, among others.

[8] Good introductions to the immense body of literature on the Fronde are provided by Ernst Kossmann, *La Fronde* (Leiden, 1954); A. Lloyd Moote, *The Revolt of the Judges: The Parlement of Paris and the Fronde, 1643–1652* (Princeton, 1971); and Boris Porchnev, *Les soulèvements populaires en France (1623–1648)* (Paris, 1963).

in that city for a century. The parlementaire Fronde at Aix was only one episode in a three-decade struggle against the crown that began with the 1630 revolt and ended with the 1659 revolt.

The parlementaire Fronde at Aix in 1649 is here discussed in terms of the uprisings that preceded and followed it, emphasizing the continuity in leadership provided by an opposition party of parlementaires. Although they were among the most militant of their colleagues in the high courts of France, there have been no studies of the Aix parlementaires in the seventeenth century, as André Bourde has observed.[9] A goal of this book has been to recreate the politics, motives, and atmosphere of the Parlement of Aix in the mid-seventeenth century. The Parlement has been treated as an institution with a corporate life and personality of its own, as well as a company of individual magistrates. Most historical studies of the Fronde have concentrated upon the Parlement of Paris. This study provides insight into the actions and motivations of a Midi parlement. As Boris Porchnev has noted, the politics of a provincial court such as Aix need investigation before we can fully understand the Fronde.[10] Another goal of this book has been a better understanding of the role of royal officials such as parlementaires in seventeenth-century revolts.

French historians Roland Mousnier, Madeleine Foisil, Yves-Marie Bercé, and René Pillorget among others have sought general models and patterns to explain seventeenth-century uprisings.[11] Classifying events and constructing hierarchies of types and subtypes to characterize the revolts as a whole have occupied their attention, and they have shown a tendency to emphasize socioeconomic causation. René Pillorget has recently completed an ex-

[9] André Bourde, "La Provence Baroque (1596–1660)," in *Histoire de la Provence* (Toulouse, 1969), ed. Edouard Baratier, p. 304. The standard studies of the Parlement of Aix are by Louis Wolff, *Le Parlement de Provence au XVIIIᵉ siècle* (Aix, 1920), and *La vie des parlementaires provençaux au XVIᵉ siècle* (Marseille, 1924); also *Les remontrances et arrêtés du Parlement de Provence au XVIIIᵉ siècle, 1715–1790* (Paris, 1912) by Pierre-Albert Robert.

[10] Porchnev, *Soulèvements populaires*, p. 151.

[11] Mousnier, *Lettres et mémoires*, introduction; and *Fureurs paysannes: Les paysans dans les révoltes du XVIIᵉ siècle (France, Russie, Chine)* (Paris, 1967); Madeleine Foisil, *La révolte des Nu-Pieds et les révoltes normandes de 1639* (Paris, 1970); Bercé, *Histoire des Croquants*; René Pillorget, *Les mouvements insurrectionnels de Provence entre 1596 et 1715* (Paris, 1975).

tensive study of Provençal revolts from 1596 to 1715. Breaking away from the controversy over Marxist class divisions, Pillorget uses a new principle of classification, the "corps politique," a group of individuals or families having a legal existence and exercising political rights. The "corps politique" of seventeenth-century Provence was the community.[12] Pillorget sees three basic types of community insurrections: violence within the community, the community against outside authority such as a seigneur, bishop, or royal official, and communities in the plural as provincial institutions or groups protesting against royal authority.[13]

Without discounting the importance of this approach, we view the revolts at Aix from a different perspective. Looking at the provincial government as a living organism composed of independent political authorities whose identity comes through their functioning as a whole, we have studied the behavior of one member institution, the Parlement, in relation to the whole. We have also studied the court's internal politics, the behavior and relationships of its individual members. We have attempted to understand politics and personalities, the variable causes of revolts that are often ignored. We have concluded that provincial, municipal, and judicial politics—the external and internal relationships of the Parlement and its members—were as important in causing the revolts at Aix as economic problems or authority struggles with the crown. René Pillorget has created types or models to explain the basic structures of revolts in seventeenth-century Provence, and his concept of community has been used as a principle of classification. We have instead investigated the behavior of one social group within a specific community in order to show that the local politics of the parlementaires as individuals was important in causing the revolts at Aix. Investigating the local politics of other elite groups, as well as their difficulties with the crown, should prove a fruitful new approach to understanding revolts in seventeenth-century France.

Why were the Aix parlementaires militant for three decades?

---

[12] *Webster's Seventh New Collegiate Dictionary* (Springfield, Mass., 1963), p. 168, gives the primary definition of community as, "a unified body of individuals," which is further defined as, "the people with common interests living in a particular area" and "an interacting population of various kinds of individuals in a common location."

[13] Pillorget, *Les mouvements*, pp. 151–153.

10

What explains the duration and tenacity of their resistance? The proverbial volatility and violence of the southern temperament—the rowdy behavior and rough disorderliness of a company of Midi magistrates—is a possible explanation, and the turbulence and violence of seventeenth-century life is another. But the author hesitates to dismiss three decades of protest as a quirk of temperament or an accident of manners. The parlementaires' fear of losing income and prestige derived from hereditary officeholding is the cause, in Roland Mousnier's opinion, while the parlementaires' desire to protect their political authority from the crown's encroachments is well known. But none of these is entirely satisfactory in explaining why the Aix parlementaires led three revolts within three decades. The crown attacked the privileges of other seventeenth-century officials, who did not react as violently, for instance, the Trésoriers Généraux of Aix. Only four of the ten parlements in France revolted in 1649, not all with the same intensity, and the neighboring Midi parlements of Toulouse and Grenoble did not openly rebel. The other high courts were calm in 1659. So we return to our original question: why were the Aix parlementaires militant for three decades?

The answer lies in judicial politics, the alliances and feuds within the Parlement of Aix, and the interaction of its members with other provincial and municipal officials, which have so far been neglected. An informally organized opposition party developed within the Parlement after 1631 and was sporadically active until 1659. The opposition was successful when its members overcame their internal feuding, coordinated their protests, and organized to play an active political role. But their success was temporary: chronic feuding permitted their eventual dispersion and destruction. Even the sporadic existence of an opposition, however, helps to explain the intensity, length, and success of their resistance. The Aix parlementaires rebelled to protect their investments in hereditary officeholding and political authority. But their rebellion was incited by a sporadically unified opposition and intensified by judicial politics.

Although this is a study of the parlementaires, a general statement is needed on the nature of the revolts. The Aix revolts were political conflicts with strong economic and social overtones. They were not social conflicts or class struggles, although they occasionally had some of these characteristics. Tension between old

11

and new members of established social groups exploded into violence in 1649, when anciens officiers fought against the newly created Parlement of the Semester sitting for six months of the year, while factions of the nobility fought during the Fronde. But these tensions occurred between levels and subdivisions of groups, not between separate social groups. The lines between new and old officials and nobles were too blurred for separate social classification. The necessary unity, solidarity, and self-awareness were lacking. Nor were the Aix revolts solely protests against royal taxation, whether direct, as the taille, or indirect, as the new creations of judicial offices. Nor were they solely protests against troop billeting. The crown's economic demands were an important cause of the revolts, but there were also important political causes.

The political crisis at Aix throws new light on the power relationships and administrative patterns of seventeenth-century Provence, pays d'états, region of the taille réelle, and frontier province often neglected by institutional historians. French administrative history has long been constricted by an abstractly institutional approach. Officials are too often viewed legalistically through their duties and responsibilities, attached to their offices as so many stiff, elongated figures on a Romanesque portal. But the stress of a political crisis animates key provincial officials and spotlights the functioning of the provincial government. Power alignments and personal factors influencing the behavior of provincial governors, intendants of justice, Estates, archbishops, and municipal governments can be observed, albeit from the vantage point of the Parlement. The operation of the provincial government centered at Aix can be observed in the crisis of the revolts.

The book proceeds on three levels. It explores the causes of the Aix revolts, the role of the parlementaires in the revolts, and the functioning of important provincial and municipal institutions as they affected the revolts. The three levels blend because the politics and personalities of these institutions and their members, particularly the parlementaires, were a major cause of the uprisings. We hope the composite picture contributes to a better understanding of the role of royal magistrates in seventeenth-century revolts.

*Chapter One*

# PROVINCIAL AND MUNICIPAL POLITICS
# AT AIX

A remote corner of southeastern France, Provence had a two hundred-mile Mediterranean coastline stretching from northern Italy to the banks of the Rhone river. Westward beyond the Rhone was the province of Languedoc; northward through the foothills of the Alps lay Dauphiné. The seventeenth-century boundaries of Provence were the Var river on the east near Nice, the second branch of the Rhone on the west, and the headwaters of the Durance river on the north. The Durance also separated Provence from the papal principality of the Comtat Venaissin. Originating in the Alps, the Durance followed a U-shaped course two hundred miles south to empty into the Rhone below Avignon, capital of the Comtat. Provence was one of the smallest French provinces in the seventeenth century. One-half of the northwest region bordering on the Rhone, the modern department of the Vaucluse, was the papal Comtat Venaissin, with its enclave of Orange governed by the Dutch house of Nassau. Two-thirds of the southeastern Mediterranean coast, the modern department of the Alpes-Maritimes, was the Savoyard county of Nice with its enclave of Monaco, a feudal principality governed by princes of the Grimaldi family.

Aix-en-Provence, the traditional administrative capital, was approximately five hundred miles southeast of Paris. In the seventeenth century, that distance for the ordinary traveler and the regular mail took about one week to cover on horseback, depending on the season, weather, and urgency of the trip. Important news by special courier took four or five days. In 1627, a weekly post was established from Aix to Lyon and extended a few years later to Paris.[1] Because of the distance, an unavoidable delay of at least

[1] B.N., Cinq Cents de Colbert 288, fols. 11, 12–14, 18–20. Letters and packages left Aix for Lyon every Sunday and Lyon for Paris every Wednesday; cf. Emile Pérrier, *L'hôtel et le château d'un financier aixois au XVII<sup>e</sup> siècle* (Valence, 1902), pp. 237–238, reprinted from *Répertoire des travaux*

a week occurred in sending a dispatch to Paris and receiving a response.

A faster, more comfortable means of traveling to Provence than by horseback or carriage was to rent passage in a small cargo boat going down the Rhone from Lyon. The Rhone was a swift-flowing river with treacherous currents well known for navigational difficulties and danger in narrow spots, particularly in winter when the mistral blew. Travelers avoided going south by boat in early spring, when the mountain snow and ice were melting and the river was at its height. The northward return journey was made on horseback, because it was harder to go up the Rhone against the current.

Provence in late spring was a pleasant surprise to travelers from a cold, grey north still in the grip of winter: the countryside was in full bloom, a fragrant blend of the scents of juniper, thyme, laurel, rosemary, and lavender growing wild on the hillsides. Visitors, for instance Jean-Jacques Bouchard in 1630 and Madame de Sévigné in 1694, commented on the sweet smell of the Provençal countryside.[2] The maquis, the hillside underbrush, was a mass of wildflowers in May and June, white heather and myrtle, red and white rock roses, yellow broom and gorse. The sun shone every day. It was warm but not uncomfortably hot, and the air was very clear.

Travelers to Provence have left accounts of their experiences which are a good introduction to its regional peculiarities. Life in Provence had Mediterranean and Italian characteristics that seemed exotic and foreign to travelers from the north. Jean-Jacques Bouchard, traveling to Rome in December 1630, described a land of low hills, valleys, and small villages, whose inhabitants in their dress, style of dwelling, and demeanor resembled the Italian. Bouchard noted that "clothes are strongly Italian, primarily for the women, who dress in all sorts of materials and colors with-

---

*de la Société statistique*, Marseille 45 (1900–1903), 234–266. Maps of Provence may be found in: Edouard Baratier, *et al.*, *Atlas historique: Provence, Comtat Venaissin, Principauté d'Orange, Comté de Nice, Principauté de Monaco* (Paris, 1969).

[2] *Les confessions de Jean-Jacques Bouchard, parisien, suivis de son voyage de Paris à Rome en 1630* (Paris, 1881), p. 123; Louis Monmerqué, ed., *Lettres de Madame de Sévigné*, 14 vols. (Paris, 1862–1866), X, 191–194, September 9, 1694.

14

out regarding the appropriateness or the overall appearance."[3]
Thomas Platter had made the same observation when he visited
Marseille in February 1596.[4] He wrote that the women wore skirts
and blouses of stripes and wildly assorted colors, resembling par-
rots. He and Bouchard both commented that the Marseillaises were
not shy. Charles de Brosses, a president in the Parlement of Dijon,
traveling to Venice in July 1739, remarked on the Italian qualities
of speech and dress when he came ashore at Avignon. He also
noticed the Italian style of architecture and the lack of window
glass at Aix, and the numbers of people in the streets at all hours
in Marseille.[5] Bouchard found the food highly spiced, and he described a dish that he had never seen before, couscous.[6] He noted
that the Provençaux were strong regionalists: "The Provençaux
distrust all other nations, and above all those whom they call
Frenchmen, called derisively *Francimants*, who are those from the
Loire and pass in this *pays* for foreigners as much as Germans in
Paris."[7]

The French name of the province originated in its Latin name,
Provincia. Provence became a Roman colony around the first century B.C., and Marseille was a Greek settlement several hundred
years before that. By the treaty of Verdun in 843, Provence became
part of the kingdom of Lotharingia, with Burgundy and Lorraine.
Passing from hand to hand, the county of Provence officially became part of the Holy Roman Empire in the eleventh century, with
virtual autonomy and self-government, and in the twelfth century
it became a possession of the counts of Toulouse, then of the
counts of Barcelona. In 1246, Charles of Anjou, brother of Louis
IX, king of France, married the daughter of the count of Barcelona and became count of Provence. The house of Anjou ruled the
county until December 1481, when the last count of Provence,
Charles III, who was without heirs, willed the county to his cousin

[3] Bouchard, *Confessions*, pp. 143–146.

[4] *Félix et Thomas Platter à Montpellier, 1552–1559, 1595–1599: Notes
de voyage de deux étudiants bâlois* (Montpellier, 1892), p. 307.

[5] Charles de Brosses, *Lettres familières sur l'Italie*, 2d ed. (Paris, 1969),
pp. 30–37.

[6] Bouchard, *Confessions*, pp. 145–147.

[7] *Ibid.*, p. 143. The Mediterranean characteristics of Provençal life are
described by Maurice Agulhon, *La vie sociale en Provence intérieure au
lendemain de la Révolution* (Paris, 1970); and Edouard Baratier, ed., *Histoire de la Provence* (Toulouse, 1969).

Louis XI, king of France. The county was officially attached to the kingdom of France in 1486. With a long history of independence, Provence retained a distinct identity and strong feelings of regionalism. In the seventeenth century, it was one of the most individual and unruly of French provinces.

Its people spoke Provençal, an old romance tongue descended from vulgar Latin and a dialect of the langue d'oc, the language of the troubadours, with a poetic tradition dating back to the twelfth century. It is musical when spoken, with open vowels, sounded final syllables, and partial nasals, as in Italian. A Provençal accent in modern French retains these characteristics. Francis I ordered in the 1539 edict of Villers-Cotterets that French be used in official documents in Provence, and thereafter the ability to speak French became a determinant of social status.[8] The peasant spoke only Provençal, and if he knew French at all, he spoke it badly. Arthur Young, an Englishman on his way to Italy in 1790, wrote that he could not converse with the peasants from whom he rented mules and donkeys because they spoke only Provençal, and he spoke only French.[9] The Provençal bourgeois spoke good French, and was ordinarily bilingual. The noble spoke good Provençal, but he ordinarily used French, and he was not fully bilingual. The educated and wealthy spoke French at home, but they spoke Provençal to their tenant farmers and servants. The regional peculiarities of Provence must not be exaggerated, but in general the province impressed the rest of France as exotic and foreign.

There were three natural regions: Basse-Provence, Haute-Provence, and the coast. Prosperous and populated, Basse-Provence was a rolling, fertile region of plains, hills, and small valleys where wheat, vines, and olives were cultivated. The three largest cities formed an obtuse triangle at the mouth of the Rhone: the apex at Marseille, the long leg at Arles in the west, and the short leg at Aix, northeast of Marseille.

The wildest, poorest, and most desolate region was the mountainous interior, Haute-Provence, the foothills of the Alps. It was difficult to travel here because the roads washed out, and winters

[8] ADBR, Aix, B 3315; Agulhon, *La vie sociale*, p. 114.

[9] Arthur Young, *Travels in France during the Years 1787, 1788, and 1789* (Cambridge, 1929), pp. 237–238. Also see Auguste Brun, *Recherches historiques sur l'introduction du français dans les provinces du Midi* (Paris, 1923).

were colder than in the rest of Provence. Nothing grew beyond
the tree line. The peaks were bare, while the mountainsides were
covered with an aromatic heavy growth of pine, oak, and scrub
brush. Villages were walled fortresses with steep narrow streets,
winding stairs, and split-level houses that perched and sometimes
clung to inaccessible spots on cliff edges and mountain peaks.
They were built for protection in a more dangerous era. While
Basse-Provence was a region of scattered and isolated farms,
Haute-Provence was a region of walled villages surrounded by cultivated land and terraced hillsides.

The coastal region of Provence enjoyed spectacular scenery. The
traveler from Genoa to Marseille rode along a narrow, winding
road cut high into coastal mountains plunging directly into the
Mediterranean. Bare ridges and needle-sharp peaks of bleached
limestone pushed their way through the reddish soil into the sun.
Vines, olives, and small orchards of fruit trees were cultivated
along a coast dotted with fishing villages. The ports of Marseille
and Toulon were home to the royal galleys and Mediterranean
fleet.

Provence received less rain than the north, and it rained only
during the winter months. The spring, summer, and autumn were
too dry to grow most crops successfully without irrigation, which
was not widely used. There were no large forests; pasturage was
inadequate; and the province occasionally had to import wheat,
which it did not produce in sufficient quantity. Dairy products were
scarce because there was not enough pasturage for large animals.
Cooking was thus done with olive oil rather than butter and animal
fat, as in the rest of France. The stony slopes made the wooden
sabots worn by peasants elsewhere in France impractical, and so
Provence was the region of the espadrille, a shoe with canvas top
and rope bottom. The two great natural assets of Provence, its sun
and coastal scenery, had no value before 1848, when the railroad
linking Avignon and Marseille was completed, and quick, easy
access to the Côte d'Azur by railroad and Rhone steamer made
coastal Provence one of the wealthiest, most famous, and populous
regions in France. The isolation and insignificance of Provence in
the seventeenth century is hard to realize because of these modern
changes.

Distant, small, and foreign, Provence had political importance
to the central government in Paris because it was a gateway to the

17

Habsburg-Bourbon battlefields of northern Italy, and it had a long, undefended coastline. Provence was strategically situated for the transport of supplies, munitions, and recruits to the royal armies in Italy. It was invaded three times during the sixteenth century by Habsburg forces, again in 1635, and twice in the early eighteenth century. It is not an exaggeration to compare Provence to the medieval English marches on the borders of Scotland and Wales: the province was a buffer area in the crown's defensive strategy against the Habsburgs, meant to cushion French contact with the political turmoil in northern Italy. Richelieu and Mazarin were interested in obedience from this buffer area. They were impatient with its independence, and hostile to its preservation of different traditions.

The two hundred-mile coastline of Provence was virtually undefended in 1626, when Richelieu set in motion plans to rebuild its coastal fortifications, construct new fortresses, and increase the size and number of coastal garrisons. The Provençal coast had been periodically ravaged by Moslems since the early eighth century, when Saracens sailed up the Rhone and regularly plundered the Mediterranean coast. Turks threatened the trade of Marseille in the sixteenth century. Barbary pirates frequently disrupted the coastal trade with North Africa. When Henri de Séguiran made a journey of inspection along the coast in 1633 as Richelieu's new lieutenant-general of commerce and navigation for Provence, he reported that Barbary pirates had hijacked forty small and four large sailing ships from Cassis in twenty years, and that La Ciotat had posted a twenty-four hour municipal lookout for pirates.[10] Martigues lost eighty men in four months, kidnapped by pirates from Algiers and Tunis as rowers for their galleys.[11] In May 1631, intendant Aubray reported that the *Notre Dame*, a ship worth 500,000 livres, had been taken by North African corsairs; and in March 1633, pirates from Tunis and Algiers seized five ships at Toulon and one at Marseille.[12] In December 1646, raiding Barbary

[10] Henri de Séguiran, "Procès-verbal contentant l'état véritable auquel sont de present les affaires de la côte maritime de Provence," B.N., Ms. fr. 24169, fols. 2–61.

[11] Hubert Méthivier, "Richelieu et le front de mer de Provence," *Revue historique*, 185 (1939), 124.

[12] *Ibid.*; A. D. Lublinskaya, ed., *Vnutrenniaia politika frantsuzskogo absoliutizma, 1633–1649* (Leningrad, 1966), pp. 230–231, intendant de La

corsairs took several ships and six washerwomen from Marseille.[13]

The crown was anxious to maintain a strong image of authority in a frontier province, considering rightly that its image was tarnished when royal officials sworn to uphold the throne rebelled in the provincial capital. Revolts at Aix slowed the transport of troops and supplies to the Italian battlefields by disrupting or temporarily paralyzing the provincial government concentrated in the capital. Revolts demonstrated internal weakness, which invited Spanish attack, such as the landing on two unfortified islands off the coast at Cannes in September 1635, or the expedition across the Pyrénées in 1638.[14] The duc de Feria, governor of Milan, was ordered to concentrate a force of two thousand Italians and five hundred Spanish for possible use in Provence during the 1631 cascaveoux revolt. Revolts in Provence offered a base for Spanish invasion similar to the French exploitation of the Catalonian revolt in 1640. The memory of the League remained strong in Provence. As late as 1605, an ex-Leaguer intrigued to deliver Marseille into Spanish hands.[15] The king's physical presence was often necessary to remind subjects of royal authority and to enforce obedience, but the king only visited Provence officially in 1600, 1622, and 1660. He could not as easily appear in person to quell a revolt or force registration of an edict as he could in the north, and there was an unavoidable delay of several weeks in communication. Mazarin wrote on June 9, 1651, that "the two most unsafe provinces in France are Guyenne and Provence, which can receive with ease assistance from Spain and the Spanish states in Italy and whose inhabitants are naturally inclined to revolt."[16] The cardinal had

---

Potherie to Séguier, April 4, 1633. Corsair attacks caused a riot at Marseille on March 4, 1620; cf. Edouard Baratier, ed., *Documents de l'histoire de la Provence* (Toulouse, 1971), pp. 191–193.

[13] Lublinskaya, *Vnutrenniaia*, p. 320, Alais to Séguier, December 25, 1646.

[14] See Chapter Two for the 1635 invasion.

[15] Carl Burckhardt, *Richelieu and His Age: Power Politics and the Cardinal's Death*, tr. Bernard Hoy (New York, 1970), p. 283; René Pillorget, "Luttes de factions et intérêts économiques à Marseille de 1598 à 1618," *Annales: ESC*, 27 (1972), 708. Ex-consul of Aix Forbin de La Barben wrote from Tarascon in May 1631 that he feared an Italian invasion; cf. A.A.E., 800, fols. 43–44.

[16] Pierre-Adolphe Chéruel and Georges d'Avenel, *Lettres du cardinal Mazarin pendant son ministère*, 9 vols. (Paris, 1872–1906), IV, 255.

written in March 1649 that revolt seemed endemic to Provence, while intendant Sève feared the consequences of the Provençal Fronde because it left the coast exposed to Spanish galleys.[17] Remote from Paris in distance and customs, Provence had military importance and a deserved reputation for recalcitrance. These factors help to explain the crown's impatience with regional customs and insistence on political and military security at all costs.

Aix and Marseille were ancient rivals. The heart of each city illustrates their differences. The heart of Marseille was her excellent natural harbor, a long rectangle stretching inland with the island fortress-prison Château d'If guarding the entrance. Visitors Thomas Platter in 1597, Jean-Jacques Bouchard in 1630, and Charles de Brosses in 1739 found the harbor of Marseille fascinating. There was a multitude of boats at anchor: lateen-rigged royal galleys with twenty-five long oars on a side; Italian feluccas and Spanish tartanes, long-oared and lateen-rigged for coastal trading; caïques, oared Mediterranean fishing boats without sail; great merchant ships with armed escorts. The quais were busy at all hours. Exotic goods were sold directly from the ships: coral, pearls, African animals, spices, silks, drugs, tropical fruits.[18] Merchants, bankers, tax farmers, manufacturers, naval personnel, and foreigners lived in Marseille, whose atmosphere they found congenial. The city was an important Mediterranean port and manufacturing center. Its population, commerce, and industry were triple those of Aix by 1690.

The Bourg was the heart of Aix, and the site of the provincial government: the cathedral and archbishop's palace, university, town hall, and palace of justice housing the royal law courts and governor's official residence. The Bourg was a former Roman military camp, around which the city had developed in concentric rings during the middle ages. A Christian church was built within its boundaries in the fifth century A.D., and the cathedral of Saint Sauveur was begun on the same site in the thirteenth century.[19]

---

[17] *Ibid.*, III, 332; B.M., Harleian 4575, "Semestre de Provence par M. de Sève," fol. 100v.

[18] *Félix et Thomas Platter à Montpellier*, pp. 304–306; Bouchard, *Confessions*, pp. 156–207; Brosses, *Lettres*, p. 37.

[19] See Jean Pourrière, *Recherches sur la première cathédrale d'Aix-en-Provence* (Paris, 1939).

Architecturally, Saint Sauveur combined several centuries of additions in an eclectic mixture, without coherence or personality. The archbishop's hexagonal palace was next door, and across the Place Saint Sauveur was the University, financed by the province and administered by a commission of judges and important Aixois. There was one professor of theology, three professors of law, and three professors of medicine.[20] The quality of instruction and diplomas was mediocre.

Directly south of the cathedral was the town hall, with the municipal clocktower to one side. The town hall was badly rebuilt two years after the Habsburg Emperor Charles V burned it to the ground when he sacked Aix in 1536; in 1594 the main door was replaced; in 1611 the building was repaired and enlarged; in 1626 the main staircase was rebuilt.[21] The staircase collapsed ten years later, in 1636, when a mob of 2,000 thundered down after receiving public dole in the main council chamber on the second floor: they brought the staircase down with them.[22] The town hall was rebuilt and enlarged after 1653. It retains the same entrance today, its double doors guarded by ornate wrought-iron grillwork, leading to an open cobbled courtyard decorated with potted trees and flags on holidays.

The Bourg also contained the city's business districts, the tree-lined Place des Prêcheurs, and the bustling market square south of the town hall. The palace of justice opened onto the diamond-shaped Place des Prêcheurs, the shop-lined square of the Dominican preaching friars, who had a house on the other side. The scaffold for hangings and breakings on the wheel stood in the square. The Place des Prêcheurs was southeast of the town hall. In between were a maze of narrow, dark, and dirty medieval streets lined with shops and poorer dwellings. The buildings on these streets were old and close together, blotting out the sunlight. There was a strong odor from stables, pig-pens, smoke, and garbage dumped out the windows into the streets below. Jean-Jacques Bouchard noted another reason for the smell: "after Paris, Orestes (Bouchard) has seen no city more superb or civilized;

---

[20] Ferdinand Belin, *Histoire de l'ancienne université de Provence*, 3 vols. (Paris, 1886), I; Jacqueline Carrière, *La population d'Aix-en-Provence à la fin du XVII^e siècle* (Aix, 1958), p. 78; ADBR, Aix, B 3348, fol. 219v.

[21] Jean Boyer, *L'hôtel de ville d'Aix-en-Provence* (Aix, 1944), p. 6.

[22] A.C., Aix, BB 101, fol. 161, deliberations of March 13, 1636.

which has only this fault, that since the use of privies is not accepted, it is necessary to do one's business on the roofs of the houses. That causes a foul smell in the houses and in the city as a whole, mainly because when it rains, the water brings all this waste down into the streets to the extent that it's difficult to walk. They say in Provence that at Aix it rains *merde*, as it does at Marseille and Arles."[23]

The palace of justice was originally the fortified palace of the counts of Provence, who made Aix their administrative center and built a city residence in the twelfth century. When the Parlement of Provence was created in 1501, shortly after the county was inherited by the French king, it was housed in this old palace, which also contained the prison and other royal law courts. The two sovereign courts of the Parlement and the Cour des Comptes, Aides, et Finances were cheek-by-jowl in the palace with the provincial tax-collection bureau of the Trésoriers Généraux de France and the chief seneschal court of twelve in Provence. The palace of justice was also the official residence of the governor, whose suite of rooms took up one wing. But the governor lived in a town house in Aix or Marseille, and only stayed in his official residence on ceremonial occasions. The Aix city council voted 7,000 écus (21,000 livres) on June 4, 1600, to buy the governor a separate residence: he had threatened never to return to Aix because of the uninhabitable condition of the palace. It was old, ugly, uncomfortable, and badly planned. Only sketches remain to show its appearance;[24] it was ordered destroyed by Louis XVI as unsafe in 1776 on request of the judges, after a piece of plaster falling from the ceiling knocked loose a stone that broke the leg of a passer-by.[25] The revolution stopped construction of a new building.

The tone of municipal life at Aix was administrative and aristocratic. Aix was the headquarters of the provincial police, the prévôt des maréchaux. The archbishop of Aix was one of two in Provence. He chaired general meetings of the provincial Estates and interim meetings of the Estates' executive, the procureurs du pays, who

[23] Bouchard, *Confessions*, pp. 118–119.

[24] A.C., Aix, BB 99, fol. 14v; A. M. de La Tour-Keyrié, *Le vieil Aix: album de gravures représentant les monuments, objets d'art et curiosités qui existaient autrefois à Aix* (Aix, 1896), pp. 11–12.

[25] L. de Berluc-Pérussis, *Le palais comtal d'Aix* (Paris, 1902), pp. 3–5.

were the consuls and assessors of the Aix municipal government. Concentration of the provincial government in the capital was not characteristic of adjacent Languedoc, where important administrative institutions were diffuse and decentralized, scattered among several cities. But it was characteristic of Burgundy, whose capital, Dijon, was similar to Aix in being a *ville parlementaire*, a residence for magistrates staffing the royal courts.[26] The similarities were often noted. Charles de Brosses, president in the Parlement of Dijon, expressed a lively curiosity in visiting Aix in 1739 because the two cities were so often compared.[27]

In 1629, Aix-en-Provence was a rough square on a north-south orientation in an area easily circled on foot in an hour.[28] There were five quarters within the walls, seven main gates, and one suburb. The population was probably 22,000 or 23,000; it had climbed to 27,500 in 1695—30,500 including the surrounding territory. Within the city walls in 1695 there were 2,990 houses, 138 blocks, approximately 150 streets, 25 squares, and 3 parishes.[29] Aix was a fair-sized provincial town.

Socio-economic groups in Aix did not reside by quarter, as they did in Paris, but were mixed and scattered throughout the city. Each quarter had representatives from all levels in society, with one or two numerically predominant groups.[30] For instance, nobles had residences in all of the quarters, but the greatest number lived in the Augustins and Mazarin. The older northern quarters, the Bourg, Bellegarde, and Cordeliers, were the city's tightly-packed medieval core, with a large number of inhabitants whose incomes were at the lower end of the social scale.[31] The narrow winding

[26] Gaston Roupnel, *La ville et la campagne au XVIIᵉ siècle: Etude sur les populations du pays dijonnais* (Paris, 1922).

[27] Brosses, *Lettres*, p. 35.

[28] "Aix, 1646, à Paris chez Jean Boisseau, enlumineur du Roy," A.M., Aix, fol. 24; Edmond Pognon, *Exposition de cartes anciennes de Provence et anciens plans de villes provençales* (Nice, 1965), 90ᵉᵐᵉ Congrès national des sociétés savantes.

[29] Carrière, *Population*, p. 33; Jean-Paul Coste, *La ville d'Aix en 1695. Structure urbaine et société*, 3 vols. (Aix, 1970), I, 59, 61; II, 736, 1028, 1061, 1227–1231. The three parishes were Saint Sauveur, Sainte Madeleine, and Saint Esprit.

[30] Carrière, *Population*, p. 96; Coste, *Ville*, II, 1019–1044.

[31] Carrière, *Population*, pp. 37–39; Coste *Ville*, I, 59, 61. Although both Coste and Carrière use the capitation of 1695, there are slight discrepancies in their figures.

streets of the older, densely populated quarters were ideal for barricades. The majority of their inhabitants were artisans, agricultural laborers, and shopkeepers, who participated in the revolts.

The revolts occurred in the Bourg, the focus of municipal life before 1646. This quarter contained the important public buildings and the city's business districts. Angry crowds assembled in the square before the town hall, in the area before the cathedral and archbishop's palace, and in the largest public square, the Place des Prêcheurs, before the palace of justice; rebels milled in the surrounding streets. The numerous other squares in the Bourg were too small and scattered to serve as assembly points, but they contained the street fountains and wells serving as the water supply and informal meeting places.[32]

There were no important public buildings or business centers in the newer quarters south of the Bourg, and there were few public squares, street fountains, and wells. The Aixois did not gather here, as they did in the northern quarters. The Augustins, Villeverte, Mazarin, and Saint Jean were residential districts for the wealthier inhabitants, with greater surface area and lower population density than the medieval core.[33] The Saint Jean quarter was a partially unenclosed area of open fields and gardens in the southeast, similar to the northwestern Faubourg des Cordeliers, a suburb of open fields and gardens outside the walls. The detested municipal flour tax was levied at the Saint Jean gate, which all strangers entering Aix had to use.[34] Saint Jean was named after the church of the Knights of the Order of Malta, who had a chapter at Aix—galley captains and naval officers were often Provençal Knights. With a dark vaulted interior and jeweled blue and red windows, this lovely gothic church of the late twelfth and early thirteenth centuries was reminiscent of churches in the Ile-de-France.

Until 1646, the Augustins quarter was the southern boundary of Aix. The city's appearance changed dramatically in the two decades after January 1646, when Michel Mazarin, archbishop of Aix and brother of the cardinal, obtained royal letters permitting enlargement of the city by enclosing the Saint Jean quarter.[35] During

---

[32] Carrière, *Population*, 63–91; Coste, *Ville*, II.

[33] Carrière, *Population*, pp. 37–39, 63–91; Coste, *Ville*, I, 59, 61; II.

[34] Coste, *Ville*, II, 1054.

[35] A.C. Aix, AA 13, fol. 503; ADBR, Aix, B 3355, fol. 401; B. Méjanes R.A. 40, "Recueil de pièces concernant l'agrandissement de la ville d'Aix,

the next ten years, the city walls were razed and rebuilt farther south, and a new *ville Mazarine* or Mazarin quarter was constructed within the Saint Jean. Michel Mazarin stamped his name all over the new district. There was a rue Cardinale for his brother; a rue Mazarine; a rue Saint Sauveur for his archbishopric; a rue Saint Michel; a Place Saint Michel; even a Saint Michel fountain for his name saint.[36] The Saint Sauveur gate opened on August 10, 1646. The new gate was maliciously nicknamed the Orbitello by the Aixois, for the cardinal's recent defeat at the Tuscan town.

The robe nobility lived in the Mazarin on wide straight streets constructed on a gridiron pattern. Houses in the Mazarin were larger, better lighted and more comfortable than others in the city, usually two stories high with private gardens and six or eight windows on the front facade.[37] Carriage entrances had carved wooden doors and ingenious brass knockers. Coats of arms, decorative columns, sculpture, and wrought-iron balconies decorated the Italianate facades. Houses in Aix were usually constructed of buff-colored stone roofed with red tiles; orange, brown, and red were the colors of Aix in Cézanne's paintings. Older houses north of the Mazarin were narrow and tall, crowded together on narrow streets. Some were four to five stories high, with two front windows and two rooms to a floor; the oldest were three stories high with one window and one room to a floor. There was only an arm's-breadth of space between them and no interior courtyards.

The Mazarin was joined to the rest of the city by a spacious avenue for carriages, the Cours Mirabeau, its construction ordered by the Parlement in 1649 and 1651 and completed in 1660.[38] It was soon lined with elegant, stately hôtels.[39] After 1660, the Cours Mirabeau became the focus of municipal life. Wide tree-lined avenues became characteristic of Aix, providing a touch of early green in the spring. Spacious and shady, the *cours* were built for

1646–1650"; G. André, *Le neuvième agrandissement d'Aix de 1646* (Aix, 1949).

[36] Jean-Paul Coste, *Aix-en-Provence et le pays d'Aix* (Aix, 1964), p. 76.

[37] Boyer, *L'hôtel de ville*, p. 5; F.A.T. Roux-Alphéran, *Les rues d'Aix ou recherches historiques sur l'ancienne capitale de la Provence*, 2 vols. (Aix, 1846–1848), I, 124–125.

[38] Jacques Cundier, "Aix en 1683," Musée d'Arbaud, Aix; see note 35.

[39] The majority of hôtels in Aix were clustered around the Cours Mirabeau, the cathedral, and the Place des Prêcheurs; cf. Coste, *Ville*, II, 1042.

leisurely promenades and carriage drives to see and be seen. Aix became fashionable and luxurious as a residence for the nobility in the late seventeenth century. Street fountains proliferated for use and decoration, offering an illusion of coolness in the Provençal summer. There were as many as thirty-six fountains in the early eighteenth century; there are twenty-two today.[40]

Situated in a valley surrounded by low hills, Aix was a crossroads for north-south and east-west traffic in Basse-Provence. There were five major roads running into the city from Italy, Marseille, Martigues, Arles and Avignon, Haute-Provence and the Alps. The traveler by road in Basse-Provence almost necessarily went through Aix, which owed its continuing existence after its days as a Roman military camp to its location at a crossroads. But Aix was not an important commercial or industrial center. Its industry was aimed at local consumption. Manufacturing was meager; all of Provence, with the exception of Marseille, had less cottage industry than was usual in France. The essential characteristic of Aix artisans was lack of specialization. The five principal trades were textiles and leathers, house furnishings and construction, food production, innkeeping and transports, and the arts. The largest group of artisans produced wool, silk, canvas cloth, and retail clothing.[41] There were numerous book printers and sellers: Aix was a printing center, with sixteen firms during the seventeenth century.[42] The city also produced paper, playing cards, a high grade of olive oil, and olive-wood furniture for local use. These were exchanged for the manufactured goods of Marseille at the important regional Tuesday and Saturday markets in the open marketplace south of the town hall. Commercial activities were on a small scale, and supported only a fraction of the town's population.

According to a municipal law of 1636, male wage earners received ten sols a day during the winter months for eight hours labor, twelve sols a day during the spring and summer months

[40] Pierre-Joseph de Haitze, "Aix ancienne," B. Méjanes R.A. 10, fols. 85–90; Maurice Pezet, *Les hôtels et les fontaines d'Aix-en-Provence* (Paris, 1967); Coste, *Aix-en-Provence*, p. 99.

[41] Michelle Vovelle, "Le 18ème siècle provençal," in *Histoire de la Provence*, ed. Edouard Baratier (Toulouse, 1969), p. 348; Coste, *Ville*, II, 839–951; Carrière, *Population*, pp. 79–84.

[42] Jacques Billioud, *Le livre en Provence du XVIᵉ au XVIIIᵉ siècle* (Marseille, 1962), pp. 8, 10.

for ten hours labor. Women and children received half that amount.[43] A lesser occupational group at Aix were the 1,998 agricultural workers farming the open fields and gardens in the suburbs outside the walls. Most lived in the Cordeliers and Saint Jean quarters near their garden plots. They produced much of the food consumed by the city. Some lived outside the city on bastides, farms with country houses, often owned by parlementaires. At the end of the seventeenth century, bourgeois, peasants, and artisans of Aix owned 70 percent of the surrounding cultivable land, nobles 25 percent, and clergy 5 percent. Aix was one of those preindustrial provincial cities that E. J. Hobsbawm has described as living by "battening on the surrounding peasantry and . . . by very little else except taking in its own washing."[44]

Most of the 145 tailors and dressmakers lived in the Mazarin and Saint Jean quarters, where the wealthy and noble lived. There were 398 sword nobles in Aix in 1695, and they played an important role in the municipal government.[45] They lived on lands scattered throughout the province, keeping a house in the nearest town, where they usually numbered 1 or 2 percent of the population.[46] Aix, Arles, and Les Baux had the largest percentage of resident nobles, with 5 or 6 percent.[47] There were also 193 judicial or robe nobles serving in the royal courts. They lived mostly in the Saint Jean quarter, although some lived in the Augustins and Villeneuve in the Bourg.[48] There was a total of 591 nobles at Aix in 1695, an

[43] A.C., Aix, AA 14, fol. 633; BB 101, fol. 185.

[44] E. J. Hobsbawm, *The Age of Revolution, 1787–1848* (New York, 1962), p. 28; Cissie Fairchilds, *Poverty and Charity in Aix-en-Provence, 1640–1789* (Baltimore, 1976), p. 4; Carrière, *Population*, pp. 87–91; Coste, *Ville*, II, 712, 973–987; René Baehrel, *Une croissance: La Basse-Provence rurale (fin du XVIe siècle—1789)* (Paris, 1961), pp. 399–401. See Roger Livet, *Habitat rural et structures agraires en Basse-Provence* (Gap, 1962).

[45] Carrière, *Population*, pp. 70–73; Coste, *Ville*, II, 712, 749–767. This number may be inflated: see François-Paul Blanc, "L'usurpation de noblesse en Provence a l'époque de la première réformation (1666–1669)," *Annales de la Faculté de Droit et de Science Politique d'Aix-Marseille*, 58 (Paris, 1972), p. 307.

[46] Maurice Agulhon, in studying 235 Var nobles in 1787–1789, found that 118 lived inside the Var on their lands with houses in nearby towns, while 58 lived outside the Var, 33 in Aix, 6 in Marseille, 12 in Paris or Versailles, 4 in Nice or the Piedmont, 3 in other provinces, 26 unknown; cf. *La vie sociale*, p. 90.

[47] Baehrel, *Une croissance*, p. 397.

[48] Carrière, *Population*, pp. 70–72; Coste, *Ville*, II, 712, 754–755.

unusually large number, only rivaled by Arles; and 3,063 domestic and public servants, emphasizing the aristocratic tone of city life. There were 933 administrative officials.[49] There were proportionately few merchants, financiers, foreigners, army or navy men. Municipal life at Aix was dominated by nobles and officials, who participated in the revolts in large numbers.

There was a moderate increase of 4,000 to 5,000 in the population of Aix by the end of the seventeenth century. The birth rate was low. There were 100 deaths for every 188 births in 1695, and families tended to be small: 54.5 percent had 1 or 2 children; 27 percent had 3 children; and only 7 families had 10 children or more. There were few resident foreigners; only 12 are listed in the 1695 capitation.[50] Approximately 58 percent of the population was unmarried. They were members of religious orders, domestic servants, widows and widowers, indigent, and children. The large number of religious houses at Aix impressed contemporaries: there were approximately 65 religious foundations, including those outside the walls, and 1,045 members of the regular and secular clergy in 1695.[51]

The surface area of Aix increased from 32 to 75 hectares between 1583 and 1646, roughly from 80 to 186 acres.[52] Much of the expansion was new hôtels. There were nine enlargements of the city walls from the twelfth through the seventeenth centuries. This ended the city's expansion until the modern era.[53] Squares, fountains, and hôtels were added in the eighteenth century, but no new quarters.

Aix was roughly pentagonal in shape after the addition of the Mazarin quarter in the southwest. Modern aerial photographs

[49] *Ibid.* There were 394 indigent in Aix in 1695, according to the capitation; cf. Coste, *Ville*, II, 987–995; Carrière, *Population*, pp. 86–87. This figure may be too low, since many poor were supported by private charity and religious foundations. It has been estimated that nearly 20 percent of the city's population received assistance in the 1690s; cf. Fairchilds, *Poverty and Charity*, p. 75.

[50] Carrière, *Population*, pp. 33–34, 45–46, 48–49, 60–61; Baehrel, *Une croissance*, p. 657. The population of Aix decreased in the eighteenth century; it went from 27,500 within the walls in 1695 to 23,000 in 1752.

[51] Coste, *Ville*, I, 45; II, 712, 735–757; Carrière, *Population*, p. 64; Haitze, "Aix ancienne," B. Méjanes R.A. 10, fols. 58–62.

[52] Coste, *Ville*, I, 41.

[53] EDB, XIV, 438–462; Coste, *Ville*, III, a carton of seventeen maps showing the development of Aix from the middle ages to the modern period.

show two cities existing side by side, the medieval core and the seventeenth-century addition.[54] Close-packed houses with tile roofs march southward in tight semicircles from Saint Sauveur, while long double lines of trees bisect Aix and mark the Cours Mirabeau, a leafy green tunnel of aqueous light until the trees are cut back in October. The original elms were blighted in the nineteenth century, and replaced by plane trees. Beyond the Cours Mirabeau, the streets form a rectangular grid marked by squares, circles, and polygons of trees and avenues. Garden courtyards, occasionally glimpsed through half-opened doors, pierce deceptively solid blocks of houses. Although the city had two faces, these blended well, and Aix was the unified and harmonious architectural product of the seventeenth century. Modern Aix retains the appearance and some of the grace, elegance, and charm that it had two centuries ago, although its political importance as a provincial capital has long since disappeared.

Outward signs and symbols of rank and office were carefully observed in the seventeenth century, an age more sensitive to precedence in public ceremonies than our own. Public appearances of officials assumed great importance. Meticulous attention was paid to seating and marching order, dress, number of attendants, and public acknowledgment of rank through salutes—removing the hat with a flourish, bowing, and appropriate greetings. Deliberate or unintentional slights by individuals or institutions caused boycotts, insults, lawsuits, dueling, arrests. Public humiliation was a grave injury. Men risked their lives in duels to defend their honor, while crimes were punished by public acts of contrition and penance. Quarrels over precedence escalated until an outside authority intervened. It was often necessary to settle quarrels by arbitration. The political climate of seventeenth-century Aix was characterized by excessive pride, preoccupation with rank and precedence, and a heightened sensitivity to insults, which caused endless bickering among institutions and officials.

Churches and municipal ceremonies were the public places where men displayed their rank in a provincial town. Mass at Saint Sauveur began most municipal ceremonies, including election of the city council around Saint Michael's Day on September 29 and investiture on October 1; opening sessions of the royal courts

[54] Coste, *Ville*, II, 1010, 1013.

during October; opening sessions of the Estates and General Assembly when they met at Aix; Saint Sebastian's Day on January 20; Mardi Gras in February; Fête Dieu during the week after Pentecost; and closing sessions of the judicial courts around Saint John's Day on June 24.[55]

A visitor to Aix during Pentecost could see the Fête Dieu. The municipal council elected a prince d'amour and an abbé to preside over the festivities, which climaxed with a procession at noon of clergy and officials in full regalia, escorting under a canopy the sacrament from high mass at the cathedral.[56] The Fête Dieu became an annual occasion for expressing personality clashes and power struggles. From 1641 to 1648, the Parlement excluded the Chambre des Requêtes from the procession, and to its fury, the Aix seneschal court was often excluded by the higher royal courts. The Trésoriers Généraux and consuls of Aix regularly quarreled over precedence, the Parlement serving as mediator in one of their quarrels in June 1653. If an historian could photograph municipal processions, and if he could analyze the order and position of marching institutions and officials on a comparative basis annually, in the same way that groupings of Soviet officials at the May Day parade in Red Square are studied by western observers, he would have an indication of the power struggles and shifting alignments within the provincial and municipal administrations at Aix.[57]

Mardi Gras was a traditionally rowdy event, when old scores could be settled and political protests made in anonymity. Everyone went masked, and there were several days of celebrations with street dancing, satirical songs, mystery plays, a procession of costumed heads of mythical creatures, private balls, theatrical parties, and ballets. The parlementaires used the confusion of Carnival in 1648 to harass members of the Semester, while the panic sparking the 1649 revolt sprang in part from the presence in Aix of "Turks," Moslem forced labor brought from Marseille to build scenery for

[55] A.C., Aix, AA 55 (1645–1815), procès-verbaux of municipal ceremonies.

[56] See abbé Grégoire, *Explication des cérémonies de la Fête-Dieu d'Aix-en-Provence* (Aix, 1777).

[57] Delib. Parl., B. Méjanes 954, fol. 12v; Jean-Paul Charmeil, *Les trésoriers de France à l'epoque de la Fronde* (Paris, 1964), p. 444, n. 902; Lublinskaya, *Vnutrenniaia*, pp. 252–253.

a ballet that the governor intended to produce during Carnival.[58]

When members of an institution became intensely defensive, it often indicated that the institution's authority was declining and that its members had little to do but observe the outward manifestations of their disappearing authority. This happened to the Cour des Comptes during the seventeenth century. This sovereign fiscal court of Provence combined the functions of a Chambre des Comptes and Cour des Aides in judging litigation between the crown and its tax officials, auditing and maintaining fiscal records, hearing final appeals from taxpayers, and registering royal edicts affecting its competence. A bureau of Trésoriers Généraux de France was established at Aix in 1555 to supervise provincial tax collection. By royal edict in 1627, it received trial jurisdiction over fiscal cases pertaining to the royal domaine. The Cour des Comptes bitterly fought this reduction in its authority by refusing to recognize its rival as a fiscal court, even after a decree of the council of state in May 1640 permanently settled the issue in favor of the Trésoriers. Clinging to the remainder of its authority with determination, the Cour des Comptes quarreled incessantly over precedence and jurisdiction with the Trésoriers Généraux and Parlement.[59]

At a typical public ceremony, the Te Deum mass on February 6, 1660, to celebrate the king's visit to Provence, the Parlement and Cour des Comptes sat in the cathedral choir, a visible reminder of their rank, while the Trésoriers Généraux and Aix seneschal court, whose decisions were subject to appeal, sat in the side chapels.[60] The Parlement and Cour des Comptes were ancient bitter rivals. They quarreled incessantly over precedence in public ceremonies, payment of gages, royal domaine and criminal jurisdiction.[61] As the larger, older court with political authority, the

[58] Pierre-Joseph de Haitze, "Histoire de Provence sous le gouvernement du comte d'Alais," B. Méjanes 736, fol. 139; Paul Gaffarel, "La Fronde en Provence," *Revue historique*, 2 (1876), 87.

[59] Edict of Anet, August 1555, ADBR, Marseille, B 45, fols. 200–205; EDB, III, 427–432; Charmeil, *Les trésoriers*, pp. 5, 11–12, 16, 315–317; "Règlements touchant les rangs des officiers," B. Méjanes 1114.

[60] Edouard Baratier, ed., *Documents de l'histoire de la Provence* (Toulouse, 1971), pp. 216–217.

[61] J.L.H. Hesmivy de Moissac, "Difficultés entre le Parlement et les diverses autorités," B. Méjanes 936, fols. 405–617; M.A. Provence 355, "Conflits entre le Parlement de Provence et la Cour des Comptes"; Jeanne Allemand,

Parlement claimed precedence. The smaller, less prestigious Cour des Comptes, with weakened jurisdiction, spent most of its time fighting for recognition as an equal. A 1608 decree of the council of state had ordered the Cour des Comptes to sit and march on the Parlement's left, wearing black coifs. But the Cour des Comptes always attempted to sit on the right and omit the coifs, maneuvering themselves into an even line when marching; the parlementaires tried to force them behind. Scuffling occasionally broke out, as it did during municipal receptions for a new governor in 1631 and a new lieutenant general in 1635.[62] Even when it stayed on the left, the Cour des Comptes jockeyed for position with the Trésoriers Généraux.

The quarreling of the sovereign courts became buffoonery on August 28, 1683. Arriving at Saint Sauveur for high mass, the Cour des Comptes found the Parlement already seated in the choir behind locked and guarded grillwork. In a frenzy of anger, the Cour des Comptes chased the guards and climbed the grillwork. Croze de Lincel aimed a guard's musket at the first president of the Parlement, who threw himself behind the seats of the choir yelping in terror. The parlementaires beat a hasty retreat, followed by a shower of stones from the Cour des Comptes, who stoned the first president's sedan chair and the legs of his porters. Croze de Lincel ended on his knees before the high altar a month later, holding a lighted candle in public penance.[63]

During October, parlementaires in full regalia could be glimpsed on their way to the palace of justice for the rentrée, the reopening of the court after the summer recess.[64] The presidents wore round

---

"La haute société aixoise dans la seconde moitié du XVIII<sup>e</sup> siècle," 2 vols. (dissertation for *diplôme d'études supérieures*, University of Aix-Marseille, 1927), II, 424–473.

[62] Moissac, "Difficultés," B. Méjanes 936, fols. 489–490; ADBR, Aix, J.L.H. Hesmivy de Moissac, "Histoire du Parlement de Provence, 1501–1715," 2 vols. (Aix, 1776), I, fol. 465; Charmeil, *Les trésoriers*, pp. 317–318.

[63] Charmeil, *Les trésoriers*, p. 290, n. 265; Prosper Cabasse, *Essais historiques sur le Parlement de Provence*, 3 vols. (Paris, 1826), II, 60–67.

[64] Although the official date of the rentrée was October 1, it was often postponed until after the *vendanges* or grape harvest in late October: the parlementaires were property owners who wanted to supervise their harvests; cf. Louis Wolff, *Le Parlement de Provence au XVIII<sup>e</sup> siècle* (Aix, 1920), p. 177.

hats or *mortiers* of gold-trimmed black velvet with a pendulous tip, lace at the throat, and an ermine-trimmed mantle over a red robe held high by an attendant to avoid the filth underfoot. With their servants going ahead to clear the way, and their clients and suitors following after, they must have been an impressive sight as they walked through the streets of Aix. On formal occasions such as rentrées, councilors wore red robes without a mantle and flat, wide-brimmed black velvet hats called *bonnets*. For routine business, they wore black robes, hats, and white two-tailed neck-pieces known as *rabats*, their sacks of lawsuits suspended from their belts by a cord. Jean-Jacques Bouchard passing through Aix on his way to Italy in 1630 remarked: "Those of the Parlement are respected like kings and have kept the ancient custom of having themselves accompanied to the palace of justice by their clients so that each magistrate is sometimes accompanied by five or six hundred men."[65] Bouchard undoubtedly exaggerates, and a "crowd" would be more accurate, but his meaning is clear: the parlementaires were personnages of distinction in Aix, and their journey to the palace of justice on foot, particularly in red robes for the rentrée, was an occasion in a society emphasizing ceremony.

The palace of justice was entered by a wide staircase leading to an open-roofed gallery on the second floor, from which onlookers could observe the Place des Prêcheurs below. Charles de Brosses commented in 1739 that the Aix palace of justice was old and badly planned, as was the palace at Dijon, but the rooms were beautifully decorated.[66] The courtrooms of the Cour des Comptes were on the left ground floor; the Aix seneschal court was on the right; the Trésoriers Généraux de France were on the second floor back; the Parlement was on the second floor front, facing onto the loggia (see figure 2).[67] The palace had a tiled roof and three tree-lined interior courtyards in the Mediterranean manner. The roughly rectangular government courtyard, with its fountain and stables was behind the governor's apartments. The center rectangular courtyard was used by the prison. The great front courtyard,

[65] Bouchard, *Confessions*, p. 117.

[66] Charles de Brosses, *Lettres familières: Aix-en-Provence, Marseille* (n.p., 1942), pp. 15–16.

[67] Pierre-Joseph de Haitze, *Les curiosités les plus remarquables de la ville d'Aix* (Aix, 1679), pp. 5–25; La Tour-Keyrié, *Le vieil Aix*, p. 12; Coste, *Ville*, I, A 34.

L-shaped, was used by the judicial courts and formed the rear wall of the wing that included the main entrance on the Place des Prêcheurs. Arcades of shops lined the ground-floor facade and interior judicial courtyard, to the disgust of the parlementaires, who encountered shopkeepers, rug merchants, soldiers, vendors, and street peddlars doing business in the halls of justice.

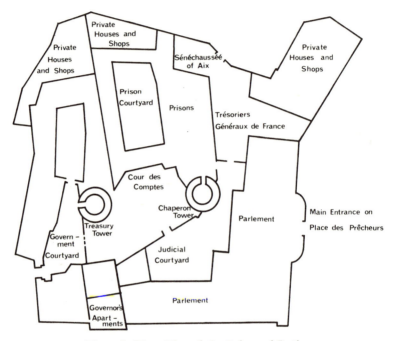

Figure 2. Floor Plan of the Palace of Justice

The main entrance was busy when the courts were in session. Thomas Platter wrote in February 1597: "A visitor sees wide streets and impressive buildings, among them the palace of the Parlement, with all the rooms giving onto a circular gallery, and its entrance on the ground floor bordered by all sorts of shops as at Paris through which, coming and going continually, are judicial personnel and businessmen. The main courtroom on the first floor is hung with violet cloth dotted with fleurs de lys. One cannot enter wearing a sword."[68] There would have been parlementaires talk-

[68] *Félix et Thomas Platter à Montpellier*, pp. 316–317.

ing, laughing, gossiping in groups on the loggia, observing the comings and goings on the staircase and in the square below: defendants, plaintiffs, lawyers, witnesses, court clerks, bailiffs, prisoners, merchants, customers, soldiers, clients, suitors, idlers, passers-by. Wealth, rank, and influence helped to turn the wheels of justice in the seventeenth century. The scene would have made an excellent sketch by Daumier.

Before gas and electricity, life was regulated by the sun, and the Parlement began at an early hour. The two most important chambers, the Grand'Chambre and the Tournelle, sat, in theory, from six to ten in the morning before Easter and five to nine after Easter. The Chambre des Enquêtes sat after the Tournelle, from 10:30 to 2:30 before Easter and 9:30 to 1:30 after Easter. However, the courts usually sat at eight in the morning, or when enough judges arrived to begin, since in a collegial system a quorum was necessary for a sitting. Afternoon sessions were avoided whenever possible.[69]

The Parlement of Aix, created by Louis XII in 1501–1502,[70] was the highest civil and criminal appellate court in Provence. Joint meetings of all its chambers were held in the ornately decorated grande salle, the courtroom of the Grand'Chambre, or oldest chamber. The Parlement was termed a sovereign court, which was technically incorrect because its decisions could be appealed to the king in his council, and its cases evoked for judgment by other royal courts. Evocations were an issue during the Fronde. The council of state claimed authority to evoke cases and annul parlementary arrêts, although the parlements refused to recognize its authority in the absence of the king.[71]

The Grand'Chambre routinely registered noncontroversial legislation. It also had the privilege of registering papal legislation from Rome and Avignon sent for publication by the archbishop of Aix.[72] It regulated the lower royal courts and exercised civil juris-

---

[69] Wolff, *Parlement*, pp. 167–169, 179. The Grand'Chambre sat on Thursday mornings. The Tournelle and Enquêtes sat on Wednesday and Saturday mornings.

[70] ADBR, Aix, B 3313, fols. 1–15.

[71] Roland Mousnier, "Le Conseil du Roi de la mort de Henri IV au gouvernement personnel de Louis XIV, 1610–1661," *Etudes d'histoire moderne et contemporaine*, 1 (1947), 29–67, reprinted in Mousnier, *La plume, la faucille et le marteau* (Paris, 1970), pp. 141–178.

[72] Wolff, *Parlement*, pp. 277–278; ADBR, Aix, B 3504–3518.

diction in the first instance over privileged persons: nobles, royal officials, higher clergy, persons with lettres de committimus giving the right of trial before the Parlement. It could hear appeal cases from the municipal police courts, but whenever it acted in this capacity, there was friction.[73]

The second-ranking court, the Chambre de La Tournelle, met in the salle dorée, decorated with heavily gilded woodwork. The Tournelle judged on appeal criminal cases involving corporal punishment, and it shared criminal jurisdiction in the first instance over privileged persons with the Grand'Chambre. It also judged important provincial cases of treason, sedition, libel, heresy, sacrilege, and blasphemy. Its jurisdiction was occasionally challenged by the intendants and governors.[74]

Created by the crown as a fiscal measure, suppressed after protest, then permanently recreated in 1574, the Chambre des Enquêtes had its jurisdiction carved from those of the two existing chambers. The Enquêtes had less prestige and importance, and its members were the youngest and least experienced in the Parlement. The appeal court for nonprivileged persons, it judged written appeals in civil cases not exceeding a hundred livres and in criminal cases not involving corporal punishment. Jealous of their jurisdictions, the older chambers evoked the Enquêtes' cases and refused to allow it to extend its competence beyond minor cases and written appeals, so it was never as busy as its rivals. It did preliminary investigations for cases adjudicated by the other two chambers, hence its name as a court of inquiry.[75] It was excluded from joint meetings until the first decade of the seventeenth century.

At the head of the main staircase was the salle des pas perdus, a noisy waiting room for litigants and witnesses that was assigned in 1641 to an unwanted new chamber. Created for fiscal reasons, the new Chambre des Requêtes was to have jurisdiction over privileged persons in the first instance, formerly the competence of the Grand'Chambre and Tournelle. The older chambers ceased squabbling and united against the intruder, harassing it, evoking its cases, and excluding it from joint meetings until 1648, when it was abolished. The Requêtes was not recreated until 1705.[76]

[73] Wolff, *Parlement*, pp. 275–287.
[74] *Ibid.*, pp. 289–293; see Chapters Three and Four.
[75] Wolff, *Parlement*, pp. 293–298.
[76] *Ibid.*, pp. 304–311; see Chapter Six.

The Chambre des Vacations was a skeleton body of fifteen judges sitting from July through October to hear cases that could not await the return of the full court. Most parlementaires were reluctant to exchange the coolness of their country estates for the sweltering heat of Aix in summer. Consequently, the Vacations councilors were usually the youngest in the Parlement, eager to gain the extra experience and gages for summer service. The Vacations judged lesser criminal cases and civil cases up to 1,200 livres. It did not register royal legislation, assign sentences of death, or judge extraordinary cases.[77]

Tempers flared easily into violence in the seventeenth century, even among the most eminent upholders of law and order, and the lack of restraint contributed to the constant quarreling among magistrates and officials at Aix. The parlementaires quarreled over precedence, rank, distribution of cases and the role of rapporteur, pensions, gages, lettres en survivance, reception of new members, competence, and legal procedure. There were accusations of malfeasance and peculation, threats of lawsuits for slander and libel, shouting matches degenerating into general free-for-alls. Royal attorneys Decormis and Porcellet hit each other with their bonnets and fists in February 1641. Cour des Comptes first president Henri de Séguiran lost his temper in the corridor of the palace of justice in April 1641, when second president de Réauville complained that his pension had not been paid and accused Séguiran of appropriating it. The first president hit Réauville so hard that he lost his hat and judicial baton, and nearly fell down. A quarrel between councilors Venel and Aymar ended in a challenge to duel in 1638. Jacques Gallifet, a rebel chief in 1649 and the son of a president of the Enquêtes, killed Séguiran's son in a duel on December 28, 1641. Parlementaires Coriolis and Périer were suspended from office in 1662 for brawling in the grande salle.[78]

Sitting in joint meetings and marching by office and order of reception, the parlementaires often disputed precedence. Alexandre de Gallifet complained in 1647 that his son Jacques, recently received with lettres en survivance as president of the Enquêtes, had a lower rank than François Thomassin, received at the same time, because Thomassin had intrigued with his relatives in

[77] Wolff, *Parlement*, pp. 311–318.
[78] Charles de Grimaldi and Jacques Gaufridy, *Mémoires pour servir à l'histoire de la Fronde en Provence* (Aix, 1870), pp. 144–145, 152–154, 156.

the Parlement to obtain the higher rank.[79] The presidents of the Enquêtes, councilors with royal letters to sit as presidents, won the right to precede the other councilors in December 1635, after bitter contention.[80] Régusse noted that, "because of a quarrel over precedence I had with one of my colleagues," six or seven months elapsed between his purchase of an office of councilor in 1633 and his reception.[81]

The presidents' red robes set them off from the black-robed company. The first president, as chief justice, customarily presided over the Grand'Chambre, but he could replace the second president as head of the Tournelle by choice. Most presidents sat in the Grand'Chambre, although one had to preside over each session of the Tournelle and sign the register for its proceedings to be valid. The presidents became acting chief justice by order of service. Presidents of the Tournelle and Enquêtes distributed cases and the role of rapporteur on a rotating basis. Intendant Champigny wrote to chancellor Séguier on February 16, 1644, that the Tournelle was protesting a councilor's distribution of cases in the president's absence.[82] Oppède wrote in 1657 that presiding over the Vacations had caused contention.[83] The dean of the company, or doyen, the councilor with the longest service, sat in the Grand'Chambre and followed the presidents in rank.[84]

The red-robed attorneys marched after the councilors. The two procureurs-généraux prepared the written work for royal cases, which the two avocats-généraux pled before the court. At Aix, the first avocat-général had precedence, but they signed written work jointly. The procureurs-généraux complained to Paris in 1646 that decrees were being signed and published by the avocats-généraux without their knowledge.[85]

---

[79] B.N., Ms. fr. 17387, fols. 113–114, Gallifet to Séguier, October 29, 1647; 17393, fols. 53–54, Gallifet to Séguier, March 10, 1649.

[80] Wolff, *Parlement*, pp. 68–70.

[81] Grimaldi and Gaufridy, *Mémoires*, p. 10.

[82] Lublinskaya, *Vnutrenniaia*, pp. 271–274.

[83] B.M., Harleian 4493, fols. 355–356. Oppède to Séguier, September 18, 1657.

[84] Wolff, *Parlement*, pp. 57–68.

[85] *Ibid.*, pp. 82, 86–89; Lublinskaya, *Vnutrenniaia*, p. 313, Champigny to Séguier, May 22, 1646, p. 315, procureurs-généraux to Séguier, October 22, 1646, p. 316, Champigny to Séguier, October 23, 1646.

The most bitter quarrels occurred during registration of royal legislation. The first president summoned a joint meeting for this purpose at the request of the royal attorneys or deputies from the chambers. The first procureur-général presented the edict and requested "pure and simple" verification and registration without remonstrance. The first president asked for opinions by order of seniority on agreement with existing laws, in a discussion that was at the same time an oral vote. The edict could be registered immediately. It could be modified during verification with the effect of a veiled veto, or it could be rejected with a remonstrance to Paris, citing the reasons. The Parlement could renew its remonstrances many times, in contrast to lesser royal courts. The delay in publication and enforcement of an edict could last years; sometimes it was permanent. The crown exerted pressure to force registration, because it preferred the Parlement's support for new legislation, ensuring enforcement by local officials.

Arrêts d'état or arrêts de règlement, so-called "decrees pronounced in red robes," were also issued at joint meetings.[86] They were public statements of the Parlement's position on judicial and administrative issues with legal questions needing clarification in the court's opinion. Printed and distributed for enforcement, these interpretations had the effect of new regulations. The Parlement's right to issue public policy statements with the force of law allowed its intervention in a wide range of issues.[87]

The Aix parlementaires were occasionally guilty of judicial misconduct, provoking popular dislike and criticism. Individual parlementaires were attacked for their corruption and greed in accepting bribes, harshness as local landlords, arrogance, absenteeism, inattention to duty, nepotism, and favoritism in giving judgments. On July 11, 1643, intendant Champigny wrote to chancellor Séguier that the Parlement refused to hear a suit by a creditor of councilor Arbaud, who had seized property of his late father worth 15,000 or 16,000 livres, which should have gone to the creditor. Champigny wrote that he would have to judge the case himself if the Parlement continued to shirk its responsibilities.[88] In August

---

[86] ADBR, Aix, B 3692–3697, "arrêts de règlement ou d'états, 1625–1661."

[87] François Olivier-Martin, *Histoire du Droit français des origines à la Révolution* (Paris, 1948), pp. 538–541; see Chapter Three.

[88] Lublinskaya, *Vnutrenniaia*, pp. 253–255.

1656, the Parlement permitted irregularities in prosecuting a councilor's son accused of murder by dueling.[89] Governor Alais in 1649 charged that the parlementaires regularly evaded payment of the taille, while their relatives escaped prosecution for crimes.[90]

In theory, the parlementaires had to appear at the palace of justice or forfeit their gages for the day, because the crown refused to pay salaries to absent judges. In practice, the Parlement refused to show the attendance register to the salt-tax receiver who paid the gages, so salaries were always paid, and there was a high rate of absenteeism. Some of the parlementaires did not set foot in the palace during the judicial year except for the obligatory autumn rentrée; this practice had political repercussions in 1630–1631. The Parlement was also attacked for the dilatoriness and costliness of its justice, since high court appeals were lengthy and expensive.[91] Popular dislike burst forth in anonymous satiric verse, wall placards, and graffiti such as the well-known jingle that appeared from time to time on the walls of Aix: "Parlement, mistral et Durance sont les trois fléaux de Provence."[92] Carnival was a popular time for verbal attacks on the parlementaires. The court issued arrêts against throwing snowballs and making obscene gestures at its members, who made good targets as they walked to the palace of justice.[93]

Whatever its faults, the Parlement was indispensable to Aix's position as the provincial capital, and essential to its prosperity, while the parlementaires dominated the city's political and social life. The Parlement and other royal courts offered employment to Aixois. Many parlementaires owned land in the vicinity, which they leased. They kept large households with numerous domestic

[89] B.M., Harleian 4489, fols. 188–190, Oppède to Séguier, August 15, 1656.

[90] B.N., Dupuy 754, fols. 218–219, "Remontrance du peuple de Provence"; see Chapter Eight.

[91] See Bernard Guenée, *Tribunaux et gens de justice dans la bailliage de Senlis à la fin du moyen age (1380–1550)* (Paris, 1963), pp. 249, 252.

[92] Emile Reybaud, *Etudes sur le Parlement de Provence: Les troubles du Semestre, 1647–1649* (Aix, 1863), p. 23; J. Marchand, *Un intendant sous Louis XIV: Etude sur l'administration de Lebret en Provence (1687–1704)* (Paris, 1889), p. 20; Guide Michelin, *Haute-Provence*, p. 40: "Parlement, mistral and Durance are the three curses of Provence."

[93] Louis Wolff, *La vie des parlementaires provençaux au XVI<sup>e</sup> siècle* (Aix, 1924), p. 43.

servants. Their hôtels along the Cours Mirabeau and the streets leading to the Place des Prêcheurs and Place Saint Sauveur were among the finest in the city.[94] The parlementaires and other magistrates provided business for the shopkeepers, merchants, and innkeepers of Aix. From November through June, the city swarmed with plaintiffs, defendants, and witnesses for the royal courts, as well as visitors who came to enjoy the high season in the capital. There were fifty-three inns, thirty-seven cabarets, and thirty-four wine shops at Aix in 1695.[95] As magistrates of a high royal court, the parlementaires were local symbols of political authority derived from an almost mythical king at Paris. As powerful officials in the provincial administration, they were an elite group of opinion and decision makers whose political influence far outweighed their numbers or individual reputations. The king was too distant to secure the personal loyalty that his local representatives enjoyed.

The city of Aix was governed by a city council composed of three consuls, an *assesseur* or assessor, and sixty councilors. There was no mayor. The consuls and assessor of Aix were elected annually during the last week of September in the main council chamber, and invested with their offices in a public ceremony before the town hall on October 1. The consuls and assessor were chosen by an indirect, two-step election procedure. The first step was to prepare a list of candidates. The day before the election a nominating assembly, composed of the present consuls and assessor, with the ex-consuls and assessor from the previous year, met to propose candidates. Nominees were recorded by the consulaires, fifty or sixty former consuls with the right to advise but not to nominate. In addition, a list of one hundred notables was drawn up, twenty from each of the city's five administrative districts (the Bourg, Bellegarde, Cordeliers, Saint Jean, and Augustins; the Faubourg des Cordeliers was excluded). The names of thirty notables were then drawn by lot from an urn. These thirty became the cités, who were announced on the next day.[96]

[94] René Borricaud, *Les hôtels particuliers d'Aix-en-Provence* (Aix, 1971); Coste, *Ville*, II, 1045–1051.

[95] Coste, *Ville*, II, 930–935; Carrière, *Population*, p. 81.

[96] EDB, XIV, 512–520; A.C., Aix, AA 6, fols. 14v–23; BB 102, fols. 24–30. Separate nominations and indirect two-step election procedures were

41

The list of nominees for consuls and assessor was presented to a special election assembly on the next day. The election assembly was composed of the consuls and assessor for that year and the previous year; the abbé and prince d'amour from the Fête Dieu procession; the 30 cités; the 60 municipal councilors (at least 32 had to be present for the election to be valid, and fines were levied to ensure their presence); the city treasurer; and the 5 captains of the municipal guard. The election assembly, numbering approximately 120, approved or rejected nominees by placing red or yellow balls in the appropriate boxes. Occasionally, the election assembly stubbornly rejected the slate presented to it, but it could not make substitutions. Thus, the nominating assembly controlled the election by choosing the candidates, drawing up the list of notables, and selecting 30 to vote on the next day.

When the election was finished, the thirty cités became the thirty new councilors, serving terms of two years each and joining thirty from the previous year (there was a total of sixty councilors on the city council). Five captains of the municipal guard, one from each district, the city treasurer, and several tax assessors were elected annually by the same procedure. The outcome of the election, *la nouvel estat de la ville*, was registered by the Parlement, which also registered any changes in the election procedure, as it did for all the communities in Provence.[97]

The symbol or badge of the consul's office was the *chaperon*, a band of red velvet worn over the left shoulder.[98] The Aix consuls and assessor were the procureurs du pays, the executive committee of the provincial Estates. In theory, the first consul was a noble with a fief; the assessor was a lawyer; the second consul was a noble without a fief; and the third consul was a bourgeois.[99] Ob-

common to the municipalities of the ancien régime; cf. Nora Temple, "Municipal Elections and Municipal Oligarchies in Eighteenth Century France," *French Government and Society, 1500–1850*, ed. J. F. Bosher (London, 1973), p. 77; Pierre-Clément Timbal, "Les villes de consulat dans le Midi de la France: Histoire de leurs institutions administratives et judiciaires," *Recueils de Société Jean Bodin*, 6 (1954), 343–370.

[97] ADBR, Aix, B 3346, fol. 322; B 3348, fols. 43, 693; B 3349, fols. 395, 470–474, 504; B 3353, fols. 1, 895.

[98] Henri de Gérin-Richard, "Enquête sur le chaperon consulaire en Provence," *Provincia* IV (1924), 1–11.

[99] A.C., Aix AA 6, fols. 17–23. In Provençal towns, the first consul was often a gentleman, the second a bourgeois, and the third a merchant. In

servance of rank was not absolute in practice, although the third consul was more often noble than the second consul was bourgeois. The assessor was a lawyer responsible for protecting the legal interests and privileges of the city and province. He was the watchdog or censor of the Estates, making reports to the general meetings on the interim activities of the other procureurs du pays. By virtue of his responsibilities, the assessor usually ranked between the first and second consul. But in a 1590 city council decision, the first consul acted as chairman in the absence of the viguier, followed by the second consul.[100] The consuls could never agree whether to march by office or rank. The assessor preferred to march by office, since in rank he might be nonnoble. Quarrels on marching order periodically enlivened city council deliberations.

The bell of the municipal clocktower rang to summon members to council meetings. The consuls had to be present at these meetings, and a quorum of thirty-two councilors was necessary for the deliberations to be valid. Frequent règlements by the city council forbidding consuls to transact important business outside the meetings show that this abuse occurred often. Consuls were forbidden to authorize expenditures over sixty livres, the number of prohibitions again indicating this occurred often. The city council often met without a quorum, and a royal edict in 1674 reinforced the rule that there had to be thirty-two councilors and the consuls present for transactions to be valid. Outgoing consuls, the consuls of the preceding year, and the consulaires could conspire to fix the municipal elections by revealing the names of the cités in advance to pressure their vote. There were a number of city ordinances forbidding this practice. Consuls and councilors were often related within a degree prohibited by city ordinances as brothers, fathers, sons, uncles, nephews, and first cousins.[101]

---

Provençal villages, the first consul was often a bourgeois, the second a merchant or artisan, the third a ménager; cf. Maurice Agulhon, "Mise au point sur les classes sociales en Provence," *Provence historique*, 20 (1970), 101–108. Also see John Cameron, "Village Government in Provence in the Late Eighteenth Century," *Proceedings of the First Annual Meeting of the Western Society for French History*, March 14–15, 1974 (Las Cruces, New Mexico, 1974), pp. 98–107.

[100] A.C., Aix, BB 90, fol. 17v.

[101] *Ibid.*, BB 99–105, municipal deliberations, 1598–1697; AA 1, 6, 14, *règlements* and ordinances; EDB, XIV, 532–536.

Friction between social groups was a decisive factor in municipal politics. The Aix municipal government was dominated by the nobility, divided into two groups: the "old" nobility of incontestable authenticity, ennobled for more than a century, and the "new" nobility, occasionally dubious, ennobled for less than a century. There were frequent quarrels springing from the old nobility's exclusion of the new from office. Quarrels between noble factions were also characteristic of municipal politics at Salon, Marseille, and Arles.[102]

The first consul of Aix, traditionally a member of the old nobility, was often titled. The second consul was traditionally a member of the new nobility, an *écuyer* or gentleman. The third consul and assessor, traditionally bourgeois, were in fact often clients or members of the nobility.[103] In voting power, the consulate was often divided three-to-one in favor of the nobility.[104] Outgoing officials nominated the new consuls and drew up the list of one hundred notables from which the thirty new councilors were chosen. Thus the aristocratic oligarchy was self-perpetuating. The old nobility attempted to name its members and clients as notables, cités, third consul and assessor, in this way continuing its control over the city government. The new nobles, represented by the second consul and a minority of councilors, protested the domination of the old nobility and avidly sought municipal office to strengthen their claims to noble rank, although Aix municipal of-

[102] René Pillorget, "Les luttes de factions à Salon de 1608 à 1615," *Provence historique*, 18 (1968), 293–311; "Luttes de factions et intérêts économiques à Marseille de 1598 à 1618," *Annales: ESC*, 27 (1972), 721–722, 729; Lublinskaya, *Vnutrenniaia*, pp. 271–274, Champigny to Séguier from Arles, February 16, 1644; Roland Mousnier, ed., *Lettres et mémoires adressés au chancelier Séguier (1633–1649)*, 2 vols. (Paris, 1964), II, 669–679, Champigny to Séguier, Arles (erroneously cited as Aix), February 16, 1644; B.N., Ms. fr. 18976, fols. 457, 459–466; B.M., Harleian 4575, "Semestre de Provence par M. de Sève," fols. 56–57.

[103] See Appendix II. In the autumn of 1694, the first consul was a baron, the assessor a lawyer, the second consul an écuyer, and the third consul a bourgeois. A survey of late seventeenth-century consulates at Aix reveals that first consuls were almost invariably nobles with fiefs; 7 second consuls included 3 nobles (2 with fiefs) and 4 écuyers; 4 third consuls included 1 écuyer, 1 lawyer, and 1 bourgeois; cf. Coste, *Ville*, II, 809–811.

[104] Nobles numerically dominated fifteen of thirty Aix consulates from 1629 to 1659. See Appendix II.

fices did not ennoble. The bourgeoisie, in theory, were represented by the third consul and assessor and at least one-half of the councilors, but in practice the third consul was frequently noble and a minority of the councilors was bourgeois.

To lessen noble control, royal letters changed the election procedure in August 1659. The crown specified that one-half of the councilors had to be bons bourgeois, one-half gens de condition, the assessor a lawyer, and the third consul a bourgeois.[105] The artisans, agricultural laborers, and domestic servants, who were a majority of the population, were not represented. It has long been recognized that French towns of the ancien régime were governed by self-perpetuating local elites. The elite at Aix was strongly aristocratic, reflecting the tone of city life. Friction occurred within the elite between the old and new nobility, not between these privileged few and lesser social groups, as one might expect.

Exclusion of a newer social group from political power by an older, entrenched group is a classic political pattern, which violence is often necessary to change. It is not surprising that there were increasing numbers of violent confrontations at Aix between the old and new nobility during the seventeenth century. On September 26, 1643, the first consul, the comte Du Bar, halted the election with angry words and walked out because his three candidates for first consul were rejected by the election assembly. He refused to return, paralyzing the municipal government because the elections could not be finished. The governor stepped in "to end the factions, monopolies, and intrigues" with royal letters dated October 6, 1643, giving him the right to appoint the Aix municipal government.[106]

The new nobility demanded three reforms in the election procedures. First, they wanted enforcement of existing prohibitions against membership on the city council of close relatives. Second, they wanted a different method of nominating and electing councilors—they wanted either the choice of a hundred notables by the

[105] A.C., Aix, AA 1, fol. 268v; AA 6, fols. 17–23; A.A.E., 1722, fols. 152–165. Municipal governments in the north were usually controlled by bourgeois oligarchies; cf. Temple, "Municipal Elections," pp. 75–84.

[106] A.C., Aix, BB 102, fols. 24–30, September 26, 1643; Lublinskaya, *Vnutrenniaia*, p. 259, Champigny to Séguier, September 28, 1643; Mousnier, *Lettres*, I, 589–590, same.

elections assembly and selection of cités by lot from that list, or the direct nomination and election of new councilors by the election assembly. Third, they wanted eligibility for the office of first consul. These changes did not challenge the basic structure of the city council or the nominating procedure, although they loosened the old nobility's grip on the municipal government. Nothing came of the proposed reforms because the city council could not agree on exact changes.

E. H. Kossmann has stated that social conflict opposing citizens to the municipalities and municipalities to the Parlement was a factor in causing the Fronde, particularly in Guyenne and Provence.[107] He describes a complex hierarchy of groups engaged in battle, the popular classes against the haute-bourgeoisie controlling the municipal government, the haute-bourgeoisie against the parlementaires, and the parlementaires against the governor.[108] This conflict may have been characteristic of Guyenne and Bordeaux,[109] but it does not describe municipal politics at Aix. Factions of old and new nobles fought for control of the Aix municipal government, but their struggles did not cause the Aix revolts or the Fronde.

The parlementaires intermarried with the noble families dominating the municipal government. Intendant Sève wrote in 1649 that among twenty-two noble families controlling the Aix municipal government, eighteen were allied to the parlementaires by marriage or sympathy.[110] Cadet branches of parlementaire families often served as consuls. Parlementaires occasionally intrigued with nobles to fix municipal elections, as in 1643, 1650–1653, 1657,

[107] E. H. Kossmann, *La Fronde* (Leiden, 1954), p. 138.

[108] *Ibid.* and p. 119.

[109] *Ibid.*, pp. 126–136; Nicolas Fessenden, "Epernon and Guyenne; Provincial Politics under Louis XIII" (Ph.D. dissertation, Columbia University, 1972), pp. 42–65. Since the governor of Guyenne, the duc d'Épernon, controlled the *Jurade* of Bordeaux, the Parlement's difficulties with the municipal government in 1648–1649 can also be interpreted as an extension of the Parlement's difficulties with the governor, cf. *ibid.*, pp. 42–65, 238–245; Robert Boutruche, *Bordeaux de 1453 à 1715* (Bordeaux, 1966), pp. 317–320, 337.

[110] B.M., Harleian 4575, fol. 55v. Parlementaire families often served as consuls and intermarried with other noble families active in municipal politics; cf. François-Paul Blanc, "Origine des familles provençales maintenues dans le second ordre sous le regne de Louis XIV: Dictionnaire généalogique" (doctoral dissertation in law, University of Aix-Marseille, 1971).

and 1673–1674.[111] The court exercised direct authority over the city in emergencies such as epidemics, invasions, or revolts, while its indirect influence included mediating disputes between municipal officials, threatening uncooperative officials with prosecution for malfeasance, serving as the appeal for the municipal police court, and registering results of municipal elections and important municipal règlements to give them added force. The comte de Grignan, lieutenant general in the late seventeenth century, avoided visiting Aix whenever possible because the city was dominated by "ambitious and jealous" parlementaires who disputed precedence with him.[112]

The crown frequently used the pretext of disruptive "cabals and intrigues" during municipal elections to name its supporters to the city council. Municipal elections were suspended and royal appointees named in fourteen of twenty-nine annual elections at Aix from 1631 to 1659 (in 1631–1637, 1643–1644, 1647–1648, 1657, and 1659). With three revolts at Aix in thirty years, the crown hoped for greater control through municipal appointments. In addition, the consuls and assessors of Aix were the procureurs du pays, and their appointment gave the crown control over the provincial Estates. The governors often suspended elections in order to name their own clients, thereby increasing their provincial power base. Vitry and Alais, governors of Provence from 1631 to 1650, regularly followed this practice.

After the 1659 revolt, the crown changed the procedure for electing the town council of Aix. Letters patent of August 1659 removed the consulaires, all living past consuls, from participation in the municipal government after their term in office, and from serving in the nomination and election assemblies or the town council. This change was intended to reduce the old nobility's control over the municipal government. Consuls leaving office were to nominate the new consuls and councilors for presentation to the election assembly. In cases of disagreement over nominations, the consuls from the two previous years broke the tie. The consuls

---

[111] Grimaldi and Gaufridy, *Mémoires*, pp. 43–44, 67–69; Pierre-Joseph de Haitze, *Histoire de la ville d'Aix*, 6 vols. (Aix, 1880–1892), VI, 95–102, 244.

[112] Jean-Claude Paulhet, "Les parlementaires toulousains à la fin du dix-septième siècle," *Annales du Midi*, 76 (1964), 189; Marchand, *Un intendant*, p. 69.

were to schedule the election assembly for the Saturday nearest Saint Michael's Day on September 29, and voting was by plurality of voice. One-half of the councilors were to be persons of condition, one-half bourgeois, and the traditional rank distinctions between the consuls and assessor were to be observed. Consuls were eligible for another term after five years had elapsed, councilors after three years. Successions of terms were prohibited. These changes were meant to lessen the strife between the old and new nobility. An interim executive committee of ten to twelve councilors was created to aid the consuls in handling daily business when the town council was not in session. The interim committee was intended to check the power of the consuls. The reforms were ostensibly to prevent municipal elections from becoming occasions for expressing tensions and hostilities.[113]

As Nora Temple has shown, the crown increased its control over municipal governments in the later seventeenth century by increasing its surveillance over revenues and expenditures. Colbert placed municipal finances under the strict supervision of provincial intendants and the contrôle générale, ostensibly to end exploitation by unscrupulous local officials and notables.[114] However, the crown also increased its control over local government by modifying, suspending, and suppressing municipal elections to end supposed abuses.

Provincial politics were rife with quarrels over authority, a chronic condition well known to historians. The overlapping authorities and confused jurisdictions of its institutions and officials were a classic problem of the ancien régime. The problem had two causes. A new office was created for fiscal reasons and given

---

[113] A.C., Aix, AA 6, fols. 17–23; AA 1, fols. 268–271; ADBR, Aix, B 3359, fol. 353. On June 10, 1659, acting intendant Oppède wrote to Mazarin: "The largest faction of council members are those who previously held the office of consul and are perpetual members of the municipal council, and from this perpetuity comes all the evils of the province. The consulaires name the cités, and so the cités are always persons badly or little-intentioned for the king"; cf. A.A.E., 1723, fol. 543. Oppède repeated his accusations and demanded the consulaires' suppression on July 22 and 29, 1659, cf., B.M., Harleian 4493, fols. 78–83, 87–90.

[114] Nora Temple, "The Control and Exploitation of French Towns during the Ancien Régime," *History*, 51 (1966), 16–34. Also see Marcel Marion, *Dictionnaire des institutions de la France au XVIIᵉ et XVIIIᵉ siècles*, 2d ed. (Paris, 1968), pp. 387–391.

slightly different jurisdiction from an older one, without abolishing the older office or assigning it another function. The results were jurisdictional disputes over duplicate powers and functions. After 1500, the growing number of offices created to fill a treasury drained by wars deepened tensions in the provincial administration. Newly created offices caused conflict, hostility, harassment of new officials, and occasional paralysis of government. Creations were bitterly fought by office-holders whose authority and prestige were threatened. The central government engaged provincial officials in endless bickering, while creating new royal officials to bind provincial institutions to the throne. The second cause of the problem was the practice, characteristic of medieval government, of attaching judicial functions to administrative agencies. For example, a *grenier à sel* was at the same time a warehouse for storing salt, a collection agency for the salt tax, and a judicial unit for the trial of offenders against the tax. Widely held judicial powers were responsible for frequent disputes over jurisdiction.

Police powers were a source of dispute because they were possessed by many institutions. A good example is the tangle of conflicting police powers at Aix. Police authority was divided between the viguier, prévôt des maréchaux, municipal police, and criminal lieutenant of the seneschal court. These four authorities also shared criminal jurisdiction—the right to prosecute disturbers of the peace—and their endless quarrels were characteristic of the provincial and municipal administrations.

Another difficulty encountered by provincial and municipal institutions was the tangle of conflicting, archaic laws to be enforced. To Roman law were added the ordinances of the medieval counts and a flood of royal legislation after the union with France. There were also ordinances of the governors, decisions of the sovereign courts, decrees of the municipal governments and various police authorities, decisions of the seigneurial courts, and provincial and local privileges written and unwritten. Taken together, these formed a bewildering and contradictory body of law that depended for enforcement upon authorities whose jurisdictions were equally conflicting, and who resisted attempts at reform as attacks on their power and prestige. The very excess of laws gave local officials great leeway in interpreting which to enforce. In attempting to bring some order into the legal maze, the central government issued a steady stream of directives on enforcement and interpretation, which only increased the chaos. A crisis in command existed in seventeenth-century Aix, an uncertainty about who should obey whom in what circumstances, and who should be prosecuted for what infractions of the law. It was the worst kind of problem in a society where authority was more apparent than real. Within a framework of national, customary, and local law, political life at Aix ebbed and flowed around the governors, intendants, Estates, sovereign courts, nobles, and municipal officials in a bewildering complexity that was a living political organism.

# Chapter Two

# THE ESTATES AND THE HABSBURG WAR

Royal financial and military demands generated by the Habsburg War were an important economic cause of the revolts at Aix: a higher taille and taillon were demanded to support more royal troops in transit. The crown's demands met strong resistance from the traditional tax-granting assembly, the Provençal Estates, and its interim executive authority, the procureurs du pays. Royal attempts to suppress resistance by suspending the Estates and intimidating the procureurs du pays became an important political cause of the revolts at Aix.

Relations between Paris and Madrid deteriorated after 1624, when Richelieu decided to break the Habsburg encirclement. He chose for attack the Spanish military route to the Low Countries, which began at Genoa and went north through Milan and Switzerland to the Rhine, then westward. An alternate Spanish troop route led through Savoy and Piedmont to the Franche-Comté, then northward. Richelieu knew that France could be directly attacked from any one of a half-dozen points on this route, and he determined to destroy it.

His first opportunity came in 1624–1626 with the military campaign in the Valtelline, a mountain valley north of Milan recently added to the Spanish military route. The French, with the Venetians and Savoyards as allies, captured Valtelline fortresses held by papal troops for the Spanish.[1] Richelieu's second opportunity came two years later, when French and Spanish candidates disputed the succession to the duchy of Mantua, strategically adjacent to the route. The French candidate, Charles, duc de Nevers, occupied the duchy's principal fortress, Casale in Montferrat, overlooking the plain of the river Po. In October 1629, the Spanish sent troops under Spinola to drive him out. Crossing the Alps before the

---

[1] Rémy Pithon, "Les débuts difficiles du ministère de Richelieu et la crise de Valteline, 1621–1627," *Revue d'histoire diplomatique*, 74–75 (1960–1961), 298–322.

snows had melted, Louis XIII and Richelieu in March 1630 brought an expeditionary force to relieve Casale. They occupied mountain fortresses in Piedmont and Savoy guarding the passes to France, later signing the Treaty of Cherasco by which these fortresses were returned for recognition of Nevers as duc de Mantua. Finally, on June 6, 1635, Richelieu openly declared war on Spain.[2]

Richelieu had agents in Italy at Genoa, Milan, Venice, Pisa, Florence, Naples, and Messina. This spy network reported early in 1634 that the Spanish were gathering a fleet to land on the Provençal coast. Invasion was rumored on September 28, 1634, when lieutenant general of the galleys Forbin reported to the governor that the Spaniards under Santa Cruz were gathering twenty-six galleys and eight galleons at Naples. The fleet would sail to Sardinia, then land on the French coast near Grasse and march east to Aix in ten or twelve days. An alternate route was to land on the coastal islands off Hyères near Toulon and march north to Aix in five or six days. The crown sent 2,400 soldiers of the Vaillac and La Tour regiments to defend Toulon and Fréjus.[3] On October 19, 1634, the governor of Provence wrote to Richelieu that there were reports of forty Spanish galleys and ten galleons at Corsica preparing to land on the coast between Hyères and Cannes.[4] Councilor Peiresc of the Parlement wrote on October 24 that the Spanish attack was imminent, according to rumors at Aix.[5] But these reports were premature. The landings did not occur.

In January 1635, Richelieu sent marine intendants Du Plessis-Besançon and d'Hémery to supervise the enlargement and repair of fortresses on the islands near Hyères. Six months later, in August 1635, a Spanish fleet of twenty-two galleys and five ships was reported at Monaco awaiting reinforcements. In a surprise attack on September 14–15, this fleet under Garcia Toledo, duc de Fernandina, landed on the Lérins islands of Sainte Marguerite and

---

[2] J. H. Mariéjol, *Henri IV et Louis XIII (1598–1643)*, vol. 6, part 2 of *Histoire de France*, ed. E. Lavisse (Paris, 1911), 278–280; ADBR, Aix, B 3350, fol. 200.

[3] A.A.E., 1702, fols. 253–263; Hubert Méthivier, "Richelieu et le front de mer de Provence," *Revue historique*, 185 (1939), 130–131, 134.

[4] A.A.E., 1702, fol. 301; Méthivier, "Richelieu," p. 132.

[5] Philippe Tamizey de Larroque, ed., *Lettres de Peiresc aux frères Dupuy*, 7 vols. (Paris, 1888–1898), III, 192.

Saint Honorat off the coast at Cannes.[6] The islands fell immediately because they were unfortified and undefended. Caught un-
prepared, the French faced the task of driving out the Spanish
before they could gather support to invade the mainland.

A month after the attack, the Atlantic fleet of fifty-nine ships
sailed into the Mediterranean under the command of the archbishop of Bordeaux and the comte de Harcourt to become a joint
invasion force with the Levant fleet of twenty galleys, thirteen
ships, and three tartanes under the command of galleys general
Pont de Courlay and lieutenant general Forbin.[7] But dissension
paralyzed French efforts to recapture the islands. The French
command was so badly split in 1636 that no plan of action could
be agreed upon. The French were also hampered by a lack of funds
with which to create and supply a landing force.[8] Their efforts to
recapture the Lérins islands had to be postponed until May 1637,
when they launched a successful attack. In June they repelled a
Spanish attempt to land at Saint Tropez on the coast, and in the
following year they defeated the Spanish in a sea battle off Genoa.[9]
In the north, the Habsburg War went badly at first, then improved,
and the Austrians withdrew from combat in the Treaty of West-
phalia on October 24, 1648. But peace with the Spanish Habsburgs was not achieved until the Treaty of the Pyrénées on November 7, 1659.

There were serious obstacles to French participation in the
Habsburg War, including a badly equipped and organized army
and an almost nonexistent navy. Money had to be found to finance
the war from a budget that did not balance in peacetime and a
country experiencing widespread protest against taxation. In 1621,
the crown suffered the first of substantial annual deficits from

[6] Méthivier, "Richelieu," p. 134. Good accounts of the 1635 invasion and
1637 counterattack are given by Honoré Bouche, *La chorographie ou description de Provence*, 2 vols. (Aix, 1664), II, 900–909; René la Bruyère,
*La marine de Richelieu: Sourdis, archevêque et amiral (6 novembre 1594–18
juin 1645)* (Paris, 1948), pp. 38–72; B.M., Harleian 4468, fols. 138–166.

[7] Méthivier, "Richelieu," pp. 135–136.

[8] *Ibid.*, pp. 137–138; A.A.E., 1704, fols. 473–477; Hubert Méthivier,
"Un conflit d'autorité en Provence sous Louis XIII: L'affaire Vitry-Saint
Chamond (Oct. 1634–Jan. 1635)," *Mélanges historiques et littéraires sur le
XVIIᵉ siècle offerts à Georges Mongrédien* (Publications de la Société
d'Etude du XVIIᵉ siècle II, Paris, 1974), pp. 17–23; see Chapter Four.

[9] Méthivier, "Richelieu," pp. 137–138.

military expenditures, which became a national crisis by 1635.[10] After 1639, the crown balanced precariously on a knife-edge between insolvency and bankruptcy. The crown's desperate attempts to secure money and supplies for the Habsburg War provoked revolts throughout France.

There was a steady flow of royal troops through Provence. Military summaries in the Estates' deliberations and the governors' memoirs, while inaccurate and incomplete, indicate approximate numbers and routes of royal troops in Provence in this period. Troops reached numerical peaks in 1629–1631, during the campaign to relieve Casale; in 1635–1637, when the Spanish attacked the Provençal coast; and in 1655–1658, with Mazarin's resumption of the Italian campaign. Troop movements were relatively light in 1640–1653, when the fighting in Catalonia drained soldiers from Provence into Languedoc. There were approximately 18,000 royal troops in transit through Provence in 1629.[11] This figure dropped somewhat in 1631 to 16,400 troops in transit, winter billets, and fortress garrisons.[12] In 1632, there were 9,000–10,000 troops in Provence.[13] The number climbed to 12,000 soldiers in billets during the Spanish invasion in 1635.[14] It fell to 6,550 in billets in 1639[15] and 4,100 in 1640,[16] remaining low

[10] A. D. Lublinskaya, *French Absolutism. The Crucial Phase 1620–1629*, tr. Brian Pearce (Cambridge, 1968), pp. 230, 232. The budget deficit in 1622 was 636,600 livres. The maréchal d'Effiat estimated that the annual deficit by 1629 was 5,000,000 livres. When France went to war, this amount was multiplied by ten; cf. Julian Dent, *Crisis in Finance: Crown, Financiers and Society in Seventeenth Century France* (London, 1973), pp. 42–43.

[11] A.C., Aix, BB 100, fol. 59; ADBR, Marseille, C 15, fols. 200v–201, 258; C 16, fols. 4v, 34–43v; ADBR, Aix, B 3348, fols. 199, 261; A.A.E., 1701, fol. 106; Bouche, *La chorographie*, II, 876; Tamizey de Larroque, *Lettres de Peiresc*, II, 25–26; P. Lacour-Gayet, R. Lavolée, eds. *Mémoires du cardinal de Richelieu*, 10 vols. (Paris, 1907–1931), IX, 155–157.

[12] ADBR, Marseille, C 17, fols. 147v–152v; C 19, fols. 167v, 181–189; Honoré d'Agut, "Discours du Parlement de Provence," B. Méjanes 906, fol. 185; René Pillorget, "Les Cascaveoux: L'insurrection aixoise de l'automne, 1630," *XVIIe siècle*, 64 (1964), 25.

[13] A.A.E., 1702, fol. 134.

[14] A.A.E., 1703, fol. 329; 1704, fols. 102, 242v; Méthivier, "Richelieu," p. 137.

[15] "Effectifs réels et solde des armées françaises en 1639 d'après le règlement du 24 juillet 1638," in Georges d'Avenel, *Richelieu et la monarchie absolue*, 4 vols., 2nd ed. (Paris, 1895), III, 442–443.

[16] A.A.E., 1707, fols. 14–15; Méthivier, "Richelieu," pp. 139–140.

until the Fronde began.[17] In 1655, there were approximately 6,630 royal soldiers in Provence,[18] increasing to 7,350 in 1656[19] and 10,000 in 1657.[20]

Soldiers were expensive and destructive. On March 2, 1629, councilor Peiresc of the Parlement complained that royal troops were stealing, kidnapping for ransom, and raping their way across Provence. Disciplinary hangings made no difference:[21] they plundered and stole because they had not been paid.[22] The Parlement's avocat-général complained to chancellor Séguier on July 24, 1635, of the soldiers' violence, theft, and disorder.[23] French-speaking soldiers were little different from foreigners to the Provençaux, and in behavior no different from the enemy. The village of Les Mées rioted in July 1637 because of the misconduct of the Boissac light horse company billeted there.[24] In May 1640, the towns of Fréjus and Draguignan rioted and killed two cavalrymen of the La Chapelle cavalry regiment.[25] Soldiers on the march also carried contagious disease. In July 1629, eight infantry regiments of the maréchal d'Estrées, who had marched his troops along the Provençal coast four months earlier, returned to Languedoc carrying plague.[26] There were false rumors in May 1640 and August 1657 that passing troops had brought plague to Provence.[27]

Basse-Provence—the Rhone valley and coast—the most prosperous, populated region, and the coastal route to Italy, had the highest concentration of troops. Regiment after regiment marched from the Huguenot campaigns in Languedoc along the Provençal coast to the battlefields of northern Italy. Soldiers from the north ferried down the Rhone to Arles were marched east to Italy or

[17] There were approximately 4,050 soldiers billeted in Provence in 1646; cf. ADBR, Marseille, C 27, fols. 255v–258; B.N., Clairambault 408, fols. 70–72.

[18] ADBR, Marseille, C 35, fols. 14–28.

[19] *Ibid.*, C 37, fols. 42–46.

[20] *Ibid.*, fols. 194–196.

[21] Tamizey de Larroque, *Lettres de Peiresc*, II, 45–47.

[22] *Ibid.*, 7.

[23] B.N., Ms. fr. 17369, fol. 85.

[24] A. D. Lublinskaya, ed., *Vnutrenniaia politika frantsuzskogo absoliutizma, 1633–1645* (Leningrad, 1966), pp. 244–245.

[25] A.A.E., 1707, fol. 94.

[26] Tamizey de Larroque, *Lettres de Peiresc*, II, 7; Pierre-Joseph de Haitze, *Histoire de la ville d'Aix*, 6 vols. (Aix, 1880–1892), IV, 144–145.

[27] A.A.E., 1707, fol. 94; Delib. Parl., B. Méjanes 954, fol. 133.

embarked at the coastal ports for Italy, then retraced their steps west and north.

Provincial and military intendants wrote to the secretary of war for money to transport and pay the troops, but funds were delayed or never arrived—the crown had no money to send. From March through June 1648, provincial intendant Sève threatened, complained, and pleaded for money to transport several hundred troops down the Rhone from Arles to Toulon for embarkation. On May 5, Sève wrote that the governor of the royal fortress at Toulon, Estampes de Valençay, desperately needed money because he was maintaining troops there from his own pocket. On June 23, Sève wrote that the troops at Toulon and Arles had finally been billeted on those cities because there was no other way to feed them. He and Estampes had exhausted their money and credit, and still no money was sent.[28] Such delays were common. As a result, soldiers stole from the families with whom they were billeted. Seventeenth-century soldiers lived under a brutal, exploitative system, and they behaved accordingly. Hungry, unpaid because of the crown's chronic insolvency, victims of officers who extorted their pay before they received it, soldiers terrorized the local population into providing what they needed.

Troop support was a major tax expenditure. The taille in Provence increased dramatically during the Habsburg War, until the annual average was well over a million livres. The taille was a direct royal tax assessed annually on nonnoble or *roturier* land and collected by the Estates regardless of the owners' rank: the clergy and nobility paid the taille in Provence on their nonnoble land. Only a small percentage of land was noble and exempt. In 1620, the Provençal Estates approved a taille of 271,000 livres.[29] In 1657, the General Assembly of the Communities (which replaced the Estates) approved a taille of 1,845,450 livres, roughly a 400 percent increase in four decades, allowing for currency devaluation.[30] The increase began in 1631, when the Estates paid a rachat for revocation of the edict of élus of 2,000,000 livres; the

[28] A.A.E., 1713, fol. 123, March 31, 1648; fol. 140, April 7, 1648; fol. 177, May 5, 1648; fol. 211, June 23, 1648.

[29] B.N., Cinq Cents de Colbert 288, fols. 1–2; ADBR, Marseille, C 12, fols. 205–241; Lublinskaya, *French Absolutism*, p. 226, n. 4.

[30] ADBR, Marseille, C 37, fols. 63–66, 336–338v.

total taille was 2,123,048 livres.[31] The taille in 1632 was 1,110,000 livres[32] and 975,000 livres in 1634.[33] The Spanish invasion accelerated the increase, and in 1636 Provence paid 2,222,287 livres in taille, much of which was a voluntary gift to fight the Spanish.[34] The taille was 1,329,048 livres in 1639,[35] 1,211,000 livres in 1641,[36] and 967,089 livres in 1647.[37] The taille averaged somewhat more than 1,000,000 livres until the end of the Fronde,[38] climbed again in 1655 to 1,918,700 livres,[39] and continued at a high level until the end of the war.[40] In general, the taille was lower from 1640 to 1653, when the theater of war shifted away from Provence, and higher in 1629–1631, 1631–1637, and 1655–1658, when there were military campaigns in the southeast.

A substantial portion of the taille was used to reimburse communities for quartering royal troops. About 150 of 630 communities were designated as stopping points for troops in transit or as billets.[41] Provence was expected to provide *étapes*, winter quarters, including lodging and *ustensile*, garrison support, *ban* and *milice*, contributions to the *solde* and supplies of troops on campaign.[42]

[31] ADBR, Marseille, C 16, fols. 124v–133; C 19, fols. 99–125, 153v; B.N., Cinq Cents de Colbert 288, fols. 15–18.

[32] ADBR, Marseille, C 20, fols. 201–278v; A.A.E., 1702, fols. 155–160.

[33] ADBR, Marseille, C 22, fols. 95v–115v.

[34] A.A.E., 1704, fol. 100; ADBR, Marseille, C 23, fols. 152–175v, 187–214v, 250–292; B.N., Cinq Cents de Colbert 288, fols. 25v–30v.

[35] ADBR, Marseille, C 26, fols. 39–40v; B.N., Cinq Cents de Colbert 288, fols. 36–37v.

[36] ADBR, Marseille, C 26, fols. 267v–271v; B.N., Cinq Cents de Colbert 288, fols. 40–42.

[37] ADBR, Marseille, C 29, fols. 1–47; B.N., Cinq Cents de Colbert 288, fols. 48–50.

[38] The taille was 1,332,000 livres in 1651; cf. B.N., Cinq Cents de Colbert 288, fols. 53–55. It was 1,243,000 livres in 1653; cf. ADBR, Marseille, C 32, fol. 216.

[39] ADBR, Marseille, C 33, fol. 146v.

[40] The taille was 1,389,000 livres in 1656; cf. *ibid.*, fol. 298.

[41] Intendant Lebret in a letter on November 29, 1717, estimated that there were 630 communities in Provence; cf. Bruno Durand in "Le rôle des consuls d'Aix dans l'administration du pays," *Mélanges Busquet, Provence historique* (December 1956), 250.

[42] Consult Camille Rousset, *Histoire du Louvois et son administration politique et militaire*, 4 vols. (Paris, 1862–1863); Louis André, *Michel Le Tellier et l'organisation de l'armée monarchique* (Paris, 1906), and *Michel*

Needless to say, communities were not fully reimbursed for military support, which in bad years was equivalent to a second taille. There were also a number of indirect taxes levied by the crown: creations of new judicial offices, augmentations des gages, levies of the taxes of franc-feif, amortissement, nouveaux acquêts, and gabelle. These soared during the Habsburg War.

Pays d'états, provinces with Estates, formed one-third of France in surface area, and it was reasonable for the crown to expect them to pay one-third of the taille. From an average annual taille of 40,000,000 livres, the pays d'états should have contributed 30 percent, or approximately 13,300,000 livres, but they paid 11 percent, or approximately 4,400,000 livres.[43] Provence and Languedoc paid the least. In 1620, Languedoc paid 223,900 livres in taille, and Provence paid 170,000 livres. Both provinces had Estates as a traditional privilege and a taille réelle, a direct tax on nonnoble, real property. In contrast, Normandy paid 2,274,000 livres.[44] The Estates of Normandy were more or less moribund, the taille collected by royal agents known as élus. In 1629, with the financial pinch of the Habsburg War, the crown determined to make privileged provinces pay their share of the taille and launched an offensive against the Estates.

The taille was assessed by feux, units of measure of the value of real property, approximately 35,000 livres each in 1634 and 50,000 livres each in 1732.[45] The affouagement was a list of 3,000 feux in 22 administrative districts known as vigueries. The affouagement listed the taxable property of communities within vigueries in terms of feux, and thus apportioned the taille to be paid among the vigueries.[46]

---

*Le Tellier et Louvois* (Paris, 1942); André Corvisier, *L'armée française de la fin du XVIIᵉ siècle au ministère de Choiseul: Le soldat,* 2 vols. (Paris, 1964); Douglas Baxter, *Servants of the Sword: French Intendants of the Army, 1630–1670* (Urbana, 1976); Bernard Hildesheimer, *Les assemblées générales des communautés de Provence* (Paris, 1935).

[43] Mariéjol, *Henri IV et Louis XIII,* p. 400.

[44] Lublinskaya, *French Absolutism,* p. 226, n. 4.

[45] Letter of intendant Lebret cited by Durand, "Le rôle des consuls," 251; Pillorget, *Les mouvements,* p. 114. A feu was 55,000 livres in 1789; cf. EDB, III, 546.

[46] An extract from the council of state's registers for July 15, 1656, cites 3,000 feux in Provence; cf. A.A.E., 1721, fols. 13–14. The 1664–1665 affouagement listed a total of 3,031 feux in the vigueries, 3,315 including

The Provençal Estates were convened annually by the governor on behalf of the crown to approve and grant the sum in taille allocated in the royal budget. The archbishop of Aix, his vicar general, 10 bishops and 2 abbots of Provence composed the first estate. Nobles owning fiefs composed the second, and attended in varying numbers: there were 160 at the Tarascon Estates in 1631 and 220 at the Brignoles Estates in 1632. Communities with the right of representation composed the third estate. There were 37 in the seventeenth century, the chief towns of the 22 vigueries and 15 additional towns of importance.[47] Each community sent 2 of its consuls as deputies, a total of 64. A syndic represented nonmember communities. The last general meeting of the Estates at Aix in February 1639 was attended by the archbishop of Aix, 10 bishops, 166 nobles, and 64 deputies from the communities.[48]

The Estates collected the taille through its member communities and vigueries. The community receiver gave the sum to the viguerie receiver, who transmitted it to the taille receiver, who turned it over to the provincial treasurer. The procureurs du pays verified the treasurer's books before their audit by the Cour des Comptes. Only then was the sum turned over to the Trésoriers Généraux de France.[49]

The provincial treasurer had a difficult task. The communities were chronically behind in their tax payments, while the clergy and nobility escaped payment through litigation, false assessments, exemptions, and intimidation. When tax money was not forthcoming, the provincial treasurer had to borrow from merchants and bankers in Marseille or Paris, whomever would lend to him on behalf of

---

the terres adjacentes; cf. B. Méjanes 792, "Mémoire du pays de Provence par Le Bret, intendant," fols. 215–261. The affouagement of 1728, in use until 1790, listed 2,927 feux in the vigueries and 284 feux in the adjacent areas, excluding Marseille; cf. EDB, III, 545–546.

[47] See M. J. Bry, *Les vigueries de Provence* (Paris, 1910), p. 219; and EDB, III, 466 for lists of vigueries and communities eligible to attend the Estates. Bry gives twenty-three vigueries, separating Barrême from Lorgues. René Pillorget, *Les mouvements insurrectionnels de Provence entre 1596 et 1715* (Paris, 1975), pp. 101–104.

[48] ADBR, Marseille, C 25, fols. 227–279v; Hildesheimer, *Assemblées générales*, pp. 69–70; EDB, III, 474. There were thirty-seven communities and vigueries represented, with one syndic for nonmember communities, and two procureurs of the communities.

[49] Consult Hildesheimer, *Assemblées générales*, pp. 115–116; Bry, *Vigueries*, pp. 219–348; Jean-Paul Charmeil, *Les trésoriers de France à l'époque de la Fronde* (Paris, 1964), pp. 155–158.

the Estates, usually in long-term notes with projected tax revenues as collateral. Prospective treasurers bid for contracts of five to twenty years to collect taxes for the Estates, a perilous occupation.[50] Intendant Lauzon announced to the procureurs du pays on December 14, 1638, that if he did not immediately receive 10,800 livres in back salary, he would seize Gaillard's household furnishings. The treasurer hurriedly borrowed this sum.[51] Gaillard went bankrupt in 1651 after three decades as treasurer. Blanc went bankrupt in 1690, followed by Creysel in 1702.[52]

The General Assembly of the Communities was a separate assembly of the third estate, meeting annually after the mid-sixteenth century. The respective authorities of the Estates and General Assembly were ill-defined, with no real division of functions or powers.[53] The communities proved more cooperative without the nobility, and meetings of the General Assembly provided a way for the crown to request approval for taxation without summoning the Estates. Separate general assemblies of the other two estates also met regularly to protect their interests. The General Assembly of the Nobility was highly litigious, claiming exemptions from the taille for its members and attempting to substantiate them before the Cour des Comptes. It was not convened after 1639, with the exception of meetings in 1656 and 1688, and was replaced by small assemblies of thirty to forty noble deputies.[54] The General Assembly of the Clergy did not meet regularly after 1635, and was replaced by small assemblies of deputies from the dioceses.[55] Of the four Provençal representative assemblies in the late sixteenth century—the Estates and the General Assemblies of the Clergy, Nobility, and Communities—only the last continued to meet regularly after the mid-seventeenth century.

---

[50] ADBR, Marseille, C 32, fols. 288–288v, 301; Hildesheimer, *Assemblées générales*, p. 125; Boisgelin, *Maurel de Villeneuve de Mons*, (Digne, 1904), pp. 27–28.

[51] ADBR, Marseille, C 25, fol. 215. Lauzon obtained a decree of the council of state in August, 1638, ordering immediate payment; cf. *ibid.*, fol. 198.

[52] See Jean Audouard, *Un krach financier au XVIIIᵉ siècle: La faillite de Pierre Creissel, trésorier général des Etats de Provence (1702)* (Paris, 1910).

[53] EDB, III, 452, 475–477. The terms Estates and General Assemblies were often used interchangeably by local officials.

[54] EDB, III, 508–521.      [55] *Ibid.*, pp. 521–532.

In July 1629, the crown issued an edict transforming Provence from a pays d'états to a pays d'élections, where the taille was collected by royal agents called élus. (Three other pays d'états, Dauphiné, Languedoc, and Burgundy, were threatened with the establishment of élus in the same year.) Ten bureaus and seats of élections with 350 élus were planned for Provence, with the chief seat at Aix.[56] It is probable that, as in Normandy, the Estates would have continued as a rubber stamp to approve taxes collected by the élus. But there existed the possibility that the Estates would be suppressed, as in Dauphiné. The élus' assessment and collection of the taille would have reduced illegal exemptions, nonpayment, and back taxes.

The edict of élus was accompanied by increases in the taillon and gabelle. The taillon was a direct land tax established by Henry II in 1549 and used to support the provincial police and coastal fortifications. It was 36,000 livres in Provence in 1627, levied with the taille as a surtax. Letters patent on May 18, 1627, announced its increase to 100,000 livres.[57] A compromise was only reached after the 1630 revolt, when the Estates at Tarascon and Brignoles accepted 70,000 livres.[58]

The gabelle was a combination sales, consumption, and circulation tax on salt. Provence was a *pays de petites gabelles*, where salt was produced naturally by evaporation in coastal marshes. The natural advantage of lower salt prices also lowered gabelle revenues. The expected total gabelle for France in 1649 was 18,293,300 livres. Of this only 806,000 livres came from Provence and Dauphiné, combined as one gabelle district in 1627. In contrast, 3,609,000 livres came from Auvergne, Velay, Vivarais, and Languedoc.[59] The crown was determined to increase gabelle revenues.

[56] B.N., Ms. fr. 24166, fol. 224; "Mémoires pour l'histoire de Provence," B. Méjanes 794, fols. 197–202; "Histoire du Parlement," B. Méjanes R.A. 54, fol. 218.

[57] ADBR, Marseille, C 15, fols. 122v–123. This was an increase of three to fourteen livres per feu.

[58] A.A.E., 1702, fols. 155–160, 179–180; ADBR, Marseille C 16, fols. 144–145v; C 20, fols. 201–278v; "Brevets de la taille," B.N., Ms. fr. n.a. 199, fols. 35v–36v; 200, fols. 84v–85v, 251v–252v.

[59] George Matthews, *The Royal General Farms in Eighteenth Century France* (New York, 1958), pp. 99–101; Dent, *Crisis in Finance*, pp. 36–37; Charmeil, *Les trésoriers*, p. 164, nn. 56, 61, 62.

The Estates at Aix in May 1628 protested royal letters of the previous year reducing the salt measure in Provence by one-third and increasing the price by 50 percent, while the Cour des Comptes and Parlement issued arrêts prohibiting levy of the new gabelle.[60] The Provençal measure for salt and wheat, the emine was valued at approximately eight gallons at Aix. In 1627, it was decided to replace the emine with the French measure, the minot used in Languedoc, about two-thirds the value.[61] The price of salt escalated at the same time. It had gone from 2 livres, 15 sols an emine in 1598, to 4 livres, 9 sols in 1622, to 6 livres, 10 sols in 1627.[62] Assessor Gaufridy protested that the increase threatened provincial liberties.[63] The Estates at Aix in 1628 also protested the creation of new judicial and financial offices, the *auditeurs des comptes tutélaires* and *experts jurés*, an edict that the Parlement had refused to register in March. They also opposed the creation of thirty-seven new offices in the Cour des Comptes and the transfer of that court's jurisdiction over the auditing of community tax payments and the royal domaine to the Trésoriers Généraux. In July 1629, the Tarascon Estates unsuccessfully offered the crown 900,000 livres to revoke the increases in the taillon and gabelle.[64] The emine was retained only with great difficulty.

Called in September 1630 by the Parlement in the governor's absence, and chaired by president Forbin de La Roque, the General Assembly of the Nobility at Pertuis was openly hostile to the élus. A month later, the General Assembly of the Communities met at Aix. Called by the Parlement and chaired by dean Ollivier, this meeting voted for the distribution of arms and copies of Provençal privileges to member communities. Assessor Martelli declared that "the edict of élections would bring the destruction of all the usages, customs, privileges, and liberties . . . to the extent that from good

[60] A.C., Aix, BB 100, fols. 56v–58v; ADBR, Marseille, C 15, fols. 131, 176v–177; B.N., Cinq Cents de Colbert 288, fol. 5; B. Inguimbertine 1841, fols. 346–346v.

[61] Pillorget, *Les mouvements*, pp. 355–358.

[62] *Ibid.*; Lublinskaya, *Vnutrenniaia*, de La Potherie to Séguier, May 23, 1633; J. Marchand, *Un intendant sous Louis XIV: Etude sur l'administration de Lebret en Provence (1687–1704)* (Paris, 1889), pp. 175–176. By 1661, the price of salt had risen to fifteen livres a minot.

[63] ADBR, Marseille, C 15, fol. 131.

[64] *Ibid.*, fols. 311–357; Agut, "Discours du Parlement," B. Méjanes 906, fol. 242; ADBR, Aix, B 3347, fol. 1217; A.A.E., 794, fol. 22.

and faithful subjects as the Provençaux have been recognized during past centuries . . . they would be changed into captives and miserable slaves."[65] The edict of élus, the increases in the taillon and gabelle, and the creations of new offices were an important cause of the revolt at Aix in 1630.

The Estates at Tarascon and Brignoles, after the revolt, agreed to pay the crown a total of 2,000,000 livres to revoke the edict of élus and to guarantee no future increases in the gabelle.[66] But two years later, in October 1634, the crown raised the gabelle from 6 livres, 10 sols an emine to 22 livres, 10 sols. Jacques Talon was sent as a royal commissioner to establish the increase, aided by governor Vitry.[67] Talon sent his letters of commission to the two sovereign courts for registration. The Parlement accepted the letters in writing; the Cour des Comptes refused them.[68] Assuming leadership of Provençal resistance to the salt increase, the Cour des Comptes issued an arrêt on October 8 forbidding Talon to execute his commission, and reestablishing the old prices. The Cour des Comptes, Estates, and cities of Aix, Arles, and Marseille sent to Paris a remonstrance on the price increase, which the Parlement refused to join.[69] Talon did not enter Aix because of popular hostility, and there was near riot when he attempted to post the new prices at the Marseille salt warehouse on the morning of October 10. The new prices were not posted at Marseille for another month.[70]

[65] ADBR, Marseille, C 17, fols. 61–61v, published by Félix Tavernier in *Marseille et la Provence sous la royauté 1481–1789* (Aix-en-Provence, n.d.), pp. 14–15.

[66] *Ibid.*, C 16, fols. 144v–145; C 20, fols. 201–278v; ADBR, Aix, B 3349, fols. 590–606.

[67] Lublinskaya, *Vnutrenniaia*, p. 240, Cour des Comptes to Séguier, October 17, 1634; B.N., Cinq Cents de Colbert 288, fols. 22–22v; A.N., E 119A, fol. 32v.

[68] Tamizey de Larroque, *Correspondance de Peiresc*, II, 184–185.

[69] ADBR, Marseille, C 22, fols. 102–102v, 134v–135; A.A.E., 1702, fols. 265–267, 270–273. The Cour des Comptes complained to Séguier about the increase on October 13, 1634, cf., B.N., Ms. fr. 17369, fol. 178.

[70] Tamizey de Larroque, *Lettres de Peiresc*, II, 184–185; A.A.E., 1702, fols. 265–267, 270–273; Dent, *Crisis in Finance*, p. 37. The 1634 gabelle increase disrupted municipal elections at Marseille on October 28. There was also violent protest against the gabelle in November; cf. René Pillorget, "Destin de la ville d'ancien régime," in *Histoire de Marseille*, ed. Edouard Baratier (Toulouse, 1973), p. 177.

The crown did not abandon its attack on the Provençal Estates after the 1630 revolt at Aix. Instead, it shifted its attention to the don gratuit. Troop expenses were higher during the five months of winter quarters, so the crown usually requested a supplement to the taille, a voluntary gift or don gratuit for winter support. Provence, at the frontier, had substantial numbers of troops in winter quarters. Only the Estates had the right to vote dons gratuits, which it disliked doing for fear of establishing an annual precedent. The Estates refused to vote voluntary gifts in 1628 and 1629. The General Assembly of 1633 refused to approve a don gratuit. There were no Estates convened from 1633 to 1639. The issue reached a climax during the Estates at Aix in February 1639, when the crown demanded 600,000 livres for military expenses within the province, 400,000 livres as a voluntary gift, 200,000 livres additional for winter quarters—a total of 1,200,000 livres—and unspecified support for winter quarters outside the province for the duration of the war. The Estates noisily protested and offered less than half what the crown requested, 500,000 livres for military expenses, which they increased to 600,000 livres after the governor's threats. They refused to vote a voluntary gift or support for the army outside Provence.[71]

In contrast, the General Assembly of Communities convened in November 1639 at Fréjus approved an additional 700,000 livres for a total grant of 1,320,048 livres, including a voluntary gift of 300,000 livres in the guise of supplementing winter quarters in Provence.[72] Thereafter, the governor convoked the more cooperative General Assemblies to approve annual grants of approximately 1,000,000 livres and disguised voluntary gifts of 300,000 livres from 1640 to 1649. The Estates were not summoned.[73] After 1648, the General Assembly requested unsuccessfully each year that an Estates be called. In 1660, it finally dropped the fiction that it was voting additional winter quarters support averaging 300,000 livres a year by voting the crown an outright voluntary gift, thus recog-

[71] ADBR, Marseille, C 25, fols. 238–245; Hildesheimer, *Assemblées générales*, p. 72; EDB, III, 474.

[72] ADBR, Marseille, C 26, fols. 22v, 39–40v. The General Assembly at Draguignan in 1640 voted 1,000,000 livres; cf. *ibid.*, fols. 158–160.

[73] See Jules Viguier, *La convocation des Etats Généraux en Provence, 1787–1788* (Paris, 1896).

nizing the Estates' permanent suppression.[74] After 1664, the General Assembly of the Communities met annually at Lambesc. The Estates did not sit again.

Not only the royal taxes of the taille, don gratuit, taillon, and gabelle were increased by the war's demands. The Habsburg War also had the effect of increasing municipal taxes, one cause of the 1659 revolt. The cities of Aix and Toulon enjoyed the traditional privilege of substituting taxes on merchandise entering their gates for the taille. Municipal taxes were heavy, bringing proportionately more money than the taille on land. There were rêves at Aix on flour, bread, beef, fresh and salted fish, oil, and wine sold in shops. The rêve on flour, collected at a toll booth inside the Saint Jean gate, increased the price of bread. The rêves at Aix were a burden on the lower classes, who were not property owners and should not have paid the taille. Exemption of nobles and clergy from the rêves, although not from the taille, increased resentment. Intendant Champigny informed chancellor Séguier in letters on September 28 and 29, 1643, that assessor Du Fort had made seditious speeches against the rêves.[75] The parlementaires in January 1649 obtained popular support for their revolt by suspending the rêve on flour.[76]

On August 30, 1653, the Cour des Comptes authorized a trial increase of five sols per quintal on flour and twelve sols per quintal on oil, making the increase permanent on October 28.[77] The municipal government cited a deficit of 37,300 livres in its budget as justification.[78] On August 14, when the Aixois learned that the municipal council had tentatively approved the increase, a crowd of protesters pushed through the Saint Jean gate without paying the tax. When the permanent increase was announced, a crowd attacked the hôtel of consul Cabassol, who had defended the tax, sacked his house and broke all the windows and doors, crying

[74] Hildesheimer, *Assemblées générales*, pp. 72–73, 144, 148. The General Assemblies voted voluntary gifts of 500,000 livres from 1672 to 1675, 600,000 to 800,000 livres from 1676 to 1692, and 700,000 livres in 1693.

[75] Roland Mousnier, *Lettres et mémoires adressés au chancelier Séguier (1633–1649)*, 2 vols. (Paris, 1964), I, 589–590; Lublinskaya, *Vnutrenniaia*, pp. 259–261; Hildesheimer, *Assemblées générales*, pp. 203–204.

[76] See Chapter Eight.

[77] A.C., Aix, AA 14, fol. 317.

[78] *Ibid.*, fol. 322; see Appendix II.

65

"Vivo lou Rey, Fuero fermo" (Long live the king, Down with taxes). They also destroyed the toll booth inside the Saint Jean gate.[79]

Monetary devaluation worsened the effect of municipal tax increases. Devaluation was a deliberate royal monetary policy, and the 1602 devaluation began an avalanche. Coins in circulation did not carry indications of value. Named for their appearance, their value was assigned by legislative act, and to depreciate the currency, the crown had only to issue an edict assigning new values to coins in circulation, which it did increasingly during the Habsburg War to obtain revenue. The book value of the livre-tournois declined 17 percent from 1593 to 1633, and 25 percent from 1634 to 1652.[80] The decline in value was also caused by counterfeiting and the introduction of debased foreign currencies by merchants, smugglers, and black marketeers hoping to make a quick profit.

Foreign coins of inferior quality were widely used in Provence, which suffered from its specialization in a Spanish-Italian trade. Spanish gold pistoles, silver reales and copper cuartillons, Italian scudi and piastres had little value. Genoese merchants had the worst reputation for currency speculation, and they were among the most numerous foreign merchants in Marseille. On October 6, 1648, president Gaufridy of the Semester Parlement wrote to chancellor Séguier that the new Spanish reale should be banned from Provence because it had recently been devalued by twenty-three sols per reale; some reports said thirty.[81] On October 27, 1648, Gaufridy wrote that Genoese merchants had introduced 70,000 bad piastres into Marseille a month earlier, causing riots.[82] Provence also suffered a steady drain of good silver coins to the small

[79] Haitze, *Histoire*, V, 297; A.C., Aix, AA 14, fol. 318; BB 102, fols. 268v–273, 278. Municipal excise taxes on meat and flour, levied to pay municipal debts at Marseille, provoked riots in 1603, 1607, and 1609; cf. Pillorget, "Destin de la ville," 172–176, and "Luttes de factions et intérêts économiques à Marseille de 1598 à 1615," *Annales: ESC* 27 (1972), 705–730.

[80] The livre-tournois went from 10.98 grams of silver in 1602 to 8.33 grams in 1641; cf. René Pillorget, "Les problèmes monétaires français de 1602 à 1689," *XVII<sup>e</sup> siècle*, 70–71 (1966), p. 120; Frank Spooner, *The International Economy and Monetary Movements in France, 1493–1725*, 2nd ed. (Cambridge, Mass., 1972), pp. 97–105, 179–195.

[81] B.N., Ms. fr. 17390, fols. 239–240.

[82] *Ibid.*, fols. 262–264.

neighboring principalities of the Comtat Venaissin, Orange, and Monaco, which minted quantities of inferior copper coins.[83] Orange had twelve presses in operation in 1628 and Avignon six: there were complaints that these presses were flooding the Rhone valley with inferior copper coins, causing riots at Marseille in 1636 and 1637.[84]

Copper coins with a small percentage of silver were known as *billon*. This "black money," deniers, double-deniers worth two pennies, liards worth three pennies, was widely used by the lower classes. On January 20, 1609, the crown gave permission for the establishment of four mints producing copper coins at Aix, Dijon, Bordeaux, and Paris.[85] Aix coined 15,000 livres in copper from 1611 to 1620. On February 17, 1617, Henri Du Plessis, sieur de Richelieu—the surname was not a coincidence—received a contract to issue copper currency in the sum of 60,000 livres within six years in the cities of Aix, Lyon, Toulouse, and Nantes.[86] In the decade from 1641 to 1650, 60,000 livres in copper were coined at Vienne and Valence, another 100,000 livres at Roquemaure near Nîmes.[87] The Rhone valley was flooded with low-quality copper coins.

On March 23, 1640, the procureurs du pays protested a February ordinance of the intendant ordering the provincial treasurer to pay 13,200 livres deducted from his tax payments as a loss from "lightweight and clipped gold coins" received in tax monies.[88] In August 1643, the crown devalued by one-half the double-tournois or double-denier, worth two pennies. The effects were felt immediately at Aix. On October 30, the town council learned that the municipality had lost 3,000 livres in the devaluation, while the city's bakers were refusing to accept the coin or using an exchange rate of twelve double-tournois to one sol.[89] Parlement presidents Régusse and Foresta de La Roquette wrote to Séguier on September 8 that the devaluation was causing riots at Arles and Marseille because the coin was frequently used by the *menu peuple*, as were

---

[83] Pillorget, "Les problèmes monétaires," 112, 116–117.

[84] Spooner, *International Economy*, pp. 178–187, 187, n. 213.

[85] *Ibid.*, p. 175.

[86] *Ibid.*, p. 177.      [87] *Ibid.*, p. 219.

[88] ADBR, Marseille, C 26, fol. 66v.

[89] A.C., Aix, BB 102, fol. 29. The livre-tournois was composed of twenty sols of twelve deniers each.

Italian coins.[90] And continued serious depreciation after 1650 adversely affected low-income groups.

On April 22, 1653, a royal edict increased the value of gold and silver coins in circulation, but their value was decreased by another royal edict three months later.[91] These manipulations caused a shortage of silver coins at Aix. There was an abortive meeting of the procureurs du pays on July 27 to discuss remedies.[92] On August 30, the Cour des Comptes announced the increase in rêves, which became permanent in October: the devaluations contributed to popular protest against the municipal tax increase. On December 23, 1658, the Cour des Comptes authorized another increase in the municipal flour tax of 2 sols, 6 deniers per quintal —for a total tax of 7 sols, 6 deniers per quintal of flour.[93] This increase contributed to popular participation in the revolt at Aix in February 14, 1659.

Written summonses to attend a meeting of the Estates or General Assembly of the Communities were dispatched by the procureurs du pays on the governor's orders. At Aix, the delegates usually met in the main council chamber of the town hall, a large square room paneled in dark wood to the height of six feet. Curtains of dark green velvet covered the doors and the wall behind the dais. The wall hangings hid an altar, where mass was said before the meeting began. The deputies rose as a mark of respect to greet the governor, perhaps the lieutenant general or another official acting as the crown's representative, when he arrived to open the meeting.

The governor sat on the dais with his back to the curtained wall in an armchair covered with a tapestry, his guard captain at his feet. The archbishop of Aix sat to his left, the provincial intendant to his right, both in armchairs. Below the archbishop was a bench for the vicar general of Aix and the two procureurs or representatives of the clergy, and below the intendant was a similar bench for the two procureurs of the nobility. An armchair for the syndic of the unrepresented communities was positioned behind the bench

[90] Lublinskaya, *Vnutrenniaia*, p. 259, La Roquette to Séguier, September 8, 1643, pp. 258–259, Régusse to Séguier, September 8, 1643.
[91] Bouche, *La chorographie*, II, 984–985.
[92] ADBR, Marseille, C 32, fol. 127.
[93] A.C., Aix, AA 14, fol. 683.

for the clergy, followed by a bench for the consuls of Aix as the procureurs du pays. Finally, there was a table covered with a tapestry for the secretary of the Estates and his clerk. The provincial treasurer sat to one side in an armchair. The deputies sat across the room in rows of stall seats used by the municipal councilors and on extra benches installed for the occasion. The positioning of seats and the order of speakers were carefully noted and frequently disputed.[94]

The opening ceremony lasted all morning. The governor spoke, then the intendant, followed by the archbishop of Aix, the assessor, and the other procureurs. The speeches were lengthy, grandiloquent, fulsome with praise for the king and each other, too ornate for modern taste. With the windows closed against "unhealthy" air, the room packed with men, and the speakers long-winded, the atmosphere was oppressive. The angry debates, name-calling, insults, and threats that would enliven the sessions had to wait for a few days.

The consuls and assessor of the Aix municipal government, the procureurs nés du pays, acted as an executive committee for the Estates and General Assemblies when they were not in session. Originally composed of deputies from ten or fifteen Provençal communities, the procuration developed during the sixteenth century. Gradually it narrowed to the Aix municipal government. The procureurs du pays met once a week at Aix, asking the governor to call a general meeting when conditions arose beyond their interim authority. Customarily, they approved assignment of royal troops billeted on the communities, reimbursement of communities for troop support, expenditure of tax monies for extraordinary expenses, and levy of temporary taxes for additional expenses. They were aided by six procureurs joints, two for the clergy, two for the nobility, and two for the communities.[95] The cumbersome machinery of particular and general meetings encouraged delay, a widely used tactic in resisting royal tax demands.

The weekly meetings were held at the palace of the archbishop of Aix, the first procureur du pays. The archbishop, an important Estates official, was replaced during absences by the vicar general. The archbishop also played an important role in the provincial General Assemblies of the Clergy. He attended the General As-

---

[94] Hildesheimer, *Assemblées générales*, pp. 107–111.
[95] *Ibid.*, p. 16; EDB, III, 452.

semblies of the Clergy of France, and was one of two representatives from Provence at the last Estates General. He enjoyed an income of 25,000 livres annually, while the cathedral chapter of Saint Sauveur had yearly revenues of 60,000 livres.[96] Through his spiritual and political authority, the archbishop of Aix was an important provincial official.

For this reason, both Richelieu and Mazarin appointed their brothers to the position. Alphonse-Louis Du Plessis de Richelieu, Carthusian prior of Bonpas in Provence and the cardinal's older brother, served as archbishop from 1626 to 1629. He then became archbishop and cardinal of Lyon.[97] He headed an Estates deputation to the king in 1628. In 1635, a joint deputation of the Parlement and General Assembly of Communities asked Richelieu to appoint him governor in place of Vitry.[98] Michel Mazarin, former general of the Dominican order and cardinal Sainte Cécile, was named archbishop of Aix in 1645. He commanded the royal armies in Italy, served as viceroy in Catalonia, and became ambassador extraordinary to the papal court at Rome, where he died in September 1648 at the age of forty-one. A blunt, outspoken Italian with little respect for the Provençaux around him, Mazarin was usually absent from Aix on diplomatic and military missions for his older brother.[99]

Personality and interest determined the political role of the archbishop, as for most provincial officials. Louis de Bretel, archbishop of Aix from 1632 to 1644, formerly a canon in the cathedral of Rouen and a clerical councilor in its parlement, was well liked for his gentle character and piety, but he was a political nonentity.[100] In contrast, politically ambitious Jérôme de Grimaldi

---

[96] J. Michael Hayden, *France and the Estates General of 1614* (Cambridge, 1974), pp. 138, 247; Pillorget, *Les mouvements*, pp. 80–81.

[97] Maximin Deloche, *Un frère de Richelieu inconnu: chartreux, primat des Gaules, cardinal, ambassadeur* (Paris, 1935); EDB, IV–2, 415; J.-H. Albanès, *Gallia Christiana Novissima*, 7 vols. (Valence, 1899–1920), I, 137–138. A portrait of Richelieu's brother shows a strong family resemblance; cf. EDB, III, plate XVI.

[98] ADBR, Marseille, C 15, fol. 133v; C 22, fols. 198–199.

[99] EDB, IV–2, 328; Albanès, *Gallia*, I, 140–141; Gabriel de Mun, "Un frère de Mazarin: Le cardinal de Sainte Cécile (1607–1648)," *Revue d'histoire diplomatique*, 18 (1904), 497–530; Georges Dethan, *Mazarin et ses amis* (Paris, 1968), 38–45.

[100] EDB, IV–2, 105; Albanès, *Gallia*, I, 138–139; Haitze, *Histoire*, IV, 235.

was implicated in the 1659 revolt. Grimaldi consecrated Michel Mazarin archbishop in 1645, then became archbishop of Aix himself ten years later. Grimaldi's energy and dedication were visible as he rode through the Aix suburbs in November 1655, to take up his new office, a crowned eagle in silver and gold shining on his cardinal's hat.[101]

The parlementaires occasionally intervened in the municipal elections of Aix to determine the choice of procureurs du pays. They also influenced the conduct of the Estates and the General Assemblies of the Nobility. A minority of parlementaires, about 25 percent, were eligible to attend as noble fiefowners.[102] Nobles were by far the largest group in the Provençal Estates, as in Brittany. They dominated the proceedings and encouraged unruliness, since voting was by head, not by order.[103] A list of 144 nobles at the last meeting of the Estates in 1639 shows that 17 were parlementaires.[104] A list of approximately 200 fiefowners eligible to attend the Estates in 1649 shows that 33, possibly 38, were parlementaires.[105] This was more than half the company. When the Estates were restored in 1787, 205 noble fiefowners had the right to attend, including 34 of 62 parlementaires.[106]

The parlementaires attending the Estates and General Assemblies of the Nobility served as a channel for the exchange of opinions and attitudes. Parlementaires eligible to sit in the Estates resented its suppression, and its convocation was one of their demands as rebels in 1649.[107] Their anger at the crown's suspension of traditional privileges in 1658–1659 was fanned by the knowledge that the Estates had been permanently suppressed and the General Assembly of the Nobility was likely to share the same fate.

The General Assembly of the Nobility chose three syndics, sometimes more, to handle its affairs when it was not in session.

[101] EDB, IV–2, 254; Albanès, *Gallia*, I, 142–144; see Chapter Nine.

[102] See Chapter Eight.

[103] Emile Camau, *La Provence à travers les siècles* (Paris, 1931–1936), p. 512.

[104] "Notes et recherches sur la ville d'Aix," B. Méjanes 1013, fols. 788–795. This list was compiled in the eighteenth century and may be inaccurate.

[105] B.N., Ms. fr. 18977, fols. 322–326.

[106] Jean Egret, "La prérévolution en Provence (1787–1789)," *Annales historiques de la prérévolution française*, 26 (1954), 99–100.

[107] See Chapter Eight.

The first two syndics were sword or traditional nobles, and the third a robe or judicial noble. Five of the robe syndics from 1576 to 1672 were parlementaires. A number of sword syndics were also parlementaires. The second syndic from 1625 to 1631 was councilor Gaspard de Glandèves-Rousset. His son was a rebel in 1659. Jean-Baptiste de Castellane de La Verdière, uncle of Maynier d'Oppède, was second syndic from 1632 to 1639. Sextius d'Escalis de Bras, from a family of Parlement presidents, was first syndic in 1639. He participated in the 1630 revolt, and his son was a leader of the 1659 revolt. Jacques de Forbin de La Barben, the first consul whose arrest in 1658 contributed to causing revolt, was first syndic in 1656 and in 1661–1667.[108]

There were several weaknesses in the Provençal Estates. Not all geographical regions in the province belonged to the Estates or contributed to the taille. The so-called *terres adjacentes*[109] were not members and did not contribute to provincial taxes before 1641, although royal letters and conciliar decrees issued in 1558, 1572, 1582, 1583, 1599, 1621, and 1641 ordered them to contribute to the taille.[110] After 1641, these areas contributed 30,000 livres to voluntary gifts, while Marseille and Arles contributed an additional 25,000 livres each. The province contributed 220,000 livres for the total of 300,000.[111] The adjacent areas did not otherwise contribute to the taille, which caused much resentment, because Marseille and Arles were two of the wealthiest cities in Provence. They did contribute to the taillon, but they did not lodge troops or contribute to the provincial militia and road repairs. Marseille and Arles sent deputies without the right to vote to the Estates and General Assemblies in alternate years. As traditionally

---

[108] Séverin Icard, "Liste des syndics de la noblesse en Provence (1548–1789)," *Mémoires de l'Institut historique de Provence*, 10 (1933), 66–72; EDB, III, 509–511.

[109] The terres adjacentes included Marseille, Arles with Trinquetaille and Fontvieille, the counties of Sault and Grignan, Les Baux, the cities of Salon, Saint Tropez, Entrevaux, the towns and villages of Allan, Aureille, Chantemerle, Colonzelles, Cornillon, Cornillac, La Charce, Lurs, Mondragon, Monségur, Notre-Dame-de-la-Mer, Pommerol, Réauville, Remuzat, Salles; cf. EDB, III, 322, and Marchand, *Un intendant*, pp. 125–142.

[110] Mireille Zarb, *Les privilèges de la ville de Marseille du X^e siècle à la Revolution* (Paris, 1961), pp. 138–139; Cremieux, *Marseille et la royauté*, I, 11–14.

[111] Lublinskaya, *Vnutrenniaia*, pp. 269–270; Champigny to Séguier, February 1, 1644, pp. 246–247; Vautorte to Séguier, March 23, 1643.

privileged areas under the personal rule of the crown, they were taxed by royal letters sent to the intendant, whose efforts to increase their contribution to the taille in 1656–1657 failed.[112]

Not all members of the Estates attended the general meetings, which were convened irregularly. Moreover, the Estates suffered from internal strife. The communities quarreled among themselves; the nobles fought with the communities; the clergy had altercations with both, usually over taille payments.[113] The Estates of Dauphiné had been easily suppressed in 1628 because they were torn by internal strife over assessment of the taille.[114] In Provence, the taille could be collected independently of the Estates through General Assemblies of the Communities, which could not occur in Languedoc. The General Assemblies became a natural bypass to the Estates, which were suppressed. The Parlement of Aix, while suffering from absenteeism and factionalism, had more natural unity than the Estates, largely because of its hereditary office-holding. The Parlement was thus more successful in resisting the crown. The political destinies of these two institutions illustrate the importance of continuity in preserving traditional privileges.

Policy decisions on taxation in Provence were made at the provincial level by a small group of royal and provincial officials. The governor, intendant, and temporary royal commissioners represented the crown's interests. The archbishop of Aix, procureurs du pays, and procureurs joints represented provincial interests. The procureurs du pays were especially important because they were responsible for the levy and payment of taxes. There were frequent conflicts between the procureurs du pays and the governor and intendants. The confrontation of 1658 illustrates both the role of the procureurs du pays in provincial taxation and the causes of the 1659 revolt.

Mazarin had reopened the campaign in northern Italy in 1656, renewing the heavy burden of taxes and troops on Provence. Governor Mercoeur issued an ordinance on January 15, 1658, in compliance with a royal military règlement of the previous November,

---

[112] A.A.E., 1721, fols. 9–14, 35–36, 58–61, 278–281.

[113] EDB, III, 448–545; Camau, *La Provence*, p. 514.

[114] François Olivier-Martin, *Histoire du Droit français des origines à la Révolution* (Paris, 1948), pp. 395–396. A. Dussert, *Les Etats du Dauphiné de la Guerre de Cent Ans aux Guerres de Religion* (Grenoble, 1923), pp. 273–320.

ordering winter quarters payment of 150 days in silver for full regimental strength. The procureurs du pays flatly refused to approve this amount and would not affix their attache to the ordinance so that it could be enforced. They offered instead the customary 140 days in copper and in kind for the regimental effective.[115] On February 8, they refused to approve an increase in the rate of troop support paid by the communities.[116] The money was needed immediately to embark troops for the Italian campaign.[117]

The General Assembly at Aubagne in September 1657—convened after the January assembly was dismissed as balky and uncooperative—granted an unusually high taille of 1,845,450 livres.[118] In return, the governor and acting intendant Maynier d'Oppède promised to reduce the number of troops. But the flow of troops through Provence continued unabated, and four months later the governor and intendant requested a tax increase to support them. The procureurs du pays refused.

To force their approval, the governor and acting intendant requested lettres de cachet for the first consul of Aix, the secretary of the General Assembly, and his clerk, who were summoned to Paris to explain their refusal to approve the governor's tax ordinances. More letters arrived within the month for the lieutenant general of Provence, a former councilor, and a president of the Parlement, while archbishop Grimaldi of Aix was threatened with citation.[119]

The mass citations were unsuccessful. The procureurs du pays still refused their approval, and the unpaid troops began to riot and pillage the countryside where they were billeted. Mercoeur reported that *canaille* hidden in the woods had sniped at his cavalry regiment, breaking the arm of one of his men.[120] The governor

---

[115] ADBR, Marseille, C 37, fol. 264.

[116] A.A.E., 1721, fols. 359–361, Mercoeur to Mazarin, February 8, 1658. Mercoeur was demanding thirty sols per cavalryman and ten sols per infantryman a day. The procureurs du pays would only authorize twenty sols and six sols, respectively.

[117] Mazarin had written to Oppède on February 1 that 3,000 men were being sent for embarkation, cf., A.A.E., 1722, fols. 35v–36.

[118] ADBR, Marseille, C 37, fol. 264.

[119] See Chapter Nine.

[120] ADBR, Marseille, C 37, fol. 375; André, *Michel Le Tellier et l'organisation*, pp. 383–404. A.A.E., 1721, fols. 135–136, Mercoeur to Mazarin, May 29, 1657.

wrote to Mazarin on March 5, 1658 that the troops were beginning to mutiny, and he added that there was no hope of getting the approval of the procureurs du pays without using force, which he advised.[121] Consuls La Barben, Séguiran, and Estienne warned the Parlement on April 10 that mutinous soldiers were in Aix and refusing to leave: seven or eight cavalrymen had taken the hôtel de Guise in the Cordeliers quarter, and armed cavalrymen were occupying other hôtels throughout the city.[122] Soldiers, demanding their back pay, swelled the crowd before the palace of justice on February 25 protesting the arrest of the ex-councilor. Unpaid, mutinous soldiers had been drifting into Aix for weeks, ignoring orders to stay with their units.[123]

On April 11, 1658, acting intendant Oppède informed the Parlement that several companies of infantry and cavalry had been ordered into Aix to halt the disorders and illegal distribution of arms from the municipal arsenal.[124] The soldiers entered Aix on the night of April 12–13 without the city's knowledge. They came through the Saint Louis gate, obtaining the key by putting a pistol to the head of the guard. The troops were camped in the Place des Prêcheurs when the city awoke the next morning.[125] Third consul Estienne warned the Parlement that the shops were closing in protest. There was fighting in the Place des Prêcheurs, and stalls were overturned[126] The troops were not withdrawn until September.[127] An angry crowd gathered on January 29, 1659, a few days before the revolt, when rumors circulated that troops would again be billeted on Aix. They dispersed only when archbishop Grimaldi swore that the rumors were false.[128]

On May 23, 1658, provincial treasurer Gaillard and Cour des Comptes first president Séguiran informed the procureurs du pays of a meeting at Oppède's hôtel on the previous evening with army

---

[121] A.A.E., 1721, fols. 437–438.

[122] Delib. Parl., B. Méjanes 954, fol. 159.

[123] A.A.E., 1722, fol. 49; see Chapter Nine.

[124] A.A.E., 1722, fols. 159v–161.

[125] A.C., Aix, BB 103, fols. 67v–69; Haitze, *Histoire*, V, 416–417.

[126] Delib. Parl., B. Méjanes 954, fol. 161; A.A.E., 1721, fols. 493–494, president Coriolis to Mazarin, April 13, 1658.

[127] Pierre-Adolphe Chéruel and Georges d'Avenel, *Lettres du cardinal Mazarin pendant son ministère*, 9 vols. (Paris, 1872–1906), IX, 716, Mazarin to Parlement of Aix, September 8, 1658.

[128] Delib. Parl., B. Méjanes 954, fol. 192, January 29, 1659.

intendant de Chouppes and army lieutenant general de Marsilly. The intendant presented two lettres de cachet ordering immediate payment in silver of winter quarters support for three infantry and four cavalry regiments. He promised to send the troops to Catalonia after the money was paid. But Gaillard and Séguiran refused to approve payment, declaring they could only disburse monies with the approval of the procureurs du pays.[129]

On May 26, Oppède unsuccessfully threatened the procureurs du pays.[130] On May 30, he summoned them to the palace of justice to announce, as acting governor, a new ordinance: Chouppes was authorized to levy a tax of fifty-nine livres per feu to pay the troops.[131] The Parlement and Cour des Comptes immediately issued arrêts annulling the ordinance, forbidding the communities to pay the tax on penalty of 10,000 livres in fine, and prohibiting the army intendant from assembling or moving troops.[132] Anonymous placards appeared all over Aix reading, "Vive le Roy et fuero les élus," with seven little bells under the lettering, the slogan of the 1630 rebel cascaveoux.[133] The procureurs du pays angrily remonstrated against the ordinance as "wounding the ancient forms and usages of this province in which a tax levy can only be made following deliberations of the Estates or General Assemblies of the Communities."[134] The tax was not collected; the crown capitulated and issued letters in October for acting intendant Oppède to call a General Assembly at Tarascon in December to approve the increase.[135] The ordinance was revoked by the council of state on February 16, 1659, two days after the Aix revolt began, as being "in violation of the usages of the province."[136]

Oppède advised Mazarin on March 19, 1658, that appointing new consuls was the only way to secure cooperation for the tax increase.[137] In early August, he advised Mazarin to remove the consulaires from the city council to increase its cooperation and

---

[129] ADBR, Marseille, C 37, fols. 372v–375.

[130] *Ibid.*, fol. 366v.

[131] *Ibid.*, fols. 371v–375; A.A.E., 1721, fols. 534–535.

[132] ADBR, Marseille, C 37, fols. 372v–375; A.C., Aix, CC 617, fol. 359, June 4, 1658.

[133] A.A.E., 1723, fol. 12.   [134] A.A.E., 1724, fol. 27.

[135] B.N., Ms. fr. 20565, fols. 20–22; ADBR, Marseille, C 38, fols. 69–144.

[136] A.C., Aix, AA 14, fol. 747.   [137] A.A.E., 1721, fols. 449–453.

reduce the nobility's control.[138] In September, he recommended the appointment of two barons as reliable consuls.[139]

But Mazarin allowed the Aix elections to take place freely on September 27, 1658. Perhaps he feared a riot if they were suspended: there had been a revolt at Marseille in July after the suspension of municipal elections.[140] Roquemartine, a relative of the imprisoned first consul, was elected to the vacant post after letters endorsing his candidacy were read from several of the intendant's enemies. Oppède recommended annulling the Aix elections because reading endorsement letters was an unusual procedure, and all four consuls were lawyers.[141] Mazarin allowed the elections to stand, but he removed the consulaires from the election assembly by letters patent drafted at Calais in June 1658.[142] These letters were never issued. The change was made by similar letters patent issued at Bordeaux in August 1659.[143]

The governor and intendant were dependent upon the procureurs du pays to approve tax levies and disburse tax monies when the Estates or General Assemblies were not in session. They used a combination of promises and threats to secure cooperation. They promised to send troops from Provence and lower taxes. They delivered long, threatening speeches, cited individuals in disciplinary legislation, exiled and arrested them, billeted troops on Aix. They issued ordinances to collect taxes and pay troops without the approval of the procureurs du pays. They rigged municipal elections and modified electoral procedures to obtain cooperative procureurs. Lifting the procuration from Aix and transferring it to another city, or changing its composition, was briefly considered in 1637.[144] But intimidation was not always successful. The crown in 1658 had to call a General Assembly to approve the tax levy, and the attempts of its agents to control the procureurs du pays caused a revolt at Aix the following February.

[138] A.A.E., 1723, fols. 92, 112. Mercoeur made the same recommendation.

[139] *Ibid.*, fol. 179, Oppède to Mazarin, September 3, 1658.

[140] See Adolphe Crémieux, *Marseille et la royauté pendant la minorité de Louis XIV*, 2 vols. (Marseille, 1917), II, 513–667; Pillorget, *Les mouvements*, pp. 723–729, 767–783.

[141] A.A.E., 1723, fols. 203–208, Oppède to Mazarin, October 20, 1658.

[142] A.A.E., 1722, fols. 162–165.

[143] A.C., Aix, AA 6, fols. 17–23; AA 1, fols. 268–271.

[144] *Ibid.*, BB 100, fol. 198v, September 29, 1637.

The economic causes of the Aix revolts should not be exaggerated. Provence suffered less from the Habsburg War than many of the northern provinces. With the exception of the Spanish landing on the coastal islands off Cannes in 1635, Provence was not invaded during the war nor fought over, as Burgundy was. Provence regularly paid a fraction of the taille paid by Normandy. The greatest increase in taxes and troops in Provence occurred around 1630, while the level of taxes and troops from 1638 to 1655 was stable and comparatively low. The overall economy of Aix during most of the seventeenth century was moderately prosperous when compared to the north. Economic historian René Baehrel states that the Provençal economy expanded slowly from 1600 to 1655, stagnated from 1655 to 1690, and declined from 1690 to 1730. As evidence for his conclusions, Baehrel gives price indexes of staple items in several towns in Basse-Provence including Aix: prices of bread, wheat, other grains, wine, oil, firewood, livestock, and wool, as well as information on daily wages, land distribution and use, numbers of workers, children, birth and death rates.[145] Pierre Goubert, in describing the Beauvaisis and southern Picardy found that the decline started earlier in the north, around 1660.[146] Aix enjoyed territorial and population expansion in the seventeenth century, while Provence had a comparatively high birth rate not affected by war, plague, or poor harvests.[147]

Baehrel has been criticized by Jean Meuvret and Pierre Goubert for using nominal or actual prices rather than metallic prices.[148]

[145] René Baehrel, *Une Croissance: La Basse-Provence rurale (fin du XVIᵉ siècle—1789)* (Paris, 1961), pp. 29–30, 232–236, 530, 532–533, 535, 547, 558–560, 565–566, 578, 584, 604, 657–658, 668, 673.

[146] Pierre Goubert, "The French Peasantry of the Seventeenth Century," *Past and Present*, 10 (1956), 57–77; *Beauvais et le Beauvaisis de 1600 à 1730* (Paris, 1960); "Le 'tragique' XVIIᵉ siècle," in *Histoire économique et sociale de la France*, II, *Des derniers temps de l'âge seigneurial aux préludes de l'âge industriel (1660–1789)*, ed. Fernand Braudel and Ernest Labrousse (Paris, 1970), pp. 329–365. Also see Roland Mousnier, *Les XVIIᵉ et XVIIIᵉ siècles*, vol. IV in *Histoire générale des civilisations* 4th ed. (Paris, 1965), pp. 162–172.

[147] Baehrel, *Une croissance*, pp. 232–236, 662; Baratier, *Histoire de la Provence*, p. 276; Marchand, *Un intendant*, p. 126; EDB, XIV, 583; see Chapter One.

[148] Jean Meuvret, "Simple mise au point," *Annales: ESC*, 11 (1955), 48–49; Pierre Goubert, *Beauvais*, pp. 372, nn. 39 and 41; 375, n. 57; 494, n. 4; 500, n. 2.

Baehrel's critics argue that nominal prices are misleading because price increases due to currency devaluation and inflation can be misinterpreted as general prosperity. Baehrel counters that metallic prices confuse an understanding of commercial flow and normal price fluctuations.[149] Baehrel seems justified in ascribing moderate prosperity to Provence in the early seventeenth century.[150] Emmanuel Le Roy Ladurie, in describing the economy of neighboring Languedoc, states that the Midi in the first half of the seventeenth century had better climate and more harvests, fewer deaths, and fewer crop failures than the north. One reason was the heavy rains that destroyed northern wheat crops, particularly from 1647 to 1653, did not fall in the Midi.[151] Le Roy Ladurie notes that the economic slowdown in Provence and Languedoc after 1660 was not a decline until the decade after 1689–1690.[152]

The tide of inflation caused by the sixteenth-century price revolution had weakened and was ebbing in Provence by 1620.[153] Prices in Provence overall rose 50 to 60 percent from 1600 to 1650, corresponding to a general price rise in France of 1 percent a year. This price rise was accompanied by monetary devaluation, which accelerated around 1640 and again around 1650.[154] But inflation stabilized after the Fronde.[155] Thus the inflationary effects of the Habsburg War should not be exaggerated. In general, the economy of Aix was moderately prosperous from 1629 to 1659.

As Roland Mousnier and his students have shown, the crown's financial and military demands during the Habsburg War were a

[149] René Baehrel, "Prix, superficies, statistique, croissances," *Annales: ESC*, 16 (1961), 699–722, 922–938; "Prix nominaux, prix métalliques et formule d'Irving Fisher," *Annales: ESC*, 17 (1962), 732–736; *Une croissance*, 2–20.

[150] Pierre Chaunu, in *Le XVIIe siècle: Problèmes de conjoncture* (Geneva, 1963), states that Baehrel has been attacked for his population figures and prices, but his findings have been substantiated.

[151] Emmanuel Le Roy Ladurie, *Les paysans du Languedoc*, 2 vols. (Paris, 1966), I, 15–91, 449–450.

[152] *Ibid.*, 635–638.

[153] Spooner, *International Economy*, pp. 20–33, 35; Goubert, "Le 'tragique' XVIIe siècle," p. 331.

[154] Baehrel, *Une croissance*, pp. 533, 547; Pierre Goubert, *L'avènement du Roi-Soleil, 1661* (Paris, 1967), p. 41; Mousnier, *Les XVIe et XVIIe siècles*, pp. 165–166.

[155] Spooner, *International Economy*, pp. 193–195.

basic cause of revolts in early seventeenth-century France.[156] It is central to Mousnier's thesis that the crown's increased demands occurred at a time of economic recession, intensifying the reaction against the crown. However, sunny Provence before 1660 seems not to have suffered as badly as elsewhere in France. The Aix revolts were not caused solely by popular economic misery or insoluble economic problems, nor were they only tax revolts or troop protests. Political issues were a major cause of the Aix revolts, in particular the crown's attacks on the Estates and procureurs du pays. These attacks were meant to suppress provincial resistance to higher taxes and more troops. They included intimidation of individuals, suppression of provincial privileges, and emasculation of provincial tax-granting assemblies. Except on the most superficial level, the parlementaires never protested these attacks or direct royal taxes, which they did not pay. But they did worry about the political implications. The crown's financial and military demands created a general atmosphere of dissatisfaction encouraging political protest at Aix.

[156] See Roland Mousnier, "The Fronde," in *Preconditions of Revolution in Early Modern Europe*, ed. Robert Forster and Jack Greene (Baltimore, 1970), pp. 131–159; *Lettres et mémoires*, I, introduction; Y. M. Bercé, *Histoire des Croquants: Etude des soulèvements populaires au XVIIᵉ siècle dans le sud-ouest de la France*, 2 vols. (Paris, 1974), I, 7–118.

# Chapter Three

# THE INTENDANTS OF JUSTICE AND THE PARLEMENT

The 1630 revolt began as an attack upon a royal commissioner sent to Aix to establish a bureau of élus.[1] Dreux d'Aubray was also ordered to establish an intendance of justice, police, and finance in Provence—which he did when he returned to Aix with a colleague and royal troops to suppress the revolt his arrival had provoked. Roland Mousnier notes that 1635 to 1648 were the critical years in the development of the intendants' authority.[2] Although intendants of justice appeared in Provence in 1630, they did not exercise wide authority until six years later. After 1636, they expanded their authority at the expense of provincial institutions and spearheaded the crown's drive for bureaucratic centralization. They became bitter enemies of the parlementaires, who resented their attacks upon the court's authority. The intendants' correspondance rang with invective: "These discontented, seditious magistrates . . . factious and quarrelsome . . . their disorders and intrigues . . . this calamitous province . . . the insolence and temerity of the Parlement."[3] The hostility at Aix between the intendants and parlementaires helped to cause the 1649 revolt.

In December 1630, Dreux d'Aubray and Charles Le Roy de La Potherie were sent to Aix to aid in suppressing the cascaveoux revolt.[4] Their letters of commission were short, describing a specific

[1] See Chapter Five.

[2] Roland Mousnier, "Etat et commissaire: Recherches sur la création des intendants des provinces (1634–1648)," in *La plume, la faucille, et le marteau* (Paris, 1970), pp. 180–181.

[3] A. D. Lublinskaya, ed. *Vnutrenniaia politika frantsuzskogo absoliutizma, 1633–1649* (Leningrad, 1966), Champigny to Séguier, pp. 254–255, July 11, 1643; p. 259, September 28, 1643; pp. 265–266, December 8, 1643; pp. 275–276, March 1, 1644; p. 304, July 2, 1645.

[4] The procureurs du pays were informed of the impending arrival of two royal commissioners on December 12, 1630; cf. ADBR, Marseille, C 16, fol. 81.

task to be performed. They were to transfer the sovereign courts from Aix because their members were guilty of encouraging rebellion, remove Tournelle president Laurent de Coriolis from office with the excuse that his blindness was hindering the dispensation of justice, although in reality it was because he was a cascaveoux leader, and sit as a court to judge the rebels. They were also "to establish an intendance of finance and justice in Provence."[5] Their report to Paris in March 1631 was signed, "intendants of justice, police, and finance and the army of Provence."[6] A new royal official had been created.

The name of Dreux d'Aubray, seigneur d'Offemont, last appears in Provençal documents in November 1631 as royal representative at the Aix General Assembly.[7] Charles Le Roy, sieur de La Potherie, remained in Provence without new letters of commission, exercising authority as intendant of justice. He stayed in Provence until the autumn of 1633.[8] Several temporary royal commissioners arrived during these years. Charles de Brûlart de Léon briefly joined de La Potherie as royal representative at the Brignoles Estates in December 1632.[9] Noel Brûlart, baron de La Borde, was

[5] B.N., Dupuy 154, fols. 111–116, published by Gabriel Hanotaux in *Origine de l'institution des intendants des provinces (1550–1631)* (Paris, 1884), pp. 295–302. Hanotaux dates the commission on September 3, 1630, which is erroneous because the revolt did not begin until September 19. The date of December 30, 1630 is used by Roland Mousnier in *Lettres et mémoires adressés au chancelier Séguier (1633–1649)*, 2 vols. (Paris, 1964), I, 147, also erroneous because the procureurs du pays learned on December 12 that the royal commissioners were arriving shortly. Madeleine Foisil mistakenly uses the date September 30 in *La révolte des Nu-Pieds et les révoltes normandes de 1639* (Paris, 1970), p. 287. The most likely date is December 5, 1630, given on their letters of commission at Marseille; cf. ADBR, Marseille, C 986.

[6] A.A.E., 798, fols. 16–17.

[7] ADBR, Marseille, C 19, fol. 105v. Aubray is best remembered for his death. He was poisoned on September 17, 1666, by his daughter, the marquise de Brinvilliers (née Madeleine d'Aubray), who poisoned her father, two brothers, and a sister because they tried to prevent her adultery with a cavalry captain. She was tried and executed in what became the most famous court scandal of the seventeenth century; cf. Mousnier, *Lettres*, II, 1184.

[8] *Ibid.*, C 22, fols. 1–14v. De La Potherie's name last appears in the Provençal documents as royal representative to the Pertuis General Assembly in August, 1633.

[9] ADBR, Aix, B 3349, fol. 606; Marseille, C 20, fols. 201–278v.

sent as gabelle commissioner in May 1633.[10] Jacques Talon visited Provence in October and November 1634 to raise the gabelle.[11] But these royal commissioners returned to Paris after accomplishing a specific mission. The intendants remained, exercising wide authority as instruments of an expanding centralization from Paris. They were used to bind a frontier province closer to the throne.

Joint intendants were sent to Provence in 1630 and 1636. Jean de Lauzon, sieur de Liré, was issued letters of commission as intendant on August 29, 1636. He soon requested a colleague's help, and was joined in December by François Bochart, seigneur de Saron-Champigny.[12] Champigny's letters of commission bore the title of "intendant of justice, police, and finance in Provence and in the royal army in Provence at Aix."[13] Temporary royal commissioners with military functions came to Provence from 1635 to 1637 during the Spanish invasion. Gaspard Du Gué was sent in April 1636 to serve as "intendant of our finances in Provence and in our armies that are or will be in this province and its coasts."[14] Henri de Séguiran, sieur de Bouc and first president of the Cour des Comptes, was chosen in 1633 to report on coastal fortifications and shipping.[15] Naval intendants Du Plessis-Besançon and d'Hémery were sent in 1635 to supervise the repair and enlargement of royal fortresses. Hémery soon returned to Paris, but Du Plessis-Besançon remained throughout 1636.[16] The authority and duties of army and naval intendants gradually diverged from those of provincial intendants.

[10] Richard Bonney, "The Intendants of Richelieu and Mazarin, 1624–1661" (Ph.D. dissertation, Oxford, 1973, soon to be published by Oxford University Press), pp. 269, 277.

[11] *Ibid.*, and p. 57; ADBR, Marseille, C 22, fols. 102–102v, 134v–135; A.A.E., 1702, fols. 265–267; A.N., E 181A, fol. 227v.

[12] Bonney, "Intendants," pp. 59, 269, 277.

[13] "Recueil d'actes notariés," B. Méjanes 1286, fol. 30, Champigny's letters of commission, December 16, 1636.

[14] Douglas Baxter, "French Intendants of the Army, 1630–1670" (Ph.D. dissertation, University of Minnesota, 1971), pp. 27, n. 5; 48, n. 24.

[15] B.N., Ms. fr. 24169, "Procès-verbal contenant l'état véritable auquel sont de present les affaires de la côte maritime de Provence par Henri de Séguiran de Bouc, premier président de la Cour des Comptes de Provence, conseiller du roy;" ADBR, Marseille, IX B2, fol. 252, September 24, 1632, Séguiran's letters of commission.

[16] Hubert Méthivier, "Richelieu et le front de mer en Provence," *Revue historique*, 185 (1939), 134.

By 1640, the pattern of one intendant serving in a généralité for an average three-year term was established. The four intendants serving at Aix from 1636 through 1648 were Lauzon and Champigny; François Cazet, seigneur de Vautorte, who served from May 12, 1640, until May 4, 1643, when Champigny was appointed to a second term; Alexandre de Sève, seigneur de Chastignonville, who served from October 29, 1647, until April 2, 1649, when the intendance of Provence was revoked by a decree of the council of state.[17] The intendant was granted 7,200 livres annually by the Estates, increased to 12,000 livres in 1645.[18]

The intendants of justice had a difficult, unenviable task. Far from home, overworked, they were detested and harassed by provincial officials who resented their attempts to regulate the financial administration, prosecute tax offenders, and discipline uncooperative officials. The intendants left little personal imprint on the documents: there are no faces behind their words. They were useful, effective cogs in the machinery of the central government but shadowy as individuals. The position was more important than the men who filled it.

The intendants came from a few hundred Parisian families ennobled through three or more generations of royal office-holding. Originally from the provinces, the ambitious founders of these administrative dynasties had gone to Paris to seek their fortune in the royal service, where they had obtained rank, power, and wealth. Future intendants studied law and usually acquired judicial experience at Paris in the Grand Conseil, Parlement, or Châtelet. Aubray and Champigny were councilors and Vautorte avocat-général in the Grand Conseil, Lauzon and de La Potherie councilors in the Parlement of Paris, Aubray civil lieutenant, and de La Potherie procureur du roi in the Châtelet. Later, they purchased the office of master of requests, since provincial intendants were chosen from the ranks of these officials. Only Cazet de Vautorte did not hold this office, which he never reacquired because he had

[17] Mousnier, *Lettres*, II, 1059, Vautorte, May 12, 1640; A.A.E., 1708, fols. 171–172v and B. Méjanes 1286, fol. 32, Champigny, May 4, 1643; A.A.E., 1712, fols. 264–267, Sève, October 29, 1647. Vautorte's commission stated that he was "intendant of the police, justice, and finances in Provence and adjacent areas and in our army that we are having assemble in the province"; cf. Baxter, "French Intendants of the Army," p. 398.

[18] B. Méjanes 1286, fols. 34–35; ADBR, Marseille, C 987, conciliar decree, November 20, 1645.

the patronage of Le Tellier. Most of the intendants spent one-third to one-half of their careers in the provinces. Alexandre de Sève served as intendant in Abbéville and Ponthieu, Dauphiné, and Auvergne before coming to Provence. Aubray had received commissions to serve in Provence in 1629 and 1630. De La Potherie, Lauzon, Vautorte, and Champigny served as intendants in other généralités after leaving Provence. Aubray, de La Potherie, and Vautorte also obtained the office of councilor of state, the next step in a successful career. They hoped to become ambassador, as did Vautorte; first president of a parlement, as did Laisné and Mesgrigny at Aix; a royal household official, perhaps even secretary of state, superintendent of finance, or minister. But few went this high in the administrative hierarchy.[19]

Decisive rulings by the council of state from 1634 to 1643 gave the intendants joint authority with trésoriers and élus to supervise provincial tax collection. The intendants were also given authority to supervise the levy and payment of winter troop support.[20] After 1643, the intendants gradually assumed control over most bureaus of finances, usurping the trésoriers' authority, as the latter had annexed the functions of the sovereign financial courts. Intendant Vautorte, in a letter to chancellor Séguier on April 7, 1643, spoke of proceeding jointly with the trésoriers of Aix in the apportionment and surveillance of the taille.[21] Trésorier Marcel complained to Séguier on July 3, 1645 about the intendant's "scandalous behavior." Marcel wrote that "Champigny in order to revenge himself on us and on me in particular, because we do not want to recognize him as our superior, took the commission for the recov-

[19] The backgrounds and careers of the intendants have been widely studied. See Mousnier, *Lettres*, I, 42–185; Bonney, "Intendants," pp. 193–240, 337–350; F. Marin de Carranrais, "Notice sur l'intendance de Provence," *Revue de Marseille* (January 1889), 3–19; (February 1889), 75–90; (April 1889), 147–164; Vivian Gruder, *The Royal Provincial Intendants: A Governing Elite in Eighteenth Century France* (Ithaca, 1968).

[20] Mousnier, "Recherches sur la création des intendants," pp. 179–199; Edmond Esmonin, *La taille en Normandie au temps de Colbert (1661–1683)* (Paris, 1913), pp. 37–102; Jean-Paul Charmeil, *Les trésoriers de France à l'époque de la Fronde* (Paris, 1964), pp. 149–226; Bonney, "Intendants," pp. 45–90.

[21] B.N., Ms. fr. 17376, fol. 28v; Provence may have been exempt from the rulings of 1642–1643; cf. private communication from Richard Bonney.

ery of this tax [a 1642 levy of 500 livres each on all trésoriers généraux in France]." The Aix trésoriers refused to pay the tax because they had not been reimbursed for 2,400 livres they had lent the crown in 1637. Irritated at the delay and lack of cooperation, Champigny arrested Marcel in his judicial robes on the steps of the palace of justice, using two of the prévôt's police and five or six servants. Champigny grabbed Marcel by the collar, put a gun to his chest, and marched him through the streets of Aix to the prison of the canons of Saint Sauveur, a stable full of pigs and chickens. Marcel was held there until the other trésoriers collected 11,500 livres to pay the tax.[22] Champigny's successful if discourteous method suggests how he swiftly resolved his difficulties.

Control over the Aix bureau of finances did not assure the intendant control over tax collection in Provence, a pays d'états in which the taille was assessed and collected by agents of the communities and vigueries without the trésoriers' supervision until the final stages. The intendants' assumption of control over the financial administration of Provence was incomplete before 1661 because of the opposition of the Estates, General Assemblies, and procureurs du pays. In addition, the Aix bureau of finances was weak. Its jurisdiction was challenged by the Cour des Comptes and Estates for over a half century, and it was one of three bureaus in France that did not send representatives to the 1648–1649 assembly of trésoriers at Paris.[23]

Provinces with Estates were notoriously uncooperative in granting and paying the taille: the Provençal Estates regularly granted twenty to fifty percent less than the crown demanded. The crown's usual response was to dismiss an uncooperative assembly and call another, as in 1657, or to order the trésoriers généraux to collect the tax without the assembly's approval, as in 1643. Bullying and intimidating the Estates, General Assemblies, and procureurs du pays were accepted techniques for obtaining their approval. Condé threatened the Tarascon Estates in 1631, as did Brûlart de Léon

---

[22] Lublinskaya, ed. *Vnutrenniaia*, pp. 305–306; Mousnier, *Lettres*, II, 762.

[23] Charmeil, *Les trésoriers*, pp. 315–318, 368; ADBR, Aix, "Recueil d'édits," fols. 200–202; Roland Mousnier, "Recherches sur les syndicats d'officiers pendant la Fronde: Trésoriers Généraux de France et Elus (1648–1653)," *XVIIᵉ siècle*, 42–43 (1959), 84. Aix, Rennes, and Metz did not participate in the assembly. Only 505 items of more than 5,000 in Series C of the Bouches du Rhone departmental archives at Marseille, C 4749–C 5254, concern the Aix bureau des finances.

at Brignoles in 1632, and Alais at Aix in 1639. Mercoeur and Maynier d'Oppède used this technique in 1658.[24] Before 1630, the governors, trésoriers généraux, and temporary royal commissioners represented the crown at tax-granting assemblies.[25] After 1630, the intendants joined the governors in presenting royal demands. A decade later, the intendants appeared alone.[26]

The Estates and General Assemblies sometimes attempted to bargain with the royal representatives on tax requests. Deputies sent to the king did not always receive a cordial reception, as we learn from the diary of Léon de Trimond, who went to Brignoles in May 1630 to see Louis XIII returning from Casale. Trimond and his fellow deputies were admitted at noon to the bishop's palace. Louis XIII was dining with Richelieu, the provincial governor, secretary of state, minister of finance, and several court nobles. The deputies removed their swords and knelt while their leader presented the Estates' petition; the minister of finance made faces and whistled while they talked. When they had finished, the king answered curtly that he had listened to their demands, now they were to go. Richelieu snapped, "Rise and go." And the secretary of state stopped them in the hall to warn them that they had twenty-four hours to leave the city.[27] In December 1642, the procureurs du pays were told not to send sieur Blanc as "the one among them who was carried away with himself in the appeal he made to the council in the previous year by speaking with too much heat."[28] A deputy from Provence was given twenty-four hours to leave Paris in October 1657 for his bluntness.[29] Jean and Louis d'Antelmi, deputies from the city of Aix and the Parlement in 1631, spent two years in the Bastille for their frankness.[30]

Intendant Vautorte was removed from Provence in 1643 for failing to control the procureurs du pays. Vautorte wrote to the superintendent of finance and secretary of state on April 7, 1643,

[24] ADBR, Marseille, C 16, fol. 115; C 20, fols. 201–278v; C 25, fols. 227–279v.

[25] *Ibid.*, C 15, fols. 120, 178, 311; C 16, fol. 59.

[26] *Ibid.*, fol. 114; C 19, fol. 99; C 20, fols. 201, 313; C 22, fol. 1; C 25, fols. 6, 102v, 124, 192–200, 227; C 26, fols. 3, 140, 215v, 235, 315, 365.

[27] "Livre de raison de Léon de Trimond," B. Méjanes 1140, fols. 3–4.

[28] ADBR, Marseille, C 986, December 10, 1642.

[29] A.A.E., 1721, fols. 243–244, October 27, 1657; ADBR, Marseille, C 988, October 11, 1657. The deputy was M. Vaucluse from Aix.

[30] See Chapter Five.

that he had been unable to coerce the procureurs du pays into authorizing the levy of a subvention générale, a national sales tax of five percent, as ordered by a decree of the council on February 5. They had demanded a General Assembly, and he attached a copy of their deliberations. Vautorte advised convocation of an assembly with these words: "On which you know very well, Sir, that we can do nothing without an assembly of the communities which grant impositions, the King until now having kept this form and privilege in the province."[31] Instead, the council of state ordered the governor and trésoriers généraux to levy the tax immediately, with or without the approval of a General Assembly. Champigny was appointed intendant in Provence the same month. Vautorte's last letter from Provence was dated June 2, and by July he was intendant in the Limousin. Vautorte's integrity may have been under question, since he was reprimanded by Séguier in 1643 for accepting gifts of money from the General Assemblies.[32] Control over the procureurs du pays and General Assemblies was a major responsibility of intendants in pays d'états. Intendants unable to perform this task were transferred to other provinces.

The intendants gradually assumed the supervision of the communities' collection of the taille by two techniques. They expanded their authority to verify and liquidate community debts and to collect royal land taxes—the franc-fief, amortissement, and nouveaux acquêts—to include regulating the taille. They also bypassed officials of the regular financial administration, using their own clerks and agents, the prévôt's police, and tax farmers' agents to collect taxes.

The assessment and levy of the taille in pays d'états contained a number of abuses: illegal exemptions and deliberate omissions of taxable property, peculation and false assessments, clandestine arrangements between landowners and community agents. The 1471 affouagement—the list of feux in vigueries—was used until

[31] B.N., Ms. fr. 17376, fols. 28–29; ADBR, Marseille, C 26, fol. 265, particular assembly of April 6, 1643.

[32] B.N., Ms. fr. 17376, fol. 42. Champigny was appointed intendant in Provence for a second term in April 1643 on governor Alais's request, and he received his commission on May 4; cf. A.A.E., 1708, fols. 169, 171–172v, 193. The province was notified of his arrival on July 3; cf. ADBR, Marseille, C 987. Vautorte's integrity was questioned; cf. Mousnier, *Lettres*, I, 155–161; Bonney, "Intendants," p. 218.

1664–1665 because of practical difficulties in revising it.[33] The cadastres, the registers of taxable property within a community evaluated in terms of feux, based on this land survey were also outdated and inequitable. Cadastral evaluations were given in old monetary units, florins, sols, deniers, as well as in écus and livres; pounds and ounces were used in central Provence.[34] The afflorinement, the register of fiefs that were taxed separately, was as obsolete. Its assessments were in terms of a fifteenth-century coin, the florin.[35]

The communities of Provence were heavily in debt after the religious wars of the late sixteenth century. Guillaume Du Vair estimated their debt in 1596 at 36,000,000 écus, much of it in interest.[36] In 1602, Aix owed 1,200,000 écus to individual lenders.[37] The communities complained that they could not pay on the principal or make back payments; they could hardly pay the interest on this immense debt. A chamber of communities was established at Aix by the crown on October 15, 1613, to adjudicate disputes over repayment.[38]

Attempting to maximize tax revenues in 1635, Richelieu established a national program of settling municipal debts and paying

---

[33] EDB, III, 545–546; René Pillorget, *Les mouvements insurrectionnels de Provence entre 1596 et 1715* (Paris, 1975), pp. 62–64; Paul Masson, *La Provence au XVIII<sup>e</sup> siècle*, 3 vols. (Paris, 1936), I, 188–189. There were affouagements in 1471, 1664–1665, 1698, and 1728.

[34] Raoul Busquet, "Les cadastres et les unités cadastrales en Provence du XV<sup>e</sup> au XVIII<sup>e</sup> siècles," *Annales de Provence*, VII (1910), 119–134, 161–184, reprinted in *Etudes sur l'ancienne Provence: Institutions et points d'histoire* (Paris, 1930), 159–167, 173–176.

[35] EDB, III. 512–513; François-Paul Blanc, "L'anoblissement par lettres en Provence à l'époque des reformations de Louis XIV, 1630–1730" (doctoral dissertation in law, University of Aix-Marseille, 1971), pp. 677–678.

[36] Charles-Alexandre Sapey, *Etudes biographiques pour servir à l'histoire de l'ancienne magistrature française: Guillaume Du Vair, Antoine Le Maistre*, 2d ed. (Geneva, 1971), p. 341, Du Vair to Henry IV, January 15, 1597.

[37] Georges Reynaud, *Guillaume Du Vair, premier président du Parlement de Provence* (Aix-en-Provence, 1873), p. 22.

[38] *Ibid.*, p. 16; B.N., Ms. fr. 18976, fols. 123–124; ADBR, Aix, J.L.H. Hesmivy de Moissac, "Histoire du Parlement de Provence," I, fol. 414; M.A., Provence 353; Sapey, *Etudes biographiques*, pp. 378–379, Du Vair to Henry IV, August 5, 1599. Du Vair proposed establishment of a two chamber tribunal to hear appeals on community debts and noted that he was directing the commissioners investigating municipal debts.

back taxes. Seven royal commissioners were appointed on January 28 and August 30 to verify and liquidate community debts in Provence.[39] They were to verify the origins of the debts, the creditors' claims, and order repayment. Royal letters on August 22 and a council decree on August 29, 1636, abolished the old chamber and established a new tribunal at Aix headed by the intendant to handle resulting litigation and punish fraud. Other members of the tribunal included first presidents Dubernet and Séguiran of the Parlement and Cour des Comptes, councilors Périer and Peiresc of the Parlement.[40] Champigny's commission as intendant on December 16, 1636, emphasized his authority to regulate community debts. First president Mesgrigny received a similar commission on July 30, 1644.[41] On December 16, 1636, Dubernet wrote that the tribunal and agents of the indebted communities had met at Cannes. Present were Lauzon, Séguiran, seven parlementaires, and two councilors of the Cours des Comptes.[42]

The tribunal soon came into conflict with the sovereign courts. On January 31, 1645, Parlement first president Mesgrigny protested to Séguier that the tribunal's membership had changed— the first presidents and councilors of the sovereign courts had been excluded. Mesgrigny protested that the tribunal should at least include judges from the Aix seneschal court. But it was composed of a royal attorney, two clerks, and several agents appointed by the intendant. In a letter on May 2, 1645, Mesgrigny added that as first president he was supposed to serve on the tribunal, but he was relieved to be excluded because he did not want to participate in usurping the jurisdiction of the royal judges, seneschal courts, and Cour des Comptes.[43] The tribunal had become the exclusive

---

[39] The commissioners included Le Roy de La Potherie and Aubray, Jacques Le Prevost, sieur d'Herbelay, Hubert, Mallier, Etienne d'Aligre, seigneur de La Rivière, and Michel Particelli, sieur d'Hémery; cf. A.N., E 124B, fol. 494v; Bonney, "Intendants," pp. 260, 277; Georges d'Avenel, *Lettres, instructions diplomatiques et papiers d'état du cardinal de Richelieu*, 8 vols. (Paris, 1853–1877), V, 942, mémoire from Richelieu to Servien, September 31, 1635.

[40] B.N., Ms. fr. 18976, fols. 123–124; M.A., Provence 353.

[41] "Recueil d'actes notairés," B. Méjanes 1286, fol. 31; B.N., Ms. fr. 24166, fol. 251.

[42] Lublinskaya, *Vnutrenniaia*, pp. 243–244.

[43] B.N., Ms. Fr. 17383, fols. 76–78, January 31, 1645; Lublinskaya, *Vnutrenniaia*, pp. 298–299, May 2, 1645.

instrument of the intendant. An arrêt of the Parlement in 1646 regulated conflict between the intendant and royal judges.[44] Champigny's ordinance on February 25, 1645, forbade the Cour des Comptes to hear any disputes between the communities and their creditors.[45]

Conciliar decrees gave the communities a year to liquidate their debts. A royal tax agent or *traitant* was sent to Provence to aid the intendant. Creditors who feared partial payment from bankrupt communities in land rather than money were the principal obstacle, and there were long negotiations. A decree on March 6, 1639, ordered the communities to pay their creditors in eight annual payments or face confiscation of community property.[46] Champigny listed eighty indebted communities on November 8, 1639. By 1647, their debts had been reduced to 3,659,643 livres. But this success was temporary. When intendant Lebret arrived in Provence in 1687, debts had climbed to 23,000,000 livres. Three years later he had managed to reduce this sum by 12,000,000 livres, but he was no more successful than his predecessors in liquidating it.[47]

The crown wanted liquidation of community debts for several reasons. Royal taxes and dues could not be collected on community property that had been alienated or mortgaged to creditors. When the communities could not collect enough taxes to meet their share of the affouagement, they alienated property to secure loans. Creditors were liable for taxes on property while enjoying its revenues, but they tended to be nobles, parlementaires, and ecclesiastical corporations, who often evaded payment of royal taxes.[48] Municipal governments deliberately spread their tax payments over a number of years by obtaining covering loans instead of paying immediately, and municipal officials grew wealthy making loans. Municipal governments had to levy new taxes to meet loans.

Communities were usually in arrears on their taille payments. Alienating property led to heavy debts and bankruptcy, which made payment of back taxes even more difficult. The crown justi-

---

[44] A.N., E 220A, fol. 447.  [45] M.A., Provence 353.

[46] B.N., Ms. fr. 18976, fols. 123–124, 129–130; A.N., E 151C, fol. 154.

[47] M.A., Provence 353; J. Marchand, *Un intendant sous Louis XIV: Etude sur l'administration de Lebret en Provence (1687–1704)* (Paris, 1889), pp. 211–222.

[48] B.N., Ms. fr. 17373, fols. 197–198.

fiably suspected the communities of using false conveyances, false declarations of alienated property, and bankruptcy to escape taille payments. The Tarascon Estates in 1631 reluctantly agreed that community debts should be registered in cadastres and liable to partial payment of the taille, but this did not go into effect until after 1637.[49] The intendant and traitant were authorized to verify debts and pressure the communities to settle and pay their back taxes or face prosecution by the new tribunal.

To force payment, the crown charged 6.66 percent interest, *au denier quinze*, on back taxes, and collected 690,000 livres interest in 1639, a high rate.[50] Interest rates before 1634 were 6.25 percent, *au denier seize*. Interest rates under Louis XIII, set by royal edict in March 1634, were 5.55 percent, *au denier dix-huit*, and interest rates under Louis XIV, set by royal edict in December 1665, were 5 percent, *au denier vingt*.[51] Champigny, in an ordinance on June 1, 1639, reinforced by Vautorte on February 16, 1641, set a schedule of payments from one to eight years depending on the size of the debt, with an annual interest rate of 5 percent on the unpaid balance.[52] The communities complained to Paris in 1642, with two-thirds of the debts remaining, on the harsh measures used by the intendant to force payment. But a decree of the council on November 5 upheld Champigny's financial penalties for nonpayment: each consul, community, and creditor was ordered to pay one year's interest on unpaid debts; the syndic for the creditors paid two years.[53] The intendant's efforts to collect the interest created strong resistance. Champigny wrote to the secretary of state on October 4, 1644, that he could not continue to collect interest without causing riots; he feared a murderous personal attack.[54] Champigny wrote on September 27 that a crowd

[49] B.B., Clairambault 395, fols. 138–141; A.N., E 142A, fol. 71; E 131A, fol. 149.

[50] B.N., Clairambault 395, fols. 138–141; A.N., E 146A, fol. 429; E 147A, fol. 341; E. 149A, fol. 345.

[51] Marcel Marion, *Dictionnaire des institutions de la France au XVIIᵉ et XVIIIᵉ siècles* (Paris, 1923), pp. 168, 300.

[52] B. Marseille 3165, "Jugement général rendu par Monseigneur de Vautorte intendant en cette Province," in Edouard Baratier, ed., *Documents de l'histoire de Provence* (Toulouse, 1971), pp. 219–220.

[53] B.N., Ms. fr. 18976, fols. 169–171, 346–374; A.N., E 170B, fol. 313; M.A., Provence 353.

[54] B.N., Clairambault 395, fols. 138–141.

of 3,000 to 4,000 angry protesters had assembled at Aix to demand a General Assembly on the issue.[55]

The intendants expanded their commission on community debts to include auditing the accounts of provincial tax farmers and particular receivers. On July 2, 1646, Champigny wrote to Séguier that agents verifying community debts were regularly auditing the accounts of all provincial tax farmers who owed the crown money.[56] Surveillance of the tax farmers was necessary, as Champigny wrote to Séguier on June 21, 1644, because they were guilty of irregularities. Champigny had recently discovered that the gabelle farmer was hoarding 2,000 emines of salt, which he intended to sell after he left office.[57]

The intendants also used their commission on community debts to regulate provincial wheat sales and exports. The Parlement had regularly issued arrêts regulating the wheat traffic, but its authority to do so was questionable. This profitable power had belonged to the governors since 1503 by royal letters that expressly forbade the Parlement's interference. The issue was a traditional source of friction.[58] Royal letters annually prohibited wheat exports from Provence because of shortages and the need to provision the royal armies. The intendants assumed this aspect of the governors' authority and challenged the Parlement's right to regulate the provincial wheat traffic.

There were shortages of wheat in Provence during the spring of 1644, after a bad harvest. Champigny wrote to Séguier on June 28 that hoarding was increasing the price and causing shortages at Marseille.[59] The Parlement had issued arrêts d'état in March regulating the sale of wheat and ordering the prosecution of hoarders.[60] But on June 7, president Régusse wrote to Séguier that Champigny and master of requests Habert de Montmor, who had been in Provence two months, sent a substitute royal attorney with Champigny's clerk and agents and the prévôt's police to seize the Parlement's arrêts and to regulate wheat prices and sales.[61] With-

---

[55] *Ibid.*; Lublinskaya, *Vnutrenniaia*, pp. 286–287.

[56] Lublinskaya, *Vnutrenniaia*, pp. 314–315.

[57] *Ibid.*, pp. 282–283.

[58] Gaston Zeller, "L'administration monarchique avant les intendants: Les parlements et gouverneurs," *Revue historique*, 197 (1947), 212–214.

[59] B.N., Ms. fr. 17376, fols. 5–6; Mousnier, *Lettres*, I, 686.

[60] Mousnier, *Lettres*, I, 685–686; Lublinskaya, *Vnutrenniaia*, pp. 279–281.

[61] *Ibid.*

out letters of commission or decrees of the council, the intendant's authority for this action was shaky. The Parlement's avocat-général ordered the province to disregard the intendant's agents, whom he described as "simple lawyers without any character of royal office . . . [who are going] everywhere in the province with great expense to the people and by their violent procedures are not only disrupting the wheat traffic from one city to another but frightening men into hiding their wheat in order not to sell it at the price set by these commissioners."[62] The intendant's agents were notorious for their rudeness, corruption, and violence. First president Mesgrigny complained to Séguier on May 2, 1645, that agents deputized by Champigny to verify community debts were stealing tax monies from the crown.[63] Intendants at Aix did not have troops to aid them in collecting taxes, as in other généralités. They used their own agents, those of the traitants, and the prévôt's police.

The Parlement ordered the return of the confiscated wheat. The Grand'Chambre demanded the right of final appeal for criminal prosecutions developing from the intendant's regulation of the wheat traffic. The demand was refused by Champigny and Montmor, who ordered the royal chancellery at Aix not to seal or issue the Parlement's arrêts or appeal demands.[64] On October 4, 1644, Champigny asked Séguier for a decree of the council to settle the dispute, with letters of evocation to another court for lawyers Vela and Pigenat, whom he described as "lawyers serving the commission for the investigation of wheat *and* the verification of debts of the communities."[65] President Régusse complained on January 31, 1645, that Champigny was overstepping his authority in exploiting and misusing decrees of the council.[66] The issue was resolved in the intendant's favor because Sève was investigating illegal wheat exports at Arles, Martigues, and Fréjus in July 1648.[67]

The intendants used commission letters to collect royal taxes in order to increase their surveillance over the taille. They received commissions to collect the amortissement in 1641, a royal tax of one-fifth to one-third the value of land held by gens de mainmorte

[62] *Ibid.*
[63] Lublinskaya, *Vnutrenniaia*, pp. 298–299.
[64] Mousnier, *Lettres*, I, 685–686; Lublinskaya, *Vnutrenniaia*, pp. 279–281.
[65] Lublinskaya, *Vnutrenniaia*, p. 287.
[66] B.N., Ms. fr. 17383, fols. 72–74.
[67] *Ibid.*, fols. 162–163, Sève to Séguier, July 7, 1648.

(usually the church); the subvention générale, a national sales tax of five percent; the droit d'avènement à la couronne and droit de confirmation in 1644, taxes paid by financial officials on the accession of Louis XIV to the throne.[68] Traitants under the intendant's supervision collected these taxes, as well as the franc-fief, an annual tax of one-twentieth the revenue of a fief payable to the crown by a nonnoble owner, and the nouveaux acquêts, a tax on gens de mainmorte who had purchased land omitted from the amortissement. Levies of these unpopular land taxes, with searches going back to 1520, were announced in 1634–1635, 1637, 1639, 1641, 1644, 1645, 1652, 1654, and 1655.[69] The intendant investigated fraudulent exemptions, which allowed him to verify cadastres. His tribunal at Aix judged litigation arising from collection of these land taxes until a sovereign chamber was created for this purpose in December 1652.[70] In 1642, the council of state ordered all communities in Provence to obtain permission from the Aix bureau of finance to levy taxes over 300 livres, increasing the intendant's control over community finances.[71]

The intendants thus expanded their authority granted in royal letters to include other responsibilities. Commissions to liquidate community debts were used to force payment of back taxes, super-

[68] In January and February 1642, intendant Vautorte sent lists to Paris of amortissements paid and owed by each community and viguerie in Provence. Jean Martinet was the traitant; cf. B.N., Ms. fr. 18976, fols. 147–152, 157–158, 161–165. Champigny wrote to Séguier on December 8, 1643, that Vautorte had forced the communities and their creditors to pay the amortissement; only ecclesiastical bodies still owed. Sieur Pidoux was the traitant; cf. Lublinskaya, *Vnutrenniaia*, pp. 265–266. The new search for the amortissement was announced on April 19, 1639; cf. A.N., E 151C, fol. 154. Vautorte wrote of his difficulties in collecting the subvention générale on February 25, 1643; cf. B.N., Ms. fr. 17376, fols. 28–29. Champigny's troubles in levying the avènement and confirmation were described in a letter from the Cour des Comptes to Séguier on April 4, 1645; cf. Lublinskaya, *Vnutrenniaia*, pp. 296–297. Printed copies of the conciliar decrees levying these taxes are available in M.A., Provence 353.

[69] Marion, *Dictionnaire des institutions*, 2nd ed. (Paris, 1968), pp. 18–19, 244–245; Roger Doucet, *Les institutions de la France au XVI^e siècle*, 2 vols. (Paris, 1948), II, 484–485; Martin Wolfe, *The Fiscal System of Renaissance France* (New Haven, 1972), pp. 357–358; Charmeil, *Les trésoriers*, p. 199; ADBR, Marseille, C 166; C 2070; C 23, fol. 299; B.N., Ms. fr. 18976, fols. 147–159, 161–165.

[70] ADBR, Marseille, C 167–188, seventeenth-century registers of the Aix *chambre souveraine des francs-fiefs, nouveaux acquêts, et amortissements*.

[71] ADBR, Marseille C 2070.

vise provincial tax farmers and receivers, and regulate the wheat traffic. Commissions to collect royal land taxes were used to supervise the assessment and collection of the taille. In prosecuting tax offenders, the intendants encroached upon the jurisdiction of the royal courts. Not only did they anger the communities and landowners in supervising provincial tax collection; they also irritated the sovereign courts.

The growing series of conflicts between the intendants and the Parlement reached a climax during Champigny's second period in office from 1643 to 1647. The Parlement complained that the intendants were encroaching upon its authority as a provincial high court. The intendants' tribunal was usurping the Tournelle's criminal jurisdiction and refusing to recognize its right to final appeal, while the intendants were using the council of state to evoke cases from the Parlement to other royal courts. The intendants also attacked the political authority of the Parlement, hoping to confine it to its jurisdiction as a provincial high court. They challenged its authority to regulate the provincial administration by arrêts d'état, for instance the provincial wheat traffic, and they gained entry to joint meetings, denying its privilege of free debate.

On January 24, 1645, the Parlement accused Champigny of "constant attacks on the authority of this company . . . judging without differentiation all sorts of cases."[72] Champigny had judged at his hôtel the case of a tailor and a process server indicted for stealing seven livres from a soldier by a confidence trick in the gardens of the archbishop's palace. Champigny condemned them to the galleys, a penalty too severe for the crime. This criminal case fell within the jurisdiction of the Aix prévôt or seneschal court, with appeal to the Tournelle, but Champigny refused to recognize their authority or allow an appeal. First president Mesgrigny complained to Séguier on January 31 that the intendant was expediting more judgments than the Parlement, Cour des Comptes, and Aix seneschal court together, arresting and condemning all sorts of people as tax offenders and wheat traffickers.[73]

[72] Delib. Parl., B. Méjanes 953, fol. 106.
[73] B.N., Ms. fr. 17383, fols. 76–78; Delib. Parl., B. Méjanes 953, fols. 104–105. The Cour des Comptes issued injunctions against the intendant's adjudications in 1645 and 1648, cf., B.N., Ms. fr. 17390, fols. 31–32.

On July 27, 1645, the Parlement wrote to chancellor Séguier that "the aforesaid sieur Champigny and his council have as a goal the destruction of the authority of the Parlement in order to make his own more illustrious. . . ."[74] On July 1, Champigny had sent his agents to transfer a prisoner—arrested for attempted extortion by a traitant—from the Parlement's prison in the palace of justice to his own. Champigny claimed jurisdiction over the case. The agents pounded on the prison door with their fists, kicked it in, then held a gun to the stomach of the jailer. The Parlement ordered their immediate arrest. A furious Champigny wrote to Séguier from Aubagne, where he claimed to have retreated for safety, accusing the Parlement of disobedience and contempt for royal authority. He declared the intimidating effect of the incident to be so great that the traitants had left Aix in fear. He complained that he could no longer find bailiffs or sergeants to serve him, and insisted that he could not exercise his office without an immediate conciliar decree—issued on July 12—releasing his agents and reprimanding the Parlement. Three parlementaires were called to Paris for explanation.[75]

Champigny had made the same complaint to Paris six months earlier in January 1645, when he demanded permission from Séguier to send the prévôt's men to free his bailiff. The Parlement had arrested his bailiff five or six days earlier for making illegal arrests. Champigny claimed that his agent had been persecuted and falsely imprisoned because the Parlement was intent on attacking and destroying his authority.[76] The quarreling of the intendants and Parlement reached a shrill crescendo by the late 1640s.

The intendants' judicial authority was derived from their letters of commission and their office of master of requests. They sat as a sovereign court to judge a case, then executed the sentence. Appeals went to the king's council in Paris. The flow of litigation before the intendants soon became a flood. Their justice was rapid and free, in contrast to the seneschal and sovereign courts, and their case loads were swollen with individual suits and complaints.[77] The sovereign courts protested that the intendants' final

[74] B.N., Ms. fr. 17383, fol. 70v.
[75] Lublinskaya, *Vnutrenniaia*, p. 304; B.N., Clairambault 400, fols. 29–30; B.N., Ms. fr. 18976, fols. 633–642; A.N., E 1689, fol. 109.
[76] B.N., Ms. fr. 17383, fol. 70v.
[77] Bonney, "Intendants," pp. 53, 68.

judgments were reducing them to the level of seneschal courts. The intendants also had the responsibility of reducing corruption, delay, and expense in the provincial royal courts. For instance, in April 1638, Champigny prosecuted Arnault de Monier, civil and criminal lieutenant at Draguignan, for corruption.[78] The intendants received special judicial authority in their letters of commission, as in those of Champigny on May 4, 1643, to prosecute *rogneurs et billoneurs*, counterfeiters and others guilty of debasing the coinage.[79]

The intendants and governors used evocation as a tactic to evade the Parlement's authority. They requested the council of state to transfer controversial cases that came before the Parlement of Aix. On October 4, 1644, Champigny requested evocation for two of his agents under prosecution by the Parlement for alleged criminal actions in regulating the wheat traffic.[80] On January 31, 1645, president Régusse complained to Séguier about Champigny's request for evocation in a case involving his bailiff, who was later tried before the Nîmes seneschal court with appeal to the Parlement of Toulouse.[81] On February 28, 1645, governor Alais wrote to Séguier requesting evocation for unpopular Requêtes councilors Gautier and Ballon.[82]

As a condition of the 1649 peace treaty, Alais obtained permanent evocation for his entourage to the seneschal court of Marseille and the Parlement of Dijon. They included forty friends, twenty-two members of the newly created court, the Semester, and twenty officers of his regiment. The Parlement argued that evocations should only be granted when a litigant had six close relatives in a court, as was customary, since mass evocations would seriously reduce its case load.[83] But the crown granted evocation for three years to Alais's supporters upon application to the council of state, despite the Parlement's remonstrance in

---

[78] *Ibid.*, p. 27, n. 1.

[79] A.A.E., 1708, fols. 171–172v; Mousnier, *Lettres*, II, 1056–1059. Intendants in Bordeaux, Toulouse, Castres, and Agen also prosecuted those guilty of counterfeiting; cf. Bonney, "Intendants," p. 172.

[80] Lublinskaya, *Vnutrenniaia*, p. 287.

[81] B.N., Ms. fr. 17383, fols. 76–78, 140–143.

[82] Lublinskaya, *Vnutrenniaia*, p. 293.

[83] B.N., Ms. fr. 20473, fols. 15–17; B.M., Harleian 4575, fols. 138–139v; Pillorget, *Les mouvements*, pp. 624–625. Communities also obtained evocations.

1650.[84] Those eligible included the families and servants of Alais's supporters, their brothers, brothers-in-law, uncles, nephews, and servants. They could evoke cases from the Aix to the Marseille seneschal court with appeal to another provincial parlement, as well as from the seneschal courts of Arles and Tarascon to the royal judge of Beaucaire, and from the admiralty to the seneschal court of Marseille, with appeal to another parlement.[85] A decree of the council on June 30, 1651, granted permanent evocation to the Parlement of Dijon for members of the defunct Semester, their families, and servants.[86] So, although the Parlement could be vindictive, evocations were used to bypass its authority.

Decrees of the council of state were one of the crown's main instruments for administrative reform. These decrees were registered by the sovereign courts to acquire the force of law, but they could be published, distributed, and enforced as administrative orders without registration, which was usual in bypassing the Parlement. The crown used conciliar decrees executed by the intendants to avoid registration, nullify the Parlement's arrêts d'état, discipline the company, and challenge its authority to regulate the provincial administration. In addition, the intendants issued ordinances and created new administrative procedures. The Parlement protested that the intendants were illegally creating new authority and acting without registered letters of commission, as in the case of the provincial traffic in wheat.[87]

The intendants also observed the Parlement's political activities. The intendants wrote weekly reports to Paris on the behavior and attitudes of local officials, sometimes suggesting punitive action. Their dispatches usually went to the chancellor and secretary of state for Provence, taking one to three weeks, and sometimes becoming lost, stolen, or illegibly soaked. Replies took the same length of time. The intendant went to important joint meetings of

[84] A.C., Aix, AA 14, fol. 574; A.A.E., 1717, fols. 90–91.

[85] B. Marseille 1797, "Arrêt du conseil d'état sur les evocations . . . March 18, 1650." Conciliar decrees were also issued on April 27, June 15, and October 29, 1649.

[86] Adolphe Crémieux, *Marseille et la royauté pendant la minorité de Louis XIV (1643–1661)*, 2 vols. (Paris, 1917), I, 378.

[87] Edmond Esmonin, "Les arrêts du conseil sous l'ancien régime," in *Etudes sur la France des XVIIe et XVIIIe siècles* (Paris, 1964), pp. 183–199; François Olivier-Martin, *Histoire du Droit français des origines à la Révolution*, 2d ed. (Paris, 1951), pp. 458, 571–573.

the Parlement: as a government informer, he monitored and reported on all controversial registrations. There was danger in freely voicing opinions critical of the crown on the floor of the grande salle because the intendant reported negative opinions to Paris. Eighty-three citations of Aix parlementaires in disciplinary decrees of the council and lettres de cachet were issued from 1631 to 1659, mostly for negative opinions expressed during joint meetings.[88]

As masters of requests and councilors of state, the intendants had the privilege of entering the Parlement as honorary guests.[89] The letters of commission for Aubray and de La Potherie did not authorize regular attendance at the sovereign courts. In fact, the Parlement on March 17, 1631, decided to permit de La Potherie to attend one session only for the purpose of greeting the company. He was to sit below the dean.[90] But soon the crown was issuing letters patent granting the intendants in Provence the authority to sit in joint meetings and to deliberate on all issues "as they consider best . . . as are all councilors provided to office." Letters patent to this effect were issued on July 27, 1636, for Lauzon; May 14, 1640, for Vautorte; June 3, 1643, for Champigny; and December 8, 1647, for Sève.[91]

The regular issuance of such letters for Provençal intendants indicates the Parlement's reputation for unruliness. Sève's letters of commission stated his authority "to enter and take seat in our courts of the Parlement and Cour des Comptes in order to confer and take resolutions for the good of our service in matters concerning the administration of justice and police or the direction of our finances."[92] Sève was also made an honorary councilor in the Parlement by letters patent; this gave him precedence over the dean.[93] The intendants' rank in the Parlement was hotly disputed. Champigny's letters had ranked him after the presidents and before the dean.[94] The intendants would not recognize the prece-

[88] See Chapter Six.

[89] Louis Wolff, *Le Parlement de Provence au XVIIIᵉ siècle* (Aix, 1920), pp. 70–71, 192–193.

[90] Delib. Parl., B. Méjanes 952, fol. 24.

[91] ADBR, Aix, B 3351, fol. 6; B 3352, fol. 835; B 3354, fol. 219v; B 3356, fol. 355; B. Méjanes 1286, fol. 33.

[92] A.A.E., 1712, fols. 264–267, October 29, 1647.

[93] ADBR, Aix, B 3356, fol. 355; Wolff, *Parlement*, pp. 70, 199.

[94] ADBR, Aix, B 3354, fol. 219v.

dence of the dean. But the Parlement insisted that the dean had the higher rank. The issue was not resolved until 1661, when the company was forced to recognize the intendants' precedence over the dean.[95]

It took courage and determination for an intendant to attend joint meetings, to enter the palace of justice, and climb the grand staircase under the glare of angry eyes, to ignore the muttered remarks and deliberate rudeness, to demand a better seat in the grande salle than the one below the dean. The intendants were not respected or popular until Colbert's time. Champigny, in thanking Séguier on June 18, 1643, for appointment to a second term in Provence, wrote: "Provence being a region attached to the formalities [traditional privileges] and the sovereign companies being well-disposed to play tricks upon the intendants who report on them, I humbly beg you to do me the favor of kindly signing some orders and commission on which I sent a memorandum to M. de La Barde, in order to avoid all the difficulties which they could create for me."[96] In letters to Séguier from 1643 to 1647, Champigny described the Parlement as full of "cabals, monopolies, intrigues, insolent young hotheads, young councilors eager to foment revolt, seditious cascaveoux." He blamed the Parlement for some of his administrative difficulties: for disrupting municipal elections at Aix in 1643, for blocking verification of community debts as creditors of the communities, for ignoring or retarding execution of conciliar decrees.[97] He began a memoir to the secretary of state in April 1645 with, "You see, Sir, that the Cour des Comptes of this province has no more respect for decrees of the council than the Parlement."[98]

The parlementaires as creditors of the communities blocked the liquidation of community debts: they wanted to be assured full payment in money. Councilor Gaspard de Cauvet, baron de

[95] Wolff, *Parlement*, pp. 187–193; J. Marchand, *Un intendant sous Louis XIV: Etude sur l'administration de Lebret en Provence (1687–1704)* (Paris, 1889), p. 189.

[96] A.A.E., 1708, fol. 193. Jean de La Barde was Chavigny's clerk and cousin. He was ambassador to Switzerland in 1648.

[97] Mousnier, *Lettres* I, 589–590, September 28, 1643; I, 619–620, January 19, 1644; II, 811, October 19, 1647; II, 762, July 2, 1645; Lublinskaya, *Vnutrenniaia*, pp. 254–255, July 11, 1643; p. 259, September 28, 1643; pp. 289–293, January 16, 1645.

[98] B.N., Clairambault 398, fols. 312–316; see Chapter Six.

Bormes, lent the community of Trets 100,000 livres. Champigny ordered in 1639 that he be repaid in eight months by renting community ovens, mills, and woods.[99] Cauvet was also a creditor of the community of Barjols.[100] Other creditors of Barjols included parlementaires Scipion de Foresta, François de Saint Marc, and Alexandre Thomassin.[101] Councilors Dedons, Venel, and Aymar d'Albi had an interest in the tax farm on grain windmills at Barjols.[102] Jacques Gaufridy in his memoirs noted a quarrel between councilors Boyer and Valbelle, in which the latter criticized Boyer, Guiran, and Leidet-Sigoyer for making 45,000 livres from the interest on community debts collected in 1639. The mazarinades protested the intendants' collection of community debts. President Henri de Forbin-Maynier d'Oppède was a creditor of Cadenet, Aix, and at least eight other communities in Provence, and he frequently lent money to other magistrates.[103] Lending money to communities and magistrates were favorite forms of parlementary investment.

Although the intendants had justifiable complaints about the parlementaires' behavior, the tone of their letters is so vehement that one suspects them of exaggerating and seeking scapegoats for their own failures. First president Mesgrigny protested to Séguier on January 31, 1645, that Champigny habitually reported only one side of an incident; disciplinary decrees were being issued on the basis of these inaccurate reports.[104] But the parlementaires were also guilty of distortions and exaggerations.

The intendants' complaints to Paris about the insubordination and disobedience of local officials show a lively concern for image. This was especially true of de La Potherie, Champigny, and Sève. With difficult duties to perform, the intendants were hypersensitive to insult and opposition They saw intrigue and sedition everywhere. Royal commissioners with questionable legitimacy in an

---

[99] B.N., Ms. fr. 18976, fols. 129–131; Marchand, *Un intendant*, p. 216.

[100] AD Var, E 1058, fol. 456v.

[101] *Ibid.*, E 1057, fol. 317v; E 1061, fols. 237, 446v; E 1064, fol. 218.

[102] *Ibid.*, E 1176, fol. 99v; E 1174, fols. 368, 373.

[103] Charles de Grimaldi and Jacques Gaufridy, *Mémoires pour servir à l'histoire de la Fronde en Provence* (Aix, 1870), p. 145; Richard Holbrook, "Baron d'Oppède and Cardinal Mazarin: The Politics of Provence from 1641 to 1660" (Ph.D. dissertation, University of Illinois at Chicago Circle, 1976), pp. 63–64.

[104] B.N., Ms. fr. 17383, fols. 76–78.

age when local credibility was much of the struggle to secure obedience, they had the unpleasant task of supervising hereditary local officials with traditional authority. Royal commissioners had to be accepted as authoritative in order to be obeyed, and the intendants pursued this goal with marked anxiety and varying degrees of success.

After the 1649 revolt, the parlementaires demanded the intendants' suppression as a condition of the February peace negotiated by cardinal Bichi. On March 10, while awaiting the crown's ratification of the treaty, the parlementaires sent two deputies to confiscate the intendant's papers, accusing him of increasing the misunderstanding between their company and the crown. The Cour des Comptes received the papers pertinent to its jurisdiction on March 16.[105] The intendant had been without authority for nine months: Sève wrote to Séguier on August 6, 1648, that the Cour des Comptes was refusing to allow him to exercise his commission on indebted communities. The Cour des Comptes had been emboldened by the crown's July revocation of intendants in all but six frontier provinces.[106] On November 17, Sève wrote to Séguier that deputies from the sovereign courts had confiscated papers pertaining to the indebted communities, and arrested his clerk.[107] The Treaty of Rueil, registered by the Parlement of Paris on April 1, 1649, recognized the suppression of all intendants in France; a decree of the council on April 2 suppressed the intendant of justice in Provence. An arrêt of the Parlement on April 12 forbade Sève to exercise his authority as intendant, and his salary was not paid after that. He left Provence in the autumn.[108]

The crown had no intention of suppressing the intendants, who had proved so useful in collecting taxes and controlling local offi-

[105] B.N., Ms. fr. 24166, fol. 269.

[106] B.N., Ms. fr. 17390, fols. 53–54; A.N., U28, fol. 194, July 18, 1648. The six frontier provinces were Lyonnais, Picardy, Champagne, Provence, Languedoc, and Burgundy.

[107] B.N., Ms. fr. 17390, fols. 305–306.

[108] Dominique Guidy, "Histoire du Parlement de Provence," B. Méjanes R.A. 54, fol. 266; Carranrais, "Notice sur l'intendance," p. 151; Bonney, "Intendants," p. 107; B. M., Harleian 4575, fol. 149; Crémieux, *Marseille*, II, 466. The procureurs du pays ignored royal letters on April 20, August 12, and October 15, 1649, ordering them to pay Sève's salary; cf. ADBR, Marseille, C 987.

cials. But it could not revoke its declarations of July 18 and October 22 abolishing the intendants, or suspend the Treaty of Rueil, for fear of violent protest. It had to find a way of reintroducing the intendants under another name, which it did in January 1650 by reviving a sixteenth-century edict sending masters of requests periodically on tour in the provinces to remedy abuses in the provincial administrations.[109] There were a number of royal officials serving as commissaires departis from 1650 to 1653; the title "intendant" was not used. These officials acted as financial and army intendants with special letters of commission. At the conclusion of the Fronde, there were again rumors that masters of requests would be sent on tour without letters of commission. Provincial intendants were gradually reestablished as visiting masters of requests or special royal commissioners. After 1653, only Provence and Brittany did not have intendants.[110]

Sève had left Provence in the autumn of 1649. On March 22, 1650, Jacques de Chaulnes was sent with a lettre de cachet to report on the behavior of governor Alais.[111] Councilor of state Miromesnil was sent to Provence in January 1651 to convoke a General Assembly.[112] But Miromesnil's stay was temporary. On March 4, the procureurs du pays requested that he not be present at the next General Assembly, and by May he was back in Paris.[113] In August 1653, Parlement president Régusse received letters of commission to convoke a General Assembly in the absence of

[109] Edmond Esmonin, "La suppression des intendants pendant la Fronde et leur rétablissement," *Bulletin de la Société d'histoire moderne* (1935), pp. 114–119, reprinted in *Etudes sur la France*, pp. 33–39; "Un episode du rétablissement des intendants: La mission de Morant en Guyenne (1650)," *Revue d'histoire moderne et contemporaine*, 1 (1954), 85–101, reprinted in *Etudes sur la France*, pp. 53–70; "Un episode du rétablissement des intendants après la Fronde: Les maîtres des requêtes envoyés en chevauchées," *Revue d'histoire moderne et contemporaine*, 12 (1965), 219–228; Mousnier, "Recherches sur les syndicats d'officiers," 94–100. In 1649, the frontier provinces of Languedoc, Picardy, Burgundy, and Champagne had army intendants; cf. Baxter, "French Intendants of the Army," pp. 139–141.

[110] Bonney, "Intendants," pp. 113–116, 122.

[111] *Ibid.*, pp. 107, 309, 312; A.A.E., 870, fol. 267v; 1713, fol. 353. A commission was drawn up for Chaulnes but never issued.

[112] B.N., Ms. fr. 20655, fol. 44; A.A.E., 1717, fols. 119–121.

[113] ADBR, Marseille, C 30, particular assembly of March 4, 1651; A.A.E., 1717, fol. 183.

governor Mercoeur, which he did at Manosque in September 1653.[114] Jean-Baptiste de Colbert was sent briefly to Toulon to supervise naval armament in June 1654.[115] The bishop of Orange, Hyacinthe Serroni, and governor Mercoeur represented the crown during General Assemblies at Brignoles in January 1654, Brignoles in February 1655, and Lambesc in February 1656.[116] Mazarin probably decided in 1654 to reestablish intendants of justice in Provence. He thus retained an Italian client, the bishop of Orange, as a transitional financial commissioner. During eighteen months, the bishop represented the crown at three General Assemblies and supervised naval armament and supply at Toulon.[117] But in July 1656, he was sent to Catalonia.[118]

In December 1656, Geoffroy Luillier, sieur d'Orgeval and master of requests, came to Provence to replace the bishop of Orange. He was to serve as royal commissioner at the next General Assembly of Communities, but rumors quickly spread that he was the new intendant of justice. Governor Mercoeur wrote to Mazarin on December 18, 1656, that "the coming of M. d'Orgeval has so angered everyone that the Parlement has been forced to issue several arrêts that he shall present his commission before entering the province, and he shall declare that he has no function as an intendant of justice."[119] The Parlement sent a remonstrance to Paris, and would only recognize Orgeval's authority as an army

[114] B.N., Ms. fr. 20655, fols. 79–84; ADBR, Marseille, C 32, fols. 169–220.

[115] Pierre-Adolphe Chéruel and Georges d'Avenel, eds., *Lettres du cardinal Mazarin pendant son ministère*, 9 vols. (Paris, 1872–1906), VI, 567. Charles Colbert visited Toulon for the same purpose in June 1655; cf. *ibid.*, VI, 709.

[116] ADBR, Marseille, C 32, fols. 239–292; C 35, fols. 54–149, 239–300; B.N., Ms. fr. 20655, fols. 107–109.

[117] A Dominican monk born in Rome in 1617, Hyacinthe Serroni was one of Mazarin's *créatures*. In December 1645, he accompanied the newly married Marie de Gonzaga (of Mantua) to Poland to reign as its queen, and became bishop of Orange in 1647, bishop of Mende in 1661, bishop of Albi in 1678, then archbishop, and died in 1687; cf. Chéruel and Avenel, *Lettres de Mazarin*, IV, 708, n. 1; 719, n. 2. He was frequently at Toulon on naval and military matters, as in September 1656, when he sent a fleet to Catalonia; cf. *ibid.*, VII, 666, 678.

[118] A.A.E., 1720, fols. 21, 39v.

[119] *Ibid.*, fols. 54–55; B.M., Harleian 4493, fol. 111, Orgeval to Séguier, December 17, 1656; fol. 115, the same, December 29, 1656.

intendant to supervise the lodging and maintenance of troops.[120]

On January 23, 1657, Parlement first president Oppède reported to Mazarin that Orgeval was received by the General Assembly at Aubagne only when accompanied by the governor or first president, never on his own, and that his authority as a royal financial commissioner was not recognized by the assembly.[121] Orgeval was described in the deliberations as "master of requests and intendant in the army."[122] The sovereign courts refused outright to register Orgeval's letters of commission as intendant, issued on January 24, 1657,[123] or to recognize his authority.[124] Oppède did nothing to compel the Parlement to recognize Orgeval's authority. It was clear by March that Orgeval would never be accepted in Provence. On March 27, Orgeval wrote to Mazarin requesting permission to attend the funeral of his father-in-law in Paris, and on April 30 he was at Senas. Oppède wrote to Mazarin on the same day that Orgeval had contributed nothing to the task of managing the General Assembly or the procureurs du pays.[125] There were no regrets on either side at his departure.

Oppède's actions and criticisms may have been colored by his own ambitions, but when Orgeval was replaced as army intendant in Picardy in 1652, it was reported that "he is a person without a brain and without order, who spends three weeks on the same affair without concluding anything. He puts the province and the men of war in despair, ruining all and sundry."[126] Orgeval was not

---

[120] B.M., Harleian 4490, fols. 133–134, Parlement to Séguier, January 8, 1657. Orgeval complained to Séguier on January 7 that only fortress garrisons and ordinary citizens would recognize him; cf. *ibid.*, fol. 178.

[121] A.A.E., 1721, fols. 76–77.

[122] ADBR, Marseille, C 37, fol. 21v.

[123] Bonney, "Intendants," pp. 317, 323.

[124] A.A.E., 1721, fols. 52–53, 54–55, Mercoeur to Mazarin, December 12 and 18, 1656; fols. 50–52, 58–61, Oppède to Mazarin, December 12 and 19, 1656.

[125] *Ibid.*, fols. 106–107, March 27, 1657; B.M., Harleian 4490, Orgeval to Séguier, April 30, 1657; Holbrook, "Baron d'Oppède and Cardinal Mazarin," pp. 219–221.

[126] Baxter, "French Intendents of the Army," pp. 166–167. Geoffroy Luillier (Lhuiller), sieur d'Orgeval et de La Malmaison, became a councilor in the Parlement of Paris in 1627, master of requests in 1632, intendant in Picardy, Champagne, and the Ile-de-France in 1633 and at Soissons in 1634–1638; cf. Bonney, "Intendants," p. 345; Mousnier, *Lettres*, II, 1044–1046, 1216.

disgraced, and it is possible that he was the victim of a patronage struggle in 1652. But the two incidents cast some doubt on his abilities.

Parlement first president Henri de Forbin-Maynier, baron d'Oppède, replaced Orgeval quietly and unofficially as acting intendant in 1657 without letters of commission. He had already exercised the functions of intendant throughout 1656, as his correspondence with Mazarin demonstrates. Oppède wrote weekly on the performance of tasks that were previously the responsibility of Champigny and Sève—coercion of registration from the sovereign courts, transport and payment of troops, intimidation of the General Assemblies and procureurs du pays to obtain their approval, appointment of municipal officials.[127] Oppède continued to act as intendant after Orgeval's departure in March 1657 because he had already capably filled that position, while the Parlement refused to register letters of commission for an intendant of justice.

Oppède acted as intendant without title and without registered letters of commission. Already first president, he was styled royal commissioner and acted as intendant until his death in 1671, when the official title was revived. The records of the intendants of Provence begin in 1671.[128] Guillaume Du Vair, first president of the Parlement and royal commissioner from 1599 to 1616, set the precedent for combining these offices.[129] Oppède's tenure set a pattern, and the offices of first president and intendant of justice were combined in Provence after 1690. Pierre Cardin-Lebret became intendant in 1687 and first president of the Parlement in 1690. His son became intendant in 1704 and first president in 1710. Jean-Baptiste des Gallois de La Tour became intendant in 1734 and first president in 1735. His son repeated the pattern in 1744 and 1747.

[127] Oppède to Mazarin, A.A.E., 1720, fol. 21, May 19, 1656; fols. 26–27, May 30, 1656; fol. 32, June 15, 1656; 1721, fols. 41–43, November 1, 1656; fols. 79–82, January 31, 1657. In contrast, first president Mesgrigny wrote infrequently to Paris on the Parlement's internal affairs in 1645; cf. Mesgrigny to Séguier, B.N., Ms. fr. 17383, fols. 76–78, January 31, 1645; Lublinskaya, *Vnutrenniaia*, pp. 293–294, March 7, 1645; pp. 298–299, May 2, 1645; pp. 300–301, July 14, 1645; A.A.E., 1710, fol. 189, June 13, 1645.

[128] EDB, III, 304–305; ADBR, Marseille, C 2176 (December 31, 1669)–C 2224, records of the intendants of Provence.

[129] Sapey, *Etudes biographiques*, pp. 1–184.

Oppède's power as acting intendant was not openly recognized until October 1658, when as royal commissioner he convened the General Assembly at Tarascon in the governor's absence. He opened this assembly in December to present the crown's tax requests and browbeat and threatened the deputies in long speeches to obtain their cooperation. On January 11, 1659, he wrote to Mazarin that he had secured the customary voluntary gift of 300,000 livres and support for the provincial infantry regiment of fifteen companies, the most controversial requests.[130] Earlier, he had bullied and intimidated the procureurs du pays to force their approval. He had arrested the first consul, cited to Paris the assembly secretary and his clerk, billeted troops on Aix, and ordered the tax levy without approval.[131] Obtaining the cooperation of the procureurs du pays and General Assemblies was a test of an intendant's abilities.

The council issued a decree on December 7, 1658, ordering the Tarascon General Assembly to nominate two bishops as procureurs joints of the clergy "until the next Estates."[132] Nomination of procureurs was a traditional privilege of the Estates, and their appointment by the General Assembly was tacit recognition of the Estates' suppression. Oppède announced that he would make the appointments himself if the assembly refused—as he did a few years later for the procureurs joints of the nobility. He wrote to Mazarin on December 19 that the archbishop of Aix and the vicar general were working to block his nominees, the bishops of Riez and Digne. Oppède's cousin, Toussaint de Forbin Janson, was bishop of Digne. A compromise was accepted, and the bishops of Digne and Vence were finally appointed.[133] Nomination of the procureurs joints of the clergy in 1658 was a victory for Oppède.

Provence had refused to accept the restoration of intendants of justice after the Fronde, so Mazarin restored the intendants as the Parlement's first president acting without title or letters of commission. Oppède proved an invaluable royal servant in this capacity. Mazarin had devised an ingenious solution to a difficult administrative problem. As a Midi pays d'états, Provence deviated in the

---

[130] *Ibid.*, fol. 289; ADBR, Marseille, C 38, fols. 74–92v, 105v, 141v.

[131] See Chapters Two and Nine.

[132] ADBR, Marseille, C 2053, fol. 296.

[133] A.A.E., 1723, fols. 234–235, 267, 273–276, 286; ADBR, Marseille, C 38, fols. 73–74, 103v, 106; EDB, III, 514–524.

development of the intendants' authority from the pattern of a northern pays d'élection described by Roland Mousnier and Edmond Esmonin. It also deviated from the northern pattern in the restoration of the intendants after the Fronde. Excessive claims have been made about the intendants' achievements in the provinces before 1661. Permanent residency of intendants in Provence after 1630 was responsible for their increased administrative importance—and a cause of the three revolts at Aix—but it is an exaggeration to claim that the intendants introduced administrative order during these years. The decades from 1630 to 1661 were crucial in shaping the intendants' authority, which developed as that of the governors declined, but the intendants in Provence before 1661 were not as powerful as some historians have believed.

# Chapter Four

# THE GOVERNORS AND THE PARLEMENT

Before 1661, provincial governors had considerable military and political authority, particularly at the frontier.[1] The formula describing the governors' duties in the royal letters appointing them to office is deceptive because the terminology remained constant while the reality of power changed. Obscured by ceremony and quirks of personality, the precise characteristics of the governor's authority in the early seventeenth century have been difficult for historians to determine.[2] A full definition is beyond the scope of this chapter, which does not explore in detail their military role, but understanding the governors' political role in the provincial government does help to explain the causes of the Aix revolts.

The Parlement of Aix and the governors were traditional political rivals: they quarreled constantly throughout the sixteenth and seventeenth centuries. The Parlement accused the governors of overstepping their police authority, infringing upon the jurisdictions of local institutions, and ignoring or suspending traditional privileges. The governors countered that the parlementaires were disobedient, intriguing against the crown to the extent of provoking rebellions, while illegally increasing their authority and refusing to pay taxes. There were elements of truth in both accusations. The antagonists engaged in a paper war of contradictory arrêts and ordinances. In dispute were the governors' suspension of municipal elections, regulation of the municipal police, taxation by ordinance, troop billeting, criminal jurisdiction over soldiers, use

---

[1] ADBR, Aix, B 3348, fols. 811–821, royal letters appointing Vitry in 1632; B 3351, fols. 284–291, Alais in 1637, fols. 937–944, Mercoeur in 1653.

[2] Consult Roger Doucet, *Les institutions de la France au XVIe siècle*, 2 vols. (Paris, 1948), I, 229; Georges Pagès, *Les institutions monarchiques sous Louis XIII et Louis XIV* (Paris, 1962), p. 81; Gaston Zeller, "Gouverneurs de provinces au XVIe siècle," *Aspects de la politique française sous l'Ancien Régime* (Paris, 1964), pp. 207–239.

of the prévôt's police, forced registration and premature publication of royal edicts.[3]

The careers of governors Guise and Vitry are well-known examples of Richelieu's policy of demanding obedience from provincial governors or their retirement from office. Richelieu removed governors who refused to obey his orders and became entangled in court intrigues or engaged in rebellion, replacing them with loyal, obedient servants. Although he opposed hereditary governorships, he never attempted to suppress the office; it was easier to replace the man. Of the sixteen governors in France in 1614, only four held office at Richelieu's death. Most had been forced into exile.[4]

Son of the Guise murdered at Blois, Charles de Lorraine, duc de Guise et de Chevreuse, was appointed governor of Provence and admiral of the Levant on October 22, 1594, at the age of twenty-three.[5] His portrait shows a small, handsome man with a bold face, dark curly hair, black goatee and mustache, lace collar, stripped doublet, and satin sash.[6] He was a gallant with many conquests among the ladies of Marseille, where he maintained an imposing hôtel facing the harbor and a large entourage of nobles. One of the wealthiest men in France, Guise gambled and spent lavishly.[7] He was frequently absent from Provence on campaign or at court from 1594 to 1624, but he was continuously resident from 1624 to 1631. The Parlement served as acting governor in his absences.

Guise exercised considerable authority as the governor of a maritime frontier province. Most of his power came from the office of admiral of the Levant, a lucrative administrative position used for

---

[3] The parlementaires of Bordeaux and the governor of Guyenne quarreled over similar issues; cf. Nicolas Fessenden, "Epernon and Guyenne: Provincial Politics under Louis XIII" (Ph.D. dissertation, Columbia University, 1972), pp. 42–65.

[4] Jules Caillet, *L'administration en France sous le ministère du cardinal de Richelieu*, 2 vols. (Paris, 1857), I, 30, 47–50; Georges Pagès, *La monarchie d'Ancien Régime en France* (Paris, 1928), pp. 110–111.

[5] ADBR, Aix, B 3339, fols. 84–92.

[6] Guise's portrait is reproduced in EDB, III, plate XVI, 400–401.

[7] Jean-Pierre Labatut, *Les ducs et pairs de France au XVIIe siècle* (Paris, 1972), pp. 277, 300; John Pearl, "Guise and Provence: Political Conflicts in the Epoch of Richelieu" (Ph.D. dissertation, Northwestern University, 1968), p. 27.

policing the coast, controlling navigation, and equipping the French fleet. The admiral collected fees for anchorage and vessel clearance, issued passports and safe-conducts for fishermen and merchants, with the right to one-tenth the value of captured ships and one-third the value of wrecks.[8] There was one admiralty court at Marseille when Guise became governor. He added courts at Arles, Martigues, Toulon, and Fréjus in 1612. The Parlement sometimes intervened in the jurisdiction of the new admiralty courts, as in 1623–1625 and 1628.[9] Each court had a lieutenant who settled commercial disputes, issued passports, and policed the ports in his area with the right to visit and register the merchandise, personnel, and armaments of all ships.[10] Guise received the crown's share in fees collected.[11] This privilege brought him considerable income. His successor, Vitry, estimated that the rights of visitation at Marseille alone were worth 30,000 écus (90,000 livres) annually, while the fees of the other admiralties averaged 5,000 to 6,000 écus each.[12]

The combat naval command for the Mediterranean was held from 1598 to 1617 by general of the galleys Philippe de Gondi, comte de Joigny, and from 1617 to 1635 by his son Pierre, duc de Retz. Guise wanted the office. He quarreled constantly with Gondi over capture of prizes, command of galley captains, and assignment of *forçat*s to ships. The Parlement supported Gondi.[13] A royal commissioner was sent to Marseille in 1620 to warn Guise that the king was aware of his attacks on the general's authority:

[8] François Paris de Lorraine, chevalier de Guise and lieutenant general of Provence, died in the château at Les Baux on June 1, 1614.

[9] Doucet, *Les institutions*, I, 244–249; Jacques Gaufridy, "Histoire de Provence sous le règne de Louis XIII," B. Méjanes 790, fol. 5; Jean-Marc David, *L'amirauté de Provence et des mers du Levant* (Marseille, 1942), pp. 36–45, 474–485; Carl Burckhardt, *Richelieu and His Age: Assertion of Power and Cold War*, tr. Bernard Hoy (New York, 1970), p. 30.

[10] David, *L'amirauté*, p. 222; Zeller, *Aspects*, p. 215.

[11] David, *L'amirauté*, pp. 117–193, 439–452.

[12] *Ibid.*, pp. 37–38; ADBR, Aix, B 3346, fols. 431v, 435, 437, 439; B 3347, fol. 1149.

[13] Pearl, "Guise and Provence," pp. 76–79; A.A.E., 1701, fols. 66–67, "Lettres du maréchal de Vitry sur l'amirauté de Provence." The Parlement accused Guise of making 200,000 livres a year from the admiralty in January, 1626; cf. Philippe Tamizey de Larroque, ed., *Lettres de Peiresc aux frères Dupuy*, 7 vols. (Paris, 1888–1898), VI, 346–352.

Guise was rumored to have driven Gondi from the province. Guise was ordered to allow the general free access to the port of Marseille, and he was told once more that command of the royal galleys was separate from his authority as admiral. The royal galleys were ordered to join the Ponant fleet under Montmorency, and Guise was to stay in his government of Provence. If he insisted on command, he was to share it with Montmorency. The tone suggests negotiation with a sovereign prince. Guise's letters to Paris were short and peremptory, without the customary deference or flattery: his military and naval power, his rank and family, his personal reputation and remoteness allowed independence. Guise permitted neither resident royal commissioners in Provence nor a lieutenant general after 1614.[14]

Guise wanted to add the governorship of Provence to his hereditary titles and to establish a family dynasty in that office. But the Parlement refused to verify or register the royal letters of December 1615 appointing his son governor of Provence and admiral of the Levant en survivance.[15] The Parlement's refusal kindled a serious quarrel, which smoldered and burst into flames during the 1630 revolt. Guise's continuous presence in Provence after 1624 contributed to his feuding with the Parlement and intensified the personal animosity between Guise and the Parlement's first president, Vincent-Anne de Forbin-Maynier d'Oppède. Guise had helped to obtain Maynier d'Oppède's appointment in 1621, but they quarreled in December 1625, perhaps because Maynier d'Oppède had switched his allegiance to Richelieu as the more

[14] A.A.E., 1700, fols. 250–253, "Instructions from the King to Guise, June 21, 1620"; *Les confessions de Jean-Jacques Bouchard, parisien, suivies de son voyage de Paris à Rome en 1630* (Paris, 1881), pp. 137, 145; Burckhardt, *Richelieu: Assertion of Power*, pp. 47–48; David, *L'amirauté*, pp. 62–71. Also see Paul Bamford, *Fighting Ships and Prisons: The Mediterranean Galleys of France in the Age of Louis XIV* (Minneapolis, 1973). In 1635, Richelieu bought the galleys command from Gondi for 560,000 livres for his nephew, François de Vignerod, marquis de Pontcourlay.

[15] ADBR, Aix, J.L.H. Hesmivy de Moissac, "Histoire du Parlement de Provence 1501–1715," 2 vols., I, fols. 457–458; ADBR, Aix, B 3344, fol. 1644, unverified and unregistered lettres en survivance for the prince de Joinville dated December 11, 1615; "Harangues de Scipion Du Périer au Parlement de Provence lors de la présentation des lettres en survivance au gouvernment dudit pays pour François de Lorraine, prince de Joinville," B.N. Dupuy 659, fol. 278; B.N., Ms. fr. 16518, fols. 105–121.

113

promising patron.[16] Guise had two deeply cherished ambitions, his son's inheritance of his offices and his own command of a fleet of galleys, both of which the Parlement had blocked.

In July 1625, the Parlement nullified Guise's ordinance levying a tax to support three coastal garrisons. The ordinance had been issued without royal letters of authorization or the approval of the procureurs du pays. In May 1626, the Parlement sent to Paris a twenty-article remonstrance on this illegal ordinance, which Richelieu forced Guise to withdraw.[17] In July, September, and October 1628, Guise protested that the Parlement refused to verify or register an ordinance levying a tax to transfer thirty galleys to Cannes and hire new recruits.[18] This ordinance had neither royal nor provincial approval. Again, Guise was forced to withdraw it. Guise and the Parlement also quarreled over criminal jurisdiction of military personnel, use of the prévôt's police, and publication of royal edicts before registration.[19]

Their feud reached a climax in August 1629, when Guise blockaded Aix during an outbreak of plague. On October 18, the Parlement complained to Paris that Guise had ringed the city with troops, established barricades on the roads leading to the city

[16] Georges d'Avenel, ed., *Lettres, instructions diplomatiques et papiers d'état du cardinal de Richelieu*, 8 vols. (Paris, 1853–1877), III, 566–568, Richelieu to Maynier d'Oppède, March 7, 1630; Pearl, "Guise and Provence," p. 132; Jacques Gaufridy, "Histoire de Provence sous le règne de Louis XIII," B. Méjanes 790, fol. 7; Tamizey de Larroque, *Lettres de Peiresc*, VI, 337–338, December, 1625; B.N., Dupuy 754, *Remontrance au peuple de Provence* (1649), fol. 218.

[17] ADBR, Aix, Moissac, "Histoire du Parlement," I, fols. 448–449; B.N., Dupuy 498, fols. 160–167; ADBR, Marseille, IX B 2, fol. 160; Roland Mousnier, *Lettres et mémoires adressés au chancelier Séguier (1633–1649)*, 2 vols. (Paris, 1964), II, 1004–1005; A. D. Lublinskaya, ed., *Vnutrenniaia politika frantsuzskogo absoliutizma, 1633–1649* (Leningrad, 1966), pp. 327–329.

[18] A.A.E., 1701, fols. 23–26, 37–28.

[19] J.L.H. Hesmivy de Moissac, "Difficultés entre le Parlement et les diverses autorités," B. Méjanes 936, fols. 313–314, 329–351; Moissac, "Histoire du Parlement," B. Méjanes 947, fol. 252; Honoré Bouche, *La chorographie ou description de Provence*, 2 vols. (Aix, 1664), II, 870; A.A.E., 1701, fol. 125, Parlement to Richelieu, June 4, 1629; Tamizey de Larroque, *Lettres de Peiresc*, II, 113, June 9, 1629. In June 1629, the governor published a royal edict announcing peace with England before the Parlement could register it.

gates, and refused to allow men or merchandise to enter or leave the city.[20] Guise claimed that quarantine was necessary to prevent the spread of the plague. Demanding withdrawal of the troops, the Parlement asserted that Guise was seeking revenge for his difficulties with the court and harassing the city rather than controlling the plague. The rigidly enforced quarantine was disrupting commerce in the area, making life miserable for those trapped in the infected city. By sealing off the administrative capital, the governor had also suspended operation of the highest provincial court and paralyzed the provincial government. He had ignored Aix's traditional exemption from troop billeting, its traditional right to cut wood within five leagues of the city walls, and the Parlement's police authority during emergencies.[21]

In September 1629, royal letters were issued for Dreux d'Aubray to serve as mediator. But since he had recently returned from Provence, master of requests Charles de Sanguin was sent instead.[22] Sanguin presented his letters of commission to the Parlement for registration on October 6, and soon reported to Paris that Guise's measures were excessive and harsh.[23] Guise received a letter from Richelieu on December 1 ordering him to lift the blockade. But he refused to do so until December 31.[24] In January 1630, Guise left for Paris to explain his tardiness in executing Richelieu's orders, and later accompanied the king on his spring campaign to Italy. Since Guise did not return to Provence until November, the Parlement acted as governor in his stead.[25] After his return, he ignored appeals from the municipal government and

[20] Delib. Parl., B. Méjanes 951, fols. 388–390, 396–397; Moissac, "Difficultés," B. Méjanes 936, fols. 329–349; B. Inguimbertine 1841, fols. 352–352v.

[21] Delib. Parl., B. Méjanes 951, fols. 404–406.

[22] Moissac, "Difficultés," B. Méjanes 936, fol. 339; Delib. Parl., B. Méjanes 951, fol. 397; P. Lacour-Gayet and R. Lavolée *Mémoires du cardinal de Richelieu*, 10 vols. (Paris, 1907–1931), IX, 157, n. 3. Richelieu wrote to Guise on September 18, 1629 that he was sending Sanguin with orders on defense of the Provençal coast; cf. Avenel, *Lettres de Richelieu*, III, 429–430.

[23] Moissac, "Difficultés," B. Méjanes 936, fol. 341; Delib. Parl., B. Méjanes 951, fols. 404, 423.

[24] Delib. Parl., B. Méjanes 951, fols. 434–434v.

[25] ADBR, Marseille, C 16, fol. 59; C 17, fols. 1–180.

Parlement to suppress the revolt which had begun at Aix in September, although this was one of his duties as governor.[26] Thus Guise maliciously took his revenge by refusing to suppress a revolt that the Parlement was unable to control.

Guise may also have hesitated to jeopardize a doubtful political future by intervening in the revolt. He may have been paralyzed by the enormity of a recent political blunder. In 1626, Richelieu had created for himself the title of Controller General of Commerce and Navigation in France, hoping to use this new office to create a combat fleet and merchant navy, fortify the coast, and streamline the existing jumble of maritime and fiscal administrations. He began by abolishing the medieval admiralties of the Ponant and the Levant. In August 1626, the duc de Montmorency, admiral of the Ponant and governor of Languedoc, accepted 1,200,000 livres compensation for the suppression of his office. Guise agreed to accept 900,000 livres. But Richelieu proceeded without paying the latter sum, which was less than Montmorency had received and inadequate in terms of lost income: Richelieu was rumored to have laughed at the amount. Guise tempered his protests because he hoped to become Richelieu's new lieutenant of galleys for the Levant. When he was not appointed, he protested his loss of office.[27] His annoyance was increased by Richelieu's interest in the remonstrances which the parlementaires regularly sent on his conduct. Guise complained that his letters fell on deaf ears.[28]

By 1629, Richelieu knew that he would have to replace Guise as governor of Provence. Guise was fifty-eight years old, and he

[26] Delib. Parl., B. Méjanes 951, fols. 542, 543v, letters from Parlement to Guise, November 6 and 17, 1630; A.M., Aix, BB 100, November and December 1630.

[27] ADBR, Aix, B 3348, fol. 947v; Charles de La Roncière, *Histoire de la marine française*, 6 vols. (Paris, 1899–1932), IV, 567–577; René La Bruyère, *La marine de Richelieu: Richelieu (9 sept. 1585–4 dec. 1642)* (Paris, 1958), pp. 37–47, 65–73; Henri Hauser, *La pensée et l'action économique du cardinal Richelieu* (Paris, 1944), pp. 24–26; A. D. Lublinskaya, *French Absolutism. The Crucial Phase 1620–1629* (Cambridge, 1968), pp. 282–289; Pearl, "Guise and Provence," pp. 66–115; David, *L'amirauté*, pp. 103–120; Burckhardt, *Richelieu: Assertion of Power*, pp. 28–91; B.M., Harleian 4588, fols. 246–247.

[28] Avenel, *Lettres de Richelieu*, III, 567, n. 2; Pearl, "Guise and Provence," pp. 122–134.

had served as governor and admiral for thirty-five years. Old dogs have difficulty in learning new tricks, and Richelieu wanted a cooperative, obedient servant. Guise remained stubbornly independent. But finding a pretext to remove an entrenched governor with friends at court was not easy. Guise himself seems to have provided the excuse.

Guise probably joined the queen mother's party to intrigue for Richelieu's dismissal sometime after he arrived at court in January 1630. He seems to have been one of the dupes on the Day of Dupes, November 10, 1630. A letter from Guise at court, dated a week earlier and sent express to the Parlement and procureurs du pays, arrived in Provence on November 17. It announced that Richelieu had fallen.[29] Receiving a summons to court on July 23, 1631, which simultaneously announced the arrival of the maréchal de Vitry to act as governor in his absence, Guise knew what to expect.[30] Bearing in mind the fate of Richelieu's other enemies, Guise obtained a three month delay to fulfill a vow to visit Notre Dame de Lorette and Rome. Permission was granted on the condition that he go to Paris when he returned.[31] Guise had been living at Marseille on his galley, anchored in the harbor, since February 1631, when he greeted Condé at Avignon under heavy personal guard to forestall an attempt to arrest him for treason.[32] Sending Condé with troops to Aix in December to suppress the cascaveoux revolt had been the announcement of Guise's fall. Facing probable imprisonment, Guise chose voluntary exile, and on August 6, 1631, he sailed from the harbor of Marseille on his galley *La Guisarde* to visit the coastal ports. On August 23, he left the harbor at Cannes steering for Italy and exile. He died in Tuscany in 1640.[33] Richelieu appointed the maréchal de Vitry as acting governor the day after Guise sailed.[34] The Parlement acted as

29 ADBR, Marseille, C 16, fol. 78; EDB, III, 375, n. 2; B.M., Harleian 4588, fols. 250v, 252, Bassompierre noted in his mémoires that Guise was at Paris in August 1630, where he was known as an intriguer against Richelieu.

30 B.N., Clairambault 380, fol. 274, king to Guise, July 23, 1631.

31 *Ibid.*, fol. 275, king to Guise, August 23, 1631; Avenel, *Lettres de Richelieu*, III, 802–803, mémoire of July 31, 1630.

32 Pearl, "Guise and Provence," pp. 215–245; A.A.E., 800, fols. 28–30.

33 *Ibid.*, p. 251; B.M., Harleian 4588, fol. 418 v.

34 ADBR, Aix, B 3348 fol. 593v, August 7, 1631. Guise suggested self-exile to Richelieu in a letter on July 29, 1631; cf. A.A.E., 1701, fol. 278.

governor until Vitry arrived in late September. Guise sent one of his gentlemen to the king in January 1632 to request a post in the royal armies fighting in Italy, but he was ordered to appear at court.[35] He was never forgiven or reinstated, although his son returned to the royal service.

Richelieu tacitly agreed to the exile of Guise as an easy solution to an awkward affair. There was no conclusive proof of treason, and it would have been difficult to convict the hero of the famous 1622 naval victory of La Rochelle, who had led numerous expeditions against the Barbary pirates, defeated the Genoese in a recent battle, and loyally served the king for thirty-five years. Guise's failure to suppress the cascaveoux revolt had condemned him, probably falsely, as a sympathizer: a 1631 memoir on the Aix revolt written for the council of state on Richelieu's orders named Guise as an accomplice of the rebels. Richelieu wrote, "It was not that he was so devoted to the Queen Mother and Monsieur but rather that he was obsessed with a passionate desire to undermine the King's authority and increase his own. For this reason, he has never failed to give secret support to any rising against the King in his province."[36] This memoir has misled historians into thinking that Guise incited the 1630 revolt at Aix, dragged Montmorency into his projects by encouraging the 1632 revolt in Languedoc, and negotiated with the Spanish and Gaston d'Orléans.[37] There is no evidence that Guise participated in the cascaveoux revolt, and it is difficult to imagine him in sympathy with the rebels.

Nicolas de L'Hôpital, marquis de Vitry and maréchal de France, replaced Guise. Vitry failed to profit by his predecessor's mistakes, and was recalled from office for his obduracy by Richelieu in 1637. His disputes with the Parlement, Estates and General

---

Vitry's letters of appointment as acting governor were registered by the Parlement in October 1631, and his letters of provision as governor were published in May 1632; cf. ADBR, Aix, B 3348, fols. 593v, 811–821.

[35] *Ibid.*, fols. 811–821; Pearl, "Guise and Provence," pp. 243–252.

[36] A.A.E., 797, fol. 109; Carl Burckhardt, *Richelieu and His Age: Power Politics and the Cardinal's Death*, tr. Bernard Hoy (New York, 1970), p. 283. The mémoire accused Guise of receiving an envoy from the duc d'Orléans and letters from an Italian at Avignon.

[37] Caillet, *L'Administration en France*, I, 47.

Assemblies, procureurs du pays and municipal governments were immediate and continuing. Headstrong and disagreeable, Vitry's violent outbursts disrupted the provincial government.

Vitry's portrait shows a short, stout man in black armor, with thick, white hair and mustaches, the florid face, heavy jowls and big nose of a heavy eater and drinker.[38] He has an angry, stubborn look. A captain of Louis XIII's guards, he killed the Italian adventurer Concini, the queen mother's favorite, on the Pont Neuf with three shots in 1617 for resisting arrest. He was rewarded by Louis XIII with the title of maréchal de France and 120,000 livres in *rentes*. Cardinal de Retz wrote in his memoirs that Vitry had little sense, and was daring to the point of recklessness; shooting Concini gave him the undeserved reputation of a man of action.[39] Vitry used similar techniques with less success in his later political career. A brutal, arrogant man with little tact or self-control, he rose too fast to assimilate his new position. Guise was the son of Henry Le Balafré, while Alais and Mercoeur were descendants of royal bastards. All three had inherited titles of duke and peer from families with generations of royal service. Vitry, on the other hand, was the oldest son of Luis Gallucio de l'Hôpital, Henry IV's guard captain, and only became a duke in 1644, shortly before his death.[40] Vitry's belligerence and brutality may have arisen from insecurity about his origins.

Vitry's suspension of municipal elections was highly controversial. Claiming that disturbances during elections and intrigues within the municipal governments made suspensions necessary, Vitry obtained royal letters authorizing his appointments, which became annual occurrences and provided him with the opportunity to exercise patronage. Packing the General Assemblies and influencing the selection of the procureurs du pays assured him greater cooperation in troop billeting and tax payments. The Parlement only protested Vitry's suspension of municipal elections when he did not obtain royal letters of authorization. The court sent a

[38] Vitry's portrait appears in EDB, III, plate XVI.

[39] *Mémoires du cardinal de Retz, de Guy Joli, et la duchesse de Nemours*, 6 vols. (Paris, 1820), I, 45–46; Georges d'Avenel, *Richelieu et la monarchie absolue*, 4 vols. 2nd ed. (Paris, 1895), II, 1.

[40] Labatut, *Les dus et pairs*, p. 123. Alais inherited the title of duke in 1650.

119

remonstrance to Paris in March 1635 on Vitry's municipal suspensions and illegal tax ordinances.⁴¹ Vitry also quarreled with the Parlement over police authority, criminal jurisdiction, and levy of taxes by ordinance without the approval of the procureurs du pays.⁴² The council of state issued decrees in December 1633 and May 1635 to resolve these quarrels.⁴³ The Parlement was forbidden to intervene in military affairs, and the governor was forbidden to intervene in municipal elections and judicial affairs.⁴⁴

Condé issued an ordinance in March 1631 depriving Aix, Tarascon, and Brignoles of their privilege of municipal elections.⁴⁵ Vitry continued this policy by suspending elections at Aix from 1632 to 1637.⁴⁶ In 1632, 1633, and 1634, Vitry wrote Richelieu that these municipal appointments were necessary to control a rebellious province.⁴⁷ In a 1634 memoir on Provence for the council of state Vitry wrote: "Considering the inclination this province has toward unreliability and quarrels, which are today fomented by the Parlement and Cour des Comptes, it would be very necessary, the King not having yet named the first consul of Aix, nor the assessor, procureurs du pays, that he immediately name men devoted to his service."⁴⁸ The Spanish invasion occurred in 1635, and municipal elections at Aix were suspended again. On June 11, 1635, the town council voted a gift of 150 to 200 pistoles to

⁴¹ B.N., Ms. fr. 17367, fol. 187, Parlement first président Laisné to Séguier, May 30, 1633; A.C., Aix, BB 101, fols. 63, 70v–72; Moissac, "Difficultés," B. Méjanes 936, fols. 375–376, 380–381; Lublinskaya, *Vnutrenniaia*, de La Potherie to Séguier, pp. 230–231, April 4, 1633, pp. 235–236, June 14, 1633, pp. 237–238, June 21, 1633; A.A.E., 1703, fols. 83–87, March 8, 1635.

⁴² ADBR, Aix, B 3349, fol. 509; "Arrêt du conseil d'état," B. Marseille 1103; Moissac, "Difficultés," B. Méjanes 936, fols. 414–433; B.N., Ms. fr. 17369, fol. 174, Parlement procureur-général to Séguier, October 20, 1634.

⁴³ A.A.E., 1702, fols. 345, 350; ADBR, Marseille, C 22, fols. 176, 208–216v.

⁴⁴ ADBR, Aix, B 3349, fol. 509; B. Marseille 1103; B. Méjanes 936, fols. 471–477.

⁴⁵ A.C., Aix, BB 100, fols. 192–195; BB 101, fols. 18v–19; Bouche, *La chorographie*, I, 889.

⁴⁶ A.C., Aix, BB 101, fols. 88, 111–113, 169, 182–183; ADBR, Aix, B 3350, fol. 581; ADBR, Marseille, C 22, fol. 187v; A.A.E., 1704, fol. 100; Moissac, "Difficultés," B. Méjanes 936, fols. 280–281.

⁴⁷ A.A.E., 1702, fol. 144, September, 1632; fol. 177, February 7, 1633; fols. 272–273, October 3, 1634; fols. 301–302, October 19, 1634.

⁴⁸ *Ibid.*, fols. 263–264.

anyone who could regain the right of municipal elections by royal letters.[49]

Vitry extorted 100,000 livres as a gift from the Estates at Brignoles in December 1632 by intimidating the deputies, although the gift was illegal according to the royal edict of 1560.[50] And he demanded money directly from the provincial tax receivers and procureurs du pays without authorization from the Trésoriers Généraux or provincial treasurer.[51] A General Assembly at Aix in January 1635 sent a remonstrance on Vitry's conduct and demanded reimbursement for the sums he had extorted by threats and his replacement by the cardinal of Lyon, Richelieu's older brother. This request was refused, but a decree of the council of state on March 8 ordered Vitry to stop disrupting the provincial and municipal administrations, while a decree on March 31 set his annual grant from the Estates at 51,000 livres.[52] The Estates had indirect influence over the governors and intendants by voting them annual grants of money.

Vitry's conduct was habitually rude and ugly. He used his guards to enforce the seigneurial rights of his friends, and he beat peasants in the countryside when he traveled with his governor's baton. When the archbishop of Aix complained that Vitry was sitting in the choir of Saint Sauveur on a dais under a canopy, a privilege reserved for the clergy, and protested the sums that he had extorted from the procureurs du pays, Vitry lost his temper, chased the chapter provost from the cathedral, threatened to break the church clock, and had his guards beat the bell-ringer.[53] In April 1633, the Parlement arrested the second consul of Aix after he quarreled with the third consul. Vitry rode into town and freed the second consul, who was his client, then brazenly toured Aix with a trumpeter. The prévôt, on the governor's orders, arrested the third consul in front of the Parlement's deputies. The second consul attended mass that Sunday in Saint Sauveur with forty of the governor's guards at his back. The furious parlementaires

---

[49] A.C., Aix, BB 101, fol. 139v.

[50] ADBR, Marseille, C 20, fols. 201–278v.

[51] Moissac, "Difficultés," B. Méjanes 936, fols. 414–433.

[52] A.A.E., 1703, fol. 83; ADBR, Marseille, C 22, fols. 176–190v, 198–199, 321–322; ADBR, Aix, B 3350, fol. 691v; A.N., E 122D, fol. 104. The governor received 36,000 livres in salary and 15,000 livres for his guard company. He was later given 1,200 livres for his secretary.

[53] Moissac, "Difficultés," B. Méjanes 936, fols. 414–433.

wrote Paris that Vitry's "bravado" was "a public scandal."[54] Vitry earned even more resentment by accompanying Jacques Talon on his mission to raise the gabelle in October 1634.[55]

After four years in office, Vitry had alienated the Parlement, intendant of justice, provincial lieutenant general, Estates and General Assemblies, procureurs du pays, archbishop of Aix, and municipal governments. On May 10, 1633, intendant de La Potherie wrote to Séguier: "For myself, I only estimate that no one has ever done more than I to get along well with a governor, but I have had unimaginable difficulties, and I do not believe that anyone has ever suffered in a province more than I have endured."[56] Talon wrote to Richelieu on November 2, 1634, that civil war would erupt if the quarrel between the governor and lieutenant general was not resolved quickly.[57]

Melchior Mitte, seigneur de Chevrières and marquis de Saint Chamond, camp marshal in the armies commanded by Guise in 1622, was appointed lieutenant general in Provence in April 1632.[58] In the previous year, he had been appointed governor of the royal fortress at Sisteron in Haute-Provence.[59] Saint Chamond was a competent diplomat who had served on important assignments for Richelieu. He was ambassador to Rome in 1625 and envoy to the queen mother at Compiègne in April 1631 after her flight from France.[60] He was serving as ambassador to Germany in July 1635, after he left Provence; the need for his services may have been one reason for his recall.[61] As ambassador to Germany, he conducted negotiations in 1636 with Count Oxenstierna, chancellor of the Swedish king, and the king of Denmark.[62] He was

[54] *Ibid.*, fols. 377–380; Delib. Parl., B. Méjanes 952, fols. 117v–124; Lublinskaya, *Vnutrenniaia*, pp. 230–231, de La Potherie to Séguier, April 4, 1653.

[55] A.A.E., 1702, fols. 265–267, 270–273; Chapter Two; and René Pillorget, *Les mouvements insurrectionnels de Provence entre 1596 et 1715* (Paris, 1975), pp. 360, 368–375.

[56] Lublinskaya, *Vnutrenniaia*, pp. 232–234. The intendant also wrote letters critical of Vitry on April 4, June 14, and June 28, 1653; cf. *ibid.*, pp. 230–231, 235–236, 238–239.

[57] A.A.E., 1702, fol. 362. Vitry wrote to Richelieu on the same subject, November 3, 1634; cf. *ibid.*, fols. 373–375.

[58] ADBR, Aix, B 3348, fols. 856–864.

[59] Avenel, *Lettres de Richelieu*, IV, 170.

[60] *Ibid.*, VII, 946; IV, 117, 140.

[61] *Ibid.*, V, 927.　　　　　　　[62] *Ibid.*, VII, 758–760, 1020, 1030.

again ambassador to Rome from 1644 to 1649.[63] Saint Chamond was probably chosen for service in Provence because Richelieu wanted someone of tact and discretion to deal with Vitry.

The lieutenant general of Provence—*lieutenant général pour le Roy en ce pays de Provence* or *lieutenant général pour le Roy au gouvernment de Provence*[64]—acted as governor during that official's absences on military campaign or at court. The lieutenant general thus resembled a modern vice president or lieutenant governor. The royal letters appointing Jean de Pontevès, comte de Carcès, to office in August 1635 and François de Simiane, marquis de Gordes, in October 1656 stated simply that they were to exercise full authority in the absence of the governor, concluding with a brief summary of the governor's powers.[65] The lieutenant general received an annual grant of 18,000 livres from the Estates with an allowance for a secretary and a guard company.[66] He shared in the command of the provincial troops with the governor, for instance during the Spanish invasion of the coast in 1635–1637.[67]

The lieutenant general had frequent authority conflicts with the governor. Their functions were overlapping and unclear, particularly when they were both in the province, and they were natural political rivals.[68] Their administrative conflicts were intensified by

[63] B.M., Harleian 4544, Saint Chamond's letters from Rome in 1644; Pierre-Adolphe Chéruel and Georges d'Avenel, eds., *Lettres du cardinal Mazarin pendant son ministère,* 9 vols. (Paris, 1872–1906), III, 1065, October 1648. Saint Chamond died in September 1649 at the age of sixty-three.

[64] ADBR, Aix, B 3350, fols. 503–509. This provincial official should not be confused with the governor, whose title included lieutenant general, or army lieutenant generals. There is comparatively little on this provincial official. See EDB, III, 284–289; Paul Masson, *La Provence au XVIIIᵉ siècle,* 3 vols. (Paris, 1936), II, 38–39; Marcel Marion, *Dictionnaire des institutions de la France au XVIIᵉ et XVIIIᵉ siècles* (Paris, 1923), p. 336; Roger Doucet, *Les institutions de la France au XVIᵉ siècle,* 2 vols. (Paris, 1948), I, 233–234.

[65] ADBR, Aix, B 3350, fols. 503–509; B 3358, fols. 1033–1039.

[66] ADBR, Marseille, C 22, fols. 321–322 and C 25, fol. 262; B.N., Cinq Cents de Colbert 288, fols. 24–24v, 36v–37v; EDB, III, 289–290. This salary was not always paid, as Pontevès de Carcès complained in March 1638, cf., ADBR, Marseille, C 25, fol. 124.

[67] B.M., Harleian 4468, fols. 138–166.

[68] Hubert Méthivier, "Un conflit d'autorité en Provence sous Louis XIII: L'affaire Vitry-Saint Chamond (octobre, 1634–janvier, 1635)," *Mélanges*

the fact that the lieutenant general usually belonged to an illustrious family of the Provençal nobility—the office had become semi-hereditary for the Pontevès de Carcès—while the governor was a *grand*, a great court noble who was not Provençal.

Saint Chamond was appointed lieutenant general six months after Vitry arrived in Provence. He was the first to fill the office in nearly thirty years; the office had remained vacant after Guise's son, François de Lorraine, chevalier de Guise, died in office in 1614.[69] Richelieu probably meant Saint Chamond, who was never resident, as a temporary replacement in case Vitry proved unmanageable.

Vitry's persistent difficulties with the Parlement led to a royal letter on September 26, 1634, calling him to Paris for explanations. Richelieu did not like Vitry's disruption of the provincial administration—but neither did he like a parlement informing on a governor.[70] Vitry replied on October 3 that he would not go until he had assisted royal commissioner Talon in raising the price of salt in Provence.[71] Saint Chamond received letters of instruction from secretary of state Servien on October 8 to act as governor in the absence of Vitry and to inspect the coastal fortifications. A secret article of Saint Chamond's instructions, which he inadvisedly made public, ordered the arrest of Vitry if the governor's loyalty became doubtful.[72]

Saint Chamond was in Provence at the end of October. He had a conflict of authority with Vitry, still in Provence, who ordered that the lieutenant general not be received when he arrived at Toulon, thereby announcing that he would not recognize Saint

---

*historiques et littéraires sur le XVIIᵉ siècle offerts à Georges Mongrédien par ses amis* (Publications de la Société d'Etude du XVIIᵉ siècle II, Paris, 1974), pp. 17–23.

[69] EDB, III, 658–660.

[70] A.A.E., 1702, fol. 345; Orest Ranum, *Richelieu and the Councillors of Louis XIII: A Study of the Secretaries of State and Superintendents of Finance in the Ministry of Richelieu, 1633–1642* (Oxford, 1963), p. 123, n. 5.

[71] B.N., Ms. fr. 17367, fol. 187; Lublinskaya, *Vnutrenniaia*, pp. 230–231, 235–236, 237–238; A.A.E., 1702, fols. 345, 350; 1703, fols. 83–87; Pillorget, *Les mouvements*, p. 360.

[72] B.N., Dupuy 501, fols. 124–134; ADBR, Marseille, C 25, fol. 71; Pillorget, *Les mouvements*, pp. 360–375.

Chamond's authority.[73] Vitry was still governor, an appointed royal official, although Saint Chamond had royal letters to act as governor in his absence. It was an awkward situation. Saint Chamond went to inspect the coastal fortifications and had another clash with Vitry over the disposition of royal troops at Hyères. Saint Chamond judged disloyal Vitry's refusal to leave Provence and to recognize his own authority to inspect the coast. He issued a call to arms to the provincial nobility to support him against the governor.[74] A memoir in October 1634 for the council of state recommended recalling Vitry for insubordination.[75]

The Parlement was delighted by the conflict, and royal commissioner Talon reported on November 2 that "neither the governors of the royal fortresses nor the soldiers know any longer whom they should obey, the governor or the lieutenant general, since the Parlement has issued a decree ordering all the nobility and royal soldiers in the province to report to M. de Saint Chamond in order to serve the King."[76] Civil war seemed likely. Vitry wrote to Richelieu on November 3 protesting that Saint Chamond had acted without authority in calling the provincial nobility to arms and starting rumors that taxes would be lowered.[77] Servien was displeased with Saint Chamond's conduct, which he found hasty and indiscreet. The Provençaux hoped that the crisis could be used to avoid the increase in the gabelle.[78]

Saint Chamond continued his tour of the coastal fortifications in December 1634, while Vitry went to Paris.[79] In January 1635, Saint Chamond convoked a General Assembly of the Communities at Aix and chaired the meeting that voted to send deputies and a petition to the king jointly with the Parlement, requesting Vitry's replacement as governor with Richelieu's older brother, the cardinal of Lyon, who had been archbishop of Aix from 1626

[73] ADBR, Marseille, C 22, fols. 159, 164.

[74] Méthivier, *Un conflit d'autorité,* 19–22; Pillorget, *Les mouvements,* pp. 367–372.

[75] A.A.E., 1702, fol. 350. A letter on November 1, 1634, from Richelieu's client, Henri de Séguiran, first president of the Cour des Comptes, mentioned the conflict as the reason for calling Vitry to Paris; cf. *ibid.,* fol. 358.

[76] A.A.E., 1702, fol. 362.     [77] *Ibid.,* fols. 373–375.

[78] Pillorget, *Les mouvements,* p. 368.

[79] A.A.E., 1702, fols. 440–461.

to 1629.[80] Saint Chamond's rashness and the impending Spanish invasion caused Richelieu to make peace quickly. Vitry returned to Provence in March. A conciliar decree was issued two months later regulating his difficulties with the Parlement.[81] Saint Chamond was recalled in March. Jean de Pontevès, comte de Carcès, was appointed lieutenant general in August 1635.[82] Carcès would have similar conflicts with governor Alais in 1649 and acting governor Aiguebonne in 1651.

Vitry's quarrelsome belligerence divided the joint military command created to retake the islands of Lérins from the Spanish. On October 8, 1635, marine intendant Du Plessis-Besançon wrote to Richelieu that Vitry had estranged the Provençal nobles who were members of the command.[83] Vitry sent a flow of critical letters to Paris on the archbishop of Bordeaux, joint commander with the comte d'Harcourt of the Atlantic fleet sent into the Mediterranean. Bordeaux quarreled with Harcourt, who formed an alliance with Vitry against the archbishop.[84] Bullying the archbishop, however, proved an error. Henri d'Escoubleau de Sourdis, archbishop of Bordeaux, had gained Richelieu's favor by humbling his old foe, the governor of Guyenne, two years earlier. Richelieu did not hesitate to punish Vitry when he learned that the governor had lost his temper, pushed Sourdis in the chest with a cane, then struck him on the shoulder during a meeting at the château of Cannes on November 25, 1636. Sourdis had a knack for provoking physical attack: the governor of Guyenne had been excommunicated for striking the archbishop and only saved his governorship by appearing on his knees in public penance. Sourdis's

[80] ADBR, Marseille, C 22, fols. 176–190v, 198–199. For Richelieu's older brother, see Maximin Deloche, *Un frère de Richelieu inconnu: chartreux, primate des Gaules, cardinal, ambassadeur* (Paris, 1935).

[81] ADBR, Aix, B 3349, fol. 509; B 3350, fol. 691v; B. Marseille 1103.

[82] ADBR, Aix, B 3350, fol. 503; A.A.E., 1703, fol. 119, April 16, 1635: Saint Chamond announced to Richelieu his intention to obey the royal letters of March 28 recalling him from Provence.

[83] A.A.E., 1704, fol. 49.

[84] B.M., Harleian 4468, fols. 139, 141; Avenel, *Lettres de Richelieu*, V, 989, Richelieu to Vitry, September 7, 1636; 1041, Richelieu to Harcourt, July 4, 1637; 769, Richelieu to Lauzon, April 16, 1637; 1024, Richelieu to Vitry, same date. Henri de Lorraine, comte d'Harcourt et d'Armagnac, was known as "cadet la perle" because he was a cadet of the house of Lorraine (son of Charles, duc d'Elbeuf) and wore a pearl in his ear.

portrait shows the handsome, aquiline face, high forehead, sharp eyes, trim mustache and beard of a seventeenth-century duelist. He was not a man to be bullied.[85]

Violent tempers and lack of self-restraint were characteristic of seventeenth-century nobles, but Vitry's bad temper had become a political liability. Richelieu sent a short letter to Vitry on December 9, 1636, which was chilling in its simplicity: "It is so unbelievable that a man of your office would have wanted to offend a person of the quality and condition of the archbishop of Bordeaux, as they say you have done, that if I had actually seen you commit this fault, I could not persuade myself of it. If this misfortune happened to you, there is nothing that can purge you of it. You would not find anyone who might excuse such an action, whatever good will he had for you."[86] Vitry weakly explained that Sourdis had come into his lodgings at seven in the morning and insulted him while he was still in bed.[87] But Vitry had also recently quarreled with the comte d'Harcourt.[88] In June 1637, sieur Guitaud, governor of the newly recaptured island of Sainte Marguerite, complained that Vitry was encouraging garrison desertions, mutinies, and refusing supplies out of personal enmity.[89] Vitry was recalled on September 18, 1637, and sent to the Bastille on October 27, where he remained until after Richelieu's death in December 1642.[90] Louis de Valois, comte d'Alais, was appointed governor on October 29, 1637. The first paragraph of Alais's provision letters states, "having been obliged by the bad conduct of the maréchal de Vitry in the office of governor of Provence to dispossess him of this office. . . ."[91]

---

[85] A.A.E., 1704, fols. 371–373; Fessenden, "Epernon and Guyenne," pp. 87–127; René La Bruyère, *La marine de Richelieu: Sourdis, archevêque et amiral (6 novembre 1594–18 juin 1645)* (Paris, 1948), pp. 27–37, 50–65. The frontispiece is a portrait of Sourdis.

[86] Avenel, *Lettres de Richelieu*, V, 709–710. On the same day, Richelieu assured Sourdis of his continued patronage; cf. *ibid.*, V, 708.

[87] Sue, *La correspondance de Sourdis*, I, 193–195.

[88] *Ibid.*, 72–76.

[89] *Ibid.*, 498–500; A.A.E., 1705, fol. 392.

[90] B.N., Dupuy 501, fols. 124–134; ADBR, Marseille, C 25, fol. 71; Chéruel and Avenel, *Lettres de Mazarin*, I, 179–180, Mazarin to Vitry, May 22, 1643, after the battle of Rocroi. Vitry died in 1644.

[91] B.N., Dupuy 501, fol. 130; ADBR, Aix, B 3351, fol. 284, Richelieu had written to Sourdis on April 16, 1637, of his intention to replace Vitry; cf. La Bruyère, *Sourdis*, p. 64.

Vitry set the stage for Alais's term as governor. The province had hoped for a sympathetic governor, only to be disappointed. Alais continued Vitry's practice of appointing municipal governments, and increased the number of provincial troops. He overreacted in difficult situations, panicking, blustering, threatening, and intimidating. He seemed convinced that force was the only way to solve administrative problems. Vitry's excesses had created a climate of exasperation that made Alais's intemperance and irritability harder to endure. In repeating the faults of his predecessor, Alais inherited all the enmity Vitry had acquired within the provincial administration, and together they helped to cause the 1649 revolt. Vitry and Alais must have merged into a composite figure in many minds. The crown had made two consecutive poor choices as governor of Provence.

The portrait of Louis-Emmanuel de Valois, comte d'Alais, shows a double chin, bags under the eyes, short mustaches, uncurled hair, and an irascible, petulant expression.[92] A wealthy man, Alais was a cousin of the royal family through his grandfather and great-uncle.[93] Bishop of Agde until 1612, he left the church for the army and fought in Languedoc, Italy, and Lorraine, becoming a colonel general of the light cavalry in 1637, a post previously held by his father and brother. He was a cultured man, an avid collector of books, with a large library, the owner of an elegant hôtel at Aix.[94] But his correspondence shows a mediocre intelligence and a weak, indecisive nature. Overweight and the butt of jokes, Alais was frequently angry and vindictive, compensating for his weakness by stubbornness and sudden, rash actions. He was dominated by a haughty wife, Henriette de La Guiche, daughter of the maréchal de Saint Géran. She encouraged his uncompromising attitude and alienated the provincial nobility by insisting upon excessive deference and formality. After Richelieu's death, Alais allied himself with the anti-Mazarin party at court led by his

[92] Alais's portrait appears in EDB, III, plate XVI, and in a mazarinade in B.M., *Parlement de Bordeaux*, fol. 53, and B. Marseille 1792, *Relation véritable de ce qui s'est fait et passée dans la ville d'Aix-en-Provence.*

[93] Alais was the second son of Charles, duc d'Angoulême, and Charlotte de Montmorency, and the grandson of Charles IX and Marie Touchet. He was the grandnephew of Henri de Valois, grand prior in the Order of Malta, legitimatized son of Henry II, and governor of Provence from 1573 to 1586.

[94] Jacques Billioud, *Le livre en Provence du XVIe au XVIIIe siècle* (Marseille, 1962), pp. 138–139.

maternal uncle and cousin, the Condés. He corresponded with Gaston d'Orléans and the comte de Chavigny, enjoyed influence with keeper of the seals Châteauneuf, and cultivated friends at court. Alais's dislike of Mazarin became common knowledge, and he showed open hostility to Mazarin's brother, the archbishop of Aix.[95] When Mazarin appointed his own client as governor of Toulon in 1646, a post that Alais wanted, their estrangement was complete.[96]

Alais and Champigny were the first governor and intendant in Provence to work closely and successfully as a team. Mutual cooperation brought mutual benefits: the governors were royal officials with traditional authority, who lent credibility to the intendants' shaky legitimacy in provincial eyes, while the intendants acted as the governors' advisors and assistants. Champigny was already intendant when Alais became governor in January 1638. They worked so well together that Alais requested Champigny's second appointment in 1643, when the council of state transferred Vautorte.[97] They collaborated until Champigny returned to the Lyonnais as intendant at his own request in 1647.[98] Champigny's forceful personality bolstered the weak, indecisive Alais with a damaging effect, because the pair's aggressive actions contributed to causing the 1649 revolt. Alais increasingly depended on Champigny's help in coercing the sovereign courts, General Assemblies, and municipal governments to obey the crown. Champigny gradually relieved the governor of his more unpleasant police responsibilities in disciplining uncooperative officials and institutions.

Alais and Champigny occasionally wrote to Paris from the same

[95] Adolphe Crémieux, *Marseille et la royauté pendant la minorité de Louis XIV*, 2 vols. (Marseille, 1917), I, 168–171, 302; Charles de Grimaldi and Jacques Gaufridy, *Mémoires pour servir à l'histoire de la Fronde en Provence* (Aix, 1870), p. 20; EDB, III, 71–72; B.M., Harleian 4575, fols. 27v, 30–31; Pillorget, *Les mouvements*, p. 551.

[96] Chéruel and Avenel, *Lettres de Mazarin*, II, 814, September 27, 1646.

[97] A.A.E., 1708, fol. 169, Champigny to Séguier, April 21, 1643, fol. 193, Champigny to Séguier, June 19, 1643; B.N., Ms. fr. 17376, fol. 42, Champigny to Séguier, July 21, 1643. Alais regretted Champigny's transfer to the Lyonnais in 1640; cf. A.A.E., 1707, fol. 5, January 2, 1640.

[98] The death of Faucon de Frainville, first president of the Parlement of Rouen, in 1647 led to the recall of his son, Jean-Louis Faucon de Ris, from the Lyonnais to take his father's place, and Champigny replaced him; cf. Chéruel and Avenel, *Lettres de Mazarin*, II, 959, October 11, 1647, Mazarin to Champigny; Mousnier, *Lettres*, II, 1080.

city, on the same day, on the same subject.[99] It is evident that they kept in close touch, because their letters refer to joint projects and shared political opinions.[100] Champigny wrote exhaustively detailed letters, while Alais's letters were shorter, less frequent, and less informative. Alais often wrote that the intendant or a secretary was sending a full account. The governor was enthusiastic about Champigny's performance. For instance, Champigny wrote to Séguier on November 3, 1643, that his correspondence had been interrupted by a trip to Monaco with Alais at the latter's request, and on May 23 and July 2, 1645, Alais wrote to the secretary of state praising Champigny's ability and zeal.[101] Alais's enthusiasm cooled after 1646, when he broke openly with Mazarin, and Champigny requested a transfer the next year.

Champigny began to regulate the provincial wheat traffic in 1644, one of the governor's duties. He also regulated municipal debts and assumed the task of supervising the Parlement. Alais had little direct contact with the Parlement, depending upon the intendant or compliant presidents such as Gaufridy or Foresta de La Roquette to transmit his orders.[102] There were the usual disputes with the Parlement. For instance, in 1644 Alais and the Parlement quarreled over jurisdiction in a criminal case involving travelers robbed by three soldiers on the Saint Maximin road east of Aix.[103] The intendants aided the governors in supervising the General Assemblies and later assumed this task alone. Vitry attended six and possibly eight of eleven Estates and General Assemblies convened during his tenure in office. Alais attended four of eleven assemblies convened from 1638 to 1648. In contrast, there were intendants present at thirteen assemblies. Champigny attended all assemblies during his two terms in office.[104]

---

[99] B.N., Clairambault 389, fols. 240–244; 391, fols. 274–276, 303; 395, fols. 138–141, 173–175; 400 fols. 29–30, 31; 401, fols. 195–197, 199.

[100] In December 1643, the governor and intendant wrote similar accounts of an incident in the Parlement and recommended Bonfils for the vacant office of président, cf., B.N., Clairambault 390, fols. 231–234. They also wrote letters describing their suspension of municipal elections at Marseille in 1644 and 1646, and at Aix in 1643 and 1645; cf., *ibid.*, 396, fols. 3–5; 401, fols. 195–197, 199; Lublinskaya, *Vnutrenniaia*, pp. 295, 317.

[101] Lublinskaya, *Vnutrenniaia*, pp. 261–263; B.N., Clairambault 399, fols. 236–238; 400, fol. 31.

[102] See Chapter Six.                [103] B.N., Ms. fr. 18977, fols. 1–4.

[104] ADBR, Marseille, C 19–29.

Alais never attended a General Assembly with intendant Vautorte, who appeared alone in the assemblies at Draguignan in December 1640, Antibes in December 1641, and Brignoles in February 1643.[105] Vautorte wrote to Paris on April 7, 1643, that the governor's presence at General Assemblies was necessary for their successful management, implying that Alais had been lax in his duties.[106] Vautorte was already under a cloud for not coercing the procureurs du pays into approving a new tax and for accepting gifts of money. He may also have been on bad terms with Alais. Suggestive are the lack of mutual references in their correspondance: Alais never referred to Vautorte, while Vautorte mentioned the governor infrequently, in a cold, formal tone. The lack of warmth in their relationship was possibly the result of a personality clash; it contrasted sharply with the friendship between Alais and Champigny. Alais may have requested Vautorte's transfer when he recommended Champigny's reappointment. Governors of frontier provinces were usually consulted about the appointment of intendants.[107]

Alais continued Vitry's tactic of appointing municipal officials. He suspended elections and appointed officials at Aix in 1643–1644 and 1647–1648, and at Marseille annually from 1643 to 1650.[108] After 1643, Alais was accompanied by Champigny to the town hall, where they read the royal letters of authorization, suspended the elections, and read the list of new appointees whom they had previously suggested.[109] By 1646, Champigny was suspending elections and suggesting appointees on his own initiative.[110]

---

[105] *Ibid.*, C 26, fols. 142, 230, 315.

[106] B.N., Ms. fr. 17376, fols. 28–29.

[107] Richard Bonney, "The Intendants of Richelieu and Mazarin, 1624–1661," (Ph.D. dissertation, Oxford University, 1973), pp. 210–211.

[108] A.C., Aix, BB 102, fols. 24–26, 29v–30; A.A.E., 1708, fol. 344; 1712, fol. 253; B.N., Ms. fr. 17390, fols. 223–224, 229–230; Crémieux, *Marseille*, I, 186–265.

[109] See note 77. Alais and Champigny together named the consuls of Arles and changed the city's electoral procedure on February 24, 1644; cf. B.N., Ms. fr. 18976, fols. 459–471.

[110] In December 1646, Champigny asked the crown to appoint the consuls of Toulon; cf. Mousnier, *Lettres*, II, 792; Lublinskaya, *Vnutrenniaia*, pp. 318–319. On April 29, 1647, Champigny wrote requesting appointment of the consuls of Draguignan; cf. B.N., Clairambault 409, fol. 318. In June

The intendants' assumption of the governors' police powers acted as a curb upon their lack of cooperation and financial excesses. The governors' peculation was a serious problem. Vitry had intimidated the procureurs du pays into giving him personal gifts of money. Alais exhibited the same type of behavior. Alais was accused in the mazarinades of permitting illegal sales and exports of wheat at Arles on payment of a fee to a traitant with whom he had an arrangement. He was also accused of making 500,000 livres a year selling wheat export licenses. He was accused of illegally imprisoning a gabelle agent for seven weeks in one of his private deals, and he was supposed to have made 28,000 livres from the transfer of the Hyères seneschal court to Toulon and 60,000 livres from the establishment of the Semester Parlement.[111] Alais's peculation may explain Champigny's regulation of the wheat traffic. Richelieu stated in his memoirs that annual assessments of the taille in Provence, Languedoc, and Dauphiné produced too much profit for the governors and their clients.[112] The mazarinades also accused Alais of packing the municipal councils of Aix, Arles, and Marseille, using municipal appointments and army commissions to reward his clients, and the threat of troop billeting to pressure municipal officials.[113] Champigny's assumption of Alais's police powers allowed him to check such abuses of authority.

At first Alais was a popular governor. He permitted municipal elections at Aix in December 1637, removing the appointees of the archbishop of Bordeaux.[114] He sent one regiment from Provence in January 1638, and two more in May and June.[115] By 1640, the troop load had been reduced to one-half that in 1635. It was reported to Paris in July 1640 that Alais wanted withdrawal

---

1647, Champigny approved Alais's recommendation for the *viguier* of Toulon; cf. *ibid.*, 390, fols. 279–280.

[111] B.N., Ms. fr. 18977, fols. 264–290; B.N., Dupuy 754, fols. 254–258; B. Marseille 1792, 1794, 1796, 1798.

[112] Burckhardt, *Richelieu: Power Politics*, p. 283.

[113] *Relation de ce qui s'est passée en la ville de Marseille*, B.N., Dupuy 754, fols. 250–253; *Marseille delivrée de la tyrannie de Monsieur le comte d'Alais, ibid.*, fols. 254–258; *Très humble remontrance du Parlement de Provence* (1649), B. Marseille 1102.

[114] A.C., Aix, BB 101, fols. 201–202.

[115] ADBR, Marseille, C 25, fols. 117v–120, 157, 179v.

of the remaining four infantry regiments, whom he had publicly compared to a gangrene devouring the province.[116]

But his sympathy and good will disappeared in January 1641, when as governor he was forced to present for registration an unpopular edict creating a Chambre des Requêtes in the Parlement. The anger and hostility of the parlementaires focused on Alais, who was unable to cope with the situation. He forced the Parlement to register the edict, but neither he nor Champigny could force the acceptance of the new chamber.[117] Alais was furious at the parlementaires' refusal to cooperate. In a 1643 memoir for the council of state he wrote:

> The public disorder and disobedience which have appeared in the Parlement since the death of the previous King is nothing else but the faction of the *sonnettes* [1630 rebels] which has been reawakened by the ambition and interests of some individuals . . . gathering the most suitable pretexts to stir up the people and renew their intrigues . . . it is extremely important to disabuse all these factious minds of their false hopes which can be done easily by a strong reprimand.[118]

Alais wrote to Paris that he feared another revolt at Aix. On September 3, 1646, an anonymous placard appeared at Aix calling the governor a tyrant ruled by his wife, and accusing him of wanting to reestablish the élus. The placard was attached to the main door of the palace of justice.[119]

Guise had maintained a company of light horse with small ordinance and guard companies for which he received sporadic support from the province.[120] Vitry demanded support for a provincial infantry regiment of ten to twelve companies, thereafter called the regiment of Provence or the governor's regiment. He also demanded support for a company of horse and foot guards, a company of gendarmes, and an ordinance company. In 1636, Vitry increased the provincial infantry regiment to twenty companies of approximately a thousand men. In 1642, Alais increased this

---

[116] A.A.E., 1707, fols. 49–50.

[117] See Chapter Six.  [118] A.A.E., 1708, fol. 241.

[119] *Ibid.*, fol. 73, Alais to Chavigny, May 14, 1642; B.N., Clairambault 388, fols. 18–21, Alais to Brienne, September 1, 1643; Grimaldi and Gaufridy, *Mémoires*, p. 172.

[120] B.N., Cinq Cents de Colbert 288, fols. 1–2.

regiment to thirty companies of approximately twelve hundred men. He also demanded support for a new provincial cavalry regiment of six companies of approximately a hundred fifty men, thereafter known as the colonel's regiment from Alais's military rank and its commanding officer, Colonel Marcin.[121] The province also supported gendarmes companies commanded by the governor, the lieutenant general, and the prince de Mourgues (Monaco), who had concluded a French alliance in 1641. These troops gave the governor opportunities for military patronage.

In 1628, Richelieu began to repair and expand the network of coastal fortifications in Provence. These numbered nineteen garrisons in January 1649, supported at an annual cost of 221,816 livres.[122] Provence had not supported coastal garrisons before 1628. Support for the Monaco garrison was discontinued after the 1649 revolt, but Provence was still supporting eighteen garrisons in 1659 at an annual cost of approximately 200,000 livres.[123] By 1649, Provence was supporting a thirty-company infantry regiment, a six-company cavalry regiment, three companies of gendarmes, the governor's guard and ordinance companies, the lieutenant general's guard company, nineteen coastal garrisons, and contributing money to the support of the royal galleys at Marseille. Provence had not supported most of these troops before 1628, and they were an unpopular financial burden. Increases or reductions in the provincial troop load—and the number of royal troops billeted in Provence—determined a governor's popularity.

Alais insisted that the troops were necessary to defend the coast, to protect the province from invasion, and to maintain order by suppressing revolts. But the calm in Provence after 1641 with the shifting of the war to Catalonia and the northeast made the maintenance of a large number of provincial troops unnecessary. The mazarinades complained bitterly about the cost and conduct of "the governor's troops."[124] Maintaining a thirty-company infantry

[121] *Ibid.*, fols. 28–30v, 43–44; ADBR, Marseille, C 25, 26, 27, 29; B.M., Harleian 4468, fol. 142.

[122] B.N., Cinq Cents de Colbert 288, fols. 1–12; A.A.E., 1715, fols. 62–72; Chéruel and Avenel, *Lettres de Mazarin*, I, 289–290, Mazarin to Alais, August 19, 1643, 582–583, Mazarin to Alais, February 10, 1643; ADBR, Marseille, C 26, 27, 29.

[123] B.N., Cinq Cents de Colbert 288, fols. 64–70.

[124] B.N., Ms. fr. 18977, *La voix du peuple de Provence*, fols. 264–270, *La justice persecutée*, fols. 270–278; B. Marseille 1102, *Très humble remontrance du Parlement de Provence*.

regiment cost the province approximately 350,000 livres a year. With the coastal garrisons and the cavalry regiment, the sum was well over 500,000 livres.[125] In 1643, governor Alais demanded 528,996 livres from the General Assembly, one-third for the support of the coastal garrisons and two-thirds for the regiment of Provence.[126] In 1648, Alais demanded 605,000 livres to support provincial troops.[127] His ordinance company cost the province 300 livres a day, and his captain of guards, sieur Mathan, 4,500 livres a year.[128] Complaints to Paris on the cost of the governor's troops escalated in 1642, and became strident after 1646. On May 19, 1648, the province sent a sixteen-article remonstrance to Paris demanding troop reductions, while the parlementaires sent deputies on the misconduct and cost of the governor's infantry regiment.[129] On September 14, 1649, the Parlement complained to chancellor Séguier that the governor's troops were costing the province more than 500,000 livres annually.[130] Alais was using the troops to increase his personal power, exploiting his role as military commander at the expense of the province.

A governor's political power depended upon the support of loyal clients. There were at least two general types of clienteles. There were noble clienteles clustered around great nobles, for instance Alais's relationship to Condé or the relationship of provincial nobles to Alais, and administrative clienteles gathered around men of power such as Richelieu or Mazarin.[131] Intendants were members of administrative clienteles. For instance, Aubray was pro-

[125] ADBR, Marseille, C 25, fols. 7v, 49–51v; A.A.E., 1708, fol. 156; 1709, fols. 724–287; B.N., Cinq Cents de Colbert 288, fols. 43–47.

[126] A.A.E., 1708, fols. 273–286; B. Marseille 1792, *Très humbles remontrances du Parlement de Provence au Semestre de Janvier* (1650), p. 5.

[127] ADBR, Marseille, C 29, fols. 38–45v.

[128] B.N., Dupuy 754, fols. 281v–282.

[129] B.N., Ms. fr. 20655, fols. 25–34; 18977, fols. 108–114.

[130] B.N., Ms. fr. 17391, fols. 45–46; B. Méjanes R.A. 3, *Mémoires d'Antoine de Valbelle*, fol. 21. Valbelle alleged that Alais demanded replacement of Vautorte as too unreliable and independent.

[131] See Julian Dent, "The role of clientèles in the financial elite of France under Cardinal Mazarin," in *French Government and Society, 1500–1800: Essays in Memory of Alfred Cobban*, ed. J. F. Bosher (London, 1973), pp. 41–69; Ranum, *Richelieu and the Councillors of Louis XIII*, pp. 27–44, 170–174; Fessenden, "Epernon and Guyenne," pp. 220–261; Pierre Lefebvre, "Aspects de la 'fidelité' en France au XVIIᵉ siècle: le cas des agents des princes de Condé," *Revue historique*, 250 (1973), 59–106.

tected by his cousin Sublet de Noyers, secretary of state for Richelieu. It was reported that Aubray was requested as intendant in Provence by Guise because "he does not have the firmness to resist the personality of Guise."[132] Le Roy de La Potherie came to Provence under the patronage of Condé.[133] Vautorte was a client of Le Tellier.[134] Champigny was protected by Sublet de Noyers and Alais.[135] Sève and Oppède were créatures of Mazarin.[136]

The governors' exercise of power in Provence depended upon creating their own noble, military, and administrative clienteles. The governors' guard, ordinance, and gendarmes companies and their large households provided opportunities for patronage. The governors appointed officers in the provincial infantry and cavalry regiments. They could influence the appointment of fortress governors and garrison officers, and obtain royal commissions to raise provincial cavalry companies. Alais attracted a large entourage of provincial nobles in this way. The chevalier Du Vins commanded Alais's troops at Aix during the 1649 revolt, then became lieutenant colonel of the governor's Angoulême regiment in 1651. The chevalier Thomas de Villages, whose brother was a supporter of Alais's enemy Antoine de Valbelle, joined the governor in exchange for becoming captain of a company in his regiment. Alais's promises of military commissions to fight the rebel parlementaires in 1649 brought nobles in droves from the Rhone valley to Provence.[137]

The governors were usually *grands*, great court nobles whose rank and family provided prestige in Provence and helped the governors to attract provincial nobles as clients. Forty-eight of the sixty-eight dukes and peers of France in the seventeenth century became provincial governors. Guise was a member of the power-

---

[132] Mousnier, *Lettres*, I, 60, n. 60; A.A.E., 796, fol. 8; 800, fol. 72, cited in Avenel, *Richelieu et la monarchie absolue*, IV, 210.

[133] Maximin Deloche, *La maison du Cardinal de Richelieu* (Paris, 1912), p. 243.

[134] Mousnier, *Lettres*, I, 155–161.

[135] Ranum, *Richelieu and the Councillors of Louis XIII*, p. 40.

[136] Dent, "The role of clientèles," p. 54; see Chapters Two, Three, and Eight.

[137] Fessenden, "Epernon and Guyenne," pp. 197–262; William Weary, "Royal Policy and Patronage in Renaissance France: The Monarchy and the House of La Tremoille" (Ph.D. dissertation, Yale University, 1972), pp. 88–116; EDB, IV–2, 497, 504; Pillorget, *Les mouvements*, p. 622; Crémieux, *Marseille*, I, 187.

ful house of Lorraine; Alais was the last Valois, his father being the illegitimate son of Charles IX; Mercoeur's father was the illegitimate son of Henry IV. Guise and Mercoeur were dukes and peers, a rank giving them automatic entry into the Parlement, while Alais and Vitry became dukes and peers after their terms in office.

Guise, Alais, and Mercoeur had large personal fortunes, which were politically useful. For instance, Guise could afford to keep a private galley at Marseille; Alais and Mercoeur kept infantry regiments in Provence during the Fronde. An inventory of Guise's household furnishings on April 23, 1641, after his death, showed their value at 410,950 livres. His wife, Henriette-Cathérine de Joyeuse, had property worth 4,307,365 livres in 1655, a year before her death. In 1649, the king granted 50,000 livres as a marriage gift to Louis de Lorraine, duc de Joyeuse and son of Guise, and to his future wife Françoise-Marie de Valois, heiress of the comte d'Alais, who became duc d'Angoulême a year later. In 1654, Louis de Lorraine, duc de Joyeuse and now duc d'Angoulême after the death of his father-in-law, owned Joyeuse and Roquemaure in Languedoc; Angoumois, the barony of Buyre in Picardy; the principality of Joinville; and the baronies of Roches and Esclaron in Champagne. The value of Joinville alone was estimated at 500,000 livres in 1664.

Mercoeur's father, César, held five duchies. From 1602 to 1665, he bought as much land as he could near his duchies of Vendôme and Penthièvre in Brittany and the principality of Martigues in Provence. Penthièvre was valued at 2,400,000 livres in 1657, Vendôme at 1,830,000 livres in 1689. Martigues was the largest titled fief in Provence, with annual revenues of 30,000 livres in 1785. Mercoeur's son, Louis-Joseph, had a total fortune of 7,092,000 livres at his death in 1712; his annual income was 347,000 livres. Vitry had a much smaller fortune, probably one-half that of Guise, Alais, or Mercoeur. The hierarchy of fortunes among *grands* began with Richelieu and Mazarin, then princes of the royal blood such as Valois and Vendôme, foreign princes of whom the house of Lorraine was among the wealthiest, and finally gentlemen such as Nicolas de L'Hôpital-Vitry.[138]

[138] Labatut, *Les ducs et pairs*, pp. 74, 124, 130, 248, 250, 260, 263, 269, 281, 284, 285, 286, 288, 300, 303, 343, 348; B.N., P.O. 1752, fol. 438; 1753, fol. 648; François-Paul Blanc, "Origines des familles provençales main-

Clients fell into different levels and groups: family and friends, household, guards and servants, financial and legal agents, political clients who owed their position to a patron, and political allies who had wealth and honors from other sources. Alais's allies and clients in the provincial administration included intendant Champigny; Parlement councilor Gaspard de Cauvet, baron de Bormes, and his brother Henri de Cauvet, baron de Marignane, former first consul of Marseille and governor of the Tour de Bouc; general of the royal galleys at Marseille, the duc de Richelieu, and galley captain Vincheguerre; Parlement first president Mesgrigny, appointed at Champigny's request but unreliable after 1645; Parlement third president Foresta de La Roquette; and Chambre des Requêtes president Gaufridy.[139] Alais had numerous allies and clients in the municipal governments. Those at Marseille included the Baussets, lieutenants of the Marseille seneschal court, the Ventos, Ciprianis, and Albertas.[140] Suggesting candidates for appointment as municipal consuls, viguiers, magistrates, bishops, and vicar generals gave the governors ample opportunity to attract administrative clients. The provincial power of the governors depended upon their command of provincial and royal troops, their military and administrative patronage to create clienteles, their rank, family, and wealth.

Alais sought the type of independence which Guise had enjoyed, and married his only child to Guise's son. But Alais, unlike Guise, was surrounded by Mazarin's clients in the provincial administration. They acted as watchdogs in monitoring and curbing his power and encouraging his political enemies. Mazarin's brother Michel, archbishop of Aix, was ordered to remain friendly with Alais.[141] Louis Le Roux d'Infréville, sent to Toulon as *commissaire général* of the navy in 1646, worked closely with the arch-

---

tenues dans le second ordre sous le règne de Louis XIV: Dictionnaire généalogique" (doctoral dissertation in law, University of Aix-Marseille, 1971), p. 679.

[139] A.A.E., 1708, fol. 193; B.N., Clairambault 388, fols. 18–21; 394, fols. 128–130; Mousnier, *Lettres*, I, 590.

[140] Crémieux, *Marseille et la royauté*, I, 217, 225; Pillorget, *Les mouvements*, pp. 551–552.

[141] Chéruel and Avenel, *Lettres de Mazarin*, II, 181–184, Mazarin to Grimaldi, June 2, 1645; 735, Mazarin to Michel his brother, April 2, 1646.

bishop to arm the French fleet and send troops to Italy.[142] He was joined at Toulon by the chevalier Gravier, sent to Provence in 1646 as a squadron leader and appointed to the post of governor of Toulon in the next month, much to Alais's annoyance.[143] President Grimaldi-Régusse of the Parlement became a client of Michel Mazarin.[144] Régusse was a friend and business partner of admiralty lieutenant Antoine de Valbelle, Alais's rival for control of the Marseille city government. Valbelle enjoyed the protection of secretary of state Abel Servien, the enemy of Léon Le Bouthillier, Alais's friend.[145] Alexandre de Bichi, cardinal-bishop of Carpentras and another of Mazarin's clients, mediated between Alais and the parlementaires in 1649 with the aid of the archbishop of Arles, François d'Adhémar de Monteil de Grignan.[146] Grignan mediated between Alais and Valbelle at secretary of state Brienne's request in 1645.[147]

Mazarin inherited and used many of Richelieu's servants, for instance Le Roux d'Infréville, Régusse, Bichi, and Alexandre de Sève. He added his own clients, who were often Italian clerics. Cardinal Jérôme de Grimaldi became archbishop of Aix. Hyacinthe Serroni was bishop of Orange. Mazarin's secretary, Zongo-Ondedei, became bishop of Fréjus in 1654. Alexandre de Bichi was bishop of Carpentras.[148]

[142] *Ibid.*, II, 725, 729, 736, 745, 748, 754, March-May 1646; Dent, "The role of clientèles," 54. Infréville visited the coasts of France for Richelieu in 1629; cf. Avenel, *Lettres de Richelieu*, VII, 977, May 31, 1629. Infréville was serving as a *commissaire général* of the navy at Toulon in December, 1639; cf. *ibid.*, VI, 640–641.

[143] Chéruel and Avenel, *Lettres de Mazarin*, II, 797, August 19, 1646; 814, September 27, 1646.

[144] Grimaldi and Gaufridy, *Mémoires*, p. 25; Chéruel and Avenel, *Lettres de Mazarin*, III, 1063, Mazarin to Régusse, October 7, 1648.

[145] Joseph Billioud, "Du commerce de Marseille à la noblesse, les Covet de Marignane (1555–1803)," *Marseille*, 39 (1959), 9; Crémieux, *Marseille et la royauté*, II, 571.

[146] See Chapter Eight; Georges Dethan, *Mazarin et ses amis* (Paris, 1968), pp. 104–123. Bichi was serving Richelieu in June 1637; cf. Avenel, *Lettres de Richelieu*, V, 1039.

[147] Chéruel and Avenel, *Lettres de Mazarin*, II, 644, Mazarin to Grignan, March 4, 1645; Pillorget, *Les mouvements*, p. 547.

[148] Dethan, *Mazarin et ses amis*, pp. 129–132; J. H. Albanès, *Gallia Christiana Novissima*, 7 vols. (Valence, 1899–1920), I, 406–407. Sève was serving Richelieu in August 1637; cf. Avenel, *Lettres de Richelieu*, V, 1052.

On September 24, 1647, Mazarin informed his client Alexandre de Sève that he had been nominated as intendant in Provence to replace Champigny.[149] Sève's relationship with Alais deteriorated as the situation at Aix worsened. On September 15, 1648, Sève wrote to Mazarin, "I can little better make Alais understand the intention of Their Majesties and Your Eminence on accommodation in the affairs of the Parlement."[150] On December 22, Sève wrote that both Alais and the Parlement knew of Mazarin's desire that they "accommodate" or compromise, and that he was working constantly for this end.[151] On January 28, 1649, Sève commended Alais for his courage during the revolt at Aix, but on the next day Sève warned Mazarin that Alais was disposed to ignore royal and provincial interests in favor of his own.[152] On February 10, Sève wrote that Alais would accept Bichi's settlement of the revolt, although he was extremely resentful, with radical thoughts on how to proceed.[153] Sève wrote to chancellor Séguier on May 4 that Alais wanted revenge, that he was angry and violent, that he was not interested in mediation. Sève expressed great alarm about Alais's conduct, which he could not control.[154] On July 6, Sève wrote that the defiance was so great on both sides, the anger of the governor was so intense, and the fickleness of the Parlement so difficult to control, that only a mediator could stop the civil war that had begun.[155] Sève repeatedly requested transfer to another province, and he left that autumn.[156] Sève's relationship with Alais had begun to deteriorate in the autumn of 1648, and totally disintegrated by the summer of 1649. He proved an ineffective check upon Alais.

To curb the governors' independence and control their excesses, Richelieu and Mazarin used three tactics. They sent provincial and military intendants, military and naval commanders, and temporary royal commissioners to Provence to assist, restrain, and report on the governors. They placed clients in key administrative positions in the provincial government, surrounding the governor much as a pack of dogs would surround a bear. They encouraged

---

[149] Chéruel and Avenel, *Lettres de Mazarin*, II, 954.
[150] A.A.E., 1713, fol. 254.      [151] *Ibid.*, fol. 334.
[152] A.A.E., 1714, fols. 15, 27.      [153] *Ibid.*, fol. 84.
[154] B.N., Ms. fr. 17393, fols. 193–196.
[155] A.A.E., 1716, fol. 81.      [156] See Chapter Three.

traditional rivalries within the provincial administration, hoping that the governor's political enemies, for instance the Parlement and lieutenant general, would help to curb his powers. These tactics met with mixed success. The governors were put between the traces, but they would not pull as ordered, and they frequently broke loose.

Mazarin attempted to retain Alais's loyalty through the marriage of his nephew to the governor's only daughter, but his efforts were destroyed by Condé's opposition in 1647.[157] For two years, Mazarin blocked the proposed marriage of Alais's daughter to the duc de Joyeuse, still hoping to force the match with his nephew.[158] This only increased Alais's hostility, and by 1649 he had openly ceased to obey Mazarin's orders. When Alais was driven from the city of Marseille in 1650, he lost Condé's support at court. Mazarin recalled Alais in August and appointed an acting governor in September 1650.[159] On December 13, 1650, the new acting governor, the marquis d'Aiguebonne, reported to Mazarin that Alais had finally left Toulon for court.[160] Alais's decision to leave Provence was affected by his father's death in September 1650, making him the duc d'Angoulême. Mazarin used the pretext of new responsibilities in refusing to permit his return to Provence.[161]

Alais ignored Mazarin's orders in 1652, and departed for Toulon without permission, accompanied by parlementaire Glandèves-Rousset, envoy of the Provençal nobles supporting Alais. But Alais was arrested on Mazarin's orders at Saint Benoit near Argenton in Poitou, and Glandèves continued alone to Aix with the news.[162] Alais was imprisoned in the château of Saint Amand. He resigned his office of governor voluntarily in September 1653 for 400,000 livres—it was reported that he made 100,-

[157] Pierre-Adolphe Chéruel, *Histoire de France pendant la minorité de Louis XIV*, 4 vols. (Paris, 1879–1880), II, 413–414; Paul Logié, *La Fronde en Normandie*, 3 vols. (Amiens, 1951), II, 32.

[158] Chéruel and Avenel, *Lettres de Mazarin*, III, 1037 and n. 1; Ernst Kossmann, *La Fronde* (Leiden, 1954), p. 124.

[159] ADBR, Aix, B 3357, fols. 227v–232; Marseille, C 987, October 11, 1650; Pillorget, *Les mouvements*, p. 652.

[160] A.A.E., 1716, fols. 407–408.

[161] Avenel, *Lettres de Richelieu*, V, 254–255, 175–176, nn. 5 and 7; 262, n. 2.

[162] Grimaldi and Gaufridy, *Mémoires*, p. 51.

000 livres on the transfer—and he died soon after, on November 13, 1653. Sixteen years later the office of governor sold for 600,-000 livres.[163]

The Parlement and procureurs du pays received letters from Paris in April 1652 announcing the appointment of Louis de Vendôme, duc de Mercoeur et d'Etampes, as acting governor.[164] Royal letters naming Mercoeur temporary governor were issued on April 18, and Mercoeur wrote to the Parlement on May 2 from Avignon to announce his arrival in Provence.[165] His father was César de Bourbon, duc de Vendôme, controller general of navigation and legitimatized son of Henry IV and Gabrielle d'Estrées. Mercoeur had married Mazarin's niece, Laura Mancini, in 1651, a *beau mariage* for Mazarin and a political coup. The cardinal may have promised Mercoeur the government of Provence as part of the marriage settlement, since the marriage was against his family's wishes. The duchesse de Mercoeur visited Provence in 1653; she had seen little of her husband until then. When her uncle learned of her pregnancy, he demanded her return to court, and she never revisited Provence.[166] Mercoeur was often in Paris until her death in February 1657.[167]

Mercoeur had a fleshy face, large nose, blond hair and mustaches, protuberant eyes, an air of determination, without the petulance of Vitry or Alais.[168] In fact, he was their political op-

---

[163] *Ibid.*, p. 57; J. Balteau, ed., *Dictionnaire de biographie française* (Paris, 1933), I, 1094–1097; Pierre-Joseph de Haitze, *Histoire de la ville d'Aix*, 6 vols. (Aix, 1880–1892), V, 234–235; A.A.E., 890, fols. 289–293, September 10, 1653, resignation; fols. 296–297, September 15, 1653, payment; Labatut, *Les ducs et pairs*, p. 260, n. 3.

[164] Delib. Parl., B. Méjanes 953, fols. 468v–469; ADBR, Marseille, C 987, April 8, 1652.

[165] ADBR, Aix, B 3357, fols. 648–654; Delib. Parl., B. Méjanes 953, fols. 468v–469.

[166] Chéruel and Avenel, *Lettres de Mazarin*, VI, 538, 543, 549, December 1653–February 1654; Grimaldi and Gaufridy, *Mémoires*, p. 65; B. Marseille 1792, *Le courrier provençal sur l'arrivée du duc de Mercoeur* (May 1652), p. 3; Kossmann, *La Fronde*, p. 145.

[167] Delib. Parl., B. Méjanes 954, fol. 120v. Mercoeur was at Paris from January through April 1657, during his wife's final illness; cf. A.A.E., 1721, fols. 78, 114; ADBR, Marseille, C 35, fols. 421v–460.

[168] Mercoeur's portrait appears in the 1652 mazarinade, *Relation du soulèvement de Provence contre le duc de Mercoeur, leur gouverneur*, B. Marseille 1792.

posite: disciplined and self-controlled, firm and shrewd, with good judgment. Mercoeur was a successful choice as governor of Provence, a good bureaucrat who knew his place in the power structure. He did not attempt to govern independently. He cleared changes in policy. He did not act precipitately. He chose reliable agents. Mercoeur governed Provence as the loyal créature of Mazarin, who rewarded him with trust. Mercoeur died in office; his three predecessors had been removed for their political blunders.

The new governor served as a natural rallying point in the pacification of a province exhausted by three years of civil war. He brought peace to Provence in the summer and autumn of 1652 by adept negotiation. Honoré Bouche, a seventeenth-century historian, wrote: "in less than four months without soldiers, without bloodshed, without great expense, he united all the warring factions, pacified the revolts, dispersed the rebels, and forced them to obey the King."[169] On the advice of his political ally, Parlement president Grimaldi-Régusse who had been a chief of the party supporting Mazarin during the Provençal Fronde, Mercoeur called a General Assembly at Aubagne in October 1652, over which he and Régusse presided. This assembly requested Mercoeur as permanent governor of Provence, and he was so named by royal letters on February 24, 1653.[170]

Born in 1612, Mercoeur pursued a military career; he fought in northern France and the Lowlands in the 1640s. He was frequently absent from Provence as one of Mazarin's commanders in the Italian and Catalonian campaigns: he was absent four months in 1653, six months in 1654, nine months in 1656, four months in 1657, and ten months in 1658.[171] Mercoeur protested these

---

[169] Bouche, *La chorographie*, II, 982; Pillorget, *Les mouvements*, pp. 684–698.

[170] ADBR, Aix, B 3357, fols. 937–944; ADBR, Marseille, C 988, February 25, 1653; B.N., Cinq Cents de Colbert 288, fols. 56–57; Grimaldi and Gaufridy, *Mémoires*, p. 56.

[171] Mercoeur was French viceroy of Catalonia, where he fought from May through August 1653; cf. ADBR, Marseille C 32, fols. 65–139; Delib. Parl., B. Méjanes 954, fol. 67. Mercoeur was again absent from Provence from June through December 1654; cf. ADBR, Marseille, C 33, fols. 345–391; C 35, fols. 1–17. He was in Provence during 1655, but in April 1656 he left to command one of the royal armies in Italy, and did not return until December; cf. *ibid.*, C 35, fols. 307v, 369. He was in Paris from March

lengthy absences. Mazarin reproached him in October 1656 for his complaints, giving him permission to leave Italy "for his health" if he insisted.[172] Guise was often away from Provence before 1624, but Vitry and Alais had been almost continuously resident for twenty years, so Mercoeur's frequent absences were noted. Mercoeur's correspondence with Mazarin from 1656 to 1659 was chiefly military in nature. He wrote at least once a week on military, naval, and administrative problems, beginning with a paragraph of effusive compliments. Mazarin's replies were handwritten and informal, occasionally showing affection for his niece's husband. Richelieu had managed his governors through his secretaries of state, but Mazarin dealt with his directly, as his correspondence demonstrates.

Because of his many absences, Mercoeur needed a dependable agent to help in governing Provence. Mazarin chose Henri de Forbin-Maynier d'Oppède, first president of the Parlement and acting intendant from 1656 until 1671. According to a fifteenth-century statute, the Grand'Chambre of the Parlement became acting governor in the absence of the governor and lieutenant general.[173] Provence had no lieutenant general from 1656 to 1659: there was a delay in receiving into office the new appointee, who was soon imprisoned for disobedience.[174] So the role of acting governor fell to the Grand'Chambre, presided over by the first president. Since Oppède had already proven his value as acting intendant—Mercoeur had praised his performance in this capacity in letters to Paris in 1657[175]—it was natural to make him acting governor, which Mazarin did.

On February 9, 1657, Mazarin wrote to Oppède that he alone was to act as governor: "it is to you alone and not to your company to direct affairs in the absence of the governor and lieutenant

---

to June 1658. Then he led an expedition to Catalonia in July, returned briefly to Marseille in August, and was absent again until January 1659; cf. A.A.E., 1721, fol. 441; 1722, fols. 390–396; 1723, fols. 60–61, 340; Delib. Parl., B. Méjanes 954, fols. 154v–191.

[172] Chéruel and Avenel, *Lettres de Mazarin*, VII, 693.

[173] Louis Wolff, *Le Parlement de Provence au XVIIIᵉ siècle* (Aix, 1920), pp. 280–282; François Olivier-Martin, *Histoire du Droit français des origines à la Révolution* (Paris, 1948), p. 540; ADBR, Aix, B 1375, statute of 1417.

[174] See Chapter Nine.

[175] A.A.E., 1721, fols. 121–124, 193–196, 282–283; 1723, fols. 77–80.

general, and you would be wrong to share that which only pertains to you."[176] Mazarin even sent a letter to the Grand'Chambre rejecting its "pretension" to command for the Parlement in the absence of the governor and lieutenant general. On March 4, 1657, Oppède as acting governor received instructions to call a General Assembly at Aubagne,[177] and one month later Mazarin directed the secretary of state to send him "written authority to command alone in the province in the absence of the governor."[178]

Oppède as "commander of the King in Provence" had the same type of authority as the marquis d'Aiguebonne, who was described by Mazarin in a letter of January 26, 1651, as "commanding for our service in Provence in the absence of the comte d'Alais, governor of the province."[179] Oppède naturally provoked resentment among the parlementaires in usurping their traditional privilege of acting as governor. And he excluded them again a year later. On March 29, 1658, Oppède was told that orders were being sent authorizing him "to command alone in Provence," and on June 20 Mazarin wrote that he was sending a royal commission to this effect.[180] As acting governor, Oppède billeted troops on Aix in April, ignoring the city's traditional exemption, and issued an unpopular tax ordinance in May.[181]

As acting intendant and acting governor, Oppède assumed more and more of the governor's provincial authority. He became responsible for controlling the General Assemblies and supervising provincial taxation, for regulating municipal elections and controlling the procureurs du pays, and for supervising the sovereign courts—made easier by his office of Parlement first president and his close friendship with Cour des Comptes first president Rainaud de Séguiran, sieur de Bouc. Oppède assumed the governor's provincial police responsibilities, although he also worked with Mercoeur in supervising the passage and billeting of royal troops,

[176] A.A.E., 1720, fol. 123.

[177] *Ibid.*, fol. 145; ADBR, Marseille, C 988, March 4, 1657.

[178] A.A.E., 1720, fol. 153, Mazarin's secretary Rose to Brienne, April 14, 1657.

[179] A.A.E., 1716, fols. 117–118.

[180] A.A.E., 1722, fol. 100; Chéruel and Avenel, *Lettres de Mazarin*, VIII, 739.

[181] See Chapter Two. There is a collection of Oppède's correspondence from 1657 to 1658, while he was acting governor, at the Bibliothèque Inguimbertine of Carpentras, 491 (L. 482).

equipping and provisioning the royal fleet. Mercoeur voluntarily withdrew from the provincial administration, focusing his attention on military and naval campaigns outside the province and politics at court. When in Provence, he was interested in military and naval matters, leaving the rest to Oppède.[182]

Finally, on April 30, 1657, in the cathedral of Saint Sauveur, Mercoeur became the cardinal de Vendôme and left Provence for Rome, never living in his newly completed hôtel on the outskirts of the city. He only returned to Aix shortly before his death on August 6, 1669. Oppède served as acting governor from 1667 to 1669.[183] Mercoeur was succeeded in office by his oldest son, Louis-Joseph, duc de Vendôme, de Penthièvre et d'Etampes, who had been born in Paris in 1654 and became governor of Provence en survivance with his father in 1658, a privilege which the Parlement had refused Guise's son. Vendôme never resided in Provence and only visited briefly in 1681, 1695, and 1702. One of Louis XIV's better generals, he fought eighteen years in the army in Flanders, commanded the left flank in the 1693 battle at Marseille, and served as commander-in-chief of the French army during the War of the Spanish Succession, capturing Madrid, where he was buried in the Escorial in 1712. Provence was governed in his absence by the lieutenant general, the Parlement first president, who was also intendant of justice, and the archbishop of Aix. Thus the intendants supplanted the governors of Provence by default in the second half of the seventeenth century. Mercoeur and Vendôme pursued successful military careers outside the province and voluntarily allowed their authority to pass, by neglect, to the intendants of justice.

This transformation in the governor's authority has been the subject of conflicting interpretations. Older historians such as Georges d'Avenel believed that the governors fell after mortal combat with the intendants of the new centralization.[184] In 1947,

[182] The cooperation of the governors and intendants was often based on a division of labor, a separation of military and civilian functions; cf. Boris Porchnev, *Les soulevèments populaires de France de 1623 à 1648* (Paris, 1963), p. 80; Roland Mousnier, "Note sur les rapports entre les gouverneurs de provinces et les intendants dans la première moitié du XVII<sup>e</sup> siècle," *Revue historique*, 227 (1962), 345, reprinted in *La plume, la faucille et le marteau* (Paris, 1970), p. 206.

[183] Wolff, *Parlement de Provence*, p. 281; EDB, IV–2, 333.

[184] Avenel, *Richelieu et la monarchie absolue*, IV, 108–129.

Gaston Zeller proposed a significant revision of this interpretation. He agreed that the intendants replaced the governors, but he believed the decline in the governors' powers had come in the sixteenth century from the encroachments of the parlements and municipal governments.[185]

However, Roland Mousnier believes the intendants did not supplant the governors before 1661, while their relationship was characterized by close cooperation and alliance.[186] He characterizes the relationship between the intendants and the governor of Languedoc in 1644–1645 as, "A constant collaboration of men who combined for the same end in a spirit of confidence and reciprocal esteem without a shadow of rivalry."[187] His interpretation is supported by Orest Ranum, who believes that Richelieu's policy toward the governors as *grands* never involved attacking their provincial power.[188] Boris Porchnev agrees that the governors, who were political allies of the intendants, did not suffer a decline in their power until after the mid-seventeenth century.[189] Several historians have noted the need for a comprehensive study of provincial governors,[190] and there has been new interest in the governors during the late sixteenth century.[191]

We believe that the years from 1630 to 1661 were decisive in the transformation in the governors' authority. Their decline was the result of a voluntary choice, not mortal combat with the in-

---

[185] Gaston Zeller, "L'administration monarchique avant les intendants, parlements et gouverneurs," *Revue historique*, 197 (1947), 180–215.

[186] Mousnier, "Note sur les rapports," pp. 339–351, reprinted in *La plume*, pp. 201–213. Ernst Kossmann made the same observation in *La Fronde* (Leiden, 1954), p. 54.

[187] Mousnier, "Note sur les rapports," *La plume*, p. 203. The relations between governor Epernon of Guyenne and intendant Verthamon were also cordial; cf. Fessenden, "Epernon and Guyenne," p. 236.

[188] Orest Ranum, "Richelieu and the Great Nobility: Some Attitudes of Early Modern Political Motives," *French Historical Studies* 3 (1963), 184–204.

[189] Porchnev, *Les soulèvements*, p. 80.

[190] Mousnier, "Notes sur les rapports," *La plume*, p. 207; A. Lloyd Moote, *The Revolt of the Judges: The Parlement of Paris and the Fronde, 1643–1652* (Princeton, 1971), p. 6, n. 5.

[191] Richard Harding, "The Provincial Governors of Reformation France: Anatomy of a Power Elite, 1542–1635" (Ph.D. dissertation, Yale University, 1974, soon to be published by Yale University Press). Mark Greengrass has a similar dissertation in progress for Oxford University.

tendants. Governors such as Mercoeur and Vendôme chose to focus their careers on military service in the royal armies and advancement at court far from Provence, over which they became nominal governors. Louis XIV encouraged this choice by enforcing the attendance of great nobles at Versailles and offering dazzling prospects for military glory in his foreign wars. The traditional rivalry between the Parlement of Aix and the governors was disruptive and exhaustive, but it did not seriously weaken the governor's power. It did, however, contribute to causing the revolts at Aix.

The governors and intendants of Provence were not political rivals engaged in a power struggle for control of the provincial government. They had collaborative working relationships, the intendants serving as administrative assistants and watchdogs for the central government. Governors Alais and Mercoeur had working partnerships with intendants Champigny and Oppède. Such relationships, however, were not without tension. The partners were not as consistently cooperative as Roland Mousnier asserts: the governors and intendants did not always work well together. There were quarrels between Vitry and de La Potherie, Alais and Vautorte, Alais and Sève, just as there were quarrels between the governors and intendants in Languedoc and Alsace.[192]

What caused these conflicts? The governors and intendants had fundamentally different interests. The tensions between them were the result of different backgrounds, values, and goals. The governors were *grands*, interested in acquiring personal prestige and power. The intendants were professional bureaucrats interested in serving the central government. Their approaches to administrative problems and their goals in governing were different. The governors accepted the useful services of the intendants and did not oppose them as agents of centralization. The intendants, lacking a provincial clientele and command over troops, necessarily cooperated with the governors. But there were occasional, inevitable stresses in their relationship.

The keystone of the governor's power was military, particularly in a frontier province sporadically in revolt throughout the seventeenth century. The governor's command over provincial and royal troops gave him political power. He could always threaten to use

---

[192] Bonney, "Intendants," pp. 169–170; Georges Livet, *L'intendance d'Alsace sous Louis XIV (1649–1715)* (Paris, 1956), pp. 78–101.

military force if a city council refused to accept appointees or a sovereign court refused to register an edict. Mercoeur's great strength as governor was the speed and firmness with which he met rebellion at Toulon in 1652 and at Aix in 1659.[193] If a governor such as Guise or Alais could not restore order, the crown sent troops under a *grand* to put down the revolt, and chose another governor.

Difficulties occurred when the governors pursued personal policies contrary to those of the crown, and used their provincial power to govern independently. Guise damaged the crown's interests in blockading Aix in 1629 and refusing to suppress the 1630 revolt. Alais billeted soldiers on Aix in the autumn of 1648 to avoid a revolt, thereby provoking the revolt that led to the Provençal Fronde. The intendants as agents of the central government tried to coerce governors such as Guise and Alais into cooperating with the crown. Attempting to curb their excesses, the intendants assumed the governors' provincial police powers. But final authority rested with the governors because the intendants did not command an effective military or police force.

The governors and intendants were expected to work as a team to execute unpopular royal demands and wring minimal cooperation from provincial institutions, while convincing Paris that delays were unavoidable and resistance was being quickly and firmly suppressed. Wedged between the crown's demands and the recalcitrance of a province sporadically in revolt throughout the seventeenth century, they were criticized and harassed from both sides. If they did not enforce royal policies, they were recalled. If they created too much opposition, they were recalled. It was a difficult task calling for men with firmness and diplomacy, whom the crown was not always fortunate in finding.

A successful governor needed a semblance of the Parlement's cooperation and support. A governor who repeatedly antagonized the court and increased its stubborn resistance became a political liability, as Guise, Vitry, and Alais learned to their cost. The Parlement of Aix was difficult at best for the crown to control. The task was made worse by a blundering governor. The Parlement's active and persistent hostility could indicate a governor's general unpopularity and ineptitude. The crown could not afford this type of servant in a troubled frontier province.

[193] Pillorget, *Les mouvements*, pp. 684–694, 796–799.

# Chapter Five

# THE CASCAVEOUX REVOLT OF 1630

Plague first appeared at Digne in Haute-Provence in June 1629. Soldiers returning from the Italian battlefields carried the disease across the Midi, and within a month, there were outbreaks at Aix, Nîmes, and Montpellier.[1] Figures are inaccurate, but Aix probably had one to two thousand dead by October.[2] There were perhaps twelve thousand dead in Provence by the end of the epidemic.[3] Digne, Apt, Carpentras, and Aix were severely hit; Arles, Marseille, and Toulon less so. The epidemic took a year to abate.[4]

The rapidity with which the plague struck and its victims died was terrifying because causes and cures were unknown. Aix was crowded with charlatans selling charms against the disease, and a visitor to the city a year later noted white crosses still marking the doors of infected houses.[5] Antoine de Ruffi reported that when the plague reached Marseille in February 1630, more than 50,000 people fled the city; some were crushed and trampled to

[1] Pierre-Joseph de Haitze, *Histoire de la ville d'Aix*, 6 vols. (Aix, 1880–1892), IV, 144–146; Philippe Tamizey de Larroque, ed., *Lettres de Peiresc aux frères Dupuy*, 7 vols. (Paris, 1888–1898), II, 7–8; Antoine de Ruffi, *Histoire de la ville de Marseille*, 2 vols. (Marseille, 1696), I, 475; René Baehrel "Epidemie et terreur: Histoire et sociologie," *Annales historiques de la Révolution française*, 23 (1951), 140.

[2] ADBR, Aix, J.L.H. Hesmivy de Moissac, "Histoire du Parlement de Provence, 1501–1715," 2 vols., I, 498; Jacques Gaufridy, "Histoire de Provence sous le règne de Louis XIII," B. Méjanes 625, fols. 29–30; "Relation de la peste de 1629–1630, par Jean-Nicolas de Mimata, chanoine de l'église d'Aix," B. Méjanes R.A. 8, fols. 208–218.

[3] F.A.T. Roux-Alphéran, *Les rues d'Aix ou recherches historiques sur l'ancienne capitale de la Provence*, 2 vols. (Aix, 1846–1848), I, 242–245; Honoré Bouche, *La chorographie ou description de Provence*, 2 vols. (Aix, 1664), II, 879.

[4] Tamizey de Larroque, *Lettres de Peiresc*, II, 249.

[5] *Les confessions de Jean-Jacques Bouchard, parisien, suivies de son voyage de Paris à Rome en 1630* (Paris, 1881), p. 119.

150

death at the gates.[6] His figures are suspect, but his meaning is clear: those who could flee did so, leaving the poor and sick behind in a city where life assumed a nightmarish quality. Municipal officials who callously abandoned the city and their responsibilities when the first corpses appeared were despised and resented.[7] But there is no evidence that this resentment exploded into violence. The 1630 revolt at Aix was not an expression of class hostility or anger at the local elite.

The plague left behind economic chaos, high prices, and general unrest. The economy of the region had already been strained by heavy troop movements. In January 1630, troops billeted in the countryside around Aix caused complaints.[8] Prices of wheat and bread rose rapidly. Wheat went from 12 livres per measure at Aix in 1625 to 20 livres in 1630, with a leap in bread prices from 13.71 deniers a measure in 1625 to 23.27 deniers a measure in 1630, a 60 percent increase in five years.[9] In March 1630, peasants of Reillane pillaged a grain convoy on its way to Aix.[10] Life in the countryside was disrupted too seriously for a normal planting, and there was a bad harvest in 1630. The Parlement issued an arrêt in June 1630 prohibiting the export of wheat outside Provence because of the bad harvest. Draguignan, Grasse, Antibes, and the coastal villages were the worst hit areas.[11]

The obligation to supply royal armies in transit to Italy worsened the shortages. On February 17, 1629, the procureurs du pays were ordered to supply 10,000 measures of wheat to the army in Italy, while on March 14 they were ordered to aid in purchas-

[6] Ruffi, *Histoire de Marseille*, I, 476.

[7] René Pillorget, "Un document concernant la peste et l'insurrection d'Aix, 1630," *Revue de la Méditerranée*, 21 (April–June, 1961), 209–221. A pamphlet entitled, *Dialogue de deux chats sur les affaires presents de cette ville d'Aix*, B. Méjanes 794, "Memoires pour l'histoire de Provence," fols. 159–131; B. Inguimbertine 1841, fols. 347–350, is cited by Pillorget as evidence of lower-class resentment at Aix during the plague. Also see René Baehrel, "La haine de classe en temps d'épidémie," *Annales d'histoire économique et sociale* (1952), pp. 351–360; "Epidémie et terreur," pp. 113–146; Lucien Febvre, "Comptes rendus," *Annales: ESC*, 6 (1951), 520–523.

[8] ADBR, Marseille, C 17, fols. 3–8.

[9] René Baehrel, *Une croissance: La Basse-Provence rurale (fin du XVIe siècle–1789)* (Paris, 1961), pp. 533, 547.

[10] A.C., Aix, BB 100, fol. 174.

[11] Delib. Parl., B. Méjanes 952, fol. 47.

ing wheat for the army.[12] An edict of June 30 forbade wheat traffic on the lower Rhone to facilitate troop provisioning at the ports of Pont Saint Esprit, Beaucaire, and Tarascon.[13] Royal edicts of August 1630 and September 1631 forbade exporting wheat or vegetables from Provence in order to supply troops returning from Italy.[14] The 1630 revolt began against a backdrop of unusually poor economic conditions at Aix, which created popular misery.[15]

The Vacations Chamber of the Parlement acted quickly in July and August to halt the plague: chasing vagabonds, soldiers, and prostitutes from the city; closing inns, wineshops, schools, and the university; forbidding fairs, dances, marriages, baptisms, and market days.[16] On August 13, 1629, the Parlement registered a municipal decree ordering former councilors to fill vacancies on the city council.[17] It confiscated goods and quarantined merchants from the Lyonnais and other stricken areas.[18] Four parlementaires were ordered to search for "infected" merchandise in the shops of Aix. By October, there were two parlementaires per quarter acting in this capacity.[19] The Parlement became a health and

[12] ADBR, Marseille, C 986. Pierre de Percey received letters to purchase more wheat for the army on December 29, 1629; cf. ADBR, Aix, B 3348, fol. 240.

[13] ADBR, Aix, B 3348, fol. 205.

[14] *Ibid.*, fols. 384v, 600. Royal edicts against the exportation of wheat from Provence were frequent during the Habsburg war because of inadequate production.

[15] For additional information on economic conditions in 1629–1630 at Aix and another account of the revolt, see René Pillorget, "Les Cascaveoux: L'insurrection aixois de l'automne, 1630," *XVIIᵉ siècle*, 64 (1964), 3–30 and *Les mouvements insurrectionnels de Provence entre 1596 et 1715* (Paris, 1975), pp. 313–355.

[16] Delib. Parl., B. Méjanes 951, fols. 373v, 375; A.C., Aix, BB 100, fols. 75–76v; *Arrêt de la cour de Parlement tenant la Chambre des Vacations concernant règlement sur le fait de la peste du 17 juillet, 1629* (Aix, 1720), B. Marseille 1799, also published by Dr. Alezais in *La lutte contre la peste en Provence au XVIIᵉ et XVIIIᵉ siècles* (Marseille, 1902), pp. 69–103. The Parlement traditionally exercised direct police authority in Aix during emergencies such as invasions, revolts, and epidemics. It exercised this authority during the plagues of 1502, 1506, 1560, 1565, 1622, 1629–1630, 1649–1650, and 1720–1721; cf. ADBR, Marseille, C 904–909.

[17] ADBR, Aix, B 3348, fols. 213, 219v, 222v; B. Inguimbertine 1841, fol. 358v.

[18] Delib. Parl., B. Méjanes 951, fols. 368v–370, 422; B. Inguimbertine 1841, fol. 359.

[19] Delib. Parl., B. Méjanes 951, fols. 369, 375, 402.

police bureau to enforce the quarantine and control looting. The bureau included the viguier, members of the Cour des Comptes, medical doctors, and representatives of the municipal government. It confiscated contaminated merchandise, issued health certificates for travel, expelled those who might carry infection, and increased the city guard.[20] Travelers had to produce health certificates signed by the Parlement and governor.[21] Letters were purified by immersion in vinegar before reading.[22]

When the Parlement reconvened in October, it voted to sit as two chambers in the cities of Salon and Pertuis, in accordance with a sixteenth-century precedent.[23] All the royal courts left Aix in October. The Cour des Comptes went to Toulon, then to Brignoles; the seneschal court to Trets; and the Trésoriers Généraux to Pertuis.[24]

The first session of the court at Salon, a town about twenty miles west of Aix, sat in the Franciscan refectory on October 29, 1629. Salon acted as the main chamber, registering or remonstrating on royal legislation, judging appeals in criminal cases, handling correspondance and finances, using the great seal. First president Vincent-Anne de Forbin-Maynier d'Oppède of the Grand'Chambre presided. He was joined by presidents Foresta de La Roquette and Monier, royal attorneys Rabasse and Decormis, dean Ollivier, councilors Albert, Agut, Bermond, Paule, Mazargues, Guiran, Ballon, Villeneuve, Antelmi, Trichaud, Foresta, Laurens, and Thoron.[25]

The first session of the chamber at Pertuis, a town about twenty miles northeast of Aix across the river Durance, met on November 15 in the Carmelite refectory, and later sat in the town hall. A *Grands Jours* chamber for cases on appeal from the seneschal courts of Digne, Forcalquier, and the towns of Haute-Provence, Pertuis was a delegation from the main chamber at Salon with full

---

[20] Gérard Sautel, *Une juridiction municipale sous l'Ancien Régime: Le bureau de police d'Aix-en-Provence* (Paris, 1946), pp. 186–187; ADBR, Aix, B 33716–33720.

[21] *Les confessions de Jean-Jacques Bouchard*, p. 99.

[22] Tamizey de Larroque, *Lettres de Peiresc*, I, 728–730.

[23] Delib. Parl., B. Méjanes 951, fol. 411v.

[24] *Ibid.*, fol. 512; A.C., Aix, BB 100, fol. 137v.

[25] "Mémoires des délibérations du Parlement," 2 vols., B. Méjanes R.A. 51, I, 667; Delib. Parl., B. Méjanes 951, 415v–420; ADBR, Aix, B 3364, Salon, November 1629–July 1630.

competence on the far side of the Durance. It was smaller in size, less prestigious, and used the small seal. Second president Coriolis of the Tournelle presided. He was joined by presidents Du Chaine and Forbin de La Roque, royal attorneys Guérin and Thomassin, councilors Leidet-Fombeton, Leidet-Sigoyer, Périer, Joannis, Thomassin-Ainac, Dedons, Arnaud, Chailan, Suffren, Saint Marc, Roux, Flotte, Gautier, Boyer, Estienne, and Espagnet.[26] Choosing their service according to rank, many of the younger parlementaires went to Pertuis. Some owned property within their jurisdiction, in particular Coriolis, Périer, Joannis, Chailan, Thomassin-Ainac, Leidet-Fombeton, and Leidet-Sigoyer.[27]

Many parlementaires did not appear at either court, preferring the comfort of their country houses. There were only five regulars at Pertuis in November 1629. On November 23, the Pertuis Chamber ordered absent councilors to appear. Most came after Christmas. Attendance at Pertuis in the spring averaged about ten parlementaires. Attendance at Salon was about the same.[28]

Salon consulted with Pertuis whenever necessary by letter and deputation. At first there was a regular, peaceful flow of correspondence between the two chambers. But during January and February 1630, the letters became increasingly acrimonious. Each chamber complained about the jealousy, insolence, and negligence of the other. Pertuis was dissatisfied with the infrequent consultations and large sums of money Salon was spending, while Salon

[26] ADBR, Aix, B 3684, Pertuis, November 15, 1629–June 12, 1630; "Mémoires des délibérations," B. Méjanes R.A. 51, I, 667; Delib. Parl., B. Méjanes R.A. 51, I, 667; Delib. Parl., B. Méjanes 951, fols. 415v–420; Pierre Louvet, "Histoire du Parlement de Provence," B. Méjanes R.A. 53, fol. 363; "Entrées et délibérations de la cour séant à Pertuis à cause de la contagion de la ville d'Aix," pièce 9 in "Recueil de pièces sur la Provence par Mssrs. de Saint-Vincens," B. Méjanes 1054.

[27] Pillorget, "Les Cascaveoux," 6, n. 3; Marie-Zéphirin Isnard, *Etat documentaire et féodal de la Haute-Provence* (Digne, 1913), pp. 6, 81, 95, 106, 121, 130, 169, 253, 373, 416.

[28] It is difficult to determine the exact membership of the Pertuis and Salon chambers because of absenteeism and exchanges of deputies and members. Coriolis, Forbin de La Roque, Thomassin-Ainac, Dedons, and Saint Marc attended the Pertuis chamber regularly. On November 23, absent councilors Arnaud, Joannis, Thoron, Suffren, and Roux were ordered to appear. The Leidets and Boyer appeared after Christmas.

154

demanded speedier replies to its letters and more deputies sent from Pertuis to discuss problems.[29]

The dispute climaxed on March 20, 1630, when Salon learned that president Coriolis had gone from his lodgings to a session of the Pertuis chamber in the robe, mantle, and cap of a first president. Pertuis had been styling itself *Le Parlement de l'Outre-Durance* for over a month. By this action, Coriolis denied Pertuis's rank as a *Grands Jours* chamber and declared it equal to Salon, splitting the Parlement into two separate courts. Salon immediately sent a deputy to Paris requesting an order of reunion. The letters were signed in Paris on April 2, received by Salon on the morning of April 29, and registered that afternoon. Procureur-général Rabasse and councilor Paule were promptly dispatched to Pertuis.[30]

They arrived in Pertuis on the evening of April 29 and presented the royal letters the next morning.[31] Coriolis replied that all members were not present and would have to be summoned before the letters could be entered in the register and the chamber dissolved. Rabasse accused him of stalling, and Paule was verbally abusive. By five o'clock that evening the letters were still unregistered. The Pertuis chamber was divided on the proper course of action. Opposed to registration at Coriolis's lodgings were Forbin de La Roque, Périer, Joannis, Espagnet, Leidet-Sigoyer, Dedons, and Chailan. In favor of registration at the town hall were Guérin, Thomassin, Leidet-Fombeton, Thomassin-Ainac, Saint Marc, and Roux. Irritated at the delay and confident of support from some of the Pertuis parlementaires, Rabasse and Paule seized the registers and rode back to Salon the next morning, effectively dissolving the chamber. Prior Coriolis, the president's youngest son, unsuccessfully tried to stop the mule carrying the records as it passed through the main square. The Pertuis parlementaires in favor of reunion later registered the letters at Salon.[32]

---

[29] Delib. Parl., B. Méjanes 951, fols. 439, 442, 445v, 446v–447, 466v; B. Inguimbertine 1841, fols. 403–412.

[30] Delib. Parl., B. Méjanes 951, fols. 471v–474v, 477v–478; ADBR, Aix, B 3348, fol. 296.

[31] Delib. Parl., B. Méjanes 951, fol. 480v.

[32] *Ibid.*, fols. 480v–487. The prior may have been the second président's nephew.

The rebellious parlementaires refused to join the main body. On May 7, after learning that Pertuis had sent councilor Espagnet to Paris to protest, Salon dispatched avocat-général Decormis to defend its actions.[33] On June 12, the Pertuis parlementaires sent a remonstrance to Paris charging Salon with arbitrary, contemptuous actions. Pertuis argued the necessity of two chambers because plague quarantines prevented travel in Provence and geographically restricted one chamber's dispensation of justice. The remonstrance ended with this complaint:

> [the Salon chamber] in place of acting with moderation and a respect for their commission, since it regarded a chamber established by Your Majesty and composed of their colleagues and magistrates of equal power and authority; they [Salon] acted so imperiously with extreme violence and an expression of contempt . . . in a manner so illegal and hurried as to bring bitterness to the execution of the letters . . . not as a simple revocation and suppression of a chamber but as a degradation of Your magistrates.[34]

Salon became a Vacations Chamber in July. When the Parlement returned to Aix on September 1, 1630, with the other royal courts, most of the Pertuis parlementaires sullenly rejoined their colleagues.

The courts' return to Aix was celebrated by a bonfire in the Place des Prêcheurs and a thanksgiving mass in Saint Sauveur. Coriolis, Forbin de La Roque, and Périer were not present at the opening session at Aix, although they had attended the last joint meeting at Salon. They refused to appear at the palace of justice until the end of September, when they were ordered by the Parlement to appear or face penalties.[35] The Parlement was sharply divided in September 1630—the Pertuis parlementaires wanted the Salon chamber reprimanded and Coriolis appointed first president. To revenge themselves on their enemies, they made use of the spontaneous popular revolt that began at Aix on September 19.

[33] Delib. Parl., B. Méjanes 951, fols. 479v–480.

[34] Dominique Guidy, "Histoire du Parlement de Provence," B. Méjanes R.A. 54, fols. 196–210; "Mémoires pour l'histoire de Provence," B. Méjanes 794, fols. 216–266; B. Inguimbertine 1841, fols. 398–402.

[35] "Mémoires des délibérations," B. Méjanes R.A. 51, II, 1–13. The Pertuis parlementaires attended the August 26–27 sessions but no others; cf. *ibid.*, I, 717.

Entering Aix through the Notre Dame gate on the morning of September 19, intendant Dreux d'Aubray came to register an unpopular royal edict establishing élus in Provence. He was greeted by the consuls of Aix, who presented him with gifts of a tapestry, jam, torches, and wine. Aubray stayed at the hôtel of governor Guise, who was absent on campaign and customarily resided in Marseille, anyway. At noon, the tocsin rang from the Grand'Horloge, the municipal clock tower. Angry young men, swords in hand, gathered at the town hall and marched up the narrow rue Droit (now the rue Gaston-da-Saporta) toward the hôtel de Guise in the Cordeliers quarter, crying "Vive le Roy! Fuero Elus et Larrons!" (Long Live the King! Down with tax officials and thieves!)[36] They were looking for Aubray, whose visit had been anticipated and feared for at least a week.

Aubray had already come to Provence in July 1629 to register the edict. Daunted by the rapid spread of the plague, he soon withdrew to Paris. But he had returned a year later, presenting his commission letters to the Salon chamber on June 3, 1630.[37] He did not go to Aix because of the plague. His intentions were the subject of wild rumors: a provincial capital five hundred miles from Paris teemed with rumors. There were rumors of the Spanish invasion a year before it occurred.[38] There were false reports in 1643 and 1645 of another creation of presidial courts, and in 1658 of a merger between the Parlement and Cour des Comptes.[39] A hazard of life before rapid communication, rumors were instrumental in triggering the three revolts at Aix.[40]

When the crowd reached the hôtel, they battered down its doors

[36] Charles Grimaldi and Jacques Gaufridy, *Mémoires pour servir à l'histoire de la Fronde en Provence* (Aix, 1870), p. 107; Haitze, Histoire, IV, 177; Honoré d'Agut, "Discours du Parlement de Provence," B. Méjanes 906, fol. 172; B. Inguimbertine 1841, fols. 461–462.

[37] Tamizey de Larroque, *Lettres de Peiresc*, II, 142–148, 246; Pillorget, "Les Cascaveoux," p. 8; Delib. Parl., B. Méjanes 951, fols. 491–491v. Aubray's letters were registered June 10; cf. *ibid.*, fol. 496.

[38] A.A.E., 1702, fols. 253–263.

[39] Delib. Parl., B. Méjanes 953, fols. 1–7; 954, fol. 149; A. D. Lublinskaya, ed. *Vnutrenniaia politika frantsuzskogo absoliutizma, 1633–1649* (Leningrad, 1966), pp. 298–299, Mesgrigny to Séguier, May 2, 1645.

[40] Georges Lefebvre has demonstrated the importance of rumors in starting revolts in "Foules révolutionnaires," *Annales historiques de la Révolution française*, 11 (1934), 1–26.

Figure 3. The Grand'Horloge and facade of the town hall

and ransacked the building. Aubray escaped across the roof to a neighboring house, and left Aix that evening.[41] He took refuge with François-Anne de Forbin de La Fare de Sainte Croix, brother of the Parlement's first president and a councilor in the Cour des Comptes. In searching for Aubray, the men attempted to break down the doors of the first president's hôtel on the Place Saint Sauveur. Finally, they made a bonfire of Aubray's luggage and coach in the Place des Prêcheurs.[42]

After driving the intendant from the city, the Aixois waited, wondering what would happen next, and whether Aubray would return. Participants in the September 19 attack vowed never to permit the establishment of élus in Provence. Public meetings against the edict were held in the Place des Prêcheurs at night, to avoid identification and permit normal daytime activity—the shops remained open. At one of these crowded, torchlit meetings, the revolt received its name. Allusion was made to the classical fable of the rats belling the cat for self-protection. Paul de Joannis, seigneur de Châteauneuf and a nephew of Coriolis, announced that he would bell the cat himself and hung a small bell from a leather strap attached to his coat. The word for such a bell in Provençal was *cascaveou*. The rebels became known as *cascaveoux*. Bells on leather straps and white ribbons were distributed, and a certain Jacques Viani inscribed rebel names on a register. At night, the noise of bells could be heard throughout the city with cries of "Fuero élus," Provençal for "Down with the élus." Slogans, posters, and verse appeared on the walls, and gunsmiths' shops were searched for arms.[43]

The rebels continued to meet at night in the Place des Prêcheurs and to destroy the property of persons thought to support the élus. The streets of Aix were filled with the sound of ringing bells as men went to and from these meetings, calling out threats and

[41] Haitze, *Histoire*, IV, 178; ADBR, Aix, Moissac, "Histoire du Parlement," I, 532.

[42] *Ibid.* Aubray went first to Cavaillon, then to Avignon; cf. ADBR, Marseille, C 16, fols. 49–50. He returned to Aix with Condé, and on March 24, Guise wrote to Paris requesting that Aubray be recalled because his presence was provocative in an already tense situation; cf. A.A.E., 1701, fols. 230–231. He left Provence in November or December 1631.

[43] Haitze, *Histoire*, IV, 182; Gaufridy, "Histoire de Provence," B. Méjanes 625, fols. 59–60. A lawyer named Rians may also have inscribed names on a register.

slogans, their torches lighting up the walls. There was a flood of anonymous wall placards, graffiti, pamphlets, and handbills. On October 1, there was a brief popular demonstration against the transfer of the Cour des Comptes to Toulon; the court had been sent to Toulon in June 1630 for refusing to register the edict.[44] Aubray had arrived in Aix with letters dated September 8, reinforced by a conciliar decree transferring the court again if it refused to cooperate, and the Cour des Comptes was at Toulon in November.[45]

On October 13, a straw effigy of the marquis d'Effiat, minister of finance, was burned in the Place des Prêcheurs with much laughter and satirical songs. On the evening of October 17, a small crowd gathered and battered down the door of councilor Louis de Paule, who escaped out the back, leaving his wife behind screaming like a fishwife. Some of the men climbed the stairs to his study, threw his furniture out the window, and burned it in the Place des Prêcheurs.[46] The crowd was incited to action by second president Laurent de Coriolis and his nephews, Paul de Joannis, seigneur de Châteauneuf Le Charbonnier, and his younger brother, known as the chevalier de Châteauneuf, who had been addressing the night meetings in the Place des Prêcheurs.[47] The attack was probably in revenge for Paule's participation in the dissolution of the Pertuis chamber. Coriolis may have been encouraged by the September 19 attack on the hôtel Maynier d'Oppède, which forced his enemy, the first president of the Parlement, to flee Aix for safety accompanied by first president Séguiran of the Cour des Comptes.[48] On October 26, a crowd ransacked the house and burned the furniture of Dumas, the prévôt's lieutenant. On October 30, a noisy demonstration began in the Place des Prêcheurs, with men shouting, "Long live the King! Down with the élus and traitants,

[44] Grimaldi and Gaufridy, *Mémoires*, p. 108; A.C., Aix, BB 100, fols. 147v–149v.

[45] ADBR, Marseille, C 16, fols. 49, 50, 53; A.C., Aix, AA 14, fol. 649; B. Inguimbertine 1841, fol. 364.

[46] Bouche, *La chorographie*, II, 882; Haitze, *Histoire*, IV, 182, 184–185; ADBR, Aix, Moissac, "Histoire du Parlement," I, 533; Agut, "Discours du Parlement," B. Méjanes 906, fols. 176–177; Jean-Scholastique Pitton, *Histoire de la ville d'Aix* (Aix, 1666), pp. 385–386.

[47] Agut, "Discours du Parlement," B. Méjanes 906, fol. 177.

[48] Haitze, *Histoire*, IV, 182; Louvet, "Histoire du Parlement," B. Méjanes R.A. 53, fol. 366.

sellers of the province!" The parlementaires had to descend into the square in their judicial robes to quiet the crowd.[49]

On the afternoon of November 3, a crowd threatened the hôtel of president Coriolis, then pillaged the houses of Chaix and Menc, members of the Cour des Comptes suspected of favoring the edict of élus.[50] Menc's extortions as a clerk had been the subject of the Estates' complaints in October 1624.[51] At daybreak on Monday, November 4, a crowd of approximately two thousand rebels led by the seigneur de Châteauneuf marched twelve miles northeast of Aix to the château de La Barben, belonging to the unpopular Aix first consul, Gaspard de Forbin de La Barben, who had deserted the city during the plague of the previous year. Cousin of the Parlement's first president, La Barben had participated in a secret meeting at Brignoles in July to find a way of forcing acceptance of the élus.[52] He had left Aix after September 8, when he was burned in effigy.[53] Marching to the sound of drums with white ribbons in their hats, the cascaveoux threatened to burn his château. They tore up his vineyards, destroyed his trees and several houses in the vicinity—one belonging to Chaix—and then straggled back to town.[54]

On the night of November 14–15, the cascaveoux sacked the house next door to councilor Nicolas de Fabri, sieur de Peiresc, a

[49] Haitze, *Histoire*, IV, 184; Agut, "Discours du Parlement," B. Méjanes 906, fol. 178; Pitton, *Histoire de la ville d'Aix*, p. 386; Delib. Parl., B. Méjanes 951, fol. 539.

[50] Delib. Parl., B. Méjanes 951, fol. 540v; "Mémoires des délibérations," B. Méjanes R.A. 51, II, fol. 32; A.C., Aix, BB 100, fol. 153.

[51] B.N., Cinq Cents de Colbert 288, fols. 7–8.

[52] B.N., Ms. fr. 24166, fol. 277; Agut, "Discours du Parlement," B. Méjanes 906, fol. 172; Pitton, *Histoire de la ville d'Aix*, p. 384; Pillorget, "Les Cascaveoux," p. 8.

[53] Haitze, *Histoire*, IV, 164.

[54] *Ibid.*, IV, 190; Pitton, *Histoire de la ville d'Aix*, p. 386; Bouche, *La chorographie*, II, 883; ADBR, Aix, Moissac, "Histoire du Parlement," I, 538. La Barben strictly enforced his seigneurial rights on pasturage and woodcutting, and peasants from his lands and neighboring villages were part of the crowd. He also denied Aix's privilege of cutting wood five leagues from the city walls by refusing to allow wood to be cut on his property. This was why they cut and burned his trees. Condé, by an ordinance on February 18, 1631, exempted the château from this privilege; cf. Gaufridy, "Histoire de Provence," B. Méjanes 625, fol. 63; Haitze, *Histoire*, IV, 189; A.C., Aix, BB 100, fol. 170.

celebrated bibliophile and savant, in the rue de La Trésorerie a few steps from the palace of justice. They thought the building had been rented to a traitant selling offices of élus. Entering Peiresc's hôtel by a side door, they searched his study and threatened to burn his library. An old friend of Aubray—with whom he had traveled to Italy and whom he had entertained on several occasions—Peiresc was suspected of having a financial interest in the sale of the new offices. The crowd also threatened to pillage other houses in the neighborhood. Peiresc withdrew to his country house of Beaugentier in the Var, north of Toulon.[55]

There was a public reaction against the cascaveoux in December 1630. A vigilante group formed to stop the night meetings, taking for their emblem a bell on a blue ribbon and the motto "Vive le Roi" (the rebels were wearing bells on white ribbons with the motto "Fuero élus"). On the afternoon of December 6, 1630, a group of blue ribbons led by the first consul of Aix, Sextius d'Escalis, baron de Bras, attacked the hôtel de Coriolis in the Cordeliers quarter. Members of the crowd included municipal consuls, councilors, and guards. They told Coriolis to leave Aix. The baron de Bras had already threatened to resign his office if the rioting could not be controlled.[56]

Laurent de Coriolis had advanced to the rank of second president in the Parlement, and he was ambitious to become first president. He resented the dissolution of the Pertuis chamber, over which he had presided, by his rival and enemy Maynier d'Oppède. Fifty-two, nearly blind, Coriolis was one of the most respected judges in the Parlement. He had associated himself with the cascaveoux from the beginning of the revolt. On September 28, 1630, Coriolis and the outgoing assessor Martelli, a staunch foe of the élus, failed in an attempt to have Corioli's youngest son, the prior de Grambois, elected to the office of assessor.[57] The assessor acted as a Roman-style censor to the provincial Estates and could be expected to protest the élus.

[55] Tamizey de Larroque, *Lettres de Peiresc*, II, 261–263; *Les confessions de Jean-Jacques Bouchard*, pp. 115, 117–118; B. Inguimbertine 1841, fols. 437–438.

[56] Delib. Parl., B. Méjanes 951, fols. 540, 549v–550v; "Mémoires des délibérations," B. Méjanes R.A. 51, II, fols. 28, 32, 53; ADBR, Aix, Moissac, "Histoire du Parlement," I, 533–546; Haitze, *Histoire*, IV, 194–196. Haitze reported a crowd of 2,000 outside the hôtel de Coriolis.

[57] A.C., Aix, BB 100, fols. 143–146.

Councilor Decormis and his brother-in-law ran to warn Coriolis of the crowd's intentions, while the parlementaires hurried through the streets in their judicial robes to stop the attack. But they were too late. Coriolis and his supporters, who included councilors Antelmi and Gautier of the Parlement, were forced to leave through the Saint Jean gate to take refuge in a religious house outside the walls.[58]

The parlementaires discovered the baron de Bras at the door of the hôtel in his *chaperon*, a sword in one hand, a pistol in the other, accompanied by a group of men armed with muskets, pistols, pikes, and swords. The baron was called before the Parlement for explanations. He claimed that he was only an observer who happened to be passing, although he and Coriolis were known to have disagreed over the cascaveoux. The Parlement refused to accept his story and ordered him to leave Aix. When he did not comply, he was summoned again before the Parlement. He appeared on the morning of December 7, surrounded by a crowd of supporters. Approaching the palace of justice, he found his way barred by a captain and two companies of the municipal guard, two parlementaires, and a bourgeois guard of concerned citizens.[59] Fearing an attack on the palace of justice, councilor Gaspard de Villeneuve, a personal enemy of the baron de Bras, and councilor Louis d'Antelmi, a supporter of Coriolis, had gone from door to door on the previous night with consuls Bonipari and Anglès to recruit several hundred citizens to protect the palace.[60]

The baron ordered his valet to shoot the captain. The servant drew, fired, missed, killed a bystander, and was immediately killed himself.[61] The slaughter enraged the crowd in the Place des Prêcheurs. The wife of Paul de Joannis goaded the angry men into chasing the baron de Bras and his supporters into the nearby Dominican church.[62] The baron, two of his servants, and a woolcloth merchant named Perrin took refuge in the belltower.[63] The crowd was breaching the walls to get at them when five parlemen-

[58] B. Inguimbertine 1841, fols. 385–386.

[59] Delib. Parl., B. Méjanes 951, fols. 550–550v, 552; Haitze, *Histoire*, IV, 191.

[60] Haitze, *Histoire*, IV, 193–197; Jean-Pierre Papon, *Histoire générale de Provence*, 4 vols. (Paris, 1786), II, 460–461.

[61] Haitze, *Histoire*, IV, 197.

[62] *Ibid.*, 198; Bouche, *La chorographie*, II, 885.

[63] Pillorget, "Les Cascaveoux," p. 24.

taires in red robes, two bailiffs, and a group of Dominican friars carrying the sacrament rescued them. The Parlement sent Bras from Aix for his own safety, escorted by Forbin de La Roque and Decormis, while Antelmi's son went to inform Guise.[64] The revolt had deteriorated into anarchy. The city government could not restore order.

The secretary of state for Provence, intendant Dreux d'Aubray, and Jean-Jacques Bouchard, who was a visitor to Aix in 1630, had no doubts about who was encouraging the cascaveoux and prolonging the revolt—a disgruntled faction of parlementaires.[65] The crown considered the parlementaires guilty of complicity in the rebellion. On December 12, the consuls of Aix learned that the king was sending four regiments under the command of his Bourbon cousin, Henry II, prince de Condé, to restore order at Aix, since neither the governor, municipal government, nor sovereign courts had done so. Condé was accompanied by two intendants who were to prosecute the rebels, a function normally assigned to the Parlement.[66] Their December 5 letters of commission stated:

> It is a deplorable thing that in a kingdom ruled by a king full of piety with laws published and judged to be pious, that one sees judges, through their contempt, falling into such serious errors as these in which one sees them plunged and that the affected vanity of making themselves head of a section of the company brings them to a monopoly, not believing their power great enough if it is not recognized; they want to appear as defenders of public liberty, but oppress their colleagues from which comes an infinity of evils which cannot be so easily suppressed.[67]

The crown rightly believed that an internal dispute of the Parlement, and an embittered minority of parlementaires, had pro-

---

[64] Agut, "Discours du Parlement," B. Méjanes 906, fol. 185; B. Inguimbertine 1841, fols. 390–391.

[65] Bouchard, *Les confessions*, p. 114; B. Méjanes 909, fol. 77.

[66] ADBR, Marseille, C 16, fol. 81; C 986, letters of December 5, 21, and 30, 1630.

[67] B.N., Dupuy 154, fols. 111–116; ADBR, Marseille C 986, December 5, 1630.

longed the revolt. The royal letters transferring the Parlement in punishment were issued on November 30, 1630.[68] A conciliar decree on December 5 outlawed president Coriolis and suspended from office president Forbin de La Roque, councilors Flotte, Espagnet, and Périer of the Parlement. They were called to Paris to explain their conduct during the revolt. Forbin de La Roque, Flotte, Espagnet, and Périer were also named as cascaveoux in the intendants' letters of commission on the same day.[69]

It was estimated at first that Condé was bringing six thousand infantry and five hundred horse; later estimates ranged from four to five thousand infantry and five to six hundred horse.[70] Condé was at Avignon by February 1631 with intendants Dreux d'Aubray and Charles Le Roy de La Potherie, where they were joined by first presidents Maynier d'Oppède and Séguiran.[71] The Estates and city of Aix sent deputies to Avignon. But Condé refused to receive them. He saw only deputies from the royal courts to inform them of their transfer from Aix: the Parlement was sent to Brignoles, the Cour des Comptes to Saint Maximin, the Trésoriers Généraux to Pertuis, and the seneschal court to Lambesc.[72]

Condé occupied Aix on the morning of March 19, 1631. His four infantry regiments were ranged in battle order on the Place des Prêcheurs, awaiting his arrival. The city was empty, since it expected to be sacked.[73] Condé had acquired a reputation for severity during his campaigns against the Huguenots in Languedoc and Dauphiné. In 1627, he had ravaged the Haut-Vivarais, and in 1628, he devastated Haute-Languedoc, taking the town of Pamiers by assault, butchering most of its inhabitants, and sacking the town

[68] ADBR, Aix, B 3348, fol. 493.

[69] Delib. Parl., B. Méjanes 952, fol. 14v; B.N., Dupuy 154, fol. 116.

[70] Bouche, *La chorographie*, II, 886; Dominique Guidy, "Histoire du Parlement de Provence," B. Méjanes R.A. 54, fol. 218; ADBR, Marseille, C 16, fol. 148; B. Inguimbertine 1841, fol. 391.

[71] Gaufridy, "Histoire de Provence," B. Méjanes 625, fol. 75; Haitze, *Histoire*, IV, 205.

[72] A.C., Aix, BB 100, fols. 168v–169. The city government was notified on February 26, 1631, that the courts had left Aix; cf. *ibid.*, fols. 172–172v.

[73] Pitton, *Histoire de la ville d'Aix*, p. 390; Bouche, *La chorographie*, II, 887; Agut, "Discours du Parlement," B. Méjanes 906, fols. 200–201; B. Inguimbertine 1841, fol. 441. Condé may have entered Aix a day earlier, on March 18, 1631.

of Réalmont. It was an effective tactic: towns besieged by Condé surrendered rather than face similar treatment.[74] On March 17, Condé appointed a new municipal government with the intendants' help.[75] Aix did not regain its privilege of municipal elections until December 1637. On March 29, Condé issued an ordinance denying Coriolis, Forbin de La Roque, Flotte, Villeneuve, Antelmi, and Espagnet of the Parlement entrance to the city of Aix, while a conciliar decree on March 31 suspended Villeneuve from office and called him to Paris for explanations.[76] Condé also issued ordinances on March 29 prohibiting the carrying and selling of weapons and the holding of public meetings. He announced that his troops would stay until further notice.[77]

Coriolis retired to his château at Corbières in Haute-Provence after the December attack on his hôtel. He left his estates when warned by a son-in-law of the approach of Condé's troops, and joined the revolt of the duc de Montmorency in Languedoc, for which he was condemned to death with his youngest son, the prior de Grambois, at Toulouse on October 29, 1632.[78] After self-exile in Spain with his son, Coriolis returned to Avignon in 1640, where he was captured and imprisoned in the Tour de Bouc. He died shortly thereafter in his mid-sixties, totally blind, with great courage.[79] Coriolis, the prior, and the two Châteauneuf brothers were excluded from the general amnesty in July 1633.[80]

Coriolis's confiscated office of president was sold to Louis de Paule in October 1632, and the rest of his confiscated property was given to the city of Aix. Gaspard de Forbin de La Barben made 6,000 livres on its sale. The Coriolis hôtel at Aix was razed.

---

[74] J. H. Mariéjol, *Henri IV et Louis XIII*, in *Histoire générale de la France*, ed. E. Lavisse, VI, part 2 (Paris, 1908), 271–272.

[75] A.C., Aix, AA 14, fol. 557; BB 100, fols. 185v–186; BB 101, fols. 18v–19; Haitze, *Histoire*, IV, 229.

[76] A.C., Aix, BB 100, fol. 195v; Delib. Parl., B. Méjanes 952, fol. 22.

[77] A.C., Aix, AA 14, fols. 557–559; BB 100, fol. 195v; "Mémoires des délibérations," B. Méjanes R.A. 51, II, fol. 60.

[78] Tamizey de Larroque, *Lettres de Peiresc,* II, 368; "Recueil de mémoires et pièces," B. Méjanes R.A. 8, fols. 90–92; Grimaldi and Gaufridy, *Mémoires,* p. 114.

[79] Haitze, *Histoire*, IV, 252–254; EDB, IV-2, 147–148.

[80] ADBR, Aix, B 3349, fols. 267v, 361v; ADBR, Marseille, C 2053, fol. 135.

Barben, who recommended Louis de Paule to Richelieu "for his loyal service" in February 1631, billed the city of Aix for 50,000 livres damage to his château. His losses were actually 3,000 to 4,000 livres.[81] Coriolis's oldest son, Honoré, was not permitted to inherit his father's office in November 1630 because of his political sympathies. But he purchased the office in 1645 after Paule's death, when he received permission to rebuild the family hôtel at Aix.[82] On July 28, 1643, intendant Champigny protested to chancellor Séguier that he had learned the prior de Grambois was in Paris attempting to have his sentence commuted.[83] The prior and his two cousins, the Châteauneuf brothers, nephews of Coriolis, later resumed quiet country life in Provence.[84]

Condé's four regiments were billeted on Aix as punishment until June 6, 1631, when they were ordered out into the surrounding countryside to become the worry and expense of the Estates.[85] Aix had to borrow 74,000 livres in April to meet the expenses of maintaining these troops. The Estates had to borrow 125,000 livres in the summer for the same purpose.[86] A conciliar decree ordered the city to pay damages to those whose property had been destroyed by the cascaveoux, for which Aix borrowed 26,000 livres in June 1632.[87] The troops billeted on Aix had freedom of action: a few days after Condé's arrival, the Cordeliers quarter rioted because soldiers guarding the city gate shot three peasants in an argument, one of whom died. A crowd of three to four

---

[81] ADBR, Aix, B 3348, fol. 1006; Haitze, *Histoire*, IV, 238-239; B.N., Ms. fr. 17367, fol. 187, first president Laisné de La Marguerie to Séguier, May 20, 1633, Forbin de La Barben had Vitry's help in the sale of Coriolis's property; A.A.E., 800, fols. 31–32, Forbin de La Barben to Richelieu, February, 1631; B.N., Dupuy 754, *Remontrance au peuple de Provence* (1649), fol. 218.

[82] ADBR, Aix, B 3355, fols. 252v, 381; M.A., Provence 348; B.N., Ms. fr. 24166, fol. 237; Coriolis's son obtained his father's office of president through the patronage of the duc d'Orléans; cf. Bouche, *La chorographie*, I, 891.

[83] Lublinskaya, ed. *Vnutrenniaia*, pp. 255–256.

[84] *Ibid.*, pp. 232–234, de La Potherie to Séguier, May 10, 1633.

[85] A.C., Aix, AA 14, fols. 561–562.

[86] *Ibid.*, BB 100, fols. 199–207v; ADBR, Marseille, C 17, fols. 157v–158.

[87] A.C., Aix, BB 101, fols. 24–26v; Haitze, *Histoire*, IV, 236–237; "Recueil de pièces relatives au Parlement," B. Méjanes 943, fols. 697–699; B. Inguimbertine 1841, fols. 431–432.

thousand attacked the soldiers guarding the gate. Two were killed, and one was wounded.[88] On April 11, 1631, a soldier who had murdered his host at nearby Trets was rescued from the scaffold by his comrades, who chased the executioner into the palace of justice, where they murdered him.[89] Soyecourt, the commanding officer at Aix after Condé's departure in April, was so unpopular that his poisoning was unsuccessfully attempted at dinner on June 16, 1631.[90]

The intendants sat as a court in July 1631 to prosecute the rebels. There were approximately forty Aixois accused of sedition. Although their occupations are not clearly indicated, the majority appear to have been lower-class.[91] It can be inferred that the September and October crowds were composed of lower-class men who worked during the day and attended political meetings at night, since the shops had remained open. The documents tell us that the rebels ransacked the gunsmiths' shops, looking for arms, which were also distributed from the municipal arsenal in the city hall[92]—poor men did not own weapons. The Bourg, where the meetings occurred, was the town's business center and residence for its poorer inhabitants. The streets were narrow, the squares

[88] Bouche, *La chorographie*, II, 887; Grimaldi and Gaufridy, *Mémoires*, p. 113; A.A.E., 800, fols. 205–206, Soyecourt to Richelieu, March 29, 1631.

[89] Grimaldi and Gaufridy, *Mémoires*, p. 113; A.A.E., 1701, fol. 238, Soyecourt to Richelieu, April 14, 1631.

[90] A.C., Aix, BB 100, fols. 228v–231v; A.A.E., 800, fols. 95–96; 1701, fol. 238. This may have been food poisoning, since sixteen to eighteen dinner guests were stricken.

[91] Accused were Paul de Châteauneuf, le chevalier de Châteauneuf, prior Coriolis, Fabri, Fuveau, Perret, Rostan or Roustain concierge, le sieur de Sigonce, Melon, Gautier, Rodier, Imbert, David, Martial Blain, Dubose, Durand the elder, the son of Ruffi, Meinier the younger—a lawyer, Barthélémy—the son of Barthélémy apothecary, Lautier, Caissani the son, Lance, Brignolles, the two Guignes brothers, Vitalis lawyer, Augustin, Stelle, Morellon, Montauroux of Grasse, Ventabren de Bourdonière, Bais, Mille, Episcopari, Peiner, le chevalier Meinier, le chevalier Puymichel, J.-A. de Saint Marc, and d'Audifredi—brother-in-law of Châteauneuf; cf. "Rolle des accusés des émotions arrivés dans la ville d'Aix," B. Méjanes 776, fol. 88. Roustain or Rostan baker and Melon were arrested by the Parlement on December 7, 1630 after they were recognized during the attack on the hôtel de Coriolis the previous day; cf. Delib. Parl., B. Méjanes 951, fol. 550v. For an account of the interrogations, see "Recueil de pièces relatives au Parlement," B. Méjanes 943, fols. 667–677.

[92] Delib. Parl., B. Méjanes 951, fol. 540; "Mémoires des délibérations," B. Méjanes R.A. 51, II, fol. 30.

few and small, with the exception of the Place des Prêcheurs, so the crowds were not enormous. The crowd of two thousand on November 4 was probably one of the largest.[93]

Twenty-five or thirty rebels were condemned *in absentia*, but only three of the verdicts were executed. Jacques Roustain was sentenced to be hanged after being tortured for the names of his accomplices. Jean-Baptise Ruffi and Jean Roustain were sent to the galleys for life after paying a fine of 4,000 livres each and attending the execution of their comrade with bare heads and feet, a rope around their necks.[94] But the hanging never occurred. The condemned man went berserk at his sentencing in the prison chapel. He attacked his guards, who finally shot him through the skylight of the chapel, where he died that evening. The remaining cascaveoux fled Aix to escape arrest; some were massacred by government troops at the "Bloody Barricade" at the foot of Sainte Victoire mountain to the east; some took refugee in the château of Les Baux, whose governor, Villeneuve's brother, was a supporter of the duc d'Orléans.[95]

Royal officials invested with judicial and military authority were held responsible for disciplining their inferiors and suppressing rebellion, much as the person walking a dog on a leash is responsible when it bites someone. In the seventeenth century, the lower classes were considered leashed animals, and when they rebelled, the crown blamed the nobles and judges of the region for not keeping them in hand.[96] Richelieu dictated a memoir on the cascaveoux revolt for the council of state in 1631, in which he accused five parlementaires of misconduct. They were Coriolis, Périer, Gautier, Flotte, and Decormis. He recommended their suspension from of-

[93] Delib. Parl., B. Méjanes 951, fol. 540v; "Mémoires des délibérations," B. Méjanes R. A. 53, fol. 366; Haitze, *Histoire*, IV, 190, 194.

[94] "Recueil de mémoires," B. Méjanes R.A. 8, fols. 88, 90, 91–92; Bouche, *La chorographie*, II, 887; Haitze, *Histoire*, IV, 227–228; B. Inguimbertine 1841, fols. 470–476.

[95] Bouche, *La chorographie*, II, 887; Haitze, *Histoire*, IV, 213; ADBR, Aix, Moissac, "Histoire du Parlement," I, 549; A.A.E., 800, fols. 186–187, Soyecourt to Richelieu from Les Baux, which he was besieging, on June 26, 1631. He asked for the governorship of the château when it fell. The governor was Antoine de Villeneuve, brother of parlementaire Gaspard de Villeneuve; cf. E. de Juigné de Lassigny, *Histoire de la maison de Villeneuve en Provence*, 3 vols. (Lyon, 1900–1902), I, 232. Also see Georges Dethan, *Gaston d'Orléans, conspirateur et prince charmant* (Paris, 1959).

[96] Orest Ranum, *Paris in the Age of Absolutism* (New York, 1968), p. 200.

169

fice and the transfer of the sovereign courts from Aix "in fear of disobedience or greater rebellion."[97] The consuls and assessor of Aix were removed from office, and new consuls were appointed. The baron de Bras was called to Paris to explain his role in the events of December 6–7, 1630. One president and three councilors of the Cour des Comptes were suspended and called to court for refusing to register the edict of élus.[98] One president and six councilors of the Parlement were suspended from office by disciplinary legislation and called to Paris to explain their participation in the cascaveoux revolt. They were Forbin de La Roque, Périer, Espagnet, Antelmi, and Villeneuve. Another president, Coriolis, was condemned to death for treason, commuted to life imprisonment, and his office and property were confiscated. Maynier d'Oppède's presence at Paris may have been responsible for these citations. The first president had fled Aix for safety in the last week of September 1630. He went to Paris in November, then to Avignon, where he met Condé in early February 1631. He died there of apoplexy on February 17.[99]

Coriolis's leadership of the 1630 revolt demonstrates the political importance of clientage ties. A network of the second president's relatives and friends in the Parlement joined him in revolt.[100] Suspended from office by the conciliar decree of December 5 and called to Paris to explain his support of the cascaveoux was Julien de Périer, nephew of Coriolis, member of the Pertuis chamber and dean of the Parlement in 1631.[101] Councilor Antoine de Gautier, son-in-law of Périer, was named a cascaveoux sympathizer in Richelieu's 1631 memoir for the council of state.[102]

[97] A.A.E., 979, fol. 133.

[98] Delib. Parl., B. Méjanes 952, fols. 14v, 22; A.C., Aix, BB 100, fol. 195v; 101, fol. 88; Bouche, *La chorographie*, II, 882; Haitze, *Histoire*, IV, 200, 225; ADBR, Aix, Moissac, "Histoire du Parlement," I, 561.

[99] *Ibid.*; A.C., Aix, BB 101, fol. 88; Agut, "Discours du Parlement," B. Méjanes 906, fol. 187.

[100] "Recueil de pièces sur la Provence," B. Méjanes 826, fols. 1–95, "Etat des parentés et alliances de messieurs du Parlement de Provence, dressé en l'année 1629."

[101] *Ibid.*, fols. 5–8; Delib. Parl., B. Méjanes 952, fol. 14v.

[102] A.A.E., 797, fol. 133, published by Georges d'Avenel, ed., *Lettres, instructions diplomatiques et papiers d'état du cardinal de Richelieu*, 8 vols. (Paris, 1853–1877), IV, 171; Haitze, *Histoire*, IV, 194; ADBR, Aix, Moissac, "Histoire du Parlement," I, 540.

Gautier was a member of the Pertuis chamber, and he had been with Coriolis at his hôtel on December 6. Gautier was not cited in disciplinary legislation.

Another cascaveoux sympathizer was Jean-Baptiste de Boyer, nephew of Coriolis and member of the Pertuis chamber.[103] The intendants reported to Richelieu in March 1631 that Boyer entered the hôtel de Monier, where they were conducting their investigation, with the power to speak for Coriolis and his two Châteauneuf nephews—who did not appear when summoned.[104] Boyer was not cited. Jean de Joannis, councilor in the Parlement, nephew of Coriolis and brother of the Châteauneufs, was forbidden purchase of his uncle's confiscated office of president in 1632 because of his political sympathies.[105] Intendant de La Potherie wrote to Séguier on March 29, 1633, that Joannis was first cousin to Dedons, Saint Marc, Périer, Boyer, and second cousin to Gautier.[106] Dedons and Saint Marc served in the Pertuis chamber and were probably cascaveoux sympathizers. Jean de Leidet-Sigoyer, a member of the Pertuis chamber, who had voted against reunion, was a first cousin of Joannis and son-in-law of avocat-général Decormis. Leidet-Sigoyer was implicated in the revolt, but not cited.[107] Pierre Decormis was named a cascaveoux sympathizer in Richelieu's 1631 memoir.[108] He had hurried to warn Coriolis of the crowd's intentions on December 6, and the crowd considered sacking his hôtel.[109] The client network of president Coriolis in 1630 included his oldest and youngest sons, his three Joannis nephews and their cousin Leidet-Sigoyer, his nephews Périer and Boyer, and Périer's son-in-law Gautier. Coriolis also had a number of sympathizers.

The conciliar decree of December 5 outlawing Coriolis also suspended from office president Forbin de La Roque and councilors Flotte and Espagnet, who were named as rebels in the

---

[103] Haitze, *Histoire*, IV, 210; "Recueil," B. Méjanes 826, fols. 5–6.

[104] A.A.E., 798, fols. 16–17.

[105] Lublinskaya, *Vnutrenniaia*, pp. 228–230, intendant de La Potherie to Séguier, March 29, 1633; "Recueil de mémoires," B. Méjanes R.A. 8, fol. 91; EDB, IV–2, 279.

[106] Lublinskaya, *Vnutrenniaia*, pp. 228–230.

[107] "Recueil," B. Méjanes 826, fol. 68.

[108] A.A.E., 797, fol. 133.

[109] B. Inguimbertine 1841, fols. 385–386.

intendants' letters of commission on December 5.[110] An ordinance of Condé later denied councilors Villeneuve and Antelmi entrance to the city of Aix, while a conciliar decree suspended Villeneuve from office.[111] Intendant de La Potherie noted in a letter to Séguier on May 10, 1633, that Espagnet and Villeneuve were deeply implicated in the revolt, Flotte less so.[112] Espagnet had been the Pertuis chamber's deputy to Paris, and his family had ties with the Coriolis.[113] Flotte was a first cousin of Gautier and a member of the Pertuis chamber. Villeneuve was a personal enemy of the baron de Bras, while his older brother Antoine was governor of Les Baux and a client of the king's rebellious brother, Gaston d'Orléans.[114] Villeneuve and Antelmi were described by a contemporary historian as "zealous for the party of the cascaveoux."[115] Antelmi had been at the hôtel de Coriolis on December 6. His son served as a deputy to governor Guise, while he himself went to Paris for the Parlement, accompanied by his brother Jean, who represented the city of Aix. He and his brother were imprisoned in the Bastille until 1633 for their bold speech.[116]

President Jean-Baptiste de Forbin de La Roque was a member of the Pertuis chamber who voted against reunion with Salon—it may have been his idea that Coriolis wear the robes of a first president.[117] Forbin de La Roque vehemently protested the edict of élus at the General Assembly of the Nobility convened at Pertuis on September 14, 1630. Royal letters dated September 12, and presented nearly a week later by intendant Aubrey, revoked the Parlement's authority to summon such an assembly. The Parlement refused to register the letters.[118] Forbin de La Roque was called to Paris by lettre de cachet for chairing the assembly. He

[110] Delib. Parl., B. Méjanes 952, fol. 14v; B.N., Dupuy 154, fol. 116.

[111] A.C., Aix, BB 100, fol. 195v; Delib. Parl., B. Méjanes 952, fol. 22.

[112] Lublinskaya, *Vnutrenniaia*, pp. 232–234.

[113] Jean Celles, *Malherbe, sa vie, son caractère, sa doctrine* (Paris, 1937), pp. 159–186.

[114] Haitze, *Histoire*, IV, 193; Juigné de Lassigny, *Histoire de la maison de Villeneuve*, I, 232.

[115] Haitze, *Histoire*, IV, 196.

[116] *Ibid.*, 202–203; "Mémoires des délibérations," B. Méjanes R.A. 51, II, fol. 60.

[117] "Entrées et délibérations," pièce 9, B. Méjanes 1054.

[118] Delib. Parl., B. Méjanes 951, fols. 516v, 524; ADBR, Marseille, C 108, fol. 36; B. Inguimbertine 1841, fol. 460. The royal letters arrived in Aix on September 26.

refused to go, with a weak excuse.[119] Forbin de La Roque may also have been responsible for arrêts of the Parlement ordering royal troops from the province, prohibiting the sale of offices of élus, and forbidding unpopular first consul La Barben to exercise his new office of governor of the Antibes fortress.[120] Forbin de La Roque left Aix for safety in January 1631 when the crowds began to attack cascaveoux in anticipation of Condé's arrival.[121] Forbin de La Roque, Villeneuve, and Espagnet were back in Aix within six months, declaring "that all they had suffered was sweet to them since it had been to defend the liberties of their province," or so it was reported to Richelieu by Louis de Paule in October 1633.[122]

There was strong opposition to the edict of élus within the Parlement. Dean Jean-Pierre Ollivier, who died soon after, presided at the General Assembly of Communities called by the Parlement at Aix on October 25, 1630. This assembly voted 45,000 livres to purchase 4,000 muskets with bandoliers, 1,000 pikes, and to distribute printed copies of Provençal privileges to member communities.[123] President Monier delivered a speech on February 13, 1631, to Condé at Avignon recalling at length the Provençal privileges of taxes granted by the Estates and requesting the crown's observance.[124] Ollivier and Monier were members of the

[119] "Mémoires pour servir à l'histoire de Provence," B. Méjanes 794, fol. 280; B.N., Dupuy 154, fols. 111–116; Pillorget, "Les Cascaveux," p. 13.

[120] ADBR, Aix, B 3665, October 11 and 20, 1630; B.N., Ms. fr. 24166, fol. 220; "Mémoires pour servir à l'histoire de Provence," B. Méjanes 794, fols. 243–249.

[121] Agut, "Discours du Parlement," B. Méjanes 906, fol. 187.

[122] A.A.E., 809, fol. 172; Georges d'Avenel, *Richelieu et la monarchie absolue*, 4 vols., 2nd ed. (Paris, 1895), IV, 184–185, n. 2.

[123] ADBR, Marseille, C 16, fols. 59, 65; B.N., Cinq Cents de Colbert 288, fols. 14–15. The precedent for this action was set by the Aix Estates in January 1624, which voted 45,000 livres to purchase arms for the communities during the Valtelline confrontation; cf. *ibid.*, fol. 6. When the Aix rebels sent deputies to the other Provençal communities in November 1630 to exhort them to aid the rebellion and levy troops, only Apt responded; cf. Pillorget, "Les Cascaveoux," p. 25; *Les mouvements insurrectionnels*, p. 329.

[124] *Remontrance faite à Monseigneur le prince* [de Condé] *dans la ville d'Avignon par Messrs. les deputés de la cour du Parlement de Provence, prononcée par M. le président Monier, 13 fevrier 1631* (Aix, 1631), "Mémoires pour l'histoire de Provence," B. Méjanes 794, fols. 188–194; "Recueil de mémoires," B. Méjanes R.A. 8, fol. 85.

1589 royalist Parlement at Pertuis, over which Coriolis's father had presided. Other members of the Parlement supporting Henry IV included the fathers of Antelmi, Périer, and Leidet-Sigoyer, who were Coriolis supporters three decades later.[125]

Coriolis posed as a defender of provincial privilege and an opponent of the élus, using this political issue for his own purposes. An anonymous pamphlet entitled *La remontrance de Laophile à Messieurs d'Aix* was secretly circulated by the Coriolis party in 1630. It described Coriolis as "the father of the people . . . this old seigneur, chief of our august Parlement and of the police of our city," while the edict of élus and its supporters were called "a second plague, infected air, a nearby storm with thunder, hail and lightning." The pamphlet attacked the blue ribbons of the baron de Bras as rebels and enemies of the king. Written in defense of Coriolis shortly after he was driven from Aix, this pamphlet's circulation was prohibited by the Parlement.[126] Several pamphlets defending the second president were circulating at Aix in 1630–1631.[127]

In Richelieu's 1631 memoir for the council of state, Coriolis was quoted as saying to the crowds, "People, arm yourselves. We must kill all those who want to establish élus." Coriolis's nephew, councilor Périer, added: "Will you endure the élus? We must kill them all and dress the young ones as women!" Councilor Flotte continued, "We must die with pikes in our hands!"[128] Another anonymous pamphlet, circulated in 1631 and entitled *Factum pour la justification du sieur Périer, conseiller au Parlement de Provence* stated that the disorders were caused by the edict of élus, which intendant Aubray had attempted to enforce contrary to provincial privilege.[129] *La vérité provençale au Roi*, a pamphlet by

---

[125] Maurice Wilkinson, *The Last Phase of the League in Provence, 1588–1598* (London, 1906), p. 22; Fernand Alphandéry, *Etude sur le Parlement de Provence au XVIᵉ siècle* (Aix, 1879), pp. 35, n. 1; 36, n. 3; Georges Reynaud, *Guillaume Du Vair: Premier président du Parlement de Provence* (Aix, 1873), p. 83, n. 19.

[126] B.N. Dupuy 659, fols. 174–178; "Mémoires pour l'histoire de Provence," B. Méjanes 794, fols. 163–170; B. Inguimbertine 1841, fols. 372–372v; M.A., Provence 355.

[127] "Recueil de pièces relatives au Parlement," B. Méjanes 943, fols. 709–749; B. Inguimbertine 1841, fols. 424–431.

[128] A.A.E., 797, fol. 133.

[129] "Actes, pièces et mémoires concernant le Parlement," B. Méjanes 930.

the sieur de Nible, probably councilor Arnaud who served in the Pertuis chamber, traced the long history of provincial privilege and demanded its observance with the abolition of the élus and preservation of the Estates.[130] The Coriolis faction was able to attract supporters inside and outside the Parlement by attacking the edict of élus.

Other members of the Coriolis network included Espagnet, Antelmi, Flotte, Villeneuve, Forbin de La Roque, and Decormis, the father-in-law of Leidet-Sigoyer. Forbin de La Roque, Flotte, and Decormis opposed the élus. Villeneuve was a personal enemy of the baron de Bras, as was Coriolis. Coriolis was also an enemy of first president Maynier d'Oppède. Private feuds were a cause of parlementaire participation in all three revolts. Seven of Coriolis's supporters had been his colleagues at Pertuis. An additional five parlementaires, Monier, Ollivier, Dedons, Saint Marc, and Arnaud, were sympathizers, although they were not implicated in the revolt. Thus the parlementaires had four overlapping motives for participating in the 1630 revolt. They were relatives and friends of Coriolis; they were embittered members of the Pertuis chamber seeking revenge; they opposed the edict of élus; and they were involved in personal feuds.

Coriolis's client network was an important source of support for the cascaveoux. Many such networks existed within the Parlement and the provincial government. The Coriolis network had at least fifteen members, among whom were Coriolis's two sons, Honoré and the prior de Grambois; his three Joannis nephews, the Châteauneuf brothers and the Parlement councilor; their first cousin, Jean de Leidet-Sigoyer, and his father-in-law Pierre Decormis; Coriolis's other nephews, Périer and Boyer, with Périer's son-in-law Gautier; and Forbin de La Roque, Flotte, Espagnet, Villeneuve, and Antelmi. There were at least five more sympathizers within the Parlement.

An invisible web of parlementaire influence composed of networks of sons, brothers, uncles, nephews, cousins, in-laws, and friends stretched through the Provençal administration. Forty-five of the seventy families holding office in the Parlement from 1640 to 1650 had members serving in other institutions. There were

---

[130] "Mémoires pour l'histoire de Provence," B. Méjanes 794, fols. 171–185; B.N., Dupuy 659, fols. 167–174; "Recueil de pièces relatives au Parlement," B. Méjanes 943, fols. 681–697.

twenty parlementaire families in the Cour des Comptes, ten related to Trésoriers Généraux by marriage, another ten in the seneschal courts, a few juges royaux and judges in the admiralty courts. Twenty-four families had members who were consuls of Aix; eight had members who were consuls of Marseille and Arles. Twelve families were represented in the higher clergy, mostly as canons of Saint Sauveur and Knights of Malta, some as bishops, abbots, and priors. Other family members were viguiers, royal fortress governors, officers in the provincial regiments and governor's guard, noble syndics, noble and clerical procureurs for the Estates.[131]

Coriolis's supporters within the Parlement attempted to control the issuance of remonstrances and arrêts, and their machinations affected the court's conduct during the revolt. In contrast to its prompt response to the plague a year earlier, the Parlement took no serious measures for six weeks to control the cascaveoux rioting. The Parlement contented itself with interrogating municipal officials, sending letters to the governor and remonstrances to Paris, establishing investigative committees, and issuing arrêts that were not enforced. The Parlement summoned the municipal government for explanations on September 19, November 4, and December 6–7.[132] It sent two councilors to Guise at Marseille on November 2 to request his help in suppressing the revolt.[133] On October 31, the Parlement issued an arrêt ordering the consuls to make an inventory of the arms missing from the municipal arsenal. One councilor was assigned to each quarter to see the peace was kept.[134] Investigative committees of parlementaires were established after the events on November 4 and December 6.[135]

In fact, the Parlement issued remonstrances and arrêts in October and November that encouraged the cascaveoux. It sent a remonstrance to Paris on October 18, 1630, protesting the edict of élus and describing the poor economic conditions at Aix, which

---

[131] EDB, IV–2, *Dictionnaire biographique*; François-Paul Blanc, "Origines des familles provençales maintenues dans le second ordre sous le règne de Louis XIV: Dictionnaire généalogique" (doctoral dissertation in law, University of Aix-Marseille, 1971).

[132] Delib. Parl., Méjanes 951, fols. 519–521; "Mémoires des délibérations," B. Méjanes R.A. 51, II, fols. 5, 7, 32–33.

[133] "Mémoires des délibérations," B. Méjanes R.A. 51, II, fols. 30–31.

[134] *Ibid.*; Delib. Parl., B. Méjanes 951, fol. 40.

[135] Delib. Parl., B. Méjanes 951, fols. 519–521, 540v–542.

the edict threatened to worsen: "Among the disasters which menace this province . . . justice is threatened because, since the ancient order is changed by new citations, the sovereign companies are held in so much contempt that the people trample underfoot their authority and abandon themselves to all sorts of license; we report the cause to be none other than the edict of élections."[136] The parlementaires argued that they could not keep the peace at Aix because of the new edict. They also sent letters of protest to the king and the keeper of the seals on October 18, when they issued an arrêt making purchase of an office of élus punishable by a fine of 10,000 livres.[137] On October 28, the General Assembly of Communities sitting at Aix added its remonstrance to the one already sent by the Parlement. The Parlement sent another remonstrance to Paris on November 22.[138]

The Parlement did not take serious repressive measures to halt the cascaveoux rioting until November 8, 1630, when it issued an arrêt prohibiting night assemblies and carrying weapons on penalty of death, a punishment too severe to be enforced. The Parlement had issued a similar arrêt on September 19 without effect. On November 13, the Parlement posted the prévôt and his men in the Place des Prêcheurs to prevent night meetings, and on November 14, it posted two members of the municipal guard in every street.[139] On November 19, the Parlement named five hundred family heads from the tax rolls as a bourgeois guard to supplement the municipal police by patrolling the streets in pairs. Their number was increased on December 5.[140] The court appointed an additional two hundred family heads to aid in maintaining order after its departure for Brignoles in February 1631.[141] The court could

[136] *Ibid.*, fols. 533v–534; "Recueil de pièces relatives au Parlement de Provence," B. Méjanes 943, fols. 653–665.

[137] Delib. Parl., B. Méjanes 951, fols. 533v–534; ADBR, Marseille, C 16, fols. 61, 63v; B.N., Dupuy 658, fol. 294; ADBR, Aix, B 3348, fol. 493; B. Inguimbertine 1841, fol. 434.

[138] ADBR, Marseille, C 16, fols. 59, 61; Delib. Parl., B. Méjanes 951, fols. 545–545v; B. Inguimbertine 1841, fols. 420–422.

[139] Delib. Parl., B. Méjanes 951, fols. 543–543v; "Mémoires des délibérations," B. Méjanes R.A. 51, II, fol. 5; *Factum pour la justification du sieur Périer*, B. Méjanes, 930.

[140] Delib. Parl., B. Méjanes 951, fols. 542–542v, 549v.

[141] *Ibid.*, fols. 549v–550, 552; 952, fol. 7; ADBR, Aix, Moissac, "Histoire du Parlement," fols. 543, 545.

have appointed parlementaires to supervise a bourgeois guard, as it did during the revolts of 1649 and 1659. It could have closed the city gates, restricting entry and exit, with parlementaires as guards, as it did in the 1649 and 1659 revolts. It could have formed its own police bureau to work with the municipal government, as it did in 1629 and 1649. But it took none of these measures. In fact, its October remonstrances and arrêts encouraged the cascaveoux.

The Parlement was correct, but not vigorous, in attempting to suppress the cascaveoux revolt. Why did it lack the enthusiasm for effective action? The Coriolis network dominated joint meetings, aided by a high absentee rate. Coriolis became acting first president after Maynier d'Oppède was driven from Aix in late September, and he presided at joint meetings during October 1630.[142] Present at every meeting were presidents Forbin de La Roque and Monier, avocat-général Decormis, dean Ollivier, councilors Boyer, Périer, Espagnet, Flotte, Villeneuve, Antelmi, and Leidet-Sigoyer. This was a regular corps of twelve. There were usually another fourteen or so parlementaires present, some of whom had been members of the Pertuis chamber—Dedons, Saint Marc, Arnaud, Thomassin, and Leidet-Fombeton—and others who may have been against the élus.

There were twenty-five parlementaires present, from a membership double that size at the December 6 meeting, to investigate the attack on the hôtel de Coriolis. Third president Du Chaine was acting first president. Ten of the twenty-five present were Coriolis sympathizers: Forbin de La Roque, Monier, Decormis, Ollivier, Périer, Arnaud, Gautier, Joannis, Villeneuve, and Antelmi. They swayed the meeting with their oratory, and the Parlement decided to send the baron de Bras from Aix, although Coriolis's censure and removal may have been the only way to obtain peace. The court hesitated to condemn its second president for sedition. It was easier to discipline the baron.[143] At the joint meeting on December 8, there were twenty-four parlementaires present, including twelve Coriolis supporters. Coriolis himself presided at the meeting.[144]

---

[142] ADBR, Aix, B 3665, October 1630 deliberations of the Parlement.

[143] *Ibid.*, December 6, 1630; "Mémoires des délibérations," B. Méjanes R.A. 51, II, fols. 42–54. Coriolis presided on October 18, when the court voted to send a remonstrance to Paris on the élus. There were nine sympathizers present in a group of twenty-six; cf. *ibid.*, II, 13.

[144] ADBR, Aix, B 3665, December 8, 1630.

The high rate of absenteeism allowed Coriolis's supporters to dominate joint meetings. The Parlement had so few members present in 1630–1631 that it had difficulty in functioning. The magistrates remained on their estates, avoiding the discomfort of temporary lodgings in a small town and the threat of plague and rioting. They may also have been attempting to husband their economic resources in a difficult year. When the Parlement adjourned to Salon and Pertuis on October 25, 1629, its membership had dropped to one-third its normal strength.[145] Immediately before departing, the court wrote to absent members telling them to assemble at Salon, but few responded. For instance, on November 7 councilor Fabri de Peiresc wrote a letter to a friend from Beaugentier near Toulon, when he was supposed to be sitting in the Parlement at Salon.[146] Neither the Pertuis nor the Salon chamber was at full strength. They averaged about ten members a session. On November 16–20 and December 5–7, 1630, the chamber at Pertuis did not have enough members to sit.[147] The registration of Aubray's letters of commission at Salon had to wait a week in June 1630 until there were enough members present.[148]

The Parlement continued to operate at half strength after it returned to Aix on September 1, 1630. The Parlement sent letters to absent members, including most of the Pertuis parlementaires, during the last week of September, ordering them to appear. On October 30, the court issued another arrêt to this effect.[149] The Parlement was operating at half strength in November and December 1630.[150] Absences continued during 1631. There were not enough councilors present in Aix on February 7, 1631, for the court to sit.[151] On April 7, the Parlement at Brignoles issued an arrêt ordering absent councilors to appear.[152] The arrêt was repeated on May 12.[153] On August 30, when the Parlement learned that it was to act as governor until the maréchal de Vitry arrived, it ordered all absent councilors to appear or forfeit their gages,

---

[145] Delib. Parl., B. Méjanes 951, fol. 415v.

[146] Tamizey de Larroque, *Lettres de Peiresc*, II, 185.

[147] "Entrées et délibérations," pièce 9, B. Méjanes 1054.

[148] Delib. Parl., B. Méjanes 951, fols. 491, 495.

[149] *Ibid.*, fol. 521; "Mémoires des délibérations," B. Mejanes R.A. 51, II, fol. 28.

[150] ADBR, Aix, B 3665, October and November 1630 deliberations of the Parlement.

[151] Delib. Parl., B. Méjanes 952, fol. 5.

[152] *Ibid.*, fol. 22.  [153] *Ibid.*, fol. 23v.

and it sent councilor Agut to Aix to order all parlementaires in that city to report to Brignoles.[154] Absenteeism was a perpetual problem for the Parlement, and its vitiating effect should not be underestimated. The Parlement was frequently sitting at half strength, without a quorum, and rapid decision-making became difficult.

The Parlement also suffered from confusion and uncertainty about its authority to suppress the revolt. Legal precedents for controlling plague were more numerous and less controversial than those for suppressing revolts. The Parlement was on safer ground in issuing arrêts to establish a quarantine than in issuing arrêts to halt mob violence. It was also easier to enforce a quarantine. The Parlement did not possess the police force to execute its arrêts, and it was accustomed to interpreting, not enforcing the law. The court was also unsure of its authority as acting governor, since Guise had returned to Marseille in November 1630. He did nothing to end the rioting at Aix, despite requests for help from the city government and Parlement. The court could not act as governor with Guise in Marseille. It hesitated, and the rioting grew worse. The Parlement as an institution responded tardily and ineffectively to suppress the 1630 revolt because it suffered from internal divisions, sympathy for the cascaveoux, high absenteeism, and uncertainty about its authority as acting governor.

The cascaveoux revolt lasted five months because the governor took no measures to suppress it, while the municipal government and royal courts encouraged and aided the rebels. The 1649 revolt lasted two months because rebel parlementaires imprisoned the governor with the tacit acceptance of the municipal government. The 1659 revolt lasted only two weeks, despite the active support of the municipal government, because the governor raised a provincial military force and marched on Aix. The revolt at Aix in 1630 would not have been as serious or lengthy if the governor and the municipal government had taken firm repressive measures.

Appearing as unexpectedly as summer storms and disappearing as quickly, revolts were endemic to seventeenth-century France. The 1630 revolt began as a spontaneous popular protest against royal taxation. Its character changed when a group of parlementaires who had lost an internal dispute over authority assumed its

154 *Ibid.*, fols. 43v–44.

leadership. Judicial politics spilled into the streets of Aix. The crown's response to the parlementaires' protest shaped judicial politics for the next decade.

The cascaveoux revolt left a legacy of discontent. Twelve parlementaires, fifteen percent of the court's membership, were directly implicated in the revolt. Seven were cited in disciplinary legislation: Coriolis, Forbin de La Roque, Périer, Espagnet, Flotte, Antelmi, and Villeneuve. Five were implicated but not cited: Joannis, Gautier, Boyer, Decormis, and Leidet-Sigoyer. Three of the seven cited, Forbin de La Roque, Périer, and Antelmi, were to be cited again for their opposition politics within a decade. Decormis and Leidet-Sigoyer were implicated in 1630 and cited in 1638–1641, while Villeneuve and Espagnet were cited in 1648. The roots of the opposition party developing in the Parlement during the 1640s stretched back to the cascaveoux revolt, as we shall see in the next chapter.

181

# Chapter Six

# THE OPPOSITION PARTY

Active opposition to the crown continued in the Parlement after the cascaveoux revolt, and within nineteen years there was another revolt. The parlementaire opposition never had formal organization or discipline, public recognition or majority membership. But if less than a party, it was more than a faction. It was capable of coordinated political activity. It had continuity of membership, goals, and tactics. It enjoyed self-recognition as a group attempting to dominate the Parlement's decision making and thereby influence royal policy in Provence.

There were frequent references in the intendants' and governors' correspondance to political parties within the Parlement. Champigny wrote on July 11, 1643, of the conflict between the older and younger parlementaires, accusing the latter of spreading rumors and trying to incite revolt.[1] On September 28, he wrote that "the youth of the palace" had intrigued to fix the annual elections at Aix.[2] A year later he reported success in handling a General Assembly "despite all the intrigues and tricks of the parlementaires and their cabal."[3] On November 4, 1646, he accused "the cabal of the Parlement" of intervening to fix elections at Marseille.[4] Intendant Sève often mentioned a "party," "faction," or "cabal" of parlementaires opposing the Semester.[5]

The opposition parlementaires were allied by kinship as well as by age. On November 19, 1647, Champigny advised against appointing François Thomassin to the office of president of the Enquêtes because he had sixteen close relatives in the Parlement,

---

[1] A. D. Lublinskaya, ed., *Vnutrenniaia politika frantuzskogo absoliutizma, 1633–1649* (Leningrad, 1966), pp. 254–255; Roland Mousnier, ed., *Lettres et mémoires adressés au chancelier Séguier (1633–1649)*, 2 vols. (Paris, 1964), I, 590–591.

[2] Lublinskaya, *Vnutrenniaia*, p. 259; Mousnier, *Lettres*, I, 589–590.

[3] Lublinskaya, *Vnutrenniaia*, p. 269.

[4] *Ibid.*, p. 317.

[5] B.M., Harleian 4575, "Semestre en Provence par M. de Sève," *passim.*

several of them leaders of "the palace youth," whom he would surely join.[6] Increasing their number to twenty-six, Champigny in the next year described the Thomassins as leaders of "a cabal among the palace youth."[7] Intendant de La Potherie in March 1633 warned against granting an office to the son of condemned cascaveou Coriolis, who already had too many kin in the Parlement.[8] Champigny on July 28 and August 8, 1643, warned about the proliferation of the court's kinship networks.[9] On December 22, he reported intensified quarreling, intrigues, and factions among "the palace youth."[10]

The opposition was capable of violence. Claude Luguet, a Marseille tax farmer who came to Aix in July 1639 to purchase one of the new offices of auditeurs and experts, was murdered by the opposition as a tactic of intimidation. Around nine o'clock on the evening of July 31, Luguet sat writing at his desk in an inn. Guests and servants had gone to the roof to watch a religious procession offering public prayers for rain. Six masked men in black entered the inn. Two watched the door; two watched the stairs; two climbed to Luguet's room and stabbed him to death as a warning to other prospective purchasers. The murderers were not recognized, and an investigation that night by intendant Champigny, the consuls of Aix, and members of the Parlement and Aix seneschal court failed to uncover their identities. The authorities made no real effort to find the murderers, who were never discovered. The traitant, Daunila, fled the city.[11]

It was widely believed that the opposition parlementaires were responsible for the murder. Richelieu's niece, Marie-Madeleine de

[6] Lublinskaya, *Vnutrenniaia*, p. 322; Mousnier, *Lettres*, II, 811 (Mousnier gives the date as October 19, 1647); B.N., Ms. fr. 18977, fol. 35, September 20, 1647.

[7] B.N., Ms. fr. 18977, fol. 81. Thomassin was cited in disciplinary legislation in 1645; cf. Lublinskaya, *Vnutrenniaia*, pp. 299–300, Cour des Comptes to Séguier, May 30, 1645.

[8] Lublinskaya, *Vnutrenniaia*, pp. 226–228; Mousnier, *Lettres*, I, 227.

[9] Lublinskaya, *Vnutrenniaia*, pp. 255–256; Mousnier, *Lettres*, I, 590–591.

[10] Lublinskaya, *Vnutrenniaia*, p. 268; B.N., Clairambault 390, fols. 231–232.

[11] Pierre-Joseph de Haitze, *Histoire de la ville d'Aix*, 6 vols. (Aix, 1880–1892), IV, 327–329; A.A.E., 1706, fol. 359; Jean-Scholastique Pitton, *Histoire de la ville d'Aix* (Aix, 1666), p. 395; "Vente d'offices et journée des barricades du 20 janvier 1649 à Aix-en-Provence," *Provence historique*, 15 (1965), 27; ADBR, Marseille, IX B 2, fol. 434v.

Vignerod, duchesse d'Aiguillon, complained to first president Dubernet at Paris that the parlementaires had helped to hide the
murderers.[12] In 1769, Aix bibliophile Méjanes found a marginal
note on one of the manuscripts of Jacques Gaufridy in his own
hand, reading: "Councillor Louis de Saint Marc . . . admitted long
after the event that he was one of the six masked men." Méjanes
was told the same thing by the grand prior of Saint Gilles, who had
heard it from Saint Marc himself.[13] Louis Decormis was accused
of the murder in a 1650 mazarinade.[14] Both parlementaires were
members of the opposition. The tactic created fear among the
Parlement's political enemies. In October 1644, intendant Champigny wrote that he dreaded an assault similar to the one on
Luguet,[15] while in a 1643 memoir governor Alais wrote that he
feared the revival of cascaveoux intrigues. The governor accused
the parlementaires of "cabals, intrigues, and cascaveoux plots" in a
letter to the secretary of state on September 1, 1643.[16]

The opposition party at Aix developed from the crown's attempts to force registration of edicts creating new judicial offices
—offices created in fiscal desperation. The crown had exceeded
its budget for the Habsburg War, and the finance minister wrote
on October 11, 1639, that he had raised 30,000,000 livres through
the sale of new judicial offices, but he needed 22,000,000 livres
more.[17] These new offices created dissatisfaction in Provence, beginning soon after the 1630 rebellion.

As punishment for its share in the cascaveoux revolt, the crown
sent the Parlement to Brignoles in 1631. The court sat there for
the first time on February 25.[18] Royal letters authorizing its return
to Aix were issued on April 28. But they were only presented for
registration by the intendant on October 21, three days after the

[12] Haitze, *Histoire*, IV, 328–329.

[13] F.A.T. Roux-Alphéran, *Les rues d'Aix ou recherches historiques sur
l'ancienne capitale de la Provence*, 2 vols. (Aix, 1846–1848), II, 24.

[14] B.M., *Parlement de Bordeaux* (1650), fol. 53, *Les pensées du provençal
solitaire*, p. 8; see Chapter Seven.

[15] B.N., Clairambault 395, fols. 138–141.

[16] A.A.E., 1708, fol. 241; B.N., Clairambault 388, fols. 18–21.

[17] Orest Ranum, *Richelieu and the Councillors of Louis XIII* (Oxford,
1963), pp. 137–139.

[18] Delib. Parl., B. Méjanes 952, fol. 8.

Parlement had returned to Aix.[19] The intendant had delayed presentation in a futile attempt to force the registration of a March edict creating eight new offices of councilor.[20]

The Parlement had already decided not to vote on the registration, and had sent Aubray a letter to this effect. He refused to allow the return to Aix until the edict had been verified and registered. As a counteroffensive, he went to the Cour des Comptes at Saint Maximin to obtain registration, but without success.[21] Returning to Aix without permission, the Parlement on November 5 refused to register the new edict and another edict creating two new councilors in each seneschal court in Provence.[22] The first edict was finally registered in 1636, after the number was reduced to four.[23] The Parlement steadfastly refused to register edicts creating two clerical councilors in the company[24] and two more seneschal courts in Provence.[25]

There was a major confrontation in March 1638. The crown demanded registration of an edict creating presidial courts at Aix, Forcalquier, and Draguignan.[26] Never before established in Provence, presidial courts were intermediary between the seneschal courts and the Parlement, whose members feared a reduction in case loads and profits from litigation. The Parlement flatly refused to register the edict. It was finally registered by the Grand Conseil at Paris on December 10, 1638.[27] A conciliar decree later in the month informed the Parlement that the Grand Conseil would

---

[19] *Ibid.*, fol. 70; ADBR, Aix, B 3348, fol. 598; "Table des lettres royaux," B. Méjanes 860, reg. 29, fol. 1033.

[20] ADBR, Aix, B 3351, fol. 82v; Honoré d'Agut, "Discours du Parlement de Provence," B. Méjanes 906, fol. 217.

[21] Philippe Tamizey de Larroque, ed., *Lettres de Peiresc aux frères Dupuy*, 7 vols. (Paris, 1888–1898), II, 282, May 23, 1631.

[22] Delib. Parl., B. Méjanes 952, fol. 74.

[23] B.N., Ms. fr. 24166, fol. 243; Agut, "Discours du Parlement," B. Méjanes 906, fol. 235; ADBR, Aix, B 3351, fols. 82v, 145, 162, 190, 195.

[24] Delib. Parl., B. Méjanes 951, fol. 444v; 952, fol. 75v.

[25] ADBR, Aix, B 3351, fol. 687; A.A.E., 1702, fols. 150–152; Lublinskaya, *Vnutrenniaia*, pp. 226–228, de La Potherie to Séguier, March 14, 1633; pp. 234–235, the same, May 23, 1633.

[26] Delib. Parl., B. Méjanes 952, fol. 344v; Agut, "Discours du Parlement," B. Méjanes 906, fols. 235–236.

[27] A.A.E., 1706, fol. 357.

administer the oath of loyalty to new presidial judges if the Parlement refused.[28]

In January 1639, first president Dubernet, accompanied by dean Périer and Enquêtes president Gallifet, carried to Paris a remonstrance on the presidial courts. Remonstrances had already been sent by the seneschal courts, the Estates, and the cities of Aix, Arles, and Marseille.[29] They made no difference. On March 26, the Parlement learned that former intendant Lauzon was arriving in two days at Forcalquier to sell thirty-two presidial offices. A few months later he went to Draguignan to establish the second court.[30] But he never came to Aix because Dubernet secretly negotiated the edict's revocation.

The negotiations were completed in July 1639. The Parlement accepted a host of minor offices in exchange for revocation of the presidial courts. The new creations included 189 conseillers auditeurs and experts jurés in the lower royal courts, 30 new burcaus of clerks for the communities, and a number of new judicial clerks.[31] Dubernet presented these edicts to the Parlement on October 12, and they were promptly registered the next day.[32] The Parlement agreed to accept these new offices, which it had refused ten years earlier, because they were less prejudicial to its interests than presidial courts.[33] It also agreed to register a 1638 edict creating inventory commissioners in the royal courts[34] and to accept eight new members (reduced to five at verification).[35]

To preserve its own interests, the Parlement willingly sacrificed the privileges and interests of others, in particular the procureurs du pays. It sought their help in offering the crown a rachat for

---

[28] ADBR, Aix, "Recueil d'édits," fol. 194.

[29] Delib. Parl., B. Méjanes 952, fol. 369; A.A.E., 1706, fol. 357.

[30] Delib. Parl., B. Méjanes 952, fols. 375–376; Agut, "Discours du Parlement," B. Méjanes 906, fols. 236–237; Pitton, *Histoire de la ville d'Aix*, p. 400.

[31] ADBR, Aix, B 3352, fols. 252, 287, 316v, 701v; A.A.E., 1706, fol. 357.

[32] Delib. Parl., B. Méjanes 952, fols. 396–396v; "Table des lettres royaux," B. Méjanes 860, reg. 33, fol. 1075.

[33] ADBR, Marseille, C 15, fol. 131.

[34] A.A.E., 1710, fols. 337–338.

[35] Delib. Parl., B. Méjanes 952, fols. 357–360v; Agut, "Discours du Parlement," B. Méjanes 906, fol. 239; ADBR, Aix, B 3351, fol. 677.

revocation, sending two deputies to the procureurs du pays on March 25, 1638, to request money and a joint remonstrance. First consul Espinouse and assessor Gaufridy were sent to Paris empowered to offer payment.[36] The procureurs du pays cooperated because they opposed elimination of their traditional privilege of becoming *juges nés des comptes tutélaires* two years after leaving office.[37] When the rachat was rejected, Dubernet secretly promised acceptance of the unpopular new offices if the crown would revoke the presidial courts.

The procureurs du pays learned of the creation of auditeurs and experts on October 12.[38] They immediately protested to the Parlement, demanding a joint remonstrance, but the edict was registered, anyway.[39] In November, the Parlement refused to show its registers to the procureurs du pays, probably because the secret negotiations were recorded.[40] Finally, the procureurs du pays asked the governor to convoke an Estates. A General Assembly of the Communities met at Fréjus in November 1639, but a conciliar decree in March annulled the assembly's declaration that the new offices were "prejudicial to the province in raising the cost of justice."[41]

The Parlement also betrayed the interests of the Cour des Comptes. The other sovereign court at Aix had many of the same grievances: a flood of new offices after 1631,[42] excessive augmentations des gages,[43] citation in disciplinary legislation.[44] Moreover, the jurisdiction of the Cour des Comptes had been seriously attacked by the Trésoriers Généraux, the intendants, and the new

---

[36] ADBR, Marseille, C 25, fols. 291–293.

[37] Charles de Grimaldi and Jacques Gaufridy, *Mémoires pour servir à l'histoire de la Fronde en Provence* (Aix, 1870), p. 232; B. Marseille 1792, *Très humbles remontrances du Parlement de Provence au Semestre de Janvier* (1650), p. 6.

[38] ADBR, Marseille, C 25, fol. 351.

[39] *Ibid.*, fols. 351v–353; Delib. Parl., B. Méjanes 952, fol. 396.

[40] ADBR, Marseille, C 26, fol. 13v.

[41] ADBR, Aix, B 3352, fol. 673; Delib. Parl., B. Méjanes 952, fol. 398v.

[42] ADBR, Marseille, C 15, fol. 131; Lublinskaya, *Vnutrenniaia*, pp. 226–228, de La Potherie to Séguier, March 14, 1633; A.A.E., 1702, fols. 150–152; EDB, III, 441.

[43] EDB, III, 439–447.

[44] Haitze, *Histoire*, IV, 200, 225; V, 418; Lublinskaya, *Vnutrenniaia*, pp. 299–300. Cour des Comptes magistrates were cited in 1631, 1645, and 1657.

Cour des Aides at Vienne.[45] Surprisingly, however, the magistrates of the Cour des Comptes did not support the parlementaires in their revolts. In fact, their names are conspicuously absent from the documents.[46] Why? The most likely reason was the traditional hostility between the two courts, which surfaced in the Parlement's registration on October 12, 1639, of three edicts (1626, 1627, 1633) transferring the Cour des Comptes's jurisdiction over the royal domaine to the Trésoriers Généraux. The Cour des Comptes had steadfastly refused these edicts and considered their registration a betrayal.[47] It retaliated by registering edicts creating a Chambre des Requêtes and a Semester in the Parlement.

Intendant Aubray exploited the mutual distrust in 1631 when he asked the Cour des Comptes at Saint Maximin to register an edict the Parlement had rejected. Their lack of unity again surfaced in 1634, when the Parlement refused to join the Cour des Comptes in protesting an increase in the gabelle and accepted the royal commissioner's letters it had refused.[48] The crown could not always profit from the rivalry between the two courts: both refused to register the edicts of the gabelle and auditeurs and experts in 1628–1629, the edict of élus in 1630, and the edict of lods et ventes in 1655–1657. But the crown was able to play off the sovereign courts enough to use their rivalry as a tactic in the battle over registrations, and to profit from their refusal to unite during the revolts.

The Parlement also sacrificed the interests of the seneschal courts. On October 12, 1639, it registered edicts of 1626 and 1632, creating two councilors in each seneschal court and two new seneschal courts at Sisteron and Castellane, ignoring vehement protest by the other seneschal courts.[49] This callousness had political repercussions. Few magistrates of the Aix seneschal court joined the parlementaires in the revolt of 1649. The Parlement

---

[45] See Chapters One, Two, Three, and Seven.

[46] The politics of the Aix Cour des Comptes and Trésoriers Généraux de France need investigation, although their deliberations do not seem to exist.

[47] Jean-Paul Charmeil, *Les trésoriers de France à l'époque de la Fronde* (Paris, 1964), p. 316; see Chapters One and Two.

[48] See Chapter Two.

[49] ADBR, Aix, B 3351, fol. 717; B 3352, fols. 275v, 305v; A.A.E., 1702, fols. 150–152. The seneschal courts at Digne and Forcalquier each offered 10,000 livres in rachat to the crown in 1637 to avoid the creation of the new seneschal court at Sisteron; cf. ADBR, Aix, B 3351, fol. 692v.

defended its own privileges and interests, showing no concern for those of the other royal courts at Aix, whom it did not hesitate to sacrifice. These retaliated in kind, and the crown profited from their disunity.

Joseph Dubernet, baron de Sérin and councilor in the Parlement of Bordeaux, was appointed first president of the Parlement of Aix on February 20, 1636 through the patronage of Henri d'Escoubleau de Sourdis, archbishop of Bordeaux.[50] Dubernet was unpopular because he halted rambling speakers, although he permitted long trials.[51] Dubernet was accused of investing money in traitant Daunila's sale of offices of auditeurs and experts at Aix in July 1639.[52] Lauzon, unaware, was still selling offices in the presidial court at Draguignan.[53] The parlementaires disliked Dubernet's presumption in secretly negotiating another creation of new offices.

The opposition included Forbin de La Roque, Boyer, Leidet-Sigoyer, and Guiran. Their dissatisfaction focused on Dubernet.[54] Leidet-Sigoyer and Arnaud were suspended from office by lettre de cachet in July 1638 for giving negative opinions on registering the edict of presidial courts.[55] These two councilors were again suspended from office on November 22, 1639, with second president Forbin de La Roque, presidents of the Enquêtes Guiran and Gallifet, avocat-général Decormis, and dean Périer for giving negative opinions on registering the edicts revoking the presidial courts and establishing the auditeurs and experts. The suspensions were "founded on what the King has been given to understand, that various actions and intrigues are occurring in this company against the service of His Majesty."[56] Five of the cited parlementaires had

[50] ADBR, Aix, B 3350, fol. 746; B.N., Dupuy 672, fol. 148; 754, fols. 218–219; Haitze, *Histoire*, IV, 277.

[51] Pierre-Joseph de Haitze, "Histoire de Provence sous le gouvernement du comte d'Alais," B. Méjanes 736, fols. 15–16.

[52] Pierre-Joseph de Haitze, *Portraits ou éloges historiques des premiers présidents du Parlement de Provence* (Avignon, 1727), p. 113; Grimaldi and Gaufridy, *Mémoires*, p. 228;

[53] Delib. Parl., B. Méjanes 952, fol. 398v.

[54] B.M., Harleian 4575, "Semestre de Provence par M. de Sève," fols. 3–3v.

[55] Delib. Parl., B. Méjanes 952, fols. 361–362, 367. They were restored to office on December 7, 1638.

[56] *Ibid.*, fol. 399v; A.A.E., 1705, fol. 308.

participated in the cascaveoux revolt. They were Forbin de La Roque, Boyer, Leidet-Sigoyer, Decormis, and Périer.[57]

First president Dubernet's portrait shows a strong brow and determined chin. He was described as a capable but stubborn magistrate.[58] Governor Alais was an open enemy of Dubernet after their wives quarreled in 1640.[59] Their enmity worsened the Parlement's factionalism. Alais announced himself in favor of a new chamber in the Parlement in exchange for revocation of Dubernet's auditeurs and experts.[60] He complained to Paris in May 1642 that Dubernet was dividing the Parlement, attempting to usurp the governor's authority, and exerting undue influence over the intendant. He alleged that Dubernet was misrepresenting provincial conditions in his reports to Paris.[61] Régusse noted in his memoirs that Alais requested Dubernet's dismissal from the king at Perpignan and from Richelieu at Tarascon in 1642.[62] The Parlement had been complaining about its first president since 1640.[63]

The governor may have considered replacing Dubernet with his rival, second president Forbin de La Roque. But the second president refused to accompany Alais to Tarascon in 1642, thus losing his chance for appointment.[64] Dubernet was sent to Bourges by lettre de cachet on June 26, 1642, and resigned his office shortly thereafter. Dubernet later became first president of the Parlement of Bordeaux.[65] Forbin de La Roque, an opposition leader, became acting first president of the Aix Parlement.

The hostility and dissatisfaction among the parlementaires of Aix intensified in the 1640s. In January 1641, the crown issued

---

[57] Périer died while at Paris serving as the Parlement's deputy.

[58] Jacques Cundier, *Portrait des premiers présidents du Parlement* (Aix, 1724), p. 45, B. Méjanes 963.

[59] Pitton, *Histoire de la ville d'Aix*, pp. 401–402.

[60] B.M., Harleian 4575, fol. 4; Grimaldi and Gaufridy, *Mémoires*, pp. 15–16.

[61] A.A.E., 1708, fols. 9–10, 73.

[62] Grimaldi and Gaufridy, *Mémoires*, p. 19.

[63] Haitze, *Histoire*, IV, 390.      [64] *Ibid.*, 391.

[65] Henri Thourel, *Jacques de Gaufridi et le Semestre de Provence* (Aix, 1880), p. 38; Pierre-Adolphe Chéruel and Georges d'Avenel, *Lettres du cardinal Mazarin pendant son ministère*, 9 vols. (1872–1906), I, 289–290, August 19, 1643, Mazarin to Alais.

an edict creating a new chamber in the Parlement similar to those already at Paris and Rouen, while another edict abolished the auditeurs and experts. The Chambre des Requêtes had two presidents, fourteen councilors, one procureur-général, and twenty-one lesser personnel. Sale of the new offices was expected to bring the crown 370,000 livres.[66]

The joint meeting on January 11 to register this edict was canceled when the Grand'Chambre would not attend, announcing that its presidents were absent from the palace.[67] The next day Du Chaine, Foresta de La Roquette, Forbin de La Roque, Arnaud, Leidet-Sigoyer, Gautier, Ballon, Oppède, and Signier declared they were sick and would not attend the joint meeting, which voted against registration.[68] Forbin de La Roque, Leidet-Sigoyer, and Gautier had been cascaveoux. A remonstrance was sent on January 23.[69] Deputies were sent to Paris—Thomassin, Valbelle, Lombard, Foresta, and Porcellet—but their mission was futile. The council of state had already issued a decree forbidding the Parlement to assemble or to send deputies, in an unsuccessful attempt to block a remonstrance.[70] The crown then sent a lettre de cachet forbidding the Parlement to remonstrate on the edict or decree. Councilors Laurens and Antelmi were suspended from office for giving negative opinions on registration;[71] Antelmi had been cited in 1631 and Laurens in 1638–1649.

[66] ADBR, Aix, B 3353, fol. 61; "Recueil d'édits," fols. 203–210; ADBR, Marseille, C 2053, fol. 180; B. Marseille 1792, *Très humbles remontrances du Parlement de Provence au Semestre de Janvier* (1650), p. 16.

[67] Grimaldi and Gaufridy, *Mémoires*, p. 150. There were 31 parlementaires present on January 4, 1641, when the court learned of the new edict. There were only 10 parlementaires present on January 11, when its registration was discussed; cf. ADBR, Aix, B 3666; Delib. Parl., B. Méjanes 952, fol. 424v. Alais and Vautorte described the registration in "Relation de ce qui s'est passée au parlement de provence sur la presentation de l'Edit de la Chambre des Requêtes au mois de mars 1641," B. Apt, "Collection sur la Provence," pièce 30, unpaginated.

[68] ADBR, Aix, J.L.H. Hesmivy de Moissac, "Histoire du Parlement de Provence, 1501–1715," 2 vols., II, 4–5; Delib. Parl., B. Méjanes 952, fol. 426.

[69] Delib. Parl., B. Méjanes 952, fols. 430v–433v.

[70] *Ibid.*, fols. 436–436v; B. Apt, pièce 30, "Relation." Alais gives the dates of the lettre de cachet forbidding the court to send deputies and a remonstrance as January 25 and February 4.

[71] Delib. Parl., B. Méjanes 952, fols. 437v–439v.

On March 3, 1641, governor Alais summoned the presidents and royal attorneys to his hôtel to inform them that he had again received the edict from Paris. He was ordered to register it immediately, and intendant Vautorte was ordered to record the names of dissenters. The next day the Parlement sent Forbin de La Roque and Decormis to the governor to request a copy of the edict for verification. Alais indicated there was no hope of modifying or refusing it.

On March 8, Alais and Vautorte delivered a lettre de cachet assembling the Parlement. The atmosphere was tense in the grande salle. Angry, feuding with first president Dubernet, Alais was determined to register the edict. The Tournelle and Enquêtes protested that the chambers could not legally be assembled because joint sessions had been prohibited by royal letters and a conciliar decree that had not been revoked. The Enquêtes, as the youngest chamber, was particularly agitated, fearing financial ruin with the addition of another chamber.[72] The Parlement's secretary Estienne and his clerk Bonnet refused to read the edict aloud and walked out of the palace of justice. They were later sent to the prisons of Fort l'Evêque.[73]

Alais announced that he had been warned of an attempt by "the cabal against the edict" to forestall its registration by obstructing the reading. The Tournelle and Enquêtes cried out their support of Estienne. Alexandre Thomassin, who was chosen because he had already resigned his office in favor of his son—the confiscation of Coriolis's office was still fresh in everyone's mind—stated the opposition's case "with great passion," interrupting Alais with "contempt and insolence." Decormis, for the royal attorneys, recommended a remonstrance. They prepared to leave the grande salle but were stopped by the warning that Vautorte was recording the names of those who refused the edict. A vote was held. Presidents Du Chaine, Forbin de La Roque, Foresta de La Roquette, de Paule, dean Boyer, councilors Gautier, Ballon, Leidet-Fombeton, Arnaud, Mazargues, and Villeneuve of the Grand'Chambre, with Enquêtes president Gallifet, were the only ones to vote for registration. Paule made a long speech advising obedience. But

[72] *Ibid.*; Agut, "Discours du Parlement," B. Méjanes 906, fols. 259–265; B. Apt, pièce 30, "Relation."

[73] Delib. Parl., B. Méjanes 952, fols. 457–457v; ADBR, Aix, B 3353, fol. 74; B. Apt, pièce 30, "Relation."

the Tournelle and Enquêtes carried the vote and opposed registration. Their names were recorded by Alais and Vautorte. They voted for another remonstrance.[74]

The governor then ordered acting first president Du Chaine (who died a few months later) to send for a clerk to register the edict. There was loud booing and hissing from the Tournelle and Enquêtes, who refused to allow the clerk to enter the grande salle. Alais was furious. Speechless with rage, he stormed from the room to have his secretary, Germain de Volleronde, register the edict, assisted by the intendant. Alais then issued an ordinance forbidding the Parlement to assemble or send deputies to the king. On March 10, Alais wrote Richelieu that he wanted all members of the Tournelle and Enquêtes suspended, the offices of secretary Estienne and councilors Thomassin, Antelmi, and Laurens permanently suppressed as "chiefs of the cabal," Estienne and his clerk imprisoned, and Volleronde's registration declared valid by royal letters and a conciliar decree.[75]

Richelieu did not go this far, but he sent a conciliar decree on March 30 declaring the governor's registration valid if the Parlement refused to register the edict. He also suspended from the office fourteen of the opposition parlementaires who had defiantly voted no. They were Alexandre and Jean-Baptiste Thomassin, Marc-Antoine d'Albert, Charles de Lombard, Henri de Forbin-Maynier d'Oppède, François Thomassin, César Milan, Jean-Baptiste de Valbelle, Jacques d'André, Gaspard de Cauvet, Jean d'Arbaud, Louis de Saint Marc, François de Périer (son of the deceased dean), and Pierre de Barrême.[76] Ten belonged to the Chambre des Enquêtes. Only five went to Paris, returning on January 2, 1642, with royal letters and a conciliar decree restoring them all to office.[77]

The Parlement insisted that the new chamber did not exist because the joint meeting on March 8 was illegal, prohibited by royal

[74] Pierre Louvet, "Histoire du Parlement de Provence," B. Méjanes R.A. 53, fols. 397–399; B. Apt, pièce 30, "Relation."

[75] A.A.E., 1707, fol. 268.

[76] ADBR, Aix, B 3353, fols. 74, 336; A.A.E., 1707, fols. 268, 328; Grimaldi and Gaufridy, *Mémoires*, pp. 132, 153.

[77] ADBR, Aix, B 3353, fol. 336; Grimaldi and Gaufridy, *Mémoires*, p. 157. Councilors Antelmi, Laurens, Oppède, Cauvet, and Barrême went to Paris.

letters and an unrevoked conciliar decree. The edict creating the Requêtes had not been verified, and its registration by the governor's secretary was illegal. Its registration by the Parlement on April 15 was forced—the Parlement had consented because it feared to set the precedent of registration by the governor. It protested the registration on April 23.[78] Alais sought harsher punishment.[79]

Opposition to the new chamber was intense. President Foresta de La Roquette wrote Séguier on August 24, 1643, that he and five or six of the oldest councilors were willing to accept the Requêtes, but the rest of the court refused adamantly.[80] Detaching itself from the intrigues surrounding Dubernet, the opposition focused on fighting the Requêtes. It began a campaign of petty insults and harassments. It delayed reception of members and evoked cases so the new chamber had nothing to do, refused to allow the Requêtes to attend joint meetings or public ceremonies in red robes, and would not permit the transfer of Requêtes judges into other chambers without examination and loss of rank, as if they were joining the company for the first time.

The Chambre des Enquêtes became the heart of the opposition. Régusse, an opposition leader, wrote in his memoirs that he and friends in the Enquêtes voted together in joint meetings. This allowed them to dominate meetings, since the other chambers were split into factions. Régusse wrote:

I was working, therefore, in order that the Chambre des Enquêtes became the most important of the palace because intrigue divided the others in different inclinations and particular interests, while this one was united with one voice and we always agreed in joint meetings. We had as a goal not to engage in the intrigues of governor Alais and first president Dubernet, but to declare ourselves for what appeared most advantageous for the dignity of the company and the good of the province.[81]

Political activism among the younger magistrates also characterized the Parlements of Paris, Rouen, and Bordeaux, where the

---

[78] Delib. Parl., B. Méjanes 952, fol. 441; Grimaldi and Gaufridy, *Mémoires*, p. 153; Agut, "Discours du Parlement," B. Méjanes 906, fols. 265–275; A.A.E., 1707, fol. 328.

[79] A.A.E., 1707, fols. 281–282.

[80] Lublinskaya, *Vnutrenniaia*, p. 257.

[81] Grimaldi and Gaufridy, *Mémoires*, p. 16.

Chambre des Enquêtes was more radical than the older Grand'-Chambre.[82]

Two offices of president and twelve offices of councilor in the Requêtes were sold by August 1641. The new members were not received until a year later, despite royal letters and conciliar decrees ordering their immediate reception. Two offices of councilor and the office of procureur-général did not sell. Insisting the new chamber did not exist, the Parlement would not permit the customary reception before a joint meeting in the grande salle. The new members were received in the glacial atmosphere of the salle dorée before a substitute procureur-général, his assistant, two councilors, and intendant Vautorte.[83] "Insolent," "crazy," "thief," and "partisan" reverberated around the room during the reception in May 1642.[84] The Requêtes was assigned the salle des pas perdus, a noisy waiting room at the head of the main staircase, and its members were forbidden to enter the other courtrooms.[85]

The Requêtes was never summoned to joint meetings. Whenever it appeared, the other magistrates left, saying the agenda was finished.[86] Attendance would have meant recognition of the chamber's existence. Intendant Vautorte reported to Séguier and Mazarin on June 2, 1643, that the other chambers refused to summon the Requêtes to swear oaths of loyalty to the new king, insisting they were not members of the company or even royal officials. The Requêtes swore their oaths after the others had left.[87]

A conciliar decree in April 1642—registered eighteen months later—ordered the Requêtes's full participation in the court.[88] It was ignored. The Requêtes was regularly excluded from public ceremonies in red robes, as the governor wrote the secretary of

[82] Monique Cubells, "Le Parlement de Paris pendant la Fronde," *XVII*ᵉ *siècle*, 35 (1957), 172; A. Lloyd Moote, *The Revolt of the Judges: The Parlement of Paris during the Fronde, 1643–1652* (Princeton, 1971), p. 100; Sal Westreich, *The Ormée of Bordeaux: A Revolution during the Fronde* (Baltimore, 1972), pp. 4, 13; Paul Logié, *La Fronde en Normandie*, 3 vols. (Amiens, 1951), II, 11–12, 50.

[83] A.A.E., 1707, fol. 286, Alais to Richelieu, August 24, 1641; Agut, "Discours du Parlement," B. Méjanes 906, fols. 284–320; Louvet, "Histoire du Parlement," B. Méjanes R.A. 53, fols. 400–401; ADBR, Aix, B 3353, fol. 340v.

[84] B.N., Ms. fr. 18976, fols. 173–182.

[85] *Ibid.*, fols. 425–433.          [86] *Ibid.*

[87] Lublinskaya, *Vnutrenniaia*, pp. 249–250; A.A.E., 1708, fol. 183.

[88] B.N., Ms. fr. 18976, fol. 417; ADBR, Aix, B 3354, fol. 304.

state on September 1, 1643.[89] The Parlement sent deputies in black robes of the Vacations to avoid including the new chamber.[90] The Requêtes was not summoned to accompany the court to the mass celebrating the Gravelines victory.[91] The new chamber was regularly excluded from the Fête Dieu, the parlementaires claiming there was not enough space in the choir of Saint Sauveur.[92] The Parlement threatened the canons of Saint Sauveur with a boycott if the new chamber were invited to the archbishop's funeral in 1644.[93]

The opposition emptied the Requêtes's judicial calendar and evoked its cases to the Grand'Chambre and Tournelle.[94] Champigny wrote Séguier on December 8, 1643, that the other chambers were transacting almost no business, to force the Requêtes into idleness. He wrote that they spent their time intriguing, and the Parlement was so divided and disordered that it had ceased to function.[95] This charge was not without foundation: a side effect of the campaign against the Requêtes was the Parlement's near paralysis. The assembled chambers adjourned meetings with an unfinished agenda whenever the Requêtes appeared, scheduling meetings later, and disrupting the court calendar. Jacques Gaufridy reported that Dubernet refused to distribute cases for ten months after the parlementaires were suspended in March 1641 so they would not lose their share of judicial fees. When the suspensions were lifted, the Parlement was eight-hundred cases in arrears.[96]

Evocations disrupted the court's functioning. On February 24, 1643, Gaufridy wrote Séguier thanking him for a conciliar decree

[89] B.N., Clairambault 388, fols. 18–21.

[90] B.N., Clairambault 393, fols. 234–236, Champigny to Brienne, May 19, 1644; 388, fols. 111–114, Alais to Brienne, September 5 and 8, 1643.

[91] Grimaldi and Gaufridy, *Mémoires*, pp. 159–160; B.N., Ms. fr. 17380, fols. 132–133, Champigny to Séguier, September 13, 1644, fols. 156–157, Gaufridy to Séguier, September 20, 1644.

[92] B.N., Ms. fr. 17388, fols. 19–20, Gaufridy to Séguier, May 25, 1648; 17376, fol. 38, Parlement to Séguier, June 10, 1643; B.N., Clairambault 393, fols. 354–355, Champigny to Brienne, May 30, 1644; 405, fols. 486–488, Champigny to Brienne, May 26, 1644.

[93] *Ibid.* 17381, fols. 154–155, Gaufridy to Séguier, April 15, 1644; 17380, fols. 156–157, Gaufridy to Séguier, September 20, 1644.

[94] B.N., Ms. fr. 18976, fols. 425–426.

[95] Lublinskaya, *Vnutrenniaia*, pp. 265–266.

[96] Grimaldi and Gaufridy, *Mémoires*, p. 158.

preventing the Enquêtes from judging a case belonging to the Requêtes, adding that "because of the open hate which the Parlement shows, there is no one in Aix who dares to plead before us if it is possible to go before other judges."[97] In a memoir of February 1647, the Requêtes cited three evocations of its cases to other chambers, two to the Aix seneschal court, and five exclusions from joint meetings within six months.[98]

The Parlement refused to permit the transfer of Requêtes members to other chambers without loss of rank and a new examination. There was a nasty seating dispute during the reception into the Tournelle of Requêtes councilor Clapiers de Puget on December 15, 1643.[99] Eighteen months and nearly thirty royal letters and conciliar decrees were necessary to transfer Requêtes councilor Tressemanes-Chasteuil into the Enquêtes.[100] He was finally received on June 13, 1645, after being tricked into taking an examination and given the lowest rank in the Parlement, which he only kept after the 1649 revolt by paying 200 pistoles.[101] Charles de Tabaret, president of the Enquêtes, was cited to court by lettre de cachet in 1645 for objecting to the reception. Intendant Champigny named Antelmi, Laurens, Louis Decormis, Régusse, and Forbin de La Roque as cascaveoux and leaders of the party refusing to accept the Requêtes.[102]

[97] B.N., Ms. fr. 17376, fols. 9–10.

[98] *Ibid.* 18976, fols. 195–197.

[99] B.N., Ms. fr. 17376, fols. 107–112, Régusse to Séguier, December 15, 1643, fols. 114–115; Champigny to Séguier, December 15, 1643; B.N., Ms. fr. 18976, fols. 629–630; B.N., Clairambault 390, fols. 176–182, Régusse to Brienne, December 15, 1643; fols. 231–232, Champigny to Brienne, December 22, 1643; Lublinskaya, *Vnutrenniaia*, p. 266, Foresta de La Roquette to Séguier, December 22, 1643.

[100] B.N., Ms. fr. 17383, fols. 91–92, Tressemanes to Séguier, February 7, 1645; fols. 160–161, Gaufridy to Séguier, March 7, 1645; fols. 218–219, Gantès to Séguier, April 4, 1645; Lublinskaya, *Vnutrenniaia*, pp. 297–298, Tressemanes to Séguier, April 14, 1645.

[101] Lublinskaya, *Vnutrenniaia*, pp. 302–303, Tressemanes to Séguier, June 13, 1645, p. 302, Champigny the same, pp. 300–301, Mesgrigny the same; ADBR, Aix, Moissac, "Histoire du Parlement," II, 148.

[102] ADBR, Aix, Moissac, "Histoire du Parlement," II, 60–61; B.N., Clairambault 390, fols. 231–232, December 22, 1643; 393, fols. 128–130, June 21, 1644; fols. 338–341, May 29, 1644; 394, fols. 354–355, May 30, 1644; Mousnier, *Lettres*, I, 619–620, January 19, 1644; Lublinskaya, *Vnutrenniaia*, p. 269, February 1, 1644, pp. 271–274, February 14, 1644.

Parlementaires cited in disciplinary legislation did not always go to Paris, although they did not appear at the palace of justice. Only five of the fourteen cited in 1641 went to Paris, one of the four cited in 1643, and two of the eleven cited in 1645. They sent excuses based on the distance and expense, their health and personal affairs. The crown did not force their appearance.

The Requêtes was excluded from the reception of Charles de Grimaldi-Régusse as president in the summer of 1643. As a result, four lettres de cachet were issued calling Régusse, Valbelle, Lombard, and (François) Thomassin to Paris for explanations. Valbelle and Thomassin had already been cited in 1641. On November 3, Champigny wrote that none had left Aix. He recommended their suspension from office until they went to Paris.[103] Régusse finally went in 1644 to obtain their restoration.[104]

Ten parlementaires were suspended from office and called to Paris on July 13, 1645, because the Vacations Chamber had arrested two *archers* executing the intendant's orders. Cited were first president Mesgrigny, avocat-général Decormis, presidents Forbin de La Roque and Régusse, councilor Guérin of the Grand'Chambre, councilors Oppède, Saint Marc, Périer, Signier, and Raffelis of the Enquêtes.[105] Régusse, Oppède, Saint Marc, Raffelis, and Signier had been cited in May for conspiring to exclude the Requêtes from the Fête Dieu procession.[106] Only Régusse and Oppède went to Paris in January 1646 to obtain restoration.[107]

Absenteeism was a chronic problem, as attendance records of joint meetings demonstrate. One-half of the court's membership was usually absent from the palace of justice.[108] One-third was

[103] Grimaldi and Gaufridy, *Mémoires*, p. 21; ADBR, Aix, B 3354, fol. 103; B.N., Ms. fr. 17376, fols. 47–49, Régusse to Séguier, August 2, 1643; Mousnier, *Lettres* I, 590–591, Champigny to Séguier, August 8, 1643; B.N., Clairambault 389, fols. 238–239, Champigny to Brienne, November 3, 1643; Lublinskaya, *Vnutrenniaia*, Champigny to Séguier, November 3, 1643.

[104] Grimaldi and Gaufridy, *Mémoires*, p. 22.

[105] Delib. Parl., B. Méjanes 953, fol. 143; Grimaldi and Gaufridy, *Mémoires*, pp. 162–164; A.A.E., 1710, fol. 190; B.N., Ms. fr. 18976, fols. 633–642; A.N., E 1689, fol. 109, conciliar decree of July 12, 1645. Forbin de La Roque's name is missing from the list of cited parlementaires in Grimaldi and Gaufridy and B.N., Ms. fr. 18976. Raffelis's name is missing from Delib. Parl., B. Méjanes 953.

[106] B.N., Ms. fr. 18976, fols. 633–642.

[107] Delib. Parl., B. Méjanes 953, fols. 165, 168v–169.

[108] ADBR, Aix, B 3663–3668.

always absent. Those attending were often incompetent. The essential work was done by a dedicated minority of parlementaires, as shown by the first president's memoir on the company for Colbert in 1663. Of seven presidents, Oppède praised only two: Régusse as "knowledgeable about judicial affairs" and Forbin de La Roque as "dedicated to his profession." Second president Foresta de La Roquette was "weak and without spirit or intelligence, a good servant of the King whom one can lead where one wants." President Coriolis-Villeneuve was "a man of good family, the brother-in-law of Forbin de La Roque, not highly intelligent in law, would be capable of harm but behaves well at present." President Du Chaine "did not leave his house more than once a year if he was not presiding at the Parlement." President Thomas de La Garde was described as "a young man who has never been a councilor . . . without experience." President Simiane de La Coste "did not yet count for anything." Maynier d'Oppède heavily criticized the councilors, too.[109]

The opposition obtained a voting majority because of the high absentee rate. It was easy for a small group of political activists who attended regularly, spoke freely, and voted as a bloc to dominate joint meetings, particularly if they could attract the support of uncommitted members. Attendance at meetings in the 1640s averaged about thirty parlementaires, excluding the Requêtes. This was one-half of the 1640 membership of fifty-nine parlementaires. An opposition bloc of about fifteen parlementaires, most of whom were members of the Enquêtes, regularly attended and were cited by the crown in disciplinary legislation for their negative opinions.[110]

The support of the company's officers had psychological value. The first and second presidents, the first avocat-général and dean were members of the opposition. They voted first. The first president convened joint meetings over which he presided, replaced

[109] B.N., Mélanges de Colbert 7, fols. 49–55; G. B. Depping, *Correspondance administrative sous le règne de Louis XIV*, 4 vols. (Paris, 1851), II, 94–96.

[110] ADBR, Aix, B 3666, 1639–1648. The Parlement of Rouen after the creation of its semester in 1641 (suppressed in 1643 and reestablished in 1645) was divided into quarreling factions of *anciens* and *nouveaux* parlementaires. Mazarin feared that the disaffected anciens officiers, many of whom were members of the Chambre des Enquêtes, would rebel; cf. Logié, *La Fronde en Normandie*, I, 100–110.

during absences by the second president. The first avocat-général
at Aix had the highest rank of the royal attorneys, while the dean
was the councilor with the longest service. The crown expected
help in controlling the Parlement from the first president, whose
office was not venal. Since the first president usually presided over
the Grand'Chambre, where routine legislation was registered, his
support made it easier for the crown to obtain registration. The
younger councilors requested joint meetings to discuss controversial registrations, and tried to influence the voting by their
eloquence.

Four of the first presidents of Aix in the early seventeenth century were royal commissioners and intendants of justice: Guillaume Du Vair, Hélie de Laisné, Jean de Mesgrigny, and Henri
de Forbin-Maynier d'Oppède.[111] First presidents such as Oppède
were valuable to the crown when they could control the Parlement
and remain on good terms with the governor, while Laisné, Dubernet, and Mesgrigny were replaced because they could not.
Laisné resigned in 1635 after the Parlement's conflicts with governor Vitry, although the official reason was his intention to become
a priest, and he was serving as intendant of justice at Grenoble
in April 1638.[112]

Mesgrigny, formerly intendant in Auvergne and the Bourbon-
nais, was chosen first president upon the recommendation of his
old friend Champigny and governor Alais.[113] But soon after his
arrival at Aix in the summer of 1644, Mesgrigny came under the
influence of opposition leader Forbin de La Roque.[114] On March
14, 1645, Champigny wrote to Séguier, "It is necessary to make

[111] Mousnier, *Lettres*, I, 88; II, 1204–1205, 1221–1223.

[112] Richard Bonney, "The Intendants of Richelieu and Mazarin, 1624–
1661" (Ph.D. dissertation, Oxford University, 1973), p. 343; Cundier,
*Portraits*, B. Méjanes 963, p. 42; ADBR, Aix, B 3349, fol. 509; B.N., Dupuy
562, fol. 122; J.L.H. Hesmivy de Moissac, "Difficultés entre le Parlement
et les diverses autorités," B. Méjanes 936, fols. 471–477.

[113] Cundier, *Portraits*, B. Méjanes, 963, p. 48; B.N., Clairambault 388,
fols. 18–21, Alais to Brienne, September 1, 1643; 393, fols. 54–56, Alais
to Brienne, April 16, 1644; Mousnier, *Lettres*, I, 590, and Lublinskaya,
*Vnutrenniaia*, pp. 255–256, Champigny to Séguier, July 28, 1643; B.N.,
Clairambault 394, fols. 128–130, Champigny to Séguier, June 21, 1644.
Mesgrigny's provision letters as first president were dated September 17,
1644; cf. ADBR, Aix, B 3354, fol. 440.

[114] B.N., Clairambault 394, fols. 128–130, Champigny to Brienne, June
21, 1644.

known to the first president that his present conduct and the contempt in which he holds conciliar decrees are injurious to royal authority and of very perilous consequences for his service."[115] Alais criticized Mesgrigny's conduct in a letter to Séguier on June 17; so did Requêtes president Gaufridy on March 7.[116] Mesgrigny explained that he was only trying to unite a divided parlement and serve the king obediently.[117] But he was cited in disciplinary legislation in 1645 and 1648. Mesgrigny's loyalty had shifted to the company he had joined, and he had ceased to be a valuable servant. The royal attorneys were not reliable. The procureurs-généraux who presented edicts for registration supported the crown, but first avocat-général Pierre Decormis and his son Louis participated in all three revolts, while avocats-généraux Galaup-Chasteuil and Gautier were rebels in 1659.

The opposition parlementaires used several tactics to evade unwanted edicts. They delayed presentation and voting on registration. On December 20, 1644, Champigny wrote to the secretary of state that since he could not find a royal attorney willing to present a disciplinary decree for registration he would have to do it himself.[118] On May 19, 1644, the intendant wrote that he had tried unsuccessfully for a week to have a joint meeting scheduled.[119] In January 1648, the first president and royal attorneys refused to schedule or attend a meeting to register the edict creating the Semester.[120]

If a joint meeting was scheduled, the opposition could force its cancellation by refusing to attend or vote, thus failing to obtain a quorum. Refusal was termed *faire religion* and was tried unsuccessfully by Régusse on April 19, 1644.[121] Kinship was often used to force cancellations: parlementaires could excuse themselves from attendance if they were close relatives of a litigant or candidate. At

[115] Lublinskaya, *Vnutrenniaia*, p. 295.

[116] *Ibid.*, p. 303; B.N., Ms. fr. 17383, fols. 160–161.

[117] Lublinskaya, *Vnutrenniaia*, pp. 298–299, Mesgrigny to Séguier, May 2, 1645.

[118] B.N., Clairambault 396, fols. 307–309.

[119] *Ibid.*, 393, fols. 234–236.

[120] Delib. Parl., B. Méjanes 953, fols. 190–197v; B.M., Harleian 4575, fols. 10v–17v.

[121] B.N., Clairambault 393, fols. 83–86, Régusse to Brienne, April 19, 1644.

the joint meeting on October 23, 1645, to receive Lazare Du Chaine as president, about twenty-five parlementaires excused themselves for reasons of kinship. They opposed Du Chaine because he was only twenty-three, with one year's experience in the new seneschal court at Castellane; he had received letters of dispensation for age and service. The meeting was cancelled because the remaining twelve councilors were not a quorum.[122] Councilors Glandèves, Clapiers de Puget, Barrême, and Aymar d'Albi of the Enquêtes were called before a mercuriale for not attending meetings on November 21 and 22, 1645, to receive Forbin de La Roque's son, a Requêtes councilor, as president en survivance. Glandèves and Clapiers excused themselves as the candidate's first cousin. Barrême said that his nephew was the candidate's brother-in-law. Aymar d'Albi announced that he was first cousin to Barrême's nephew.[123]

The crown sent royal letters and conciliar decrees ordering immediate registration, but the distance between Aix and Paris allowed the parlementaires to ignore these more openly than they might otherwise have done. Lettres d'attache often accompanied the edict, verified its validity, and ordered the royal attorneys to present it at once for registration. These were followed by lettres de jussion with the written effect of a lit de justice, a direct command by the king to register an edict. Five or six lettres de jussion could be sent. Finally, lettres de cachet or disciplinary decrees of the council of state were delivered by the intendant of justice, who harangued the assembly on the consequences of refusing registration. The edict of October 1632 creating two new seneschal courts in Provence was registered six years later, in October 1638—after eight royal letters and three conciliar decrees ordering registration.[124] On November 8, 1644, Requêtes councilor Tressemanes wrote to the secretary of state that, "All the decrees of the council, lettres de jussion, and lettres de cachet seem to make no difference."[125] Tressemanes wrote to Séguier on February 7, 1645, that

---

[122] *Ibid.*, fols. 405–407; Mousnier, *Lettres*, II, 792; Lublinskaya, *Vnutrenniaia*, pp. 310–311. Royal letters on August 11, 1645, and February 26, 1646, ordered Du Chaine's reception; he was received in 1646; cf. ADBR, Aix, B 3355, fols. 585, 586v, 587v.

[123] B.N., Ms. fr. 18976, fols. 395–402.

[124] ADBR, Aix, B 3351, fols. 687, 700v, 703, 704, 706v, 709, 711, 713, 716; "Table des lettres royaux," B. Méjanes 860 reg. 32, fol. 1071.

[125] B.N., Clairambault 396, fols. 29–31.

fifteen months of conciliar decrees had no effect on the Parlement.[126] On April 4, procureur-général Gantès wrote that a conciliar decree and royal letters of March 2 ordering Tressemanes's immediate reception into the Enquêtes had been presented to the Parlement and registered without effect.[127]

The crown might order the Parlement to sit through a summer recess until an edict was registered, as it did in the summer of 1628 to force registration of the edict of auditeurs and experts.[128] In June 1631, the Parlement at Brignoles was ordered to sit through the summer until it registered the creation of eight new councilors.[129] In July 1638, the Parlement was ordered by royal letters to sit until the edict of the presidial courts was registered.[130] On all three occasions, the Parlement sat through the summer and refused to register the edicts. On May 23, 1633, intendant de La Potherie recommended to Séguier that he refuse the Parlement the right to consider other cases and adjourn for the summer recess until it registered the creation of eight new offices.[131]

The opposition subverted this tactic by delaying presentation until summer, because the Vacations Chamber could not register edicts. The maneuver postponed registration until autumn. It was successfully used in May 1633 and June 1643.[132] On July 29, 1644, a royal attorney presented to the Vacations a conciliar decree ordering Tressemanes's immediate reception. Replying that it did not have authority to register letters of provision or receive new members, the chamber postponed reception until the Parlement reconvened in the autumn—although the Vacations had received president Régusse into office the previous summer.[133]

As additional pressure, the crown refused to pay gages for obligatory sessions. It refused to pay gages for the 1628 summer session, and councilor de Paule was sent to Paris in May 1632

---

[126] B.N., Ms. fr. 17383, fols. 91–92.

[127] *Ibid.*, fols. 218–219.  [128] ADBR, Aix, B 3347, fol. 1187.

[129] *Ibid.*, B 3348, fol. 558v.  [130] *Ibid.*, B 3351, fols. 510, 642.

[131] Lublinskaya, *Vnutrenniaia*, pp. 234–235, de La Potherie to Séguier, May 23, 1633.

[132] *Ibid.*, pp. 250–251, Champigny to Séguier, June 6, 1643.

[133] B.N., Clairambault 394, fols. 317–319, Champigny to Brienne, August 9, 1644; A.A.E., 1709, fol. 129, extract from registers of Parlement, June 14, 1644; B.N., Ms. fr. 17376, fols. 47–49, Régusse to Séguier, August 2, 1643.

to protest nonpayment of gages for the summer of 1631.[134] Gallifet was sent to Paris in July 1632 to protest unpaid gages of suspended parlementaires for the court during the summer recess of 1628 and from March to October 1631, when the Parlement was at Brignoles.[135] The crown did not pay gages to the anciens officiers in 1648, when they did not sit.[136]

The Parlement could delay voting on an edict by prolonging discussion on registration. Intendant Champigny wrote Séguier on June 14, 1644, that the joint meeting called to register the transfer of the Hyères seneschal court to Toulon had spent several hours listening to objections to avoid voting.[137] His charge was confirmed by Forbin de La Roque on May 31. The president explained to Séguier that the parlementaires had listened to the complaints of lawyers from Toulon accusing the company of private interests in the transfer—an unusual display of patience. As a result, a vote was never taken.[138]

The Parlement could make crippling changes in an edict during verification. These modifications had the effect of nullification. The edict transferring the Hyères seneschal court to Toulon was received by the governor in August 1643, and presented to the Parlement for registration on November 12. Three days before the edict was presented, Champigny wrote Séguier that he had transferred the court in August, when the edict arrived.[139] A furious Parlement invalidated the transfer, refused to register the edict, and sent a remonstrance to Paris.[140] A year later, the Parlement finally registered the edict, after inserting a clause during verification that annulled all of Champigny's ordinances on the transfer.[141]

[134] Delib. Parl., B. Méjanes 952, fols. 101, 97.

[135] *Ibid.*; A.A.E., 1702, fols. 150–152.

[136] See Chapter Eight.

[137] Delib. Parl., B. Méjanes 952, fols. 423–423v.

[138] Lublinskaya, *Vnutrenniaia*, pp. 281–282.

[139] *Ibid.*, p. 263.

[140] *Ibid.*, pp. 256–257, Alais to Séguier, August 18, 1643; Delib. Parl., B. Méjanes 953, fol. 58; A.A.E., 1709, fol. 281; B.N., Ms. fr. 18976, fol. 403.

[141] Lublinskaya, *Vnutrenniaia*, p. 288, Champigny to Séguier, November 1, 1644; B.N., Clairambault 396, fols. 3–5, Champigny to Brienne, November 1, 1644. Mesgrigny wrote Séguier on May 2, 1645 that he had persuaded the parlementaires to verify and register the edict transferring the court to Toulon with slight modifications not affecting royal revenues; cf. Lublinskaya, *Vnutrenniaia*, pp. 298–299.

Champigny recommended to Séguier on November 3, 1643, that he forbid the court to modify edicts during verification. Champigny also recommended frequent use of evocations by the council of state to control the Parlement, and he added that suspension from office and citations to Paris were useless because the parlementaires never obeyed. He recommended permanent suppression of offices.[142] The Parlement had already verified and registered an edict in November 1638 by reducing the creation from eighteen to ten new offices.[143] On May 5, 1656, the Parlement received a letter from Mazarin protesting delays in registration and modifications during verification. Royal letters on the same day ordered that "all difficulties and modifications you have added which prevent execution are to be removed, then proceed to pure and simple registration."[144]

If delay, modifications, and repeated remonstrances were unsuccessful, the Parlement could attempt to secure revocation through a rachat. Gaspard de Villeneuve, the Parlement's deputy to Paris in 1643, wrote on June 16 that the crown was willing to revoke the Requêtes for 300,000 livres.[145] Nothing more was heard of this solution. On July 28, 1643, Champigny requested that Villeneuve be sent home in order not "to encourage the youth of the company." In January 1648, the Parlement offered to pay 300,000 livres for revocation of the Semester, increased this to 600,000 livres in October, and 900,000 livres in December, without result.[146] If negotiation and payment were unsuccessful, the opposition parlementaires could attempt to block enforcement of the edict, publicizing their protest in arrêts d'état, posters, pamphlets, public speeches, or they could use intimidation such as the murders in 1639 and 1648. As a last resort, they protested in the streets of Aix.

The crown used bribery and intimidation to control the court. It granted favors to cooperative parlementaires, including titles, brevets of councilor of state, pensions, lettres en survivance, dispensations for age, experience, and kinship, exemptions from royal taxes such as the lods et ventes and franc-fief, military com-

---

[142] Lublinskaya, *Vnutrenniaia*, pp. 261–263.
[143] ADBR, Aix, B 3351, fol. 677.      [144] A.A.E., 1720, fols. 14, 15, 18.
[145] B.N., Ms. fr. 24166, fol. 242; B.N., Ms. fr. 17369, fol. 30.
[146] Delib. Parl., B Méjanes 953, fol. 188; B.N., Ms. fr. 17390, fols. 264, 307; A.A.E., 1713, fol. 341; Lublinskaya, *Vnutrenniaia*, pp. 255–256.

missions for relatives. For his support of the crown, Foresta de La Roquette received the title of baron in 1647 and marquis in 1651.[147] Grand'Chambre members Bermond and Fabri became councilors of state in 1649 and 1650 for supporting the crown.[148] Mesgrigny was granted a pension of 1,500 livres in 1644 when he was appointed first president.[149] Jacques Gaufridy, former president of the Semester, received a pension of 2,000 livres in 1658.[150] Louis d'Arnaud was freed in 1639 from the lods et ventes for his fiefs of Rousset and Vallongue, and Jean-Baptiste Thomassin in 1650 from the franc-fief for his seigneurie of Ainac.[151] Oppède became governor of Antibes in 1656, and in May of that year his brother received a commission to levy an infantry company for service in Piedmont.[152] In December 1656, his brother received another commission to levy a cavalry company.[153] Oppède's son received its command in July 1657. Mazarin notified Oppède and Forbin de La Roque on March 21, after the 1659 revolt, that as a reward for loyalty their sons would receive commissions for cavalry companies.[154]

Reversion letters permitted joint holding of an office by father and son, although ownership was separate from exercise. A father resigned his office to his son, then obtained permission in lettres en survivance to exercise the functions himself for five to twenty years. Both went to the palace of justice for important joint meetings. Although widespread in the eighteenth century, lettres en survivance were still a privilege in the seventeenth. Mazarin wrote to Bichi in March 1649 that the comte de Carcès was essential to peace negotiations with the rebel parlementaires, suggesting an offer of money, survivance in office if he had children, or other favors

---

[147] ADBR, Aix, B 3356, fol. 160; B 3357, fol. 709.

[148] EDB, IV–2, 77–79.

[149] B.N., Mélanges de Colbert 326, fols. 41v–43.

[150] J.L.G. Mouan, *Biographie du président Jacques de Gaufridy* (Aix, 1852), XVI.

[151] François-Paul Blanc, "Origins des familles provençales maintenues dans le second ordre sous le règne de Louis XIV: Dictionnaire généalogique" (doctoral dissertation in law, Aix-Marseille, 1971), pp. 553–554; De La Chenaye-Desbois and Badier, *Dictionnaire de la Noblesse*, 3d ed., 19 vols. (Paris, 1865), I, 812; ADBR, Aix, B 3325, fol. 138.

[152] A.A.E., 1720, fol. 21, Oppède to Mazarin, May 19, 1656.

[153] *Ibid.*, fol. 123, Mazarin to Oppède, January 25, 1657.

[154] *Ibid.*, fol. 249, Mazarin to Oppède, July 20, 1657.

to secure his cooperation.[155] There was protest when Forbin de La Roque's son received reversion letters as president, with his father retaining exercise for twelve years. The son, a Requêtes councilor, was to take his rank from the date he was received en survivance, not from the date he received exercise, as was customary, and he was to be received without examination. The parlementaires claimed their offices would be devalued,[156] and they refused to receive him for two years despite royal letters.[157] He was not received until November 1646.[158]

President Foresta de La Roquette opposed the reception. Having quarreled with Forbin de La Roque, he allied himself with the governor and intendant. On September 28, 1643, Champigny wrote to Séguier that La Roquette had accompanied him during the suspension of the Aix municipal elections.[159] On January 19, 1644, Alais wrote to Séguier that a conciliar decree on the Requêtes had only been registered through the zeal of La Roquette, and on May 21, 1644, Alais wrote to Séguier that La Roquette was a loyal friend of the crown.[160] Private quarrels often supplied the crown with supporters. Villeneuve became a Canivet supporting Mazarin after a 1650 quarrel with Boyer, a Sabreur, over reception into the court of Villeneuve's son-in-law Maurel.[161]

As few as ten percent of the Aix parlementaires had Paris connections. Villeneuve, Venel, Gaillard-Longjumeau, Henri de For-

---

[155] Pierre-Adolphe Chéruel and Georges d'Avenel, eds., *Lettres du cardinal Mazarin pendant son ministère*, 9 vols. (Paris, 1872–1906), III, 332–334.

[156] Melchior de Forbin de Saint André received provision letters to his father's office of president en survivance in April 1644; cf. B.N., Clairambault 393, fols. 83–86, Régusse to Séguier, April 19, 1644; Mousnier, *Lettres*, I, 619–620, Champigny to Séguier, January 19, 1644; ADBR, Aix, B 3354, fol. 363.

[157] ADBR, Aix, B 3355, fols. 587–587v.

[158] *Ibid.*, fol. 507; Lublinskaya, *Vnutrenniaia*, p. 307, Champigny to Séguier, November 28, 1645.

[159] ADBR, Aix, B 3355, fol. 201; B.N., Ms. fr. 18976, fols. 349–352, 366, 379, 381, 383–384; Lublinskaya, *Vnutrenniaia*, p. 259, Champigny to Séguier, September 28, 1643. Forbin de La Roque wrote to Séguier on June 28, 1644, asking for support against the claims of La Roquette; cf. *ibid.*, p. 283.

[160] *Ibid.*, pp. 269, 276–277; B. Marseille 1792, *Harangue faite à l'ouverture du Parlement de Provence par M. le baron de La Roquette, second président . . . octobre, 1651.*

[161] Haitze, *Histoire*, V, 207–208.

bin-Maynier d'Oppède, Charles de Grimaldi-Régusse, Jacques and Alexandre de Gallifet were among those with connections. Régusse sent Richelieu three barrels of muscat wine on January 14, 1642, in appreciation of his partonage.[162] Régusse later became the client of Michel Mazarin, archbishop of Aix, and thereby attracted the attention of the cardinal, who had many clients in Provence. Cardinal Mazarin wrote naval intendant Paul on October 12, 1656, thanking him for orange blossoms sent from Provence.[163] On March 13, 1648, Mazarin thanked his client Bichi, bishop of Carpentras, for a gift of horses.[164]

Madeleine de Gaillard-Longjumeau married councilor Gaspard de Venel in 1636 at the age of sixteen. Several years later she went to court and attracted the attention of Anne of Austria, becoming governess of Mazarin's nieces after they arrived in France in 1647, and then of the royal children, except the Dauphin. She secured a number of benefits for herself and her family: a diamond valued at 6,000 livres; rights to wood killed by ice in the Versailles forest valued at 800,000 livres, returned to the crown for the office of lady-in-waiting to the queen; rights to all icehouses in Provence, providing 20,000 livres annual income, sold to the province for 300,000 livres in 1692. Her husband sold his office of councilor to his brother-in-law, César de Gaillard-Longjumeau, to assume the office of master of requests of the queen's household. He also obtained a pension and brevet of councilor of state. Her youngest brother, Jean, was appointed bishop of Apt in 1671. Her brother-in-law, Henri d'Hervart d'Hervingquem, constructed much of the Mazarin quarter of Aix. Her first cousin, Sauveur, obtained a pension of 6,000 livres and brevet of councilor of state, while her nephew became captain of dragoons in the queen's regiment.[165]

---

[162] A.A.E., 1708, fol. 19. Jean-Jacques Bouchard in 1630 and Mme. de Sévigné in 1694 commented on the excellent wine made in Provence from the native muscat grape; cf. *Les confessions de Jean-Jacques Bouchard, parisien, suivis de son voyage de Paris à Rome en 1630* (Paris, 1881), p. 113; Madame de Sévigné, *Lettres*, ed. G. Gailly, 3 vols. (Paris, 1957), III, 870, September, 1694.

[163] Chéruel and Avenel, *Lettres de Mazarin*, VII, 670.

[164] *Ibid.*, III, 1001.

[165] *Ibid.*, II, 908, n. 1; ADBR, Aix, B 3356, fols. 691–692v; B 3358, fols. 1230v–1232v; A.A.E., 1720, fols. 184, 294v; Jean-Paul Coste, *Aix-en-Provence et le pays d'Aix* (Aix, 1964), pp. 49, 76; "Mémoire abrégé sur la vie de Magdeleine de Gaillard-Longjumeau de Ventabren de Venel," B. Méjanes 377; EDB, IV–2, 223.

She and her husband exercised influence in Provençal politics until Mazarin's death in 1661.

Gaspard de Villeneuve-Mons belonged to an old family of the Provençal nobility. In 1616, his older brother Antoine married Louise d'Albert de Luynes, sister of Louis XIII's favorite, the comte de Luynes. Antoine receive a pension of 6,000 livres and was appointed governor of Les Baux, first master of the duc d'Orléans household, marshal of royal camps and armies. He embarked on a military career under Orléans's protection, becoming governor of Honfleur, Pont L'Evêque, and Auge. Basking in his brother's reflected glory, Gaspard served as the Parlement's deputy to court for two decades. Gaspard and his brother-in-law, Melchior de Mazargues-Malijai, were highly respected Grand'-Chambre councilors.[166]

The Gallifets were ardent supporters of the rebel princes during the Fronde. Jacques de Gallifet inherited from his father Alexandre the office of president of the Enquêtes en survivance in 1647, assuming full exercise six years later. Alexandre in 1650 visited Condé at his château on the Cher near Bourges. Jacques corresponded with Gaston d'Orléans and served as the Parlement's deputy to the Parisian princes in 1651. Arrested in 1653 as a Frondeur, Jacques was imprisoned in the citadel of Sisteron. He was released in 1654 through the intercession of Conti.[167]

The crown concentrated its favors on parlementaires who had rendered useful service, and on opposition leaders who could be seduced with gifts. One of the latter was Jacques Gaufridy, whose mother and wife were the daughters of Parlement councilors. Gaufridy was ambitious to join the Parlement. His portrait shows an intelligent face with a goatee and mustache beneath a balding head. Assessor of Aix in 1628–1629 and 1638–1639, he was sent to court to protest the élus and presidial courts. A client of Alais after 1639, Gaufridy was in Paris from January 10 to December 29, 1640. The edict creating the Requêtes was announced on January 4, with Gaufridy's purchase of an office of

---

[166] E. de Juigné de Lassigny, *Histoire de la maison de Villeneuve en Provence*, 3 vols. (Lyon, 1900–1902), I, 138, 232–233; EDB, IV, 497–502.

[167] Louis Caste, "L'origine noble des Gallifet," *Mémoires de l'Institut historique de Provence*, 11 (1934), 53–80; Haitze, *Histoire*, V, 263–266, 281; EDB, IV, 225; Grimaldi and Gaufridy, *Mémoires*, pp. 43, 47, 52; Depping, *Correspondance administrative*, pp. 94–96; *Remontrances faites au roy et à la reine regente par M. Gallifet*, B. Marseille 1798.

president, and it was presumed that he had personally profited from negotiating the creation of the new chamber. Accused of abandoning provincial interests for personal gain, Gaufridy became the most unpopular magistrate in Aix. His hôtel was attacked in 1648 during Carnival, and sacked during the 1649 revolt.[168]

But favors dispensed by the crown were too infrequent to be a significant means of control at Aix. Local interests and prestige were more important. Even parlementaires with Paris connections were not consistently loyal: Villeneuve was cited in 1631 and 1648; Oppède became a rebel leader in 1649; Régusse was a rebel in 1649 and 1657–1658. Intimidation was a more successful means of control.

The crown's intimidation took several forms. Most effective were disciplinary citations in lettres de cachet and conciliar decrees, issued upon recommendation of the intendant of justice, governor, or first president. The parlementaires were suspended from office and summoned to Paris for explanations or imprisonment. This tactic proved successful. Honoré de Coriolis was politically inactive after his father's arrest as a cascaveou in 1631, while Jacques de Gallifet was inactive after his release from the citadel of Sisteron in 1654.

The crown used threats to increase the annual tax of the Paulette and to transfer the Parlement from Aix. In January 1658, first president Oppède promised Mazarin he would explore advantages that could be gained for the crown from the upcoming renewal of the Paulette.[169] On April 2, the Parlement wrote protesting Mazarin's threatened increase of the tax. In September, the court sent a letter requesting renewal at the customary rate.[170] On March 11, 1659, the Parlement agreed to punish the Aix rebels and asked to escape transfer for this reason.[171] Unpublished conciliar decrees, drafted at Pavia after the Aix revolt, transferred the Parlement to an unnamed city in order "to repress temerity and insolence."[172] The Parlement's judgment against the rebels was published on March 27, and on March 28, Mazarin announced

---

[168] J.L.G. Mouan, *Biographie du président Jacques de Gaufridi* (Aix, 1852), XVI; Grimaldi and Gaufridy, *Mémoires*, pp. 149, 254; ADBR, Aix, Moissac, "Histoire du Parlement," II, fol. 4; EDB, IV–2, 232–233.

[169] A.A.E., 1721, fols. 324–329.

[170] Delib. Parl., B. Méjanes 954, fols. 162, 184.

[171] A.A.E., 1723, fol. 404v.    [172] *Ibid.*, 1722, fols. 290–293.

that the Parlement would *not* be transferred.[173] On April 8 and 29, Oppède thanked the crown for its generosity in renewing the Paulette at the customary rate.[174] Mazarin wrote the Parlement on April 10 that renewal of the Paulette had been delayed "to encourage your company to render justice to those guilty of sedition."[175] Renewal of the Paulette was used as a means of coercion—but threats to individuals in disciplinary legislation were more frequent, selective, and thus more effective.

On January 28, 1648, the governor and three intendants forced registration of an October 1647 edict creating a Semester in the Parlement of Aix similar to those already created in the Parlements of Rouen, Rennes, and Metz. Ninety-five offices were to be sold to staff the January Semester, which was to sit from January 1 to June 30. The old Parlement would serve from July 1 to December 31, the less lucrative summer and harvest months. The Chambre des Requêtes was abolished. Its members joined the January Semester after paying conversion fees of 5,000 livres for councilors and 12,000 livres for présidents. Intendant Sève wrote that the Semester would bring 1,000,000 livres from the sale of new offices, with the additional advantage of "crushing the authority" of a Parlement that had always been uncooperative: the Semester split the unruly Parlement into two courts and added a group of magistrates loyal to the crown for personal gain, as did the Requêtes. The creation of the Semester at Aix strongly suggested a disciplinary measure, as it had at Rouen in 1641.[176]

First president Mesgrigny refused to call a joint meeting, and the royal attorneys refused to present the edict, so the registration was delayed several months. The governor finally delivered royal orders to Mesgrigny to convene the meeting on January 28, which he reluctantly did. The royal attorneys would not attend. Sève has left an eyewitness account of this dramatic registration. Bailiffs Herbin and Munier in robes with red sleeves, gold chains around their necks, arrived to open the doors of the palace of justice

---

[173] *Ibid.*, 1724, fols. 97, 100–102.

[174] *Ibid.*, 1722, fols. 479, 505.      [175] *Ibid.*, 1724, fol. 119.

[176] "Livre de raison de Léon de Trimond," B. Méjanes 1140, fol. 17; ADBR, Aix, B 3356, fols. 325v, 376–506; B.N., Ms. fr. 20561, fols. 148–149; B.M., Harleian 4575, fol. 5; Madeleine Foisil, *La révolte des Nu-Pieds et les révoltes normandes de 1639* (Paris, 1970), pp. 322–326.

about eight o'clock in the morning. Alais arrived with a large retinue of belligerent nobles. A conciliar decree forced the attendance of the procureurs du pays, but the baron de Bras, first consul, and assessor Séguiran went to Paris the next week to protest the registration. Mesgrigny would not attend, so Sève occupied the first place. He was joined by intendants Hère of Dauphiné and Breteuil of Languedoc, archbishop of Aix Michel Mazarin, royal attorney Dupuy of the Beaucaire seneschal court, who had recently purchased an office of substitute procureur-général in the Semester, and members of the Requêtes. The grande salle slowly filled with sullen parlementaires in red robes. The archbishop was in a bad mood because he favored the parlementaires.

The bailiffs demanded silence. Dupuy read the edict and the royal orders demanding its registration. Sève delivered a long apology for the Semester, arguing that it would provide faster, better justice. But he made it clear that refusal to register the edict would result in registration by the intendants. The furious and resentful parlementaires answered that the crown was cutting their judicial robes in two. To avoid a dangerous precedent, they accepted the inevitable and registered the edict. Alais immediately installed the Semester. He then turned the angry parlementaires out of the palace of justice to avoid more trouble, and there was an ugly scene. The parlementaires unsuccessfully sent deputies to Paris in protest. The crown responded with a conciliar decree of February 27 forbidding their assembly while the January Semester was sitting.[177] A conciliar decree on March 27 ordered the Semester to sit until all of its offices were sold. The anciens officiers did not sit, or receive gages or free salt in 1648.[178]

To avoid establishment of the Semester, the anciens officiers reached an agreement with the Requêtes at La Ciotat on December 25, 1647, since their quarreling had been the official justification for the Semester's creation. The parlementaires agreed to recognize the new chamber and allow it to function freely if the Semes-

[177] B.M., Harleian 4575, fols. 8v–17v; Delib. Parl., B. Méjanes 953, fol. 197; A.A.E., 1713, fols. 39–40, 82, 91, 97; B.N., Ms. fr. 17389, fol. 9; ADBR, Aix, Moissac, "Histoire du Parlement," II, 73, 76. The Parlement's deputies to Paris were Oppède Leidet-Sigoyer, Villeneuve, and Laurens, who had been cited in disciplinary legislation.

[178] A.A.E., 1713, fols. 115–118; B.N., Dupuy 672, fol. 152; see Chapter Nine.

ter were revoked.[179] Mesgrigny, Leidet-Sigoyer, and Laurens, all previously cited, were sent to Paris in October to request the Semester's revocation. The parlementaires unsuccessfully offered 300,000 livres in January 1648 for this purpose, 600,000 livres in October, and 900,000 in December.[180] Sève recommended blank disciplinary letters to remove "the most seditious" parlementaires from Aix before registration.[181]

During Carnival armed masked men harassed Semester members, as Mesgrigny wrote Séguier on February 25, 1648. Posters prohibiting the sale of Semester offices appeared, and prospective purchasers were threatened with death. Mesgrigny complained that the troops Alais brought into Aix were unnecessary and provocative: Alais nervously filled the Place des Prêcheurs with soldiers and posted cordons around the hôtels of Gaufridy and Sève. The day before Mardi Gras a group of thirty masked men in red and blue hats took advantage of Carnival crowds to insult members of the Semester in the streets. There was talk of ringing the tocsin.[182]

Sève on March 1 named parlementaires Louis de Saint Marc, Jean-Pierre de Signier, and François Thomassin as leaders of the masked men. They were identified by eyewitnesses. It was presumed the other masked men were also parlementaires or their servants. Sève requested lettres de cachet exiling Saint Marc to Entrevaux, Signier to Antibes, and Thomassin to Sisteron for their "insolence and attempted intimidation during Carnival." Sève wrote that he had proof of the participation of avocat-général Louis Decormis, whose brother, a prior, had been named by witnesses as one of the masked men. Decormis's exile was not requested because he was protected by archbishop of Aix Michel

---

[179] Jacques Gaufridy, "Histoire de Provence," B. Méjanes 625, fols. 422–423; Pierre-Joseph de Haitze, "Histoire de Provence sous lé règne de Louis XIII," B. Méjanes 736, fol. 133; A. Savine, *Relation des troubles occasionnés en Provence par l'établissement d'une Chambre-Semestre et du mouvement dit le Sabre* (Aix, 1881), B. Méjanes 801, fol. 24.

[180] Delib. Parl., B. Méjanes 953, fol. 188; B.N., Ms. fr. 17390, fols. 264, 307; A.A.E., 1713, fols. 82, 341.

[181] A.A.E., 1713, fols. 18–19, Sève to Mazarin, January 14, 1648.

[182] B.N., Ms. fr. 17389, fols. 40–41; Haitze, "Histoire de Provence," B. Méjanes 736, fol. 139. Haitze's father was a member of the governor's guard.

Mazarin.[183] Sève wrote on March 10 that vicar general Mimata had informed the Semester that the archbishop wanted Decormis judged by an ecclesiastical court.[184] His judges included canons who were the brothers-in-law of Leidet-Sigoyer and Decormis.[185] Gaufridy accused "the youth of the company" of responsibility for the Carnival incident. He was annoyed on April 6, when Decormis escaped prosecution by the Semester, and again on May 12, when Decormis was acquitted.[186] Sève wrote to Séguier on April 7 that Decormis's release was a judicial abuse and asked permission to try him.[187] Sève wrote that there were plots to murder himself and Gaufridy during their promenades in the city.[188]

In April, avocat-général Decormis complained to Séguier that Gaufridy presided at a trial on March 8 convicting three of Decormis's children for insolence.[189] On June 10, Decormis wrote to Séguier that the Semester had imprisoned the children of councilors Laurens and Agut for blocking the path of Semester councilor Suffren and insulting him.[190] Sève wrote on March 10 that Leidet-Calissane, brother of Leidet-Sigoyer, had refused to pay his conversion fee.[191] Leidet-Calissane joined the opposition, as did Requêtes's councilors Thomassin, Laugier, Ballon, and Gautier.[192]

The intendant was annoyed by the Semester's cowardice. Sève wrote to Séguier on March 24 that none of the Semester wanted to investigate the Marseille shipburning incident that had occurred: fireworks had been attached to royal galleys, merchant

---

[183] B.N., Ms. fr. 17389, fols. 56–57. The coldness between the archbishop and governor were noted by Decormis on June 7, 1648; cf. B.N., Ms. fr. 17388, fols. 53–54. Sève, Gaufridy, and Mesgrigny wrote of Michel Mazarin's sympathy for the parlementaires; cf. *ibid.*, fols. 274–275; 17389, fols. 40–41, 56–57.

[184] *Ibid.*, fols. 71–72.

[185] *Ibid.*, fols. 73–74.    [186] *Ibid.*, fols. 150–151, 270–272.

[187] *Ibid.*, fols. 156–157.    [188] B.M., Harleian 4575, fol. 19v.

[189] B.N., Ms. fr. 17389, fols. 178–179. Decormis described Gaufridy as a personal enemy attempting to use the Semester as an instrument of "revenge and oppression."

[190] B.N., Ms. fr. 17388, fols. 130–131. On July 7, 1648, Sève wrote to Séguier that two unnamed children of anciens officiers had insulted members of the Semester; cf. *ibid.*, fols. 162–163.

[191] B.M., Harleian 4575, fol. 20. Leidet-Calissane was never received into the Semester.

[192] *Ibid.*, fol. 24; B.N., Ms. fr. 17389, fols. 266–268, Sève to Séguier, May 12, 1648.

vessels, and a skiff, but only two had exploded, and none of the ships had burned. Sève wrote that the only reliable members of the Semester were Gaufridy, Dedons, Rabasse, Beaumont, Bernard, Suffren, and Trimond.[193] On May 12 Sève wrote that "the violence and frustration of the anciens officiers have caused us less trouble than the Semester's weakness and disloyalty." He recommended issuing royal letters giving Semester councilors a higher rank; the anciens officiers' suspension as a group from office and their citation to Paris; the establishment of a judicial commission of intendants and the Cour des Aides at Vienne to prosecute parlementaires who fled to the Comtat Venaissin.[194]

On March 31, Sève wrote that all dogs in the vicinity of his and Alais's hôtels had been poisoned.[195] On April 6, Gaufridy wrote to Séguier that councilor Venel, implicated in the Carnival disturbances, and five or six of his friends had ridden masked to Avignon to steal the governor's mail: Sève mentioned witnesses in his letter of May 12. Venel was interrogated by Dedons and Trimond of the Semester, but the witnesses denied knowing him; Sève said they were bribed. Venel went to Catalonia with Michel Mazarin, then spent the rest of the year at Paris.[196]

On April 7, Sève wrote that Saint Marc and Signier had refused to obey the lettre de cachet and fled to Avignon.[197] On May 5, Sève wrote that he had received the blank letters to suspend seditious parlementaires from office, and he had exiled seventeen from Aix: Saint Marc, Signier, both Thomassins, Laugier, Oppède, Antelmi, Leidet-Calissane, Villeneuve, Espagnet, Boyer, Bonfils, Lombard, Milan, Mesgrigny, Decormis, and Rascas.[198] They fled to the Comtat Venaissin. First président Mesgrigny withdrew to his estates, leaving his son in Aix as a hostage on April 29, as ordered by royal letters.[199] The stage was set for the 1649 revolt.

---

[193] Lublinskaya, *Vnutrenniaia*, pp. 323–324; A.A.E., 1713, fols. 109, 123.

[194] B.N., Ms. fr. 17389, fols. 266–268.

[195] *Ibid.*, fols. 140–141.

[196] *Ibid.*, fols. 150–151, 266–268; B.M., Harleian 4575, fol. 23.

[197] B.N., Ms. fr. 17389, fols. 156–157, 180–181; A.A.E., 1713, fols. 113, 162.

[198] B.N., Ms. fr. 17389, fols. 236–238; A.A.E., 1713, fols. 314–315; ADBR, Aix, Moissac, "Histoire du Parlement," II, 76.

[199] B.N., Ms. fr. 17389, fols. 234–235, Decormis to Séguier, May 5, 1648.

Chapter Seven

# THE OPPOSITION PARLEMENTAIRES

Who were the opposition parlementaires? What motivated them
to revolt and what attracted their uncommitted colleagues in support? At least five factors unified the opposition: rank, regional
pride, compactness, isolation, kinship and clientage ties, and political opinion. The majority of Aix parlementaires were robe nobles
ennobled between 1500 and 1600. In a group of 70 parlementaire
families holding office between 1629 and 1649, 17, or 25 percent,
were traditional or sword nobles ennobled before 1500; 34, or 48
percent, were robe nobles ennobled before 1600; 10, or 15 percent, were ennobled between 1600 and 1660; 7, or 10 percent,
were nonnobles; and the rank of 2 is unknown.[1] At Aix as at
Rennes, the line between robe and sword was not as clear as elsewhere in France.[2] By 1695, only 5 of 111 parlementaires at Aix
were nonnoble.[3]

There were perhaps thirty great old families of the sword nobility in Provence. A few of these families were represented in the
Parlement, such as the Glandèves, Porcellet, Villeneuve, Escalis-
Sabran, Agoult, and the newer Forbin, while the Pontevès, Oraison, and Castellane de La Verdière were allied by marriage. The
holders of such names often belonged to lesser family branches

[1] ADBR, Aix, B 3346–B 3356; Balthasar Clapiers-Collongues, *Chronologie des officiers des Cours souveraines* (Aix, 1909–1912); Appendix I;
François-Paul Blanc, "Origines des familles provençales maintenues dans
le second ordre sous le règne de Louis XIV: Dictionnaire généalogique"
(doctoral dissertation in law, University of Aix-Marseille, 1971); August
Du Roure, *Les maintenues de noblesse en Provence par Belleguise (1667–
1669)*, 3 vols. (Bergerac, 1923) and *Histoire véridique de la noblesse de
Provence* (Bergerac, 1912). The group of seventy parlementaires includes
the Chambre des Requêtes and excludes the Semester and first presidents.
[2] Jean Meyer, *La noblesse bretonne au XVIIIᵉ siècle*, 2 vols. (Paris,
1966), II, 927–1016; Frédéric Saulnier, *Le Parlement de Bretagne, 1554–
1790*, 2 vols. (Rennes, 1909).
[3] Jean-Paul Coste, *La ville d'Aix en 1695. Structure urbaine et société*,
3 vols. (Aix, 1970), II, 754.

216

and tended to become robe nobles by definition when they joined the Parlement. They served as a bridge between the frequently hostile worlds of robe and sword. They also played an important role in the revolts. In 1649, six of the eight leaders of the opposition parlementaires came from families ennobled before 1500. They were Pierre and Louis Decormis, Jean-Baptiste de Forbin de La Roque, Henri de Forbin-Maynier d'Oppède, Sextius and Henri d'Escalis-Sabran de Bras. The families of Charles de Grimaldi-Régusse and Laurent de Coriolis had been ennobled during the sixteenth century. Seven of these eight parlementaires had titles of baron or marquis; only Decormis did not. Rebels with illustrious old names included Jean-François de Glandèves-Rousset and Gaspard de Villeneuve.[4]

Most parlementaires from families ennobled during the sixteenth and seventeenth centuries had legal or mercantile origins. They had been lawyers, notaries, municipal officials, and seneschal judges of Aix, such as the Bonfils, Rabasse, Agut, Coriolis, Gaufridy, Gallifet, Galaup, Ollivier, and Tressemanes, while others, such as the André and Thomassin, also had mercantile origins. A large group came from commercial or financial families, including the Guiran, Mazargues, Signier, Milan, Saint Marc, Maurel and Paul. Some assumed noble rank through military offices and fief ownership, as did the Boniface, Honorat, Laugier, Raffelis, and Roux.[5] The half-century from 1550 to 1600 was the great age for entering the Provençal nobility.[6]

Recently ennobled parlementaires bought fiefs to strengthen their claims to nobility. Their goal was a crumbling château amid olive trees on a hill overlooking the Mediterranean or Durance.

[4] Blanc, "Origines des familles"; Edouard Baratier, Georges Duby, Ernst Hildesheimer, *Atlas historique, Provence, Comtat Venaissin, Principauté de Monaco, Principauté d'Orange, Comté de Nice* (Paris, 1969), "Listes de grandes familles de la noblesse provençale," pp. 139–140.

[5] Blanc, "Origines des familles"; Roure, *Les maintenues* and *Histoire véridique.*

[6] Monique Cubells, "A propos des usurpations de noblesse en Provence sous l'ancien régime," *Provence historique*, 81 (1970), 224–301; François-Paul Blanc, "L'anoblissement par lettres en Provence à l'époque des réformations de Louis XIV, 1630–1730" (doctoral dissertation in law, University of Aix-Marseille, 1971), excerpts appear as three articles in *Annales de la Faculté de Droit et de Science Politique d'Aix-Marseille*, No. 58 (Paris, 1972), pp. 131–321.

This trend began in the late sixteenth century and grew during the seventeenth.[7] Multiple fiefowners in Haute-Provence included Valbelle, Coriolis, Périer, Rascas, Joannis, Leidet, Lombard, Tabaret, and Grimaldi-Régusse. Other parlementaire fiefowners in this region were Galaup, Tressemanes, Thomassin, Trichaud, Laurens, Trimond, Du Chaine, Thoron, Boyer, Rabasse, Bermond, Laugier, Guiran, Foresta, and Maurel.[8] The afflorinement by Maynier d'Oppède in 1668 listed over thirty parlementaires owning fiefs.[9] By 1695, fifty-two parlementaires owned fiefs; fifteen had titles.[10]

There were comparatively few titles among the Provençal nobility.[11] New titles were created as a result of the Fronde, and there was a trend among the parlementaires to upgrade titles they already possessed. For instance, Laurent de Coriolis became baron de Corbières in 1625, and his grandson Pierre became marquis d'Espinouse in 1651. Charles de Grimaldi became marquis de Régusse and baron de Roumoules in 1649.[12] Jean-Augustin de Foresta became baron de La Roquette in 1647 and marquis in 1651.[13] Melchior de Forbin became marquis de La Roque and baron de Gontard in 1651.[14] Claude de Fabri, baron de Rians, became a marquis in 1657.[15] All except Fabri were presidents. By 1695, eleven of fourteen presidents of the Parlement had titles. The other three owned fiefs.[16]

[7] Marie-Zéphirin Isnard, *Etat documentaire et feódal de la Haute-Provence* (Digne, 1913); Séverin Icard, "Fiefs titrés et terres seigneuriales de la Provence, du Comtat Venaissin, et du Comté de Nice," *Mémoires de l'Institut historique de Provence*, 8 (1931), 204–219; 9 (1932), 83–98, 131–137; H. Gourdon de Genouillac, *Dictionnaire des fiefs, seigneuries, châtellenies de l'ancienne France* (Paris, 1862). Louis Wolff in *La vie des parlementaires provençaux au XVIᵉ siècle* (Marseille, 1924), pp. 10–11, states that only 15 of 172 parlementaires in the sixteenth century owned fiefs, a figure too low because a number purchased fiefs after 1575.

[8] Isnard, *Etat documentaire*.

[9] "Etat du florinage contenant le revenue noble de tous les fiefs et arrière-fiefs de Provence avec les noms du possesseurs fait par Maynier d'Oppède en 1668," B. Méjanes 630.

[10] Coste, *La ville d'Aix*, II, 754.

[11] Blanc, "Origine des familles," pp. 660–662, 672, 674.

[12] ADBR, Aix, B 3347, fol. 233; B 3357, fols. 8, 623.

[13] *Ibid.*, B 3356, fol. 160; B 3357, fol. 709.

[14] *Ibid.*, B 3357, fol. 1216.        [15] *Ibid.*, B 3359, fol. 112.

[16] Coste, *La ville d'Aix*, II, 754.

Sixteen of twenty members of the Enquêtes in the 1640s belonged to the opposition.[17] Many were youthful: new magistrates customarily joined this chamber. The 1649 rebels were young. Jacques de Gallifet and Henri de Forbin-Maynier d'Oppède were 29; Vincent de Boyer was 31; Jean-Antoine de Bonfils was 27; Pierre de Leidet-Calissane was 20; Louis de Saint Marc was 33; and Charles de Grimaldi-Régusse was 37.[18] They had bold personalities. Boyer was described as a young man "full of passion and extravagance." Oppède was "vain and ambitious." Decormis was "violent and implacable." Gallifet and Saint Marc were "young and hotheaded."[19] Gallifet killed another magistrate in a duel in 1641, while Saint Marc was implicated in the 1639 murder of Luguet. Councilors in the Enquêtes advanced to the Tournelle, then to the Grand'Chambre. The older members of these chambers were not as politically radical. Only eight of the sixteen judges in the Tournelle and seventeen of the twenty-five judges in the Grand'Chambre belonged to the opposition in the 1640s.[20]

The Parlement of Aix was composed almost entirely of Provençaux, who were known for their regional pride and distrust of strangers. When the Parlement was established in 1501, there were magistrates from Italy and other provinces.[21] The Milan, Foresta, Boniface, and Albert had recent Italian origins.[22] But by the mid-seventeenth century, the Aix parlementaires were all Provençaux, with the exception of first presidents Laisné, Dubernet, Mesgrigny, and councilor Gaillard-Longjumeau, whose family had come from Paris a half-century earlier and still had court connec-

[17] Appendix I.

[18] Clapiers-Collongues, *Chronologie*; EDB, IV-2; René Pillorget, *Les mouvements insurrectionnels de Provence entre 1596 et 1715* (Paris, 1975), p. 670. Pillorget makes the same observation about the Sabreurs in 1650.

[19] B.M., Harleian 4575, fols. 92v-93, 99; B.M., *Parlement de Bordeaux* (1650), fol. 54, *Réponse du fidèle provençal au calomniateur*, pp. 8-12, fol. 55, *Les plaintes de la noblesse de Provence*, p. 9; Pierre-Joseph de Haitze, *Histoire de la ville d'Aix*, 6 vols. (Aix, 1880-1892), IV, 395-396; Charles de Grimaldi and Jacques Gaufridy, *Mémoires pour servir à l'histoire de la Fronde en Provence* (Aix, 1870), pp. 42, 54.

[20] Appendix I.

[21] Fleury Vindry, *Les parlementaires français au XVIe siècle* (Aix, 1910), fasc. I; EDB, IV-2.

[22] Blanc, "Origines des familles"; Du Roure, *Les maintenues* and *Histoire véridique*.

219

tions. The parlementaires were ardent regionalists. They resented royal attacks upon their provincial authority.

The comparative smallness of the Aix Parlement and its distance from Paris contributed to its esprit de corps. The concentric rings made by a stone thrown into water represent the French parlements' degrees of power and influence. At the center was Paris, with two hundred members and a jurisdiction covering one-third of France. The inner circle included Rouen, Rennes, Bordeaux, Toulouse, and Dijon, with a hundred members and large jurisdictions. Next came Aix, Grenoble, Besançon, and Pau with sixty to seventy members and small jurisdictions. In the outer ring were Perpignan, Metz, Colmar, Arras, and Douai, judicial councils created when these regions were added to France.[23] Aix was a third-ranking parlement; its compactness and distance from Paris increased its unity and sense of identity.

Kinship and clientage ties were a basic element in the politics of the Parlement. Five networks or connections existed, representing twenty-two families, a little less than half the membership. The Thomassins were a prolific robe family who produced twelve parlementaires in the seventeenth century, and intermarried with most of the robe families of Aix, including the Saint Marc and Dedons. The Coriolis network led the 1630 revolt and included, among others, Joannis, Boyer, Périer, Gautier, Leidet-Sigoyer, and Decormis.[24] The two Leidet brothers headed a network opposing Oppède in 1659. It included Decormis, Rascas Du Canet, Régusse, Raffelis-Roquesante, Escalis de Bras, and Glandèves. The opposing network of Henri de Forbin-Maynier d'Oppède included Forbin de La Roque, Coriolis, Laurens, Boyer, Cauvet, Valbelle, Thomassin, Gallifet, and Saint Marc.[25] A group of parlementaires were related to the wealthy merchant families of Marseille, the Cauvet, Valbelle, Régusse, Foresta, Glandèves, and Albertas.[26] All five networks belonged to the opposition party in the 1640s.

Kinship ties were a characteristic of the class structure of the

---

[23] Jean Egret, *Louis XV et l'opposition parlementaire, 1715–1774* (Paris, 1970), pp. 11–13; Franklin Ford, *The Robe and the Sword: the Regrouping of the French Aristocracy after Louis XIV* (Cambridge, Mass., 1953), pp. 43–44.

[24] See Chapter Five.       [25] See Chapter Nine.

[26] René Pillorget, "Luttes de factions et intérêts économiques à Marseille de 1598 à 1618," *Annales: ESC*, 27 (1972), 724–725; Pillorget, *Les mouvements insurrectionnels*, pp. 228–229.

period. Their effect on political conduct was not always great unless supplemented by other types of attachment—for instance, rank, age, chamber of service, and political opinion. The last was probably the strongest cohesive force, particularly in 1649. The opposition parlementaires united to obtain modification or revocation of unpopular royal policies. They opposed forced registration of edicts, enforcement without registration, excessive evocations, and usurpation of their authority by the intendants. They fought disciplinary citations, creations of new judicial offices, and augmentations des gages. They demanded exemption from royal taxes and troop billeting.

The crown's creation of the Chambre des Requêtes and Semester produced financial panic among the Aix parlementaires. The real value of their offices fluctuated according to the law of supply and demand, and they feared a decline with the flood of new offices. Their panic was more acute because the threatened devaluation was preceded by three decades of rising prices.

Until about 1610, offices in the Parlement of Aix sold for 3,000 to 6,000 livres.[27] Pierre de Puget paid 4,500 livres for his office of councilor in 1577, and a well-known Aix lawyer, Fabrègues, refused to purchase an office of president in 1616, the year of his death, because he thought the price of 4,000 livres too high.[28] Jean-Baptiste de Cauvet paid 5,000 pistoles for an office of councilor in 1609.[29] A decade later, in 1626, Peiresc wrote that an office of president was being offered for 45,000 livres, although there were no purchasers, and in 1625, Léon de Valbelle paid 54,000 livres for an office of councilor.[30] On May 23, 1633, intendant de La Potherie wrote to chancellor Séguier that offices of councilor at Aix occasionally sold for less than 50,000 livres, although they should sell for 60,000 livres.[31] With a 60 percent

---

[27] Wolff, *La vie des parlementaires provençaux*, p. 24.

[28] *Ibid.*; Charles de Ribbe, *L'ancien barreau du Parlement de Provence* (Marseille and Paris, 1861), pp. 84, n. 1; 113.

[29] César de Nostradamus, *L'histoire et chronique de Provence* (Lyon, 1624), p. 1082; EDB, IV–2, 153. This sum may have been a gift after purchase of the office rather than its actual price.

[30] Philippe Tamizey de Larroque, *Lettres de Peiresc aux frères Dupuy*, 7 vols. (Paris, 1888–1898), VI, 116, 356; ADBR, Aix, Fonds Lombard 309E, 1072, fol. 200.

[31] A. D. Lublinskaya, ed., *Vnutrenniaia politika frantsuzskogo absoliutizma, 1633–1645* (Leningrad, 1966), p. 235.

devaluation in the livres-tournois, this was a 400 percent increase in the prices of offices in the Parlement of Aix between 1610 and 1633. There were similar increases at Paris and Rouen.[32]

Prices continued to rise. Jean-François de Glandèves and Henri de Forbin-Maynier d'Oppède purchased offices of councilor in 1637 for 60,000 and 63,000 livres.[33] Prices dropped slightly in 1640, when Pierre de Raffelis, Jacques d'André, and César de Milan each paid 54,000 livres for newly created offices of councilor.[34] A price fluctuation of 10 percent was normal, but rumors of new offices may have caused prices to fall slightly.

The creation of the Chambre des Requêtes in 1641 caused a sharp drop in prices. Charles de Tabaret bought an office of president of the Enquêtes in 1642 for 34,500 livres.[35] Charles de Grimaldi-Régusse wrote in his memoirs that he decided to purchase an office of president in 1642 because prices were so low.[36] There were similar declines at Bordeaux and Rouen after 1640.[37]

More serious was the crown's 50 percent reduction of prices in the Chambre des Requêtes to attract purchasers. Offices of councilor in the Requêtes sold for 24,000 livres in 1641, a base price of 21,000 livres and 3,000 livres in taxes.[38] But a regular office of councilor sold for 56,200 livres in 1646.[39] The prices of 52 new offices created at Rouen in 1641 were as low as those of the Aix Requêtes, selling for 25,000 livres.[40] Offices of Requêtes presidents were also set artificially low: they sold for 33,000 livres, a base price of 30,000 livres and 3,000 livres in taxes.[41] This was more than a 50 percent reduction of the regular price of an office

---

[32] Roland Mousnier, *La vénalité des offices sous Henri IV et Louis XIII*, 2d ed. (Paris, 1971), pp. 359–363.

[33] ADBR, Aix, Fonds Lombard 309E, 1077, fols. 63, 343.

[34] Paul de Faucher, *Un des juges de Fouquet: Requesante (1619–1707)* (Aix, 1891), p. 193, n. 3. These offices were part of the crue of 1637.

[35] ADBR, Aix, Fonds Berlie 301E, 228, fol. 659.

[36] Grimaldi and Gaufridy, *Mémoires*, pp. 19–20.

[37] Sal Westreich, *The Ormeé of Bordeaux* (Baltimore, 1972), p. 3; Mousnier, *La vénalité*, pp. 359–360; Paul Logié, *La Fronde en Normandie*, 3 vols. (Amiens, 1951), I, 63.

[38] ADBR, Aix, Fonds Berlie 227E, 1641, fols. 1005, 1008, 1012, 1015, 1040, 1074, 1077, 1136, 1452, 1459; 301E, 228, fol. 827; "Livre de raison de Léon Trimond," B. Méjanes 1140, fol. 7.

[39] ADBR, Aix, Fonds Berlie 301, 232, fol. 1047.

[40] Mousnier, *La vénalité*, p. 360.

[41] ADBR, Aix, Fonds Berlie 227E, 1641, fols. 1002, 1410.

of president à mortier, which Champigny, writing to Séguier on December 20, 1643, pegged at 75,000 to 78,000 livres.[42]

Prices of offices in the Semester were also set deliberately low by the crown. Councilors in the Requêtes paid 5,000 livres in 1648 for conversion of their offices into the Semester, a total price of 29,000 livres.[43] Intendant Sève wrote in his memoirs that Louis de Flotte, seigneur de Meaux, negotiated for a Semester office in the early months of 1648, attracted by the low price of 28,500 livres. However, president Jacques Gaufridy convinced the traitant to raise the price, arguing that low prices devalued converted Requêtes offices.[44] Gueidon paid 33,000 livres for an office of Semester councilor in 1648.[45] After Gueidon's murder in March, the price dropped to 22,000 livres, and the traitant was considering lowering it to 20,000 livres to attract purchasers.[46] Charles de Tressemanes-Chasteuil sold his converted Requêtes office of councilor in July 1648 for 37,000 livres.[47] Offices of Semester president were selling for 45,000 livres in 1648, a base price of 33,000 livres and a 12,000 livres conversion fee.[48]

The parlementaires were understandably frightened by the crown's artificial reduction of prices, but the decline was temporary. One month after the parlementaires' revolt in January 1649, prices rose: César de Gaillard-Longjumeau paid 58,000 livres for his brother-in-law Venel's office of councilor in February 1649.[49] Office prices were high after the Fronde, when the Parlement's prestige was at its peak. François de Maurel paid 72,000 livres for an office of councilor in 1654.[50] In 1656, Alphonse-Louis

[42] Lublinskaya, *Vnutrenniaia*, p. 268.

[43] "Livre de raison de Léon Trimond," B. Méjanes 1140, fol. 11; ADBR, Aix, B 3356, fols. 344–355, 376, 384–385v.

[44] B.M., Harleian 4575, fols. 25–25v.

[45] René Pillorget, "Vente d'offices et journée des barricades du 20 janvier 1649," *Provence historique*, 15 (1965), p. 33, n. 36.

[46] Jean-Scholastique de Pitton, *Histoire de la ville d'Aix* (Aix, 1666), pp. 419–421.

[47] ADBR, Aix, Fonds Berlie 301E, 234, fol. 971.

[48] M. Arbaud, Provence 349, *Factum pour le sieur procureur-général du Parlement de Provence*; ADBR, Aix, B 3356, fols. 381–382v; B. Marseille 1792, *Très humbles remontrances du Parlement de Provence au Semestre de Janvier* (1650), p. 15.

[49] ADBR, Aix, Fonds Berlie 301E, 235, fol. 195.

[50] Marquis de Boisgelin, *Maurel de Villeneuve de Mons* (Digne, 1904), pp. 30–31; Haitze noted that 1654 was a year of high prices; cf. *Histoire*, V, 312.

d'Arnaud paid 60,000 livres for a similar office.[51] In 1659, offices of councilor sold for 78,000, 80,000, and 81,000 livres.[52] Decormis was offered 52,000 écus (156,000 livres) for his office of president à mortier in 1655, which he did not accept, and Oppède sold his office of president to Escalis de Bras in December 1654 for 144,000 livres.[53]

Prices of Aix parlementary offices were high in the late seventeenth century. Offices of councilor sold for 64,000 livres in 1684, 60,000 livres in 1693, and 62,000 livres in 1698.[54] An office of president sold for 120,000 livres in 1674.[55] By royal edict on October 18, 1678, prices of offices in the Parlement of Aix were set at 120,000 livres for presidents à mortier, 70,000 livres for presidents of the Enquêtes, 64,000 livres for lay councilors, 45,000 livres for clerical councilors, 45,000 livres for avocats-généraux, and 40,000 livres for procureurs-généraux.[56] Prices declined slightly in the eighteenth century, when they averaged 80,000 to 100,000 livres for offices of president and 30,000 to 40,000 livres, sometimes 50,000 to 60,000 livres, for offices of councilor.[57]

[51] Pierre Farel, ed., *Mémoires de Vitrolles* (Eugène François Auguste d'Arnaud, baron de Vitrolles), 2 vols. (Paris, 1950), I, 40.

[52] Faucher, *Un juge de Fouquet*, p. 195, n. 1; "Livre de raison de Léon Trimond," B. Méjanes 1140, fol. 21; Charles de Ribbe, *Les familles et la société en France avant la Révolution*, 2 vols. (Tours, 1879), I, 177; Clapiers-Collongues, *Chronologie*, p. 100.

[53] Haitze, *Histoire*, V, 332; private communication from Richard Holbrook, who has recently finished a dissertation entitled "Baron d'Oppède and Cardinal Mazarin: The Politics of Provence from 1640 to 1661" (University of Illinois at Chicago Circle, 1976). The figure is based on Oppède's "livre de raison," fol. 130, conserved at the Château Saint Marcel, Marseille. Prices of offices in the Parlement of Rennes reached their peak from 1650 to 1664; cf. Meyer, *La noblesse*, II, 938.

[54] "Livre de raison de François-Boniface Laydet, seigneur de Fombeton (1675–1756)," B. Méjanes 1439, fol. 90; Louis Wolff, *Le Parlement de Provence au XVIIIe siècle* (Aix, 1920), p. 35; J. Marchand, *Un intendant sous Louis XIV: Etude sur l'administration de Lebret en Provence (1687–1704)* (Paris, 1889), pp. 22–23.

[55] A.A.E., 1728, fol. 249.

[56] Wolff, *Le Parlement de Provence*, p. 31.

[57] *Ibid.*, pp. 33–37; Pierre-Albert Robert, *Les remontrances et arrêtés du Parlement de Provence au XVIIIe siècle, 1715–1790* (Paris, 1912), pp. 21–27; Jeanne Allemand, "La haute société aixoise dans la seconde moitié du XVIIIe siècle (1750–1789)," 2 vols. (Ph.D. dissertation, University of Aix-Marseille, 1927), I, 143–144.

The volume of sales followed the rhythm of prices. Trading was brisk in the decades when values were high: 1620–1640, 1650–1660, 1680–1700. Between twenty and thirty offices of councilor changed hands in each of these decades, although one-third to one-half were inherited, not sold. Trading was slower from 1600 to 1620, in the 1640s, and from 1660 to 1680: ten to fifteen offices of councilor changed hands in these decades, of which one-half were inherited.[58]

The parlementaires were members of a company, an association of magistrates with vested interests in office-holding. The crown paid the parlementaires gages, the annual interest on the capital sum they had invested in the purchase of their office. Gages were usually 1 to 4.5 percent of the market price of the office.[59] The highest level of gages paid in the seventeenth century was 5.5 percent.[60] In 1647, annual gages for the Aix parlementaires ranged from 2,062 livres for the first president, 1,650 livres for the presidents, 1,225 livres for the royal attorneys, 1,350 to 1,050 livres for presidents of the Enquêtes, 1,125 livres for presidents of the Requêtes, 643 livres for the councilors.[61]

Gages were paid by rank for three quarters of the year, the fourth being the summer recess, and they were drawn on gabelle revenues for Provence.[62] There were serious irregularities in payment because the crown was chronically short of funds. The parlementaires did not receive full gages in 1628, 1631, 1639, 1648, and 1654.[63] They were fortunate if they received three-fourths of their gages two or three years late.[64] The Cour des Comptes com-

---

[58] Clapiers-Collongues, *Chronologie*, pp. 75–102.

[59] Wolff, *Le Parlement de Provence*, pp. 227–229; Allemand, "La haute société," pp. 150–151; Mousnier, *La vénalité*, pp. 426, 455–462; Faucher, *Un juge de Fouquet*, p. 195.

[60] Ford, *Robe and Sword*, p. 152.

[61] "Recettes et dépenses pour les généralités de Toulouse, Bourgogne, Provence, Dauphiné en 1647, Gages des officiers de la cour de Parlement de Provence," B.N., Ms. fr. n.a. 173, fols. 396–403v. Gages were the same in 1658; cf. A.A.E., 1722, fols. 301v–303.

[62] A.A.E., 1702, fol. 8. The Estates contributed to the gages.

[63] Wolff, *Parlement*, pp. 232–233; Delib. Parl., B. Méjanes 952, fols. 83v–85v, 97, 100–101, 411, 423; 953, fols. 209v–210, 215v–216; 954, fol. 41; Lublinskaya, *Vnutrenniaia*, pp. 277–278.

[64] Allemand, "La haute société," p. 147; Wolff, *La vie des parlementaires*, pp. 111–112.

plained in 1651 that its members were still owed 6,000 livres in gages a year for 1640–1642 and 1646–1647, a total of 24,500 livres.[65] The crown had promised in 1649 to reimburse members of the Requêtes and Semester for their suppressed offices. But it still owed them 30,000 livres in 1654, and they were not fully paid until 1658.[66] On March 6, 1657, first president Oppède wrote to Mazarin and Séguier that twelve masked men had surrounded the traitant's hôtel to demand immediate reimbursement, attempting to break down the door and shooting when he climbed out the window.[67]

Augmentations des gages also reduced the parlementaires' income. Increases in gages meant that the crown had raised the original price of the office, since gages were a percentage of the total price. If the parlementaires wanted to keep their offices, they had to pay this forced loan, which was thereafter reflected by an increase in their gages. The 1637 augmentation, the first since 1618 for the Aix parlementaires, increased the gages of presidents by 300 livres, a forced loan of 1,500 livres; royal attorneys and Enquêtes presidents by 200 livres, a forced loan of 1,400 and 1,200 livres; councilors by 120 livres, a forced loan of 695 livres.[68] The 1637 augmentation for the Cour des Comptes was a 14 percent tax on offices: a 1,293 livres increase for the first president, a forced loan of 9,000 livres; a 500 livres increase for the royal attorneys, a forced loan of 3,500 livres; 476 livres increase for councilors, a forced loan of 3,150 livres; and 362 livres for auditors, a forced loan of 2,430 livres.[69] Another augmentation in 1639, added to this one, increased the parlementaires' gages by

[65] "Registre des délibérations de la Cour des Comptes du 4 mars 1649 jusqu'au 10 septembre 1971," B. Méjanes R.A. 57, fol. 26. Prices of offices in the Cour des Comptes were slightly lower than those in the Parlement. In December 1656, the Cour des Comptes pegged office prices at 75,000 livres for presidents, 36,000 livres for councilors, and 12,000 livres for correctors; cf. *ibid.*, fol. 391.

[66] "Livres de raison de Léon Trimond," B. Méjanes 1140, fol. 20; M. Arbaud, Provence 349, *Factum pour le sieur procureur-général du Parlement de Provence*. The crown reimbursed the price of the Requêtes office and the conversion fee, but not the 3,000 livres in taxes paid by all purchasers.

[67] A.A.E., 1720, fols. 136–137.

[68] EDB, III, 376; ADBR, Aix, B 3345, fol. 463; B 3351, fol. 677.

[69] EDB, III, 444.

more than half.[70] An augmentation des gages in 1649, as part of
the peace settlement after the revolt, totaled 44,955 livres.[71]

An indirect effect of the flood of new offices was to increase the
cost of justice. New officials meant more fees and bribes for litigants. Old officials raised their fees, since these were shared from
a common purse. Magistrates thus passed along new royal taxes
and offices to those using the royal courts as a form of indirect
taxation on litigation. In 1639, the procureurs du pays protested
that new judicial offices were increasing the cost of justice.[72] The
Estates often complained to the Parlement and crown about excessive judicial fees.[73]

The increase in the number of parlementary offices also reduced
individual income from épices, fees for what was done outside the
courtroom: preparing files, briefs, and summonses; taking deposi-
tions and examining witnesses; conducting preliminary interrogations. The amounts of épices were fixed periodically by the first
president, and litigants received a bill from the épices clerk, presented by a court bailiff. One-fifth of the fee went to the rapporteur, the member of the chamber who summarized the case, and
the rest went into a common purse.

Councilor Leidet-Fombeton noted in 1700 that he received 99
livres a quarter in épices.[74] The épices of an Aix councilor in the
seventeenth century averaged 180 to 250 livres a year, a low sum
compared to other parlements; Aix heard comparatively few
cases.[75] A doubling of the number of parlementaire offices within
a decade, when the case load remained constant, reduced the
amount of épices each parlementaire received. The case load may
actually have declined in the 1640s, when the number of working
days were reduced by the strife over the Chambre des Requêtes.

---

[70] "Recettes et dépenses," B.N., Ms. fr. n.a. 173, fols. 396–403v.

[71] ADBR, Aix, J.L.H. Hesmivy de Moissac, "Histoire du Parlement de
Provence, 1501–1715," 2 vols., II, 101; B.N., Ms. fr. 18977, fols. 5, 145.

[72] ADBR, Aix, B 3352, fol. 673; Delib. Parl., B. Méjanes 952, fol.
398v.

[73] Wolff, *Le Parlement de Provence*, p. 235; ADBR, Marseille, C 25,
fols. 351v–353.

[74] "Livre de raison de François-Boniface Laydet, seigneur de Fombeton,"
B. Méjanes 1439, fol. 149.

[75] Wolff, *Le Parlement de Provence*, p. 240; *La vie des parlementaires*,
p. 113; Marchand, *Un intendant*, p. 23.

Jacques Gaufridy reported that first president Dubernet did not distribute cases for ten months in 1641 after a mass disciplinary citation, putting the court eight hundred cases in arrears when the suspension was lifted.[76] Bribes or pots de vin, a hidden source of income difficult to document, were probably also reduced.

Disciplinary citations were inconvenient and expensive. Gages, épices, and bribes were not paid while the parlementaires were suspended, a period that averaged six to twelve months, while they might have the additional expense of a trip to Paris. The parlementaires suspended in 1648 each received 1,500 livres indemnification from their company.[77] The deputies to Paris in 1643 for Louis XIII's succession to the throne were compensated at the rate of 2,000 livres for presidents and 1,000 livres for councilors.[78] The Aix parlementaires averaged 1,500 to 2,000 livres a year in revenue from their office, which they lost when they were suspended.[79]

The parlementaires received a number of important royal tax and military exemptions that supplemented their income. They were exempt from the ban-et-arrière-ban, the obligation of fief-owners to fight for the king when called upon by the governor to do so.[80] They were exempt from the gabelle and received free salt, franc-salé, from the warehouse at Berre. In 1600, presidents received ten minots of free salt a year, raised to twelve in 1649, while councilors and royal attorneys received five, raised to six in 1649.[81] Parlementaires received as much as 1,500 livres of ice, franc-glacé, in summer. Presidents received 20 livres a day, while councilors and royal attorneys received 10 livres a day.[82] But the parlementaires claimed other important exemptions challenged by the crown.

The Aix parlementaires claimed exemption from the droit de

[76] Grimaldi and Gaufridy, *Mémoires*, p. 158.

[77] Prosper Cabasse, *Essais historiques sur le Parlement de Provence, 1501–1790*, 3 vols. (Paris, 1826), II, 278.

[78] *Ibid.*, 254.

[79] Allemand, "La haute société," pp. 105–106; Faucher, *Un juge de Fouquet*, p. 195; Wolff, *Le Parlement de Provence*, p. 240; Farel, *Mémoires de Vitrolles*, I, 40.

[80] Wolff, *Le Parlement de Provence*, p. 222; Jean-Richard Bloch, *L'anoblissement en France au temps de François I* (Paris, 1934), p. 60.

[81] Wolff, *Le Parlement de Provence*, pp. 223–224.

[82] *Ibid.*, pp. 226–228.

franc-fief, a royal land tax payable by nonnoble owners of fiefs at the rate of one year's revenue every twenty years, computed as one-twentieth of the annual revenue paid in January.[83] They claimed exemption because they owned ennobling royal offices. But they did not definitively receive this privilege until a conciliar decree of September 6, 1674. Enough parlementaires were recently ennobled fiefowners for the levy of the franc-fief, annual after 1656, to be a burden protested in the mazarinades.[84]

The parlementaires also protested levies of the amortissement and nouveaux acquêts, lucrative royal taxes on purchases of mainmorte land. The Parlement issued an arrêt on June 26, 1634, suspending new searches of these taxes and the franc-fief until a remonstrance could be sent to Paris.[85] On July 24, 1635, the avocat-général protested to Séguier on the manner in which these taxes were collected.[86]

The parlementaires, as royal officeholders, claimed exemption from seigneurial taxes, in particular the lods et ventes payable to the crown by new purchasers of nonnoble domaine lands at a variable rate. The crown in 1626 refused to recognize the Aix parlementaires' exemption from this tax.[87] The refusal was doubly injurious because nobles were exempt. Royal letters in January 1655 increased the rate of the lods et ventes to one year's revenue, with payment extended over three years. The Parlement and Cour des Comptes refused to register these letters. Eleven parlementaires had recently purchased domaine land, including several presidents.[88] The Cour des Comptes ignored four conciliar decrees and the Parlement two royal letters ordering immediate registra-

---

[83] Marion Marcel, *Dictionnaire des institutions de la France au XVII<sup>e</sup> et XVIII<sup>e</sup> siècles*, 2d ed. (Paris, 1968), P. 244; Martin Wolfe, *The Fiscal System of Renaissance France* (New Haven, 1972), p. 357; Jean-Paul Charmeil, *Les trésoriers de France à l'époque de la Fronde* (Paris, 1964), p. 199; B. Marseille 1792, *Très humbles remontrances du Parlement de Provence au Semestre de Janvier* (1650), p. 5.

[84] Wolff, *Le Parlement de Provence*, pp. 224–225.

[85] Marcel, *Dictionnaire*, pp. 18–19, 401; Charmeil, *Les trésoriers*, p. 199; Wolfe, *Fiscal System*, p. 358; Roger Doucet, *Les institutions de la France au XVI<sup>e</sup> siècle*, 2 vols. (Paris, 1948), II, 484–485; ADBR, Marseille, C 166.

[86] B.N., Ms. fr. 17369, fol. 85.

[87] Wolff, *Le Parlement de Provence*, p. 225.

[88] A.A.E., 1720, fols. 360–361. The parlementaires were Coriolis, Valbelle, Mazargues, Saint Marc, Oppède, Gautier, Ballon, Laurens, Signier, Bonfils, and Michaelis.

tion.[89] In December 1656, three parlementaires were called to Paris for their opposition, while six members of the Cour des Comptes received lettres de cachet in June 1657 for their opposition.[90] On June 25, 1657, the letters were sent to the Trésoriers Généraux for enforcement without registration by either sovereign court.[91] The crown granted the parlementaires exemption from the lods et ventes in a conciliar decree on March 17, 1660.[92]

The Aix parlementaires claimed exemption from the taille by grants of Louis II, count of Provence, in 1414, and Louis XII, king of France, in 1504.[93] There were frequent complaints by the Estates and communities on the parlementaires' exemption.[94] A conciliar decree on June 3, 1606, ordered the parlementaires to pay the taille but allowed exemptions of 75 to 150 livres per magistrate.[95] These exemptions were a comparatively small reduction in the parlementaires' taille payments because most of their property was recently purchased, nonnoble land. The parlementaires usually avoided payments to the community tax receiver, or they concluded an arrangement with him to remove their taxable property from the cadastre, as did Régusse in 1645.[96] These evasions might have been more difficult if the crown had established élus in 1629. Higher royal taxes on land, either direct or indirect, reduced parlementaire incomes.

The Aix parlementaires were subject to troop billeting. Other provincial parlementaires and the nobility and clergy of Provence were exempt from this burden, but the Aix parlementaires did not escape it until February 1, 1650.[97] The consuls of communities

[89] *Ibid.*, fols. 14–15, 28, 359.

[90] *Ibid.*, fol. 98; Haitze, *Histoire*, V, 418. The parlementaires cited were Régusse, Agut, Leidet-Calissane. The Cour des Comptes magistrates cited were Castel, Lombard, Croze-Lincel, Thomassin-Taillac, Menc, Meyronnet.

[91] A.A.E., 1720, fol. 359.

[92] Wolff, *Le Parlement de Provence*, p. 225. Also see ADBR, Aix, B 3598.

[93] *Ibid.*, pp. 225–226.

[94] *Ibid.*; ADBR, Aix, B 3340, fol. 517; A.M., Aix, CC 169. Aix sued the Parlement in 1525, 1580, and 1599 to force its payment of rêves, levied in lieu of the taille, from which it claimed exemption.

[95] Wolff, *Le Parlement de Provence*, pp. 225–226; ADBR, Aix, B 3340, fol. 510v.

[96] Grimaldi and Gaufridy, *Mémoires*, p. 35.

[97] ADBR, Aix, B 3357, fol. 80v.

230

billeted troops on them before 1650, and they were included in the military règlements of 1641 and 1644.[98] Governor Alais coercively used troop billeting. In the summer of 1649, he besieged and occupied several châteaux belonging to the parlementaires and their supporters: château Renard of councilor Aymar d'Albi, château de La Barben belonging to a Forbin kinsman of Oppède, château Meyrargues of councilor Léon de Valbelle, château Roquemartine belonging to Forbin de La Roque. The Aix deputies to Paris in 1649 listed troop billeting as a grievance.[99]

The crown's creations of new offices threatened the parlementaires with devaluation of their capital investments in office-holding and reduced their income from office by nonpayment of gages, augmentations des gages, loss of épices, disciplinary suspensions, refusal to recognize their exemption from the taxes of franc-fief, amortissement, nouveaux acquêts, lods et ventes, taille, and troop billeting. These financial hardships were one reason for the parlementaires' revolt in 1649.

Devaluation of offices and reduction in income were serious because most Aix parlementaires had modest fortunes. Provençal nobles were fewer in number and poorer than those in many other provinces. There were perhaps 500 noble families in Provence in the late seventeenth century, not all authentic, compared to 4,500 noble families in neighboring Languedoc, a province four times larger. An intendant in Languedoc wrote at the time that few noble families in that province had annual incomes of more than 20,000 livres. This was also true in Provence, where much of the wealth was in the hands of Marseille merchants.[100] The general poverty of the Provençal nobility was reflected in the modest fortunes of the parlementaires. However, the Aix company had a wide range of incomes, and some judges were wealthy.

There were three levels of fortunes. The lowest level, and the majority of parlementaires, had annual incomes from 5,000 to 10,000 livres and net worths of 100,000 to 200,000 livres. The intermediate level was moderately wealthy, with incomes ranging from 10,000 to 20,000 livres and net worths of 200,000 to

[98] Wolff, *Le Parlement de Provence*, p. 223.
[99] B.M., Harleian 4575, fols. 143v–144v; see Chapter Nine.
[100] Paul Masson, *La Provence au XVIII⁰ siècle*, 3 vols. (Paris, 1936), II, 335, 340–341; Pillorget, *Les mouvements*, pp. 81–83.

400,000 livres. The highest level—and the smallest group—were parlementaires with incomes over 20,000 livres and net worths of more than 400,000 livres. Parlementaires Raffelis, Trimond, and Glandèves-Rousset illustrate the first group; Peiresc and Lombard the second; Oppède, Cauvet, Valbelle, Régusse, and Maurel the third.[101]

Pierre de Raffelis, sieur de Roquesante, was the younger son of a family assuming nobility in the sixteenth century through judicial office-holding, and living nobly. In 1640, his father purchased for him an office of councilor for 54,000 livres with 2,000 livres annual income. Pierre married in 1647. His marriage contract stipulated that he receive 100,000 livres from his father, of which 54,000 livres had already been paid. But after his father's death in 1652 he received only 24,000 livres. His wife brought a dowry of 25,000 livres. In 1656, he bought a house near the palace of justice. In 1670, he inherited from his wife (who had inherited it the previous year) the château and fief of Grambois with an estimated annual income of 725 livres. He had ten children needing portions. His total income probably averaged 5,000 to 8,000 livres a year, of which one-fourth to one-third came from his office. His net worth was 100,000 to 160,000 livres. A cold, taciturn man who read much, Raffelis became one of Fouquet's judges. He gained Louis XIV's disfavor when he voted for life imprisonment, not death, and was exiled to Normandy until 1668.[102]

Parlementaire dowries averaged 9,000 to 12,000 livres in the late sixteenth century. Madeleine de Coriolis brought her third husband, François de Malherbe, 11,400 livres in 1581.[103] Fran-

---

[101] Monique Cubells is presently doing a comprehensive study of the fortunes of the Aix parlementaires in the eighteenth century. Robert Forster in "The Provincial Noble: A Reappraisal," *American Historical Review*, 68 (1962–1963), 691, describes 10,000 livres a year as an adequate income for a provincial noble in the late eighteenth century. It provided summer and winter residences, four to six servants, a coach, a complete pantry, wardrobe and linen closet, a respectable library, and an occasional trip.

[102] Faucher, *Un juge de Fouquet*, pp. 175–373; "Etat du florinage," B. Méjanes 630, fol. 70; Blanc, "Origines des familles," pp. 468–471; EDB, IV–2, 403. Georges Mongrédien, *L'affaire Foucquet* (Paris, 1956); Jules-Auguste Lair, *Nicolas Foucquet, procureur-général, surintendant des finances, ministre d'état de Louis XIV*, 2 vols. (Paris, 1890).

[103] Wolff, *La vie des parlementaires*, p. 89; Jean de Celles, *Malherbe, sa vie, son caractère, sa doctrine* (Paris, 1937), pp. 64–65.

çois-Louis de Leidet-Fombeton married for a dowry of 9,000 livres in 1599.[104] Dowries escalated in the seventeenth century. Councilor Peiresc wrote in 1626 that parlementaire dowries were averaging 15,000 to 21,000 livres.[105] The son of dean Ollivier married for a dowry of 18,000 livres in 1625.[106] Flotte de Meaux, a Semester councilor, married for a dowry of 21,000 livres in 1632. The wife of Grasse de Saint Césaire, a Semester president, brought her husband 23,000 livres in 1642.[107] The son of councilor Laurens married in 1648 for a dowry of 33,000 livres, while the son of president of the Enquêtes Tabaret married in 1668 for a dowry of 18,000 livres.[108]

Brides usually brought coffres as part of their dowries. The nine chests of Cathérine de Maurel, who married a councilor in the Parlement in 1664 when she was barely fifteen, were opened at her death in 1725. Their contents included silverware, porcelain, crystal, perfume bottles, enamel boxes, a tea set, napkins, sheets, aprons, handkerchiefs, a silver writing set, books, hats, bonnets, lace cuffs, a black taffeta coif, ribbons, skirts in white satin and black velvet with fringe, in ermine and black damask with gold fringe, matching blouses and cloaks, a silver and blue satin dress, ounces of silk fringe, shoes—the accumulation of a lifetime.[109]

Léon de Trimond paid 24,000 livres for an office of councilor in the Requêtes, to which a 5,000 livres conversion fee for the Semester was added in 1648. He was reimbursed 25,000 livres in 1658. He married in 1626. His wife brought a dowry of 8,000 livres: 3,000 in *rentes* on two communities, 1,000 livres in capital, 700 livres in coffres. When his father died in 1658, he inherited the bulk of the estate, including the fiefs of Tartonne and La Tour-Lauze in Haute-Provence, which his family had held since the fourteenth century. Tartonne brought 1,200 livres annually. Trimond was also a coseigneur of Aiglun in Haute-Provence. He owned a hôtel at Aix, property at Les Mées worth 37,000 livres,

---

[104] Auguste Du Roure, *Généalogie de la maison de Forbin* (Paris, 1906), p. 37.

[105] Tamizey de Larroque, *La correspondance de Peiresc*, VI, 342–343.

[106] *Ibid.*, 73–74.

[107] Emile Isnard, marquis de Gras, *Histoire de la maison de Grasse*, 2 vols. (Paris, 1933), II, 186, 192.

[108] *Ibid.*, 209; ADBR, Aix, Fonds Berlie 301E, 234, fol. 1.

[109] Emile Perrier, *Les coffres d'une grande dame provençale* (Valence, 1902).

vineyards at Manosque, and several bastides. He bought an office of councilor in the Parlement for his son in 1659 for 80,000 livres. His son married in the next year for a dowry of 28,000 livres. Trimond's annual income was close to 10,000 livres, his net worth 200,000 livres.[110]

Loans at five percent to communities and to other magistrates for purchasing their offices were favorite forms of parlementaire investment. Trimond made numerous such loans. *Rentes* on the Paris hôtel de ville were not popular: the Provençaux preferred to invest locally. Intendant Lebret wrote to the contrôleur-général in December 1689 and January 1690 that he was unable to sell 140,000 livres in Paris *rentes*, although he was doing his best. He had bought a considerable amount himself as the first purchaser, but still the Provençaux hesitated.[111]

Most parlementaires derived their income from office and land, as did Pierre Decormis, whose family were écuyers of Aix in the thirteenth century. Decormis owned Beaurecueil, four miles east of Aix, subinfeudated in 1570 to the fief of Tholonet. Beaurecueil included a two-storey stone château, built at the foot of a mountain around a courtyard of plane and chestnut trees. Decormis also owned a hôtel at Aix. He became coseigneur of Fabrègues by marriage in 1600, and added Roqueshaute in 1615. His son Louis, en survivance in 1635 and president in 1650, acquired the fief of Bregançon. The combined annual income of Beaurecueil and Roqueshaute was 1,600 livres. Decormis was assessor of Aix in 1601 and 1611; his brother Artus held the same office in 1605 and 1617, his nephew Antoine in 1640. Avocat-général from 1618 until his death in 1646 at seventy-five, Pierre Decormis was a strict observer of the formalities, never appeared in public without his robe, and followed younger councilors wearing only their neckpieces on promenades in the Place des Prêcheurs until they took refuge in shops or went home.[112]

---

110 "Livre de raison de Léon Trimond," B. Méjanes 1140; Isnard, *Etat documentaire*, pp. 4, 402, 414; "Etat du florinage," B. Méjanes 630, fol. 56; EDB, IV–2, 476; Blanc, "Origine des familles," p. 561.

111 Marchand, *Un intendant*, p. 198.

112 J.-B. Henri Bourrillon, *Notice historique sur la paroisse et le château de Beaurecueil* (Marseille, 1891); EDB, IV–2, 149; "Etat du florinage," B. Méjanes 630, fol. 97; Clapiers-Collongues, *Chronologie*, pp. 21, 163; Blanc, "Origine des familles," p. 187; F.A.T. Roux-Alphéran, *Les rues d'Aix ou recherches historiques sur l'ancienne capitale de la Provence*, 2 vols. (Aix, 1846–1848), II, 12–14.

Jean-François de Glandèves-Rousset also belonged to an old family of the Provençal nobility with a limited income. His father, Gaspard, was the fifth son of François de Glandèves, seigneur de Cuges. Gaspard received as his portion an office of Parlement councilor in 1599. In 1602, he married Véronique de Russan, who inherited as coseigneur from her father the fief of Rousset near Aix, with an estimated annual income of 3,600 livres. Their joint income was probably about 6,000 livres a year. Gaspard had little other property. After his death in 1623, his office was sold to Léon de Valbelle for 54,000 livres. His daughter Alphonsine received 1,800 livres toward her dowry. His sister received 300 livres, and a younger son, who was a Knight of Malta, received 100 pistoles. The bulk of his property—a house at Aix, additions to the château at Rousset, silver plate, tapestries, cash—went to his wife.

Véronique de Russan held the fief and château in her own name. She bought her son Jean-François an office of councilor in 1637 for 60,000 livres. He made a good marriage to Anne d'Escalis de Bras in 1651, but their joint income was limited to the revenue from his office, her dowry, and use of the house at Aix. His mother was long-lived, and she had a strong personality. Her son-in-law, Requêtes councilor Charles de Laugier, sieur de Montblanc, who had recently usurped noble rank, and was willing to marry Alphonsine with a small dowry in 1641, reported to intendant Sève in 1648 that he could not agree to the Semester's investigation of Gueidon's murder because he would lose his mother-in-law's good will! Véronique de Russan kept her son on short financial strings. Oppède reported that Jean-François had to sell his office of councilor in 1656 to pay his debts. Glandèves's six children, mostly girls, were placed in religious houses as the least expensive way of providing for them. The fief of Rousset was not confiscated after Glandèves's participation in the 1659 revolt because it was held by his mother. He died there in 1685.[113]

[113] B.N., Ms. fr. 17389, fols. 266–268, Sève to Séguier, March 24, 1648; Isnard, *Etat documentaire*, pp. 239, 325–326; "Etat du florinage," B. Méjanes 630, fol. 96; ADBR, Aix, Fonds Lombard 309E, 1071, fol. 139; 1077, fol. 63; Clapiers-Collongues, *Chronologie*, p. 99; ADBR, Aix, B 3358, fol. 796v, May 1, 1656; A.A.E., 1721, fols. 227–230, Maynier d'Oppède to Mazarin, October 2, 1657; Auguste Du Roure, *Généalogie de la maison de Glandèves* (Paris, 1907), p. 71; *Généalogie de la maison de Laugier, seigneurs de Montblanc et la Garde* (Paris, 1906), pp. 15–17; abbé Claude Bonifay, *Histoire de Cuges: La seigneurie, la commune* (Marseille, 1948), pp. 80–87;

Glandèves's financial plight illustrates the dilemma of noble families. Nobles with property and titles to bequeath sought large families because the infant mortality rate was high. But numerous children meant portions that fragmented the family fortune. The average family size at Aix in 1695 was two or three children; only seven families had ten or more.[114] Families with numerous children tended to be noble, and many were parlementaires. For instance, the hôtel Maynier d'Oppède in 1695 had thirty-one residents, including six children and twenty-one servants. Their next-door neighbor, Grimaldi-Régusse, had eight children and seven servants. The third house on the street sheltered the widow of Parlement councilor Aymar d'Albi, baron de Châteaurenard, his five children, brother, and five servants.[115] In 1695, there was an average of 9 servants in households of Parlement présidents; 5 in those of councilors; 5 and 2.5 in those of Cour des Comptes presidents and councilors, respectively; 2.5 in those at Trésoriers Généraux; and 1 in the households of lawyers and bourgeois.[116] A good marriage saved the fortunes of many robe families. For instance, Pierre de Coriolis, grandson of the cascaveou chief, married the daughter and heiress of Villeneuve-Espinouse in 1651, thereby acquiring the important fief of Espinouse, which became a marquisat in 1651, and at least three other fiefs.[117] In 1672, Claude de Milan married the daughter and heiress of Forbin de La Roque, thereby acquiring several fiefs and an office of president in the Parlement.[118]

Nicolas-Claude de Fabri, sieur de Peiresc, was moderately wealthy. He inherited an office of councilor from his uncle. He also inherited the fiefs of Calas, Peiresc, Valavez, and the barony and château of Rians, with an annual income of 3,225 livres. He owned the fief and abbey of Guître near Bordeaux, a hôtel at Aix,

---

EDB, IV–2, 245–246; Blanc, "Origine des familles," pp. 285–290; see Chapter Nine.

[114] Ribbe, *Les familles et la société*, II, 175–180; Robert Forster, *The House of Saulx-Tavanes: Versailles and Burgundy, 1700–1803* (Baltimore, 1970); Jacqueline Carrière, *La population d'Aix-en-Provence à la fin du XVII*ᵉ *siècle* (Aix, 1958), p. 45.

[115] *Ibid.*, pp. 42–43.

[116] Coste, *La ville d'Aix*, II, 717, 960.

[117] Isnard, *Etat documentaire*, pp. 114, 161, 347, 441.

[118] Roure, *La maison de Forbin*, p. 30.

and the country house of Belgentier near Toulon, famous for its gardens and fountains. His annual income was variously estimated at 18,000 to 21,000 livres and 24,000 to 27,000 livres. He spent much on books, medals, paintings, and antiquities. Tall and thin, with a long melancholy face, he was a famous bibliophile known for his collections and correspondence with the leading savants of Europe. His brother, Palamède de Fabri, chevalier, who used the titles seigneur of Valavez and baron of Rians, was a deputy of the second estate of Provence to the last Estates General in 1614. Peiresc died in 1637.[119]

Charles de Lombard, seigneur de Gourdon, came from a family of chief lieutenants of the Grasse seneschal court. He was moderately wealthy. Lombard increased an inherited fortune by careful management. In 1650, his net worth was estimated at 316,640 livres, with an annual income of 15,200 livres. He bought; he never sold. The fief of Gourdon provided revenues of 1,200 livres a year. He owned all or part of the fiefs of Le Castelet, Beauvest, Barrême, La Colle, and Malignon. In 1641, he bought part of the fief of Saint Césaire for 21,000 livres. In 1647, he bought the fief of Barjols for 15,100 livres, which he exchanged with the bishop of Fréjus in 1653 for the château and fief of Montauroux, with an annual income of 1,350 livres. Lombard had claimed this fief for several years, and in 1649, he tried to have his créatures elected to the city council. The case was eventually referred to the Grand Conseil after he tried to revive certain lapsed fiscal rights of the bishopric in his own name. In 1666, he bought Château Arnoux.[120]

Henri de Forbin-Maynier d'Oppède also obtained much of his

[119] Phillipe Tamizey de Larroque and Alexandre Moutett, *Autour de Peiresc* (Aix, 1898), p. 19; *Les confessions de Jean-Jacques Bouchard, Parisien, suivies de son voyage de Paris à Rome en 1630* (Paris, 1881), pp. 131–132; B.N., Ms. fr. 4332, fols. 206–208, will of Peiresc; G. Naudé, "Notice sur Peiresc," B.N., Ms. fr. n.a. 4217; Pierre Humbert, *Un amateur: Peiresc (1580–1637)* (Paris, 1933); Georges Cahen-Salvador, *Un grand humaniste: Peiresc* (Paris, 1951); portrait in EDB, III, plate VII; J. Michael Hayden, *France and the Estates General of 1614* (Cambridge, 1974), p. 262.

[120] ADBR, Aix, B 3358, fol. 12v; Fonds Berlie 301E, 233, fol. 329; Raymond Collier, *La vie en Haute-Provence de 1600 à 1850* (Digne, 1973), p. 315; Pierre-André Sigalas, *La vie à Grasse en 1650* (Grasse, 1964), pp. 124–129; Pillorget, *Les mouvements*, p. 611; B.M., Harleian 4575, fol. 96; "Etat du florinage," B. Méjanes 630, fols. 49, 52, 105–106, 129; Blanc, "Origine des familles," pp. 346–347; EDB, IV–2, 306–307; Isnard, *Etat documentaire*, p. 99.

income from land. But he belonged to the small group of wealthy parlementaires. The Mayniers were an old family of the robe nobility in the Comtat Venaissin, where they had held the château and barony of Oppède since 1500. In 1578, the granddaughter of the last baron married into one of the most illustrious noble families of Provence, the Forbins, and her husband, Jean de Forbin, seigneur de La Fare, assumed her family name in order to inherit the title. His grandson, Henri de Forbin-Maynier d'Oppède, had an approximate annual income of 45,000 livres and a fortune recently estimated at 572,588 livres, an admittedly incomplete and conservative figure. Oppède's fortune may have been as great as 900,000 livres, nearer that of the wealthy comte de Grignan, who enjoyed 50,000 to 60,000 livres annual income and a net worth of 1,700,000 livres.[121]

Oppède's mother paid 63,000 livres for an office of Parlement councilor for her son in 1637, the year in which he married Marie de Pontevès for a dowry of 100,000 livres. His two sisters were married with dowries of 60,000 and 42,000 livres, respectively. In 1654, Oppède sold an office of president in the Parlement for 144,000 livres, having purchased the office of first president for 180,000 livres and spent another 60,000 livres, perhaps more, in bribes. His father, Vincent-Anne, had purchased the same office for 105,000 livres in 1620. Oppède's oldest son, Jean-Baptiste, purchased an office of Parlement president for 120,000 livres in 1674 and married in that year for a dowry of 220,000 livres. Three of Oppède's daughters married with dowries of 45,000 livres each, and three became nuns. Two of his sons became Knights of Malta; a third was a canon of Saint Sauveur.

Oppède's library of 160 books was valued at 1,083 livres in 1676. Part of his library must have been sold, because it was valued at 4,500 livres five years earlier, at his death. He had 46 paintings valued at 2,329 livres in 1677. After 1647, he had extensive work done on his hôtel at Aix, which dated to the late fifteenth century—an arcade constructed, the woodwork repaired, the walls replastered, and decorative ironwork added. The furnishings were valued at more than 5,000 livres. He kept 8 carriage horses

[121] Richard Holbrook, "Baron d'Oppède and Cardinal Mazarin," Appendix III, pp. 428–434; Roger Du Chêne, "Argent et famille au XVIIᵉ siècle: Mme de Sévigné et les Grignans," *Provence historique*, 15 (1965), 205–228; 16 (1966), 3–41, 587–620.

and 2 saddle horses. Oppède's property in Provence included the fiefs of La Fare and Peyrolles held directly from the king, the fief of Berre held from the duc de Vendôme, the fiefs of Rouret, Vitrolles, Varages en Beaudun, and Saint Julien. He also had land at Marseille, and he was an extensive creditor of magistrates and communities. His property in the Comtat Venaissin included the château and fief of Oppède near Cavaillon and land at Cadenet and Cavaillon.[122] Oppède was wealthier than any parlementaire we have yet discussed, and he lived in a manner befitting his wealth.

The Escalis-Sabran were another old noble family of the Comtat Venaissin. They had been barons of Ansouis since the fifteenth century and barons of Bras since the sixteenth century, and their income was mostly from land. They held at least nine fiefs in Haute-Provence and others in Basse-Provence and the Comtat. Marc-Antoine d'Escalis-Sabran de Bras was first president of the Parlement from 1616 to 1621. His son Sextius was first consul of Aix in 1630, 1647, and 1649. His grandson Henri purchased Oppède's office of Parlement president in 1655.[123]

The wealthier parlementaires often had fortunes from commerce and finance—for instance, the Cauvets. Savoyard merchants Jean and Martin Cauvet came to Marseille in the sixteenth

[122] Roure, *La maison de Forbin*, pp. 49–51; Pierre Daverdi, *Oraison funèbre de Henri de Forbin d'Oppède*, notes by A.-J. Rance Bourrey (Marseille, 1889); marquis de Forbin d'Oppède, *Monographie de la terre et du château de Saint Marcel du X$^e$ au XIX$^e$ siècle* (Marseille, 1888); *Monographie de la terre et du château de La Verdière et des familles qui l'ont successivement possédé sans interruption du X$^e$ au XIX$^e$ siècle* (Marseille, 1880); *Inventaire analytique des titres de la maison de Forbin recueillis au château de Saint Marcel* (Marseille, 1900); "Etat du florinage," B. Méjanes 630, fols. 43, 90; ADBR, Aix, Fonds Lombard 309E, 1077, fols. 324, 343; 1069, fol. 517; Isnard, *Etat documentaire*, p. 368; EDB, IV–2, 207–214; A.A.E., 1713, fol. 125, March, 1648; Jacques Billioud, *Le Livre en Provence du XVI$^e$ au XVIII$^e$ siècle* (Marseille, 1962), p. 176; Clapiers-Collongues, *Chronologie*, pp. 5, 6, 8, 9; Blanc, "Origine des familles," pp. 243–248; Richard Holbrook, "Baron d'Oppède and Cardinal Mazarin," pp. 20–39; 423–425, appendix I; 426–427, appendix II; 428–434, appendix III.

[123] Blanc, "Origine des familles," pp. 513–515; EDB, IV–2, 184–185; Isnard, *Etat documentaire*, pp. 54, 64, 163; "Etat du florinage," B. Méjanes 630, fols. 19, 25, 28, 78; Grimaldi and Gaufridy, *Mémoires*, p. 40; see Chapters Five, Seven, and Nine.

century and prospered. Naturalized in 1563, Jean made a fortune importing wheat, drugs, spices, and alum used in dying cloth. From 1582 to 1591, he exported German pewter to Turkey. The pewter was used as an alloy with copper in making bronze cannons, and thus he entered the munitions trade. His fortune was estimated at 900,000 livres in 1595, when the family, already living nobly, began buying fiefs, holding military and judicial offices, and making good marriages to assume nobility. Jean bought part of the barony of Trets in 1597 for 23,000 écus (69,000 livres). His son, Jean-Baptiste, bought the barony of Marignane in 1603 with estimated annual revenues of 7,600 livres—its château now serves as the town hall—and an office of Parlement councilor in 1609. In 1629, he bought the château and fief of Valaux for 157,000 livres, with annual revenues of 5,500 livres. In 1634, he bought the fief of Sillans for 108,000 livres, which he later sold. He also owned the château and fief of Gignac.

Jean-Baptiste's older son, Henri, in 1637 married Melchione d'Escalis de Bras. Henri bought the château and fief of Saint Cannat, which was sold for 106,000 livres in 1646, and the Iles d'Or off the coast at Hyères. Residing in the family hôtel at Marseille, Henri became governor of the Tour de Bouc fortress in 1644. His younger brother, Gaspard, inherited their father's parlementary office in 1638, the year in which he married the sister of Henri de Forbin-Maynier d'Oppède. Gaspard inherited the château and barony of Bormes from his mother. He also received the château and fief of Vitrolles. Gaspard belonged to the opposition until his brother's death in 1647, when he became leader of the Provençal party of nobles supporting Alais.[124]

The Valbelles were another wealthy family of Marseille merchants who assumed nobility in the sixteenth century by naval and military office-holding, living nobly, buying fiefs, and making good

---

[124] Joseph Billioud, "Du commerce de Marseille à la noblesse, les Covet de Marignane (1555–1803)," *Marseille*, 39 (1959), 3–16; Blanc, "Origine des familles," pp. 189–190; EDB, IV–2, 153–154; ADBR, Aix, B 3352, fol. 121; Auguste Du Roure, *Inventaire analytique de titres et documents originaux tirés des archives du Château de Barbegal* (Paris, 1903), pp. 15–16; ADBR, Aix, Fonds Berlie 301E, 217, fol. 483; "Etat du florinage," B. Méjanes 630, fols. 52, 90, 91; Roure, *La maison de Forbin*, p. 49; Adolphe Crémieux, *Marseille et la royauté pendant la minorité de Louis XIV*, 2 vols. (Paris, 1917), I, 217, 225. On the nobility of the Cauvets, see Pillorget, *Les mouvements insurrectionnels*, p. 226, n. 313.

marriages. They had accumulated a fortune in the eastern trade in drugs and spices. In 1586, Barthélemy de Valbelle, who later became a client of the duc de Guise, acquired the office of lieutenant of the Marseille admiralty court. He owned the fief of Pallières, and the château and fief of Cadarache overlooking the Durance, with its dependant fiefs of Carsis and Veauvezet. Cadarache rented for 2,700 livres in 1675; its estimated income in 1668 was 3,300 livres. It included several bastides, paper mills (rented for 2,000 livres), and a château.

Barthélemy had eleven children. His oldest son, Léon, inherited Cadarache. In 1620, Léon purchased the fiefs of Bevons, La Tour de Bevons, and Saint Symphorien from Vincent-Anne de Forbin-Maynier d'Oppède. In 1625, when his father died, Léon bought an office of councilor in the Parlement from the widow of Gaspard de Glandèves. In 1637, he inherited from his cousin, the last of the Alagonia family of the Provençal sword nobility, the château and fief of Meyrargues—4,068 hectares along the Durance—and 30,000 ducats annual income from lands in the Kingdom of Naples, plus two houses at Aix and their furnishings. He later constructed a fine hôtel at Aix on the Cours Mirabeau. Meyrargues in 1672 included a village of 218 families, 18 bastides, and 2 paper mills. It brought 13,800 livres annual revenue. Its château had 30 inhabitants—Léon himself, who died the next year; his oldest son, wife, and six children; eighteen servants, including a housekeeping couple, clerk, driver, gamekeeper, stableman, and seven footmen. Oppède in 1663 described Léon de Valbelle as one of the wealthiest men in the Parlement.[125]

Léon's cousin in the Parlement was Jean-Baptiste de Valbelle, sieur de Saint Symphorien, an inherited fief in the viguerie of Sisteron in the foothills of the Alps. Probably he was part owner; some fiefs in Haute-Provence were divided many times. His father, Léon de Valbelle, écuyer, was a deputy of the second estate, rep-

[125] G.B. Depping, *Correspondance administrative sous le règne de Louis XIV*, 4 vols. (Paris, 1851), II, 94–96; Ivan Rampel, *Un vieux domaine provençal: Cadarache* (Marseille, 1945); Raphael Bourrillon, *Meyrargues des origines jusqu'à nos jours* (Forcalquier, 1956); Emmanuel Davin, "Une grande famille provençale: Les Valbelle," *Bulletin de la société des amis du Vieux Toulon*, 68 (1941), 98–112; Dr. Gabriel, "Origine de la maison de Valbelle," *Provence historique*, 7 (1957), 22–34; "Etat du florinage," B. Méjanes 630, fols. 8, 9, 76, 83, 96, 97; Isnard, *Etat documentaire*, pp. 55, 368, 431; Blanc, "Origine des familles," p. 569; EDB, IV–2, 481–483.

resenting Marseille at the last Estates General in 1614; he had also served as first consul of Marseille in 1616 and 1630. Jean-Baptiste's mother was Marguerite Doria, member of the Marseille branch of a famous old noble family of Genoa. Having bought an office of councilor in the Parlement in 1637, Jean-Baptiste married Marguerite de Vintimille, daughter of the comte d'Ollioules, who brought as her dowry the barony and château of Tourves in the Var, a sizeable property which was later erected into a marquisat. The château had fifty rooms around an inner courtyard, a columned facade with a balcony, and a lovely park. It was decorated with a great number of paintings. An inventory of Jean-Baptiste's *cabinet* in his Aix hôtel listed sixty-two paintings, including one by Mignard, two by the elder Brueghel, one by Corregio, one by Rubens, one by Giotto, two by the elder Holbein, with twenty-one bronzes and twenty-four marble statues. Evidently Jean-Baptiste, who owned at least another six fiefs, was a wealthy man, if not as wealthy as his cousin Léon. Jean-Baptiste's son, who inherited his father's office in the Parlement in 1677 and became a president in 1686, had an impressive library in his Aix hôtel, the fine leather bindings stamped with his arms, a combination of those of the comtes de Forcalquier, the vicomtes de Marseille, and the Valbelles, who used a rampant greyhound in silver on an azure field.[126] Jean-Baptiste used the title of marquis of Tourves. By the late seventeenth century, this branch of the Valbelle family had moved into the highest circles of the robe.

The fortune of Charles de Grimaldi (Grimaud) was chiefly financial: Oppède in 1663 disdainfully described him as "a man of all kinds of traités and partis." He came from a wealthy La Ciotat family near Marseille. His aunts received dowries of 70,000 livres, his sister a dowry of 75,000 livres. Grimaldi inherited the property of his paternal grandfather and maternal uncle, who

---

[126] EDB, IV–2, 481; Octave Tessier, *Un grand seigneur au XVIIIᵉ siècle, le comte de Valbelle* (Paris, 1890), pp. 99, n. 1, 199–200; "Etat du florinage," B. Méjanes 630, fols. 9, 39, 83, 96; B. Méjanes 1038, "Inventaire du cabinet des livres, peintures et rares curiosités appartenant à Monseigneur le baron de Saint-Symphorien, rangé en son hôtel, rue Bellegarde, dans le mois de janvier 1656, par son très humble et obéissant serviteur Geoffroy"; Hayden, *France and the Estates General of 1614*, p. 262; Clapiers-Collongues, *Chronologie*, pp. 24, 89, 107; Jacques Billioud, *Le livre en Provence du XVIᵉ au XVIIIᵉ siècle* (Marseille, 1962), p. 196; ADBR, Aix, B 3351, fol. 162.

died without heirs; his office of councilor came from his uncle. From his father, he inherited the château and fief of Régusse, erected into a marquisat in 1649 with an estimated annual income of 3,600 livres. He bought a hôtel at Aix, the fiefs of Villeneuve Catelas with an income of 1,200 livres and Roumoules, erected into a barony in 1649, and an office of Parlement president. He owned at least eight other fiefs with a total annual income of 10,000 livres. He was able to levy and support an infantry regiment and cavalry company in 1649, as could Oppède and Escalis de Bras.

Régusse wrote in his memoirs that his fortune came from maritime commerce and investments in treaties and community debts. His fortune was probably as large as that of Oppède. Under a pseudonym, he was a partner with Antoine de Valbelle, Marseille admiralty lieutenant and brother of the councilor, in the treaty on the five percent tax on imports from Alexandria, which was abolished by mob action in 1644, encouraged by their political enemies, Alais and Champigny. Régusse was also a partner under a pseudonym with Valbelle in the three percent tax on imported Egyptian merchandise, levied to amortize debts contracted by French ambassador Crézy at Constantinople. He participated in treaties for the levy of the droit de franc-fief and droit de 22½ on communities and nonnoble inheritances in Provence; he estimated in 1644 that he lost 40,000 livres on these treaties. He unsuccessfully offered 165,000 livres for the office of Parlement first president in 1653. He eventually received from the crown a pension of 2,000 livres and a brevet of councilor of state for his long service. The daughter of Madame de Sévigné called Régusse, "une barbe sale et un vieux fleuve!" Régusse had eight children. The oldest son inherited his office. He bought an office of captain in the provincial infantry regiment for one son, a priory in Normandy (later exchanged for one in Dauphiné), and the office of chief lieutenant of the Brignoles seneschal court for the other two sons.[127]

---

[127] Depping, *Correspondance administrative*, II, 94–96; Grimaldi and Gaufridy, *Mémoires*, pp. 4, 7, 8, 10, 11, 19–20, 23, 35, 97; ADBR, Marseille, IX B 2, fols. 494, 499, 529, 541, 557; Isnard, *Etat documentaire*, pp. 75, 126, 182, 322; "Etat du florinage," B. Méjanes 603, fols. 22, 44, 93, 126; EDB, IV–2, 254; ADBR, Aix, B 3357, fol. 8; René Pillorget, "Destin de la ville d'ancien régime," in *Histoire de Marseille*, ed. Edouard Baratier (Toulouse, 1973), pp. 178–179; *Les mouvements insurrectionnels*, pp. 554–

The career of the Maurel brothers was a seventeenth-century success story. They made a financial fortune, bought fiefs, arranged good marriages for their children, acquired parlementaire office, and entered the nobility within a generation. Antoine and Pierre Maurel had been prosperous cloth merchants at Aix for twenty years when they jointly bought the newly created office of provincial postal controller for 24,498 livres each in 1633. Antoine in 1640 bought an office of Trésorier Général, probably for 40,000–45,000 livres. He bought an office of councilor auditor in the Cour des Comptes in 1641 for 40,000 livres. In 1640, he bought the fief of Valbonette, in 1642 the fiefs of Chaffaut and Malemoisson, later adding the fief of Sainte Croix. In 1618, Antoine married Jeanne Moricaud, daughter of an Aix merchant. They had six children. Their oldest son, André, became a councilor in the Parlement in 1651. Their fifth child, Gabrielle, married Requêtes councilor Charles de Tressemanes-Chasteuil in 1646.

Antoine's younger brother, Pierre, had the more spectacular career. Pierre bought an office of *trésorier particulier du taillon* in 1637, which he exchanged for an office of *trésorier général du taillon* in 1638, and resigned after he bought an office of councilor auditor in the Cour des Comptes in 1639. He bought land on the Cours Mirabeau in 1647 to construct a hôtel for an estimated cost of 45,000 livres. Its furnishings included rooms in red, blue, yellow, and green, with matching bedspreads, drapes, chair covers, and tapestries, walls covered in gold-stamped leather, chairs and stools by the dozens, marble-topped tables, gilt-framed mirrors and paintings, silver candlesticks, cut glass chandeliers, and walnut tables, chests, and cabinets (local furniture was made of olive wood.) The value of the hôtel furnishings was estimated at 45,000 livres in 1671, not including the silverware. In 1650, Pierre bought the château and fief of Pontevès, as well as the fief of Sainte Cathérine, for 159,000 livres. Their estimated annual income was 7,000 livres. In 1670, he estimated the value of Pontevès at 300,000 livres; in 1674, after his death, its value was placed at 290,000 livres. It was estimated that he had spent 59,576 livres renovating and furnishing the château, which he used as a country

---

561; M. Monmerqué, ed., *Lettres de Madame de Sévigné*, 14 vols. (Paris, 1862–1866), VI, 423–424, May 27, 1689. Sources for a detailed study of Régusse's fortune are provided by Pillorget, *Les mouvements insurrectionnels*, p. 712, n. 16.

house. Most parlementaires, for example Gaufridy, Gallifet, Du Chaine, and Decormis, had a hôtel in Aix and a country house nearby, but the furnishings were not as luxurious as those of Maurel. In 1656, he bought the fiefs of Valonne and Châteauneuf-sous-Valonne, later adding that of Maubousquet.

In 1653, Pierre bought an office of Trésorier Général, which he held for five years, buying another in 1665 for 33,840 livres, which he held until his death in 1672. In 1655, he bought an office of councilor corrector in the Cour des Comptes for 23,000 livres. In 1657, he signed a contract as treasurer of the provincial Estates for six years. His fortune was then estimated at 900,000 to 1,200,-000 livres. Maurel renewed the contract in 1662 and 1668, being the only provincial treasurer in nearly a century to avoid bankruptcy. An inventory of his property in 1670 placed his wealth at 2,039,345 livres. Six months before his death in 1672, Pierre de Maurel received royal letters "rehabilitating" himself, his brother, and their families, thus entering the nobility.

Pierre had three wives and eighteen children. His first wife, daughter of a wealthy cloth dyer, gave him four children. His oldest son, François, married the daughter of councilor Gaspard de Villeneuve-Mons and bought an office of councilor in the Parlement in 1654 for 72,000 livres, which he sold to his brother Antoine in 1662 for the same amount. François received 162,000 livres from his father in his marriage contract. Antoine received 192,000 livres when he married a daughter of the Thomassins in 1655. Pierre's second wife, Suzanne, was the daughter of Parlement councilor Henri de Laurens (whose son in 1665 married a daughter of Oppède). She gave him two children. The oldest, Pierre, became a councilor in the Cour des Comptes and married a daughter of parlementaire Louis Decormis. Pierre's third wife, Diane de Pontevès, gave him twelve children. Two daughters married sons of parlementaires; four became nuns; two sons died in infancy; one was an imbecile; the other three sons received 100,000 livres each.[128] The Maurels supported Oppède in 1659.

[128] Boisgelin, *Maurel de Villeneuve de Mons*; Emile Perrier, *L'hôtel et le château d'un financier aixois: Pierre Maurel de Pontevès* (Valence, 1902); Depping, *Correspondance administrative*, II, 94–96; Tamizey de Larroque, *La correspondance de Peiresc*, VI, 707; A.M., Aix, CC 356; ADBR, Aix, B 3350, fols. 443, 446; A.A.E., 1721, fols. 291–294, Maynier d'Oppède to Mazarin, December 18, 1657; Isnard, *Etat documentaire*, pp. 90, 105, 215, 432, 459; "Etat du florinage," B. Méjanes 630, fols. 9, 32, 49; Blanc, "Origine des familles," p. 373.

Oppède, Cauvet, the Valbelles, Régusse, and the Maurels belonged to a small group of wealthy parlementaires. Their political opinions and affiliations varied. The majority of Aix parlementaires were not wealthy. Their annual incomes were less than 10,000 livres, of which 1,500 to 2,000 livres came from their offices. Devaluation was a serious financial matter for them. In fact, the fortunes of the Aix parlementaires may have been more modest than their colleagues in larger, northern courts.[129] The creation of the Semester was an important motive for revolt in 1649. Most of the Aix parlementaires were robe nobles, although an important minority were from families of the sword nobility. The Maurels demonstrated that it was still possible for nonnobles to enter the Parlement in the mid-seventeenth century, and their careers indicate the path of upward mobility.

Another problem, easily overlooked but connected to the increases in the number of parlementaire offices, was the anxiety of existing office-holders to ensure that their company be "well-composed."[130] The parlementaires feared that offices bought for social prestige derived from exclusivity would be debased if there were large numbers of offices available. Parlementaire offices in the seventeenth century were becoming a monopoly. Dynasties of robe nobles held office, such as the Coriolis, Thomassin, Gallifet, and Périer. The parlementaires were becoming a closed social caste. Of seventy families holding office in the 1640s, at least thirty had held office for half a century.[131] Thirty-four of the parlementaires serving in this decade had received their offices from fathers, five from uncles, two from fathers-in-law, and one from a cousin. This was

[129] Bluche and Meyer have noted the extreme variability of parliamentaire fortunes; cf. *Les magistrats du Parlement de Paris*, pp. 143–155, and *La noblesse bretonne*, II, 969–976. The range at Aix was as great as that at Paris and Rennes, but there were probably more parlementaires at Aix whose fortunes were modest. Office prices were also slightly lower than in some other parlements, for instance Rouen and Toulouse; cf. Mousnier, *La vénalité*, pp. 359–361, 471–474, and Jean-Claude Paulhet, "Les parlementaires toulousains à la fin du dix-septième siècle," *Annales du Midi*, 76 (1964), 189–204.

[130] Fear for the composition of a sovereign court has been discussed by Charles Carrière, "Le recrutement de la Cour des Comptes, Aides et Finances d'Aix-en-Provence à la fin de l'ancien régime," 81ᵉ Congrès National des Sociétés Savantes, Rouen-Caen, 1956, *Actes*, pp. 141–159.

[131] Vindry, *Les parlementaires francais*; Clapiers-Collongues, *Chronologie*.

a total of forty-two hereditary officeholders, more than half of the Parlement's membership.[132] Twenty-nine newcomers joined the company in the 1650s. Eleven were sons, one a grandson, one a son-in-law, and one a brother of parlementaires.[133] In 1695, 43 of 111 parlementaires had inherited their offices from their fathers.[134]

The parlementaires feared that the Chambre des Requêtes and Semester would dilute the company's exclusivity and weaken its prestige. The Chambre des Requêtes was not a serious threat because eight of its fourteen members were closely related to parlementaires; only two were from families new to judicial office-holding.[135] But the Semester doubled the number of existing offices and offered an opportunity for wholesale entry into the company of men with nonnoble and nonjudicial origins, social undesirables. This wholesale entry was avoided in 1648 because the parlementaires so intimidated new purchasers that only eight offices were sold. But the possibility of social dilution made everyone uneasy about the company's future.

The concern to maintain social prestige was more intense than the fear of losing rank from the crown's revocation of the Paulette. The Paulette was renewable every nine years, usually after considerable bargaining as from 1629 to 1630, 1638 to 1640, 1647 to 1649, and 1658 to 1659.[136] The prolonged bargaining and the crown's threats to increase the annual tax of the Paulette created hidden tension. It is no coincidence that there were major confrontations between the Aix parlementaires and the crown in these years. But pressure from Paulette negotiations should not be exaggerated as a motivation for revolt: it was less important in causing the Aix revolts than contemporary historians have recognized.[137]

[132] Appendix I; Clapiers-Collongues, *Chronologie*; ADBR, Aix, B 3346–3356.

[133] Clapiers-Collongues, *Chronologie*, pp. 94–100.

[134] Coste, *La ville d'Aix*, II, 778.

[135] Appendix I; EDB, IV–2; Blanc, "Origine des familles."

[136] See Mousnier, *La vénalité*, pp. 232–409; A. Lloyd Moote, *The Revolt of the Judges: The Parlement of Paris and the Fronde, 1648–1653* (Princeton, 1971), pp. 125–141; A.A.E., 1721, fols. 324–329, 520–523, 526–529; 1723, fol. 505; 1724, fols. 97–119; Chapter Six.

[137] Mousnier, *La vénalité*, pp. 649–650, and "The Fronde" in *Preconditions of Revolution in Early Modern Europe* (Baltimore, 1970), ed. Robert Forster and Jack P. Greene, p. 146; Pillorget, *Mouvements insurrectionnels*, pp. 319–320, 765–766, 800.

Paulette negotiations were concluded several months before the 1630 revolt began: the royal decree reestablishing the Paulette was issued on February 1, 1630, and extended to the sovereign courts on June 23, three months before the cascaveoux revolt began.[138] The majority of Aix parlementaires had been ennobled before 1600 and were not personally threatened by Paulette negotiations: the Aix company had a higher percentage of members belonging to the old nobility than did northern courts such as Paris or Rouen. Individual citations in disciplinary legislation proved a more threatening and effective means of coercion.

Parlementaires with illustrious noble names and large landholdings mustered armed clients to form private armies. It is significant they were among the most ardent of the opposition. Decormis, Forbin de La Roque, Aymar d'Albi, Valbelle, Oppède, Escalis de Bras, Régusse, and Glandèves-Rousset raised troops in 1649 to fight the governor, while Cauvet de Bormes recruited troops for Alais. We have already seen how Coriolis called relatives and clients to his aid in 1630. Oppède did the same in 1651 and 1659, Decormis in 1649 and 1659, Escalis de Bras in 1659. Many of the rebels in the streets of Aix were relatives, friends, and clients of parlementaires. The number of sword nobles and fiefowners in the Aix company increased its unruliness. Kinship and clientage ties were an important motive for participation in the revolts.

Of the seventy families in the Parlement in the 1640s, forty-one belonged to the opposition. Only fifteen were royalists.[139] The royalists are difficult to characterize as a group because they were not a political party, not even a faction. They were not capable of coordinated political activity; they were not unified; they had no self-recognition. In fact, their chief characteristic was lack of cohesion. The royalists were motivated by immediate personal gain. They supported the crown individually for reasons of self-interest, and their political behavior was unpredictable. They were members of the Chambre des Requêtes and Semester; appointees such as the first presidents; the royal attorneys; parlementaires with close relatives in newly created offices; parlementaires who had received favors from the crown or were engaged in private feuds.

---

[138] A.A.E., 795 bis, fols. 44–49, 179–183.

[139] Forty-seven of the parlementaires holding office in the 1640s belonged to the opposition; twenty-one were royalists. See Appendix I.

Royal attorneys Rabasse and Gantès were royalists in 1649, as were councilors Ballon and Gautier, who had sons in the Requêtes. Gaufridy and Oppède were seduced by royal favors. Foresta de La Roquette was engaged in a private feud. The royalists were often new judges and nobles, members of contested chambers, who had more to gain by supporting the crown than by opposing it. A diverse group, new to the robe and motivated by personal interest, the royalists lacked the tight web of kinship ties unifying the opposition. Robert Mandrou has noted that there was conflict between sword and robe nobles within the parlements.[140] At Aix, there was conflict between old and new officeholders.

Threatened devaluation of offices and reduction of income for parlementaires of modest fortune were important motives for revolt in 1649. So were fears of tarnished social prestige and weakened political authority. But the Aix parlementaires had other personal and political motives for revolt, which have been overlooked. Kinship and clientage ties were an important determinant of political behavior. Youth and membership in the Enquêtes created esprit de corps, as did the anger and inconvenience of disciplinary citations. Personality clashes and internal quarrels over precedence and authority became entangled in the struggles with the crown; in fact, the crown encouraged these divisions to weaken the Parlement. Quarrels with other provincial officials and institutions also contributed to causing the revolts. In an article on the parlementaire Fronde at Paris, Roland Mousnier writes, "We should above all like to know whether the economic and financial factors were the determining cause of everything else, whether they determined the feelings, the mentality, and the actions of men. In the present state of knowledge, we cannot say."[141] We have tried to answer this question for the magistrates at Aix and to suggest other determining factors.

We need to revise our understanding of the motives of rebellious officials. Parlementaires went into the streets of Aix to

[140] Robert Mandrou, *La France au XVIIᵉ et XVIIIᵉ siècles* (Paris, 1970), p. 129; *Classes et luttes de classes en France au début du XVIIᵉ siècle* (Florence, 1965), pp. 42–48, 120, 129. Mandrou was specifically interested in sword and robe precedence disputes, of which there were few at Aix.

[141] Roland Mousnier, "Quelques raisons de la Fronde: Les causes des journées révolutionnaires parisiennes," *XVIIᵉ siècle* (1949), pp. 33–78, reprinted in *La plume, la faucille et le marteau* (Paris, 1970), p. 299.

lead angry crowds, risking office and fortune, for many reasons. Several of their motives for revolt are well-known: they feared the consequences of royal policies threatening their financial investments in office-holding and their social prestige, and they worried about the political future of their company. But they also had personal and political motives that have been ignored: they followed brothers and fathers-in-law into the streets of Aix, joined other members of their chamber, vented anger at recent citations, continued private and institutional feuds, and aired quarrels over precedence and authority. These motives could be as compelling for individuals as economic considerations.

# Chapter Eight

# THE 1649 REVOLT AND THE FRONDE
## AT AIX

A royal attorney in the Marseille seneschal court was one of the first to buy an office in the Semester Parlement. Philippe Gueidon came to Aix on March 15, 1648, to obtain provision letters as a Semester councilor from the royal chancellery.[1] The opposition parlementaires threatened his life, hoping to frighten him into returning to Marseille. Gueidon announced that he feared nothing, particularly idle threats. Although warned by the intendant to stay in a private house, he took a room at The Black Mule Inn near the southeastern city wall and boasted that he would be the plank over which other purchasers would cross.[2]

At eight o'clock on the evening of March 18, Gueidon was sitting at dinner in The Black Mule with a number of other guests. Suddenly, masked men ran into the inn. Posting one man at the door as guard, three or four others burst into the room and shot Gueidon. When he fell on the table, they stabbed him twice in the back. One of the assailants cried, "The first one who moves is dead." While the spectators stared, immobilized, another overturned the table to block the door and discourage pursuit. Then the masked men vanished into the night. Gueidon was carried from the room, never to recover from his wounds; he died four months later.[3]

---

[1] Philippe Gueidon (or Gueydon) was *avocat et procureur du roi au siège de Marseille* by royal provision letters of December 8, 1640; cf. ADBR, Aix, B 3353, fol. 18.

[2] B.M., Harleian 4575, "Semestre de Provence par M. de Sève, conseiller d'état," fols. 18v, 20–20v; ADBR, Aix, A. Savine, *Relation des troubles occasionnés en Provence par l'établissement d'une Chambre-Semestre et du mouvement dit le Sabre* (Aix, 1881), p. 34. Sève noted eight masked men, four at the door and four in the room, who shot Gueidon three times.

[3] On April 7, 1648, Sève wrote Séguier that there was little hope Gueidon would live. Achart reported this as the opinion of Gueidon's

251

Anonymous posters and placards appeared all over Aix in the next few days warning other purchasers of a similar fate. The parlementaires' intimidation was successful. On March 31, Achart, the agent selling the offices, wrote to Tabouret, the traitant who had contracted the sale at Paris: "Don't hope to sell offices unless Gueidon's murderers are punished; everyone is mute and no longer speaks of buying our merchandise."[4] On April 7 he wrote, "It seems we must give the offices for nothing."[5] Avocat-général Decormis wrote to Séguier on May 5 that everyone was too frightened to buy Semester offices.[6] On July 21, Achart wrote, "No one asks of us our merchandise."[7] A decree of the council of state on March 27 ordered the Semester to sit until all its offices sold, however long that might take, the acceptable minimum being two presidents and thirty councilors.[8] But the Semester had only two presidents and twenty councilors—the rest of its offices never sold.[9]

An inquiry into the murder was held during the night of March 18-19 by governor Alais, intendant Sève, the Aix consuls, first president Mesgrigny, the royal attorneys, and Semester judges Gaufridy, Rabasse, and Trimond. Interrogations were also held on March 22 and 24.[10] One of the masked men had dropped a pistol at the door as he left. At dawn on the morning of March 19 a gunsmith and his son identified the pistol as one of a pair they had cleaned and repaired for Louis Estienne, sieur de Vaillac, thirty-three year old captain in an infantry regiment. Estienne and his brother were questioned, as well as their servants. They said they had dined together at six, then retired to their separate rooms. Estienne had gone out around eight, wearing only his sword, to visit a lady whom he refused to name. He denied owning the pistol,

---

brother; cf. B.N., Ms. fr. 17389, fols. 156–157; Jean-Scholastique Pitton, *Histoire de la ville d'Aix* (Aix, 1666), p. 425. On May 18, Decormis wrote to Mazarin that Gueidon was not improving; cf. B.N., Ms. fr. 17389, fol. 303. Gueidon died in July.

[4] Pitton, *Histoire de la ville d'Aix*, p. 424.

[5] *Ibid.*, p. 425.

[6] B.N., Ms. fr. 17389, fols. 234–235.

[7] Pitton, *Histoire de la ville d'Aix*, p. 420.

[8] A.A.E., 1713, fols. 115–118; B.N., Dupuy 672, fol. 152.

[9] See Appendix III.

[10] B.N., Ms. fr. 18977, fols. 41–74; A.C., Aix, BB 102, fols. 130–131; A.A.E., 1713, fols. 103–104; B.M., Harleian 4575, fols. 22–23v; Pitton, *Histoire de la ville d'Aix*, p. 427, Achart to Tabouret, May 12, 1648.

as did his servants, and he denied any knowledge of the murder. The servants at The Black Mule were questioned without result. Alphonse Romain, kitchen apprentice aged eighteen, said that he knew nothing and had not opened his mouth nor moved a finger throughout the episode because he was so frightened![11]

Estienne was brought to trial in April 1648 before the Semester in closed chambers, with Sève presiding.[12] Two hundred of the governor's troops guarded the prisoner at the palace of justice. Alais had brought several companies of his own regiment into Aix to forestall threats of armed rescue. He wanted an example made of Estienne on the scaffold in the Place des Prêcheurs.[13] But Semester councilors Thomassin, Laugier, Ballon, Gautier, and Paul voted to dismiss the case on grounds of insufficient evidence. Dedons, Beaumont, and Suffren insisted on conviction.[14] Cappel, the defense lawyer, protested that as an honorary councilor and master of requests, the intendant could attend the trial with the right to speak, but he could not preside. Cappel's protests were ignored.[15] Confusion and irregularity characterized the trial. On May 12, Semester president Gaufridy complained that the opposition parlementaires were attempting to bribe and frighten witnesses, as well as steal the evidence—the pistol.[16] Avocat-général Decormis wrote to Séguier on May 12 at the trial's conclusion that five Semester councilors were still in favor of freeing Estienne. To prevent this, the other three confiscated the court records so that a verdict of innocent could not be entered.[17]

A second trial was held before the intendants from Languedoc,

[11] B.N., Ms. fr. 18977, fol. 61, interrogation of Alphonse Romain on March 24, 1648 by Balthazar de Rabasse and Léon de Trimond.

[12] Pitton, *Histoire de la ville d'Aix*, pp. 425–426, Achart to Tabouret, April 14, 1648.

[13] *Ibid.*, pp. 423–424; Achart to Tabouret, March 31, 1648; pp. 426–427, the same, May 5, 1648; Pierre-Joseph de Haitze, "Histoire de Provence sous le gouvernement du comte d'Alais," B. Méjanes 736, fol. 147. Haitze's father was a member of Estienne's guard. Estienne came from a judicial family, and his brother was a councilor in the Aix seneschal court; cf. René Pillorget, "Vente d'offices et journée des barricades du 20 janvier, 1649, à Aix-en-Provence," *Provence historique*, 15 (1965), 34.

[14] Savine, *Relation des troubles*, p. 39; B.N., Ms. fr. 17389, fols. 270–272; B.M., Harleian 4575, fol. 24.

[15] B.N., Ms. fr. 18977, fol. 70.

[16] B.N., Ms. fr. 17389, fols. 270–272.

[17] *Ibid.*, fols. 272–273.

Lyonnais, Dauphiné, Provence, and six councilors from the new Cour des Aides at Vienne, unpopular because it reduced the jurisdiction of the Cour des Comptes by assuming competence over the gabelle. This time Estienne was found guilty. In May 1648, guarded by three companies of the governor's regiment, he was sent to the château of Tarascon, a squat, ugly pile of yellow masonry at the edge of the Rhone.[18] None of the other murderers was ever discovered. Sève named a list of six suspects, including Aix lawyer Potonier, parlementaires Decormis and Venel, Séguiran (who was the son of the Cour des Comptes first president), Aix cadets Chaix and Bompar. The parlementaires' complicity in the murder was widely suspected but never proved.[19] It is likely that Estienne was a scapegoat: the evidence was insufficient for conviction, and the trial was hasty and irregular.

Alais and Sève obtained lettres de cachet exiling seventeen parlementaires from Aix for opposition to the Semester and suspected complicity in the murder of Gueidon.[20] Twelve of these parlementaires had been cited before. They were Saint Marc, Signier, François and Jean-Baptiste Thomassin, Milan, Oppède, Antelmi, Villeneuve, Espagnet, Boyer the younger, Lombard, and Mesgrigny. Louis Decormis's father had been cited. Bonfils and Rascas were cited for the first time. Laugier and Leidet-Calissane were cited as renegade members of the Semester. These opposition parlementaires escaped to the Comtat Venaissin, where they were

---

[18] *Ibid.*, fol. 303; "Remontrances au Roy sur la commission de Valence par la Cour des Aides," B. Méjanes 776.

[19] B.M., Harleian 4575, fol. 20v. Sève believed that fifteen or twenty magistrates were involved in the murder.

[20] A.A.E., 1713, fol. 113; B.N., Ms. fr. 17389, fols. 266–267; 18977, fols. 39–40; Pitton, *Histoire de la ville d'Aix*, p. 424, Achart to Tabouret, April 7, 1648. Sève suspected eight parlementaires of complicity in the murder: Espagnet, Lombard, Rascas, Bonfils, Milan, Antelmi, Boyer, and Decormis; cf. B.M., Harleian 4575, fol. 23v. Oppède and Villeneuve had been parlementaire deputies to court in February. Leidet-Calissane refused to pay the conversion fee for his Requêtes' office and joined the opposition. Alais issued an ordinance on April 15, 1648, forbidding the province to hide or aid eleven parlementaires, namely, Oppède, Villeneuve, Antelmi, Lombard, Boyer the younger, Bonfils, Milan, Decormis, Signier, Saint Marc, and Cauvet. The last name was probably an error, since he had been an Alais supporter since his brother's death in 1647; cf. Octave Gensollen, "Note pour servir à l'histoire du Parlement de Provence (1648)," *Répertoire des travaux de la société de statistique de Marseille*, 48 (1911–1920), 1–2.

sheltered by Alexandre Bichi, cardinal-bishop of Carpentras. They led the revolt at Aix ten months later. Alais sent an envoy to the papal legate requesting that he expel them, but the request was ignored. The legate did try to prevent their open recruiting.[21]

Sève reported the parlementaires' efforts to raise troops in the Comtat in letters to Séguier on August 11 and 18.[22] Oppède returned to Provence with fifteen horsemen in August to recruit. Lombard, Decormis, Signier, Villeneuve, Boyer, and Potonier were recruiting at Carpentras, Cavaillon, and Orgon in August 1648. Sève sent to Paris nine eyewitness accounts of their activities.[23] Sève had written to Séguier on August 11 that the parlementaires had recruited thirty soldiers at Carpentras, others at Cadenet and Barbentane. They borrowed money for this purpose from Sextius d'Escalis, baron de Bras.[24] Marseille admiralty lieutenant Antoine de Valbelle, a political enemy of Alais and a brother of councilor Léon de Valbelle, lent them 60,000 livres.[25] By the autumn of 1648, the opposition parlementaires claimed to have recruited two thousand men. Sève thought the number closer to five hundred. On August 25, he estimated they had three to four hundred men.[26]

The 1648 activities of the opposition parlementaires occurred in two phases, intimidation and armed revolt. The edict creating the Semester was registered on January 28, and a conciliar decree on February 27 forbade the anciens officiers to sit as a court until July 28 or until all the Semester offices were sold.[27] But the opposition parlementaires by intimidation halted the sale of Semester offices, so they did not sit in July. Seventeen of the radicals were exiled. Rumors were soon circulating that they would abolish the

[21] B.N., Ms. fr. 17389, fols. 156–157, 180–181; 17390, fols. 79–82.

[22] B.N., Ms. fr. 17390, fols. 79–82; A. D. Lublinskaya, ed., *Vnutrenniaia politika frantsuzskogo absoliutizma* (Leningrad, 1966), p. 352.

[23] B.N., Ms. fr. 18977, fols. 83–85, 87–99, 100–102, August 6, 10, 11, 14, 1648. Sève in a letter to Séguier on July 7, 1648, named Chaix and Potonier as lawyers guilty of the Gueidon murder. They had fled Aix and joined the parlementaires in the Comtat; cf. B.N., Ms. fr. 17388, fols. 162–163. In his mémoires, Sève wrote that Potonier, Chaix, Bompar, and other cadets of Aix had gone to the Comtat; cf. B.M., Harleian 4575, fol. 23v.

[24] B.N., Ms. fr. 17390, fols. 79–82.

[25] Pillorget, "Vente d'offices," 36; Charles de Grimaldi and Jacques Gaufridy, *Mémoires pour servir à l'histoire de la Fronde en Provence* (Aix, 1870), p. 32.

[26] B.N., Ms. fr. 17390, fols. 79–82; A.A.E., 1713, fols. 243–246.

[27] A.A.E., 1713, fol. 97.

255

Semester by arrêt, and Councilors André and Barrême were sent to the Parlement of Paris for aid.[28] By August, the anciens officiers were recruiting troops. It was clear they considered armed revolt the only way to secure reestablishment.

The Days of the Barricades took place at Paris on August 26–28. Achart reported on September 8 that the news of the uprising had caused a big stir at Aix.[29] Alais was frightened by the parlementaires' recruiting, and panicked. Having already brought troops into Aix in March, later withdrawing them, he now brought five hundred men of the Antibes garrison into Aix.[30] On August 13, he ordered the town council to instruct the captains of the municipal guard to enroll an extra hundred men each from the tax rolls.[31] He soon brought another thousand troops into Aix—infantry and cavalry companies from the provincial regiments and his own guards and gendarmes.[32] He billeted these troops on the town despite its traditional exemption. On September 30, he suspended municipal elections. Decormis wrote to Séguier that Alais had entered the town hall that morning while the voting assembly was still at mass, accompanied by two hundred soldiers. He intended to present royal letters naming the new municipal officials, but the sight of his soldiers created a fear of mass arrests, and the municipal councilors fled helter-skelter into the street.[33] The incident increased Alais's reputation for irresponsibility and violence.

[28] Pitton, *Histoire de la ville d'Aix*, p. 420, Achart to Tabouret, July 28, 1648.

[29] Pitton, *Histoire de la ville d'Aix*, p. 421.

[30] Pillorget, "Vente d'offices," 31, n. 25.

[31] A.C., Aix, BB 102, fol. 138.

[32] B.N., Ms. fr. 24166, fol. 258; "Livre de raison," B. Méjanes 1140, fol. 24; Savine, *Relation des troubles*, p. 56; "Mémoires d'Antoine Félix," B. Méjanes R.A. 25, fol. 80; Dominique Guidy, "Histoire du Parlement de Provence," B. Méjanes R.A. 54, fol. 260; Grimaldi and Gaufridy, *Mémoires*, p. 31; Paul Gaffarel, "La Fronde en Provence," *Revue historique*, 2 (1876), 95. Guidy estimated that Alais brought 200–300 cavalry and 200–300 infantry into Aix; Grimaldi estimated 1,500 soldiers; other estimates were 2,000 soldiers. However, a 1649 mazarinade printed by Alais stated that he had billeted 200 cavalry and 200 infantry in Aix; cf. B.N., Ms. fr. 18977, fol. 290.

[33] B.N., Ms. fr. 17390, fols. 229–230; A.A.E., 1712, fol. 253. The royal letters were dated September 22, 1648.

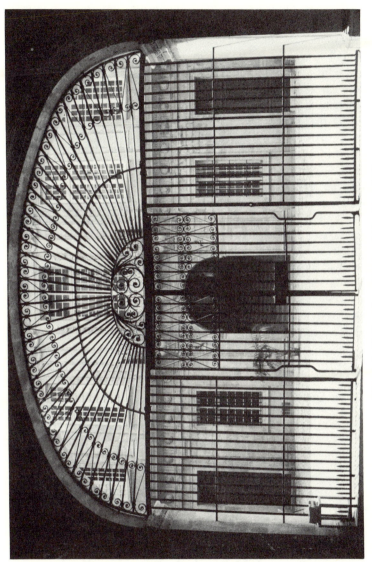

Figure 4. Grillwork entrance of the town hall

The parlementaires' cause was not popular at Aix. Sève wrote to Mazarin on January 28, 1648, when the edict of the Semester was registered, that the nobility, clergy, Estates, and consuls of Aix opposed the edict, but the common people were indifferent.[34] On August 11, Sève wrote to Séguier that most Aixois were unsympathetic to the parlementaires, with the exception of the younger nobles or cadets.[35] The deliberations of the town council were conspicuously silent on the parlementaires' troubles.[36] Sève wrote on January 18, 1649, that the Aixois did not answer the parlementaires' call to arms. They were not interested in defending the privileges of an elite.[37] However, Alais's highhandedness provoked popular resentment and provided the parlementaires with much-needed support.

Encouraged by his wife, Alais stubbornly refused to negotiate with the exiled parlementaires, athough this was contrary to Mazarin's wishes. The cardinal told Sève in September to reconcile Alais and the parlementaires by creating one large parlement, if necessary.[38] The parlementaires had already indicated their willingness to accept the Semester as a new creation if it were abolished as a separate court.[39] On August 13, the parlementaires wrote to Séguier that they were sending councilors Boyer and Leidet-Sigoyer to the governor "to represent the sincerity of our intentions."[40] Councilor Pierre de Barrême, sent as a deputy to the governor, reported to Séguier on October 13 that when he entered the palace of justice, he was insulted by one of the guards and threatened with death by a Semester councilor and his cousin.[41] Barrême left the palace. When he returned, as he wrote a week later on October 26, Alais refused to receive him. The governor

[34] A.A.E., 1713, fols. 39–40.

[35] B.N., Ms. fr. 17390, fols. 79–82; B.M., Harleian 4575, fol. 66.

[36] A.C., Aix, BB 102, fols. 129–153.

[37] B.M., Harleian 4575, fol. 43. Marine intendant Le Roux d'Infréville confirmed this in reporting to Mazarin from Toulon on 1, February 1649. He wrote that the Provençaux were not supporting the parlementaires; they would not take arms for a particular, elitist cause.

[38] *Ibid.*, fols. 25v–26, 27v.

[39] Pitton, *Histoire de la ville d'Aix*, p. 421, Achart to Tabouret, September 8, 1648.

[40] Lublinskaya, *Vnutrenniaia*, p. 324.

[41] A.A.E., 1713, fols. 274–275.

refused to receive other deputies from the parlementaires on October 27.[42]

Doubting Alais's good will, Mazarin sent royal commissioner Le Ferron to negotiate with the exiled parlementaires, aided by Cour des Comptes first president Séguiran and the archbishop of Arles.[43] Le Ferron arrived in Aix on October 20. He pressed for return of the exiles and their restoration to office. Alais and the intendant complained that Le Ferron was discrediting them and demanded his recall.[44] Mazarin told the parlementaires on November 3 that he had ordered Alais to receive their deputies, and on November 13 Mazarin warned Alais to weigh the consequences of his actions.[45]

Estranged from Mazarin and encouraged by his cousin Condé, Alais bided his time and pretended a desire for reconciliation, hoping soon to be rid of the cardinal and the anciens officiers.[46] On November 10, Sève wrote to Séguier that Le Ferron had delivered the royal letters allowing the exiles' return. They triumphantly re-entered Aix with a hundred of their friends to enjoy a great welcome from their supporters, who had been gathering in the city. A victory bonfire was lit in the Place des Prêcheurs.[47] The parlementaires offered the crown 600,000 livres for revocation of the Semester in October.[48] On November 8, Decormis wrote that Alais had agreed to the proposal; Decormis and André were deputized to work out the details with Le Ferron. But evidently the plan failed, because a rachat of 900,000 livres, offered by the parlementaires in December, was rejected.[49]

Sève was afraid of assassination. He reported a plot to stab the governor and himself during mass, thwarted by a warning from

[42] *Ibid.*, fols. 287–288, 289–290.

[43] B.N., Ms. fr. 17390, fols. 117–118, 167; A.A.E., 1713, fol. 302.

[44] Pitton, *Histoire de la ville d'Aix*, p. 422, Achart to Tabouret, October 20, 1648; B.M., Harleian 4575, fols. 27v, 30–31.

[45] A.A.E., 1713, fols. 291–302; Pierre-Adolphe Chéruel and Georges d'Avenel, *Lettres du cardinal Mazarin pendant son ministère*, 9 vols. (Paris, 1872–1906), III, 1071.

[46] B.M., Harleian 4575, fols. 39v–40.

[47] *Ibid.*, fol. 33v; Lublinskaya, *Vnutrenniaia*, p. 326.

[48] B.N., Ms. fr. 17390, fol. 264, Decormis to Séguier, October 24, 1648.

[49] *Ibid.*, fol. 307; A.A.E., 1713, fol. 341.

second president Réauville of the Cour des Comptes.[50] The frequent complaints of Sève and Alais and the opposition's bravado were noted at Paris. On November 21, twenty lettres de cachet arrived, exiling the parlementaires again. On December 28, a decree of the council confirmed the Semester and forbade the anciens officiers to sit as a court.[51]

On January 14, 1649, news arrived of the royal family's flight from Paris.[52] Alais had the Semester issue an arrêt forbidding assemblies in public places and ordering all strangers to leave Aix within twenty-four hours. He subsequently arrested a man named La Tour, reputed to be a friend of avocat-général Louis Decormis.[53] Decormis had been creating a weapons cache at his hôtel and assembling supporters in noisy meetings. Alais passed the hôtel every morning as he went to exercise his horses, and he found the candor of the conspirators extremely annoying.[54] Supporters of the parlementaires were also assembling at the hôtels Forbin de La Roque and Maynier d'Oppède. Alais used two hundred soldiers to arrest the first cousin of president Du Chaine for refusing to execute an arrêt of the Semester; the incident involved thirty armed cadets.[55] The parlementaires accused the governor of issuing the ban on public assemblies to disperse their supporters.[56]

On January 15, Armand-Jean de Vignerod Du Plessis, duc de

[50] B.M., Harleian 4575, fol. 37. Sève wrote that Réauville was loyal to Alais on January 20; cf. *ibid.*, fol. 46v.

[51] A.A.E., 1713, fols. 314–315; B.M., *Discours fait par les députés du Parlement de Provence dans le Parlement de Paris . . . 15 et 24 janvier 1649*.

[52] A.A.E., 1715, fol. 5, Mazarin to Alais, January 9, 1649.

[53] B.M., Harleian 4575, fols. 40v–41; ADBR, Aix, J.L.H. Hesmivy de Moissac, "Histoire du Parlement de Provence, 1501–1715," II, fols. 82, 86; B.N., Clairambault 419, fols. 146–148, Parlement to Brienne, January 24, 1649; B.N., Ms. fr. 17393, fols. 9–11, Parlement to Séguier, January 24, 1649; B. Marseille 1794, *Relation de ce qui s'est fait et passée dans la province de Provence*, fol. 5; Gaffarel, "La Fronde en Provence," 87. Gaffarel noted that La Tour was a Dauphinois cousin of Decormis. Sève said that La Tour was a soldier and that Alais soon freed him.

[54] Pierre-Joseph de Haitze, *Histoire de la ville d'Aix*, 6 vols. (Aix, 1880–1892), V, 7.

[55] B.M., Harleian 4575, fols. 31–31v.

[56] B.N., Ms. fr. 17393, fols. 9–11, Parlement to Séguier, January 24, 1649.

Richelieu and intendant general of the royal galleys, arrived in Aix with his galley captains and about thirty "Turks," Moslem galley rowers. They were to build scenery for a ballet that Alais intended to present during Carnival.[57] On the same day, Alais assembled the town council, heads of the guilds and confréries at the town hall to swear an oath of loyalty to the crown.[58] He deployed five hundred soldiers to guard the palace of justice, his headquarters. On January 18, he ranged his troops in battle order on the Place des Prêcheurs.[59] Barricades with chains were erected across the streets leading into the square, and the town hall was filled with troops.

On Monday, January 18, Alais toured Aix on foot at ten o'clock in the morning, accompanied by his appointed consuls, the prévôt's police under lieutenant Artaud, his own guards, the Marseille galley captains, and an entourage of nobles. The gesture was inflammatory and the guards' behavior provocative. In the Place des Prêcheurs, the group encountered the valet of parlementaire Louis de Saint Marc sitting on a stone bench in the shade of a tree. The servant was insolent, refusing to rise, bow, and remove his hat in proper acknowledgment of Alais's presence. One of the guards slapped him several times. In the confusion, the valet was shot in the arm for resisting arrest; Sève insisted that he drew a sword. His broken arm dangling, the valet was taken to the prison in the palace of justice.[60]

Rumors flew that the parlementaires would be arrested. The shops closed, and the parlementaires' armed supporters, mostly

---

[57] B.N., Ms. fr. 18977, fol. 290; Gaffarel, "La Fronde en Provence," 87. A great-nephew of the cardinal, Vignerod had become intendant general of the galleys in December 1642 at the age of fifteen. His father, François de Vignerod, marquis de Pont de Courlay and Richelieu's nephew, was intendant general from 1635 to 1637. Pont de Courlay was dismissed for incompetence and extravagance. His son was little better.

[58] ADBR, Aix, Moissac, "Histoire du Parlement," II, 83; Gaffarel, "La Fronde en Provence," 87–88; B.M., Harleian 4575, fol. 41. Sève gives the date as January 17.

[59] B.N., Ms. fr. 17393, fols. 48–49.

[60] B.M., Harleian 4575, fol. 41; B.N., Ms. fr. 17393, fols. 9–11, Parlement to Séguier, January 24, 1649; B.N., Clairambault 419, fols. 73–74, archbishop of Arles to Brienne, January 19, 1649; ADBR, Aix, Moissac, "Histoire du Parlement," II, 84; Haitze, *Histoire*, V, 13–14. The archbishop wrote that the servant resisted arrest. Haitze condemned the guard as trigger-happy.

nobles and gentlemen, gathered at the hôtel Maynier d'Oppède.[61] This building was chosen because the adjacent square, holding two thousand men, could be easily barricaded and defended. The parlementaires' supporters numbered eight hundred by evening and increased to fifteen hundred by the next morning.[62] Jacques de Gallifet was put in charge of posting marksmen and building barricades on surrounding streets. He used wheelbarrows, benches, plows, whatever would be difficult for the governor's cavalry to force. Louis Decormis and his brothers brought between fifty and three hundred men into Aix from their nearby estates. Oppède also brought men into Aix. Decormis, Saint Marc, Signier, and Boyer in red robes, with guns at their belts, went into the Bourg to rally support, crying "Follow the parlementaires not the governor!"[63] They seized the cathedral and the Notre Dame city gate. The canons of Saint Sauveur, many from robe families, rang the tocsin to summon Aixois to their support.[64] A confrontation seemed likely.

But meanwhile, volunteer mediators worked to restore peace. The comte de Carcès, who was lieutenant general of Provence; François d'Adhémar de Monteil de Grignan, the archbishop of Arles; and Cour des Comptes presidents Séguiran and Réauville went to the hôtel Maynier d'Oppède to hear the parlementaires' demands, then spent the afternoon and night with the governor at the palace of justice. Carcès remained behind at the hôtel to calm the parlementaires. Alais wanted to attack the hôtel immediately and was only dissuaded after long argument. The archbishop of Arles wrote that he spent twenty-four hours without food or sleep in the effort to convince Alais to temporize. Finally, written promises were secured from both sides. The parlementaires promised to disarm. The governor agreed to send his troops from Aix. The barricades came down in the Place Saint Sauveur and

[61] B.M., Harleian 4574, fol. 42; B.N., Ms. fr. 17393, fols. 9–11; Pitton, *Histoire de la ville d'Aix*, pp. 408–409.

[62] B.N., Clairambault 419, fols. 73–74; *Relation de ce qui s'est fait et passée dans la province de Provence*, B. Marseille 1794, fols. 5–6.

[63] B.M., Harleian 4575, fol. 43; "Livre de raison," B. Méjanes 1140, fol. 23; ADBR, Aix, Moissac, "Histoire du Parlement," II, 86; Pitton, *Histoire de la ville d'Aix*, pp. 410–411; Haitze, *Histoire*, V, 15, 19. Sève wrote there were only 400 men at the hôtel Maynier d'Oppède.

[64] Pillorget, "Vente d'offices," 43.

Place des Prêcheurs, and letters of explanation were sent to Paris.[65] Oppède gave a banquet in the courtyard of his hôtel, provisioned for siege with a large quantity of easily spoiled meat.[66]

Saint Sebastian's Day on January 20 had been celebrated as a day of thanksgiving for over a century. The festivities began with high mass in the cathedral followed by a public procession. On Wednesday, January 20, 1649, a Te Deum mass was said in Saint Sauveur at eight o'clock in the morning. Then the cathedral bells rang, and the procession formed to march around the city inside and outside the walls, bearing a gold cross containing the relics of Saint André and Saint Sebastian carried by the consuls en chaperon. The archbishop led the procession. The parlementaires marched behind by twos according to length of service, followed by the canons of Saint Sauveur, other royal judges, municipal councilors, and representatives of the university, confréries, and guilds. The Aixois straggled along at the rear.[67]

Contrary to the terms of the peace agreement, Alais kept twenty-five musketeers as guards at the palace of justice, and he sent one hundred cavalrymen to mingle with the crowds, hiding twenty to thirty soldiers in the town hall, perhaps in the Grand'Horloge, the municipal clocktower.[68] After the procession had gone through the Notre Dame gate, a few soldiers left their hiding place for fresh air, and were seen by loiterers in the Place Saint Sauveur at the end of the street. They cried, "à la larmo, à la larmo," and wild rumors began to circulate. The parlementaires would be arrested; the duc de Richelieu's "Turks" were massacring citizens; Alais's soldiers had closed the gates and would murder everyone in the city; wood assembled for ballet scenery would be used for scaffolds.[69] The tocsin rang. The parlementaires returned to the

[65] B.N., Clairambault 419, fols. 73–74, 75.

[66] Pillorget, "Vente d'offices," 45.

[67] B.M., Harleian 4575, fol. 44v; B.N., Ms. fr. 17393, fols. 9–11, Parlement to Séguier, January 24, 1649; B.N., Clairambault 419, fols. 146–148, Parlement to Brienne, January 24, 1649.

[68] A.C., Aix, AA 14, fols. 1–3; "Livre de raison de Léon de Trimond," B. Méjanes 1140, fol. 21.

[69] Pitton, *Histoire de la ville d'Aix*, p. 412; Gaffarel, "La Fronde en Provence," 87; Honoré Bouche, *La chorographie ou description de Provence*, 2 vols. (Aix, 1664), II, 942–950.

city at a run, their red robes flapping, to rally their supporters at the hôtel Maynier d'Oppède.

There had been little popular response to the parlementaires' appeal for aid two days earlier. President Régusse and intendant Sève reported that the opposition parlementaires had distributed 500 écus (1,500 livres) in sums of 30 sols each to Aixois who would join them.[70] The baron de Bras, former first consul, distributed 1,000 reales for this purpose.[71] The opposition promised popular reforms—the parlementaires suspended the rêve on flour after they assumed control of the city; they returned the 1647 consuls to office, removing the governor's appointees and promising free elections; they demanded reductions in provincial troops and disbandment of the governor's regiment from the crown.[72] The money, promises of reform, and general excitement helped to attract Aixois to the parlementaires' support on January 20.

The parlementaires rebuilt barricades across the narrow, winding streets leading into the Place Saint Sauveur, then marched down the hill to confront the governor's troops at the town hall and palace of justice. The soldiers at the palace barricades refused to fire upon the parlementaires, who were an impressive sight as they burst into the Place des Prêcheurs fully armed, in their red robes. There was great confusion in the palace of justice, which was taken without bloodshed. Alais, Sève, and the duc de Richelieu were imprisoned. The chevalier Du Vins, commander of the governor's troops, wanted to storm the nearby hôtel of the comte de Carcès, where rebels were gathering, but concern for public opinion held him back. While he hesitated, Carcès and his supporters slipped away to the hôtel Maynier d'Oppède.[73] The consuls and assessor of Aix whom Alais had appointed were driven into the cathedral for refuge and saved only by the quick thinking of canon Jean-Baptiste Du Chaine, cousin of the parlementaire and vicar general of the Aix archdiocese in later years. He hid the

---

[70] Grimaldi and Gaufridy, *Mémoires*, p. 30; B.M., Harleian 4575, fol. 44.

[71] Pitton, *Histoire de la ville d'Aix*, p. 411.

[72] ADBR, Aix, B 3356, fol. 683; A.A.E., 1714, fols. 138–141; Pillorget, "Vente d'offices," 45, 52.

[73] ADBR, Aix, Moissac, "Histoire du Parlement," II, 87–91; Haitze, *Histoire*, V, 28–30; B.M., Harleian 4575, fols. 46v–48.

consuls in the sacristy, protected by thick wooden doors. They stayed in the sacristy for three days until they were transferred to the palace of justice prison under heavy guard. Their *chaperons*, symbols of municipal office, were paraded through the city on pikes.[74]

The rebels also sacked the hôtel of Gaufridy. Unable to break down the new door, they crossed the roof from a neighboring hôtel, ransacked the mansion, took Gaufridy's money, and destroyed his books and furniture. Gaufridy wrote to Séguier in March 1649, asking for reimbursement.[75] The rebels burnt Alais's portrait, paraded Gaufridy's judicial robes on a pike, and murdered his children's tutor, whom they found in the house.[76] They probably would have thrown Gaufridy from a window if they had found him. The rebels made an unsuccessful attempt to sack the hôtel of Semester councilor Trimond, and they sacked the hôtels of consul Rostolan, who had recently lowered the daily wage rate, his cousin Benoît, and Achart, the traitant's agent selling Semester offices. In Achart's hôtel, they found 20,000 livres and his letters, which they scattered through the streets. The rebels also pulled down Alais's coat of arms from the newly opened Valois city gate, later renamed Villeverte, and destroyed the toll booth for the rêve inside the Saint Jean gate.[77]

Alais was visiting papal legate Antoine Barberini at the house of the Capucins when the revolt began. He immediately returned to the palace of justice, where he was joined by Sève and the duc de Richelieu. Gaufridy and other members of the Semester took refuge in the palace of justice or religious houses. Some may have hidden in a cemetery. The comtesse d'Alais was at mass in the church of the Ursulines and rejoined her husband safely without an escort, although Alais had sent a group of nobles under Antoine Grasse Du Bar, seigneur de La Malle and captain in the

---

[74] Delib. Parl., B. Méjanes 953, fols. 206–206v; Haitze, *Histoire*, V, 28–29; B.N., Ms. fr. 17393, fols. 9–11; Pitton, *Histoire de la ville d'Aix*, pp. 413–414.

[75] B.N., Ms. fr. 17393, fols. 48–49.

[76] Pillorget, "Vente d'offices," 52.

[77] Haitze, *Histoire*, V, 41–42; ADBR, Aix, Moissac, "Histoire du Parlement," II, 90–91; Delib. Parl., B. Méjanes 953, fol. 208v; A.M., Aix, BB 102, fol. 73; Gaffarel, "La Fronde en Provence," 91–96. The letters appear in Pitton, *Histoire de la ville d'Aix*, pp. 420–425.

governor's regiment, to escort her to safety. Someone shot Grasse Du Bar through an open window, a wound that proved fatal.[78] A musket ball flying through an open window pierced the hat of Semester councilor Suffren.[79] A captain in the governor's regiment was shot in the leg, and one of Alais's guards was shot dead. However, violence was minimal, and there were only six or seven persons killed during the revolt.

The opposition parlementaires planned, provoked, and executed the 1649 revolt. They attacked the palace of justice after Alais withdrew most of his troops from the city, having previously rallied their armed supporters. They fought in their judicial robes for psychological effect. They controlled the crowds. There were no grisly murders, no massacres, no widespread looting, no fires, no prisoners released from jail, no food riots, no serious reprisals. There were comparatively few deaths; most were accidental. Violence was restricted to abusive language, erection of barricades, and selective property destruction. Peace was quickly restored after the revolt. The parlementaires' goal was to imprison the governor and force concession from Mazarin.

The 1649 revolt has an air of precision and workmanship that contrasts sharply with the 1630 and 1659 revolts, when the parlementaires made use of protests begun by other groups. The 1649 revolt was a premeditated protest by the parlementaires against the crown's policies and agents. It was not an attack by peasants and artisans on the local elite—it is misleading to infer similarities between the Aix revolt and the Bordeaux Ormée of 1652.[80] Jacques Gaufridy understood the nature of the Aix protest when he wrote, "Revolts do not always come from a gathering of the people; they are more often fomented by men of power, and mu-

---

[78] B.M., Harleian 4575, fol. 46; Savine, *Relations des troubles*, p. 57; Haitze, *Histoire*, V, 30–31; comte de Grasse, "Documents inédits concernant l'histoire du Semestre en Provence, 1648–1650," *Bulletin de la Société d'Etudes scientifiques et archéologiques de Draguignan*, 32 (1918–1919), 6–8; ADBR, Aix, Moissac, "Histoire du Parlement," II, 92.

[79] B.M., Harleian 4575, fol. 46v. Other accounts of the 1649 revolt are provided by René Pillorget, "Vente d'offices," 25–63 and *Les mouvements insurrectionnels de Provence entre 1596 et 1715* (Paris, 1975), pp. 569–600.

[80] Sal Westreich, *The Ormée of Bordeaux: A Revolution during the Fronde* (Baltimore, 1972), p. 135.

266

tinous multitudes usually follow the movements of two or three."[81]

There was less popular support for the parlementaires in 1649 than in 1630 because economic conditions were better. An epidemic of plague came to Marseille in July 1649 and spread to Aix in January 1650, forcing the Parlement to leave for Salon in March. But this was a year after the revolt.[82] There were bad harvests in Provence from 1647 to 1649, and there were high wheat and bread prices at Aix in 1648, when prices rose to the same level as in 1630–1631. But bread prices at Aix were usually high because they were pegged to expensive local wheat prices. The years from 1629 to 1649 were ones of consistently high prices.[83] There were other bad harvests in Provence, for instance in 1637, 1643–1644, and 1647–1649, when wheat and bread prices rose to a high level without violent protest at Aix.[84]

Thirty-two parlementaires, approximately half the company, participated in the 1649 revolt and the events immediately preceding it. Nearly all were members of the opposition, and most had been exiles in the Comtat Venaissin. These included Louis Decormis, Henri de Forbin-Maynier d'Oppède, Louis de Saint Marc and his brother-in-law Jean-Pierre Signier, Vincent de Boyer, Jean-Antoine de Bonfils whose father Joseph, criminal lieutenant of the Aix seneschal court, joined him in the streets of Aix on January 20, and Rascas Du Canet, who was accompanied by his brother. Intendant Sève named Decormis, Oppède, Forbin de La Roque, and Régusse as rebel leaders.[85] Lombard and Villeneuve had recruited troops. Venel was implicated in the events surrounding Gueidon's murder. André, Barrême, Leidet-Sigoyer, and Boyer

[81] Jacques Gaufridy, "Histoire de Provence sous le règne de Louis XIII," B. Méjanes 625, fol. 261.

[82] Bouche, *La chorographie*, II, 956.

[83] René Baehrel, *Un croissance: La Basse-Provence rurale (fin du XVIe siècle—1789)* (Paris, 1961), pp. 61, 78–80, 535, 547; Louis Tilly, "The Food Riot as a Form of Political Conflict in France," *Journal of Interdisciplinary History*, 2 (1971), 34–35.

[84] Roland Mousnier, ed., *Lettres et mémoires addressés au chancelier Séguier (1633–1649)*, 2 vols. (Paris, 1964), I, 685, Champigny to Séguier, July 3, 1644; I, 686, Champigny to Séguier, June 28, 1644; B.N., Ms. fr. 17376, fols. 5–6, Vautorte to d'Hémery, February, 1643; fol. 28, the same, April 8, 1643; B.N., Clairambault 390, fol. 119, Alais to Brienne, December 8, 1643.

[85] B.M., Harleian 4575, fol. 49v.

served as deputies to Alais and the Parlement of Paris. These sixteen opposition parlementaires stormed the palace of justice and town hall on January 20. They were joined by Lazare Du Chaine, Jacques de Gallifet, whose father Alexandre was president of the Enquêtes, and his brother-in-law Henri de Clapiers, sieur de Vauvenargues.[86]

As soon as the fighting stopped, volunteer mediators began to negotiate a peace. Serving in this capacity were the comte de Carcès, the archbishop of Arles, Cour des Comptes first president Séguiran, and seigneur de Barbentane. The parlementaires sent deputies to Alais on the afternoon of January 20: Régusse, Villeneuve and his brother-in-law Mazargues, Foresta de La Roquette, and Leidet-Calissane. More deputies were sent on the afternoon of January 21: Du Chaine, Espagnet, Guérin, and Antelmi.[87] Still in red robes, the parlementaires held a meeting in the town hall by torchlight on the night of January 20. Lieutenant general Carcès represented the crown and lent the proceedings an air of legitimacy. The parlementaires issued arrêts to restore peace. Street patrols were established for each quarter. Citizens were forbidden to assemble for illegal purposes, ordered to lay down their arms, remove barricades, and open shops. Louis Decormis ordered every house in Aix to have a light in its window or pay a 1,000 livres fine. Guards were posted inside and outside the palace of justice, and chains were left across the streets leading into the Place des Prêcheurs.[88]

After the meeting, a victory bonfire was lit in the Place des Prêcheurs. Forbin de La Roque, Boyer, and Decormis delivered speeches with the bonfire as backlighting. An oath of loyalty was sworn, and the parlementaires' names were inscribed on a list. There were twenty-eight signers: Forbin de La Roque, Régusse, Decormis, Leidet-Sigoyer, Leidet-Calissane, Du Chaine, Foresta de La Roquette, Dedons, Valbelle, Bonfils, Boyer, Laurens, Ville-

---

[86] A.A.E., 1714, fol. 38, Le Roux d'Infréville to Mazarin, February 1, 1649; fols. 71–78, Cardinal Bichi to Mazarin, February 9, 1649; Haitze, *Histoire*, V, 33, 35, 38; Pillorget, "Vente d'offices," 53.

[87] Delib. Parl., B. Méjanes 953, fol. 201v. Sève wrote that Leidet-Sigoyer, Venel, and Laurens (previously cited) were sent with Régusse as deputies to Alais on January 20; cf. B.M., Harleian 4575, fol. 48v.

[88] Delib. Parl., B. Méjanes 953, fol. 201v; Haitze, *Histoire*, V, 47–48; Gaffarel, "La Fronde en Provence," 96–98.

neuve, Mazargues, Espagnet, Guérin, Antelmi, Clapiers de Puget, Rascas, Saint Marc, Lombard, Albert, Agut, Thomassin, Arbaud, Aymar d'Albi, Signier, and Glandèves.[89] The majority were members of the opposition. Exceptions were Foresta de La Roquette, Du Chaine, Mazargues, Dedons, Albert, and Clapiers de Puget, who had been swept up by events of the day rather than by political conviction. Deputies were sent to make certain no prisoners had escaped from the jail in the palace of justice.[90]

Alais, Sève, and the duc de Richelieu were placed under twenty-four hour guard in the palace of justice. Oppède and Venel slept in Alais's room the first night, while Jacques de Gallifet insisted on searching it for arms.[91] Feeling against the governor was intense. Régusse was asked to search Alais's hôtel for arms and stand guard duty. He refused the task as dishonorable, and was forced to leave Aix overnight for safety.[92] Four parlementaires a week served as Alais's guards.[93] The guards, particularly Oppède and Jacques de Gallifet, insulted Alais and allowed him no privacy. They awakened him in the middle of the night. He was forbidden permission to exercise his horses, even to walk through the streets.[94] The comtesse d'Alais and her daughter were allowed to leave Aix, as were the Semester councilors and Alais's guards, who were escorted by Glandèves and Séguiran's son.[95]

First president Mesgrigny had not exercised his office for months, so second president Forbin de La Roque, who was to die in office on November 5, 1649, presided over the joint meeting at the palace of justice on the morning of January 21.[96] The parlementaires issued arrêts creating a bourgeois guard of seven companies, one for each quarter. The Saint Jean gate was closed. Guards

[89] Haitze, *Histoire*, V, 47; Gaffarel, "La Fronde en Provence," 96–97.

[90] Delib. Parl., B. Méjanes 953, fol. 208.

[91] B.M., Harleian 4575, fols. 49, 51v.

[92] Grimaldi and Gaufridy, *Mémoires*, pp. 33–34.

[93] Delib. Parl., B. Méjanes 953, fols. 209, 215, 216v.

[94] Haitze, *Histoire*, V, 52; B.N., Ms. fr. 18977, fol. 290; A.A.E., 1714, fol. 71, Bichi to Mazarin, February 9, 1649; B.M., Harleian 4575, fol. 51; B.N., Ms. fr. 18977, fol. 290, *Justification des armes de Monsieur le comte d'Alais* (Marseille, 1649).

[95] B.M., Harleian 4575, fol. 50.

[96] M.A. Provence 348, *Harangue prononcée par Monsieur le président de La Roque à l'ouverture du Parlement de Provence, 21 janvier 1649.* He gave a similar speech on April 15, which was also printed and distributed.

were posted at the other city gates, and no one could enter or leave without the written permission of Oppède or Aymar d'Albi. Only two gates were open during the first week of February. The prévôt was informed that his company of *archers* was under the parlementaires' command, and lieutenant Artaud was arrested. The rêve on flour was suspended, and the export of grain from Provence was forbidden. Régusse, Rascas, Glandèves, Saint Marc, and Bonfils were appointed to enforce these arrêts.[97] Deputies were sent to the procureurs du pays and the cities of Arles and Marseille. But Sève reported to Mazarin that the parlementaires were not successful in eliciting support from the rest of the province.[98]

Forbin de La Roque also presided over the joint meeting of the Parlement on January 22. There were thirty-eight parlementaires present. Twenty-five were opposition members who had been cited in disciplinary legislation and participated in the events of January 20–21. Six had recently joined the rebels. Six more were present in the palace of justice for the first time on January 22: Bermond, Foresta, Roux, Chailan, Trichaud, and Ollivier. Another eighteen parlementaires, about one-third of the company, were absent, including the first president, three royal attorneys, one president à mortier, one president of the Enquêtes, and twelve councilors, as well as the members of the Requêtes and Semester. Only seventeen parlementaires attended the meeting on January 28.[99] Many judges stayed away from the palace of justice. Others arrived to drift irresolutely in and out of meetings. The opposition activists were a minority even in January 1649.

The Aix parlementaires closely followed the union of the Paris sovereign courts in May 1648 and the debates on the nature of judicial authority. Opposition councilors Barrême and André were sent to request the aid of the Parlement of Paris on July 28, 1648, after the anciens officiers realized they would not be allowed to sit as a court.[100] In Aix there were rumors of the union of the two

---

[97] B.M., Harleian 4575, fol. 51; Delib. Parl., B. Méjanes 953, fols. 201v–202, 206–209; Haitze, *Histoire*, V, 45–51; B.N., Clairambault 419, fols. 146–148.

[98] A.A.E., 1714, fols. 31, 33.

[99] ADBR, Aix, B 3367, January 22 and 28, 1649.

[100] Pitton, *Histoire de la ville d'Aix*, p. 420, Achart to Tabouret, July 28, 1648.

parlements.[101] But Alais wrote to Mazarin on August 21 that the deputies had returned without a solid promise of help.[102] Barrême and André returned to Paris in December as the situation at Aix worsened, and on January 15, 1649, they attended a session of the Parlement of Paris to present their company's grievances and to request an arrêt condemning the Semester. They complained about the citation of parlementaires in disciplinary legislation, even the first president, and the exiles sent to the Comtat Venaissin by lettres de cachet.[103] But they did not receive a definite offer of help.

Barrême and André returned to Paris for a third time after the revolt. They addressed the Parlement of Paris on January 28, a speech that summarized the grievances and goals of the Aix parlementaires.[104] They demanded revocation of the Chambre des Requêtes as illegal because it had been registered by the governor's secretary without verification and its members had been improperly received. They demanded revocation of the Semester as illegal since it had been registered by the governor and intendants without verification. These demands were later met by the Bichi Treaty and the royal edicts enforcing it. The Chambre des Requêtes and the Semester were unconditionally abolished upon payment of 500,000 livres—300,000 livres for one and 200,000 livres for the other—and the old parlementaires were restored to office. The Semester councilors were to receive 100,000 livres in compensation for their lost offices.[105] The parlementaires agreed to the creation of one president, six councilors, and twenty-one lesser personnel in the

[101] A.A.E., 1713, fols. 219–220, Gaufridy to Mazarin, July 25, 1648.

[102] *Ibid.*, fol. 239.

[103] M.A., Provence 348 and B.M., *Discours fait par les députés du Parlement de Provence dans le Parlement de Paris . . . 15 et 18 janvier 1649* (Paris, 1649).

[104] A.N., U29, "Registre du Conseil secret du Parlement de Paris," fol. 60v, "Articles accordés par les députés du Parlement de Provence . . . 24 janvier 1649"; B. Marseille 1791, *Discours fait par les députés du Parlement de Provence dans le Parlement de Paris . . . 15 et 28 janvier 1649* (Paris, 1649). Other sources of the parlementaires' demands include A.A.E., 1713, fols. 36–37; 1714, fols. 84, 101–102; Haitze, *Histoire*, V, 43, 62–67; Delib. Parl., B. Méjanes 953, fol. 207.

[105] A.A.E., 1714, fols. 101–102, 112, 114–117, 121–123; ADBR, Aix, B 3356, fols. 625v, 662v; Delib. Parl., B. Méjanes 954, fols. 42, 57v, 60. The parlementaires were to pay 100,000 livres immediately, and the province the rest within four years.

court with an augmentation des gages for the Tournelle, Enquêtes, and Vacations.[106] The parlementaires also demanded immediate payment of their gages and free salt for 1648, when the Semester had sat, and they issued an arrêt on January 21 ordering the salt tax farmer to pay without delay.[107] Mazarin never protested the payment.

The Aix parlementaires protested that the governor was persecuting their company, billeting an alleged 3,500 soldiers on their city and its environs. They demanded that the governor and the crown recognize the traditional privilege of the procureurs du pays to approve troop billets by adding their attache to the governor's ordinances, as well as the traditional exemption of royal magistrates and the cities of Aix, Arles, Marseille, and Tarascon from troop billeting. Mazarin never acted to safeguard these traditional privileges and exemptions, but the Aix parlementaires were specifically exempted from troop billeting by royal letters in February 1650.[108]

The parlementaires also requested the disbanding of the governor's provincial regiments and the appointment of another governor. A year earlier, on January 28, 1648, president Régusse had written Mazarin that four concessions were necessary to avoid violence at Aix—the recall of Alais, the disbanding of the provincial infantry regiment and substitution of a new, smaller regiment raised by a new governor, the suppression of the Semester, and the replacement of the duc de Richelieu as intendant general of the galleys.[109] Cardinal Bichi's memoir for the council of state in February 1649 recommended disbanding the provincial regiment, levying a new force, and sending Alais from the province for the rest of the year.[110] A royal edict in March disbanded the provincial infantry and cavalry regiments, sent these troops into other provinces, and levied a new infantry regiment of fifteen companies. But

---

[106] ADBR, Aix, B 3356, fol. 662v; Moissac, "Histoire du Parlement," II, 101; B.N., Ms. fr. 18977, fols. 5, 145. The new offices were sold by January 1650. The augmentation des gages was 800 livres for presidents, 600 livres for councilors, and 400 livres for presidents of the Enquêtes.

[107] Delib. Parl., B. Méjanes 953, fols. 201v–202.

[108] ADBR, Aix, B 3357, fol. 801.

[109] A.A.E., 1713, fols. 36–37. Also see Régusse's letter to Mazarin on February 25, 1649; cf. A.A.E., 1714, fols. 138–141.

[110] A.A.E., 1714, fols. 109–112. Also see his letter of February 25, 1649; cf. *ibid.*, fols. 127–135.

provincial taxes for thirty infantry companies were to be levied as usual, and the difference diverted to support other troops. The governor's horse and foot guards and gendarmes company were reduced to their pre-1630 level, and the province was freed from support of the Monaco garrison.[111] The parlementaires requested that an Estates be called at Aix to authorize provincial tax levies for troop support, as was customary. Mazarin promised to call a provincial Estates, as he promised to call an Estates General,[112] but he did neither. Alais and the duc de Richelieu remained in Provence.

The parlementaires complained about repeated interference in the municipal elections of Marseille, Aix, Arles, and other Provençal towns. They demanded the removal of the governor's appointees from municipal office at Aix and the restoration of elections according to traditional forms. An arrêt on January 21 returned to office the freely elected 1647 first consul and assessor of Aix, the baron de Bras and sieur de Séguiran; the governor's 1648 appointees were imprisoned. Recognition of this arrêt became a clause in the Bichi Treaty. A royal edict in March 1649 assured Provençal cities and communities the continuation of their traditional form of municipal elections, with the Parlement registering the results for validity.[113]

The parlementaires requested revocation of the intendant of justice's letters of commission, charging that he had usurped the authority of provincial officials and suspended traditional privileges. His commission was revoked by a conciliar decision on April 2, 1649, and a parlementary arrêt on April 12 prohibited exercise of his office.[114] The February memoir of Cardinal Bichi

---

[111] ADBR, Aix, B 3356, fol. 683; A.A.E., 1714, fols. 138–141; 1715, fol. 92.

[112] A.N., U29, fols. 60–60v; François-André Isambert, ed. *Recueil général des anciennes lois françaises*, 29 vols. (Paris, 1821–1823), XVII, 144–146.

[113] ADBR, Aix, B 3356, fol. 683; A.C., Aix AA 14, fol. 571; B.N., Ms. fr. 18977, fols. 155–158; 24166, fol. 268.

[114] Guidy, "Histoire du Parlement," B. Méjanes R.A. 54, fol. 266; Haitze, *Histoire*, V, 76. The intendant of justice had not exercised his office since November 17, 1648 when, according to the provisions of the royal ordinance of October 22 abolishing intendancies in the frontier provinces, deputies from the Parlement and the Cour des Comptes had confiscated his papers; cf. B.N., Ms. fr. 17390, fols. 305–306, Sève to Mazarin. On April

recommended general amnesty for all rebels, which was granted by royal letters in March 1649. The Bichi Treaty stated that no resentment was to be held by either party.[115] Royal letters in March nullified all arrêts of the Semester and ordinances of the governor from January 1648 to January 1649, as the parlementaires had requested.[116]

In their Paris cahier, the Aix parlementaires protested the excessive use of disciplinary citations and judicial evocations, which they wanted limited to litigants with six relatives in the Parlement. They demanded the return to the Cour des Comptes of jurisdiction over the gabelle in Provence, recently transferred outside the province to the Cour des Aides at Vienne. They demanded more responsibility in the provincial government for the lieutenant general of Provence, Jean de Pontevès, comte de Carcès, and they demanded that the governorships of the fortresses of Saint Tropez and Antibes be awarded to their noble supporters Jacques de Forbin, seigneur de La Barben, and Jean-Baptiste de Castellane, seigneur de La Verdière, relatives of Oppède. Later, they requested a provincial office for their noble deputy to Paris, Jean-Baptiste de Puget, seigneur de Barbentane, who also served as mediator. Mazarin ignored these patronage requests. The rebels freed Louis d'Estienne, sieur de Vaillac, from the prisons of the château at Tarascon by arrêt on January 21. Mazarin did not protest his release.[117]

After a lengthy debate on the cahier presented by the Aix deputies, a majority of legal conservatives in the Parlement of Paris refused aid and would not issue arrêts of condemnation. One side in the debate maintained that the Parlement of Paris, as the oldest and most important parlement in France, had the right to sanction or reject royal edicts affecting the provincial parlements. The other side maintained that the Parlement of Paris did not have the au-

---

23, 1649, the Parlement issued an arrêt forbidding the intendant to preside over the provincial General Assemblies of the Clergy and the Nobility at Marseille because he was without authority in Provence; cf. Delib. Parl., B. Méjanes 953, fol. 225v.

[115] A.A.E., 1714, fols. 101–102, 114–117; ADBR, Aix, B 3356, fol. 699; A.C., Aix, AA 14, fols. 565–571.

[116] ADBR, Aix, B 3356, fol. 699; A.C., Aix, AA 14, fols. 565–571; A.A.E., 1714, fols. 101–102.

[117] Haitze, *Histoire*, V, 43, 65–66; A.N., U29, fols. 60–60v.

thority to interfere in the jurisdiction of another sovereign court. This side won the debate, and the Parlement of Paris adopted a narrow interpretation of its authority. It promised to send a remonstrance on the Aix Semester to the king, but it offered no other help, since the edict establishing that court had not been presented for registration at Paris. There were no other attempts to unite the two parlements, although they corresponded through 1651. The chances for cooperation had been slight in any event, because Aix hesitated over a proposal for joint action. Opposition parlementaires Decormis and Gallifet favored union, but Sève wrote to Mazarin on January 29, 1649, that he thought union unlikely because the majority of parlementaires, headed by president Oppède, opposed it.[118]

On the evening of February 6, 1649, Cardinal Bichi, bishop of Carpentras and friend of Mazarin, arrived in Aix to help negotiate a peace. He was greeted by the archbishop of Arles, Le Ferron, Carcès, Séguiran, and Réauville, whose efforts to mediate a satisfactory settlement had been in vain. Grateful for his shelter of the exiles in the previous year, the parlementaires sent a full deputation to greet him, including Espagnet, Rascas, Dedons, Foresta de La Roquette, Signier, Laurens, Leidet-Sigoyer, Glandèves, and Aymar d'Albi.[119] The edict that Bichi brought abolishing the Semester and restoring the old parlementaires to office was registered the next day.[120] On February 18, a tentative agreement acceptable to the governor and the parlementaires was reached, signed on February 21, and sent to Paris for ratification.[121] Mazarin threatened to send 10,000 troops into Provence from Dauphiné, Languedoc, and Guyenne if peace were not restored quickly.[122]

---

[118] A.A.E., 1714, fols. 15–16, 31; B.N., Clairambault 419, fols. 200–201v; Grimaldi and Gaufridy, *Mémoires*, p. 33; Isambert, *Recueil général*, p. 147.

[119] A.A.E., 1714, fols. 21, 23, 58; Delib. Parl., B. Méjanes 953, fols. 210–211; Philippe Tamizey de Larroque, "Les correspondants de Peiresc: Le Cardinal Bichi, évêque de Carpentras," *Revue de Marseille et de Provence*, 30 (1884), 289–304; Georges Dethan, *Mazarin et ses amis* (Paris, 1968), pp. 104–129; J. Balteau, ed., *Dictionnaire de biographie française* (Paris, 1933–in progress), VI (1954), 398.

[120] Delib. Parl., B. Méjanes 953, fols. 211–211v; ADBR, Aix, B 3356, fol. 625v; A.C., Aix, AA 14, fol. 566.

[121] A.A.E., 1714, fols. 112, 114–117; Delib. Parl., B. Méjanes 953, fol. 213.

[122] Chéruel and Avenel, *Lettres de Mazarin*, II, 332–334.

The twenty-one article settlement, known as the Bichi Treaty, was ratified by the crown and returned to Aix on March 27, 1649, when it was registered by a joint meeting of thirty-four parlementaires presided over by Forbin de La Roque and the comte de Carcès.[123] Lettres de cachet, delivered a week earlier by the prévôt, sent hostages to Carpentras under Bichi's protection for two weeks to assure observance of the treaty and release of the prisoners.[124] Alais, Sève, and the duc de Richelieu were released on March 27, and they left immediately for Roquevaire. Alais was in such a hurry to leave Aix that he mounted and rode out in the rain, followed by a laughing, jeering crowd to the Saint Jean gate. Sève wrote on March 9 and 23 that many Aixois opposed the governor's release.[125] The city gates were opened, and on March 28 the parlementaires in red robes attended a Te Deum mass of celebration.[126]

The Aix parlementaires presented fifteen demands to the crown in 1649. Twelve concerned their privileges as an elite group at Aix—the suppression of new offices in their company, payment of gages and free salt for 1648, reduced use of disciplinary lettres de cachet and judicial evocations, provincial offices for their supporters, freedom for Estienne de Vaillac, a general amnesty, exemption for parlementaires from troop billeting, nullification of the Semester's arrêts and governor's ordinances in 1648, exemption from troop billeting for their city of Aix, removal of the governor and intendant, return of jurisdiction to the Cour des Comptes as the other sovereign court at Aix. Only three of their demands demonstrated concern for the preservation of traditional provincial privileges—the approval of the procureurs du pays for troop bil-

[123] ADBR, Aix, B 3367, March 27, 1649.

[124] Delib. Parl., B. Méjanes 953, fol. 218; A.C., Aix, CC 596, fol. 598v; Haitze, *Histoire*, V, 61–62. Councilors Lombard, Saint Marc, and Boyer were the Parlement's hostages. Henri d'Escalis de Bras, son of the 1647 consul, Joannis, seigneur de Châteauneuf, and Balthazar de Mernouillon, écuyer, were the city's hostages. They stayed twelve days at Carpentras.

[125] B.M., Harleian 4575, fol. 66; Haitze, *Histoire*, V, 69; B.N., Clairambault 420, fols. 89–90, 239–241.

[126] Delib. Parl., B. Méjanes 953, fols. 219–219v. The parlementaires had been enforcing many of the treaty's provisions by judicial arrêt since January 21, so their victory celebration was *pro forma*; cf. Delib. Parl., B. Méjanes 953, fols. 201v–202, 206–210; A.A.E., 1714, fols. 27, 101–102; A.C., Aix, BB 102, fol. 149v; B.N., Ms. fr. 17390, fols. 305–306.

leting, free municipal elections, and a reduced provincial troop load authorized by the provincial Estates. Reform is commonly defined as the improvement or correction of abuses with the implication of change for the better. In this sense, the Aix parlementaires presented a reforming program to the crown. But their reforms were narrow and self-serving, protecting their own particular privileges and interests as a provincial elite. The parlementaires focused their protest on the governor and intendant as royal representatives rather than on the crown itself. By refusing to attack the monarchy and its absolute policies directly, the Aix parlementaires vitiated the impact of their demands for change. They evaded the main issues.[127]

Mazarin wisely met many of the parlementaires' specific grievances. But he carefully ignored others such as recalling the governor and intendant general of the galleys, appointing the parlementaires' friends to office, safeguarding the traditional authority of the procureurs du pays, recognizing traditional exemptions from troop billeting, and convoking a provincial Estates. Moreover, the parlementaires had to pay a rachat, accept an augmentation des gages, and a creation of new offices. Nonetheless, their power and prestige had reached its zenith with the signing and ratification of the Bichi Treaty, which forced the crown to make concessions. Cardinal Mazarin repudiated these concessions one by one after the Fronde, as he consolidated and strengthened his position, until none was left. Ten years later he destroyed the parlementaire opposition.

In June 1649, the revolt at Aix developed into the Provençal Fronde, provoked by the angry vindictiveness of Alais. The governor had been forced to agree to the Bichi Treaty while a prisoner, but he had no intention of honoring his promise. Humiliated and angry, he wanted revenge. His wife encouraged his resentment. Condé at Paris laughed at his predicament, and satiric verses at his expense were sung in the streets of both capitals. After his release, Alais visited the coastal towns and main cities of Provence to assure their loyalty. He established his headquarters at Toulon, where he was joined by Sève. The intendant wrote Mazarin that

[127] Theme of paper presented at the annual conference of the French Historical Society at the University of California, Berkeley, in April 1977. 96–97; B.M., Harleian 4575, fols. 71–72.

Alais had formed a party to fight the parlementaires and was gathering troops for this purpose.[128]

On April 17, 1649, Sève wrote that the parlementaires were wearing white and red ribbons. The comte de Carcès had begun a fashion of shaving his beard and wearing only mustaches, adopted by Forbin de La Roque, three or four other parlementaires, and the noble cadets of Aix, who joined the rebels in great numbers. The support of the comte de Carcès helped to attract the cadets. Sevè maliciously noted that Carcès had been clean-shaven for a long time to hide his white hair. Alais and his supporters were wearing full beards and blue ribbons.[129] White and blue had been the colors of the 1630 revolt.

Sève reported on April 17 that Alais had called General Assemblies of the Nobility and Clergy at Marseille to gain their support, although the meetings were ostensibly to choose deputies for an Estates General that Mazarin promised to convene at Orléans. Alais designated Oppède to preside over a General Assembly of Communities at Aix, recognizing the communities' support of the parlementaires.[130] Oppède sent deputies to Arles to enlist that city's support. On May 4, Sève wrote that Alais had opened the Assembly of the Nobility at Marseille. There was great concern over its purpose and use. The procureurs du pays sent deputies to Paris on the subject, and the comte de Carcès planned to attend with three hundred armed men. Sève presided over the Marseille assemblies, although the Parlement had issued an arrêt against this on April 23 because the intendant was without authority in Provence. [131]

On April 14, Oppède wrote that Alais's followers had signed an offensive and defensive pact. The governor had illegally retained four hundred infantry from his disbanded provincial regiment to serve in the Antibes and Toulon garrisons, to which he added the new infantry regiment of fifteen companies. Alais summoned the

---

[128] B.M., Harleian 4575, fols. 69, 73, 92v, 103, 115; A.A.E., 1714, fols. 27, 243; Lublinskaya, *Vnutrenniaia*, p. 327; Grimaldi and Gaufridy, *Mémoires*, pp. 240–241; Pitton, *Histoire de la ville d'Aix*, pp. 415–416.

[129] B.N., Ms. fr. 17393, fols. 108–110; Lublinskaya, *Vnutrenniaia*, pp. 327–329; B.M., Harleian 4575, fols. 61, 80v; A.A.E., 1718, fol. 129.

[130] B.N., Ms. fr. 17393, fols. 108–110; B.M., Harleian 4575, fols. 75–78.

[131] B.N., Ms. fr. 17393, fols. 193–196; A.A.E., 1714, fol. 309; Delib. Parl., B. Méjanes 953, fol. 225v.

provincial militia "to guard the coast," and he levied a tax of twenty livres a day on surrounding communities to support these troops without the approval of the procureurs du pays.[132] The Parlement issued arrêts on April 16 and 30 forbidding the communities to support Alais's troops or pay his taxes without royal letters and approval of the procureurs du pays.[133] On April 16, the Parlement complained that Alais had suspended municipal elections at Grasse and appointed the consuls, confirmed by Sève, who wrote to Séguier on April 5 that Alais nullified municipal elections whenever the results were unfavorable to his party.[134]

The rapid escalation of hostilities can be traced in the intendant's letters. On April 15 and 17, Sève asked to be recalled because he could control neither Alais nor the Parlement.[135] On May 4, he wrote that Alais was angry and violent, motivated by a desire for revenge, and refusing to negotiate a peace. Alais and the parlementaires had divided the provincial nobility between them, and neither side would listen. Sève again asked to be recalled.[136] On May 10, Sève wrote that the parlementaires under Carcès were levying troops and collecting weapons—he estimated two to three thousand men.[137] On May 29, he wrote that he was unsuccessfully trying to enforce the Bichi Treaty. He feared civil war because Alais was gathering and arming more men.[138] On June 13, he wrote that Alais's military offensive against the Parlement had ended all hope of peace. Encouraged by his wife and his entourage of nobles, guards, and officers from his provincial regiment, Alais had decided on war in Sève's absence.[139] Alais was silent throughout these weeks: his few uninformative letters to Paris neither explained nor justified his conduct.[140]

The nobility of Languedoc, Dauphiné, and the Rhone valley flocked to Provence, exhilarated at the prospect of a good fight.

---

[132] Lublinskaya, *Vnutrenniaia*, pp. 327–329. Régusse made the same complaint to Mazarin on February 25, 1649; cf. A.A.E., 1714, fols. 138–141.

[133] B.N., Ms. fr. 18977, fols. 104, 160, 166–167.

[134] Delib. Parl., B. Méjanes 953, fol. 224v; B.N., Ms. fr. 17393, fols. 96–97; B.M., Harleian 4575, fols. 71–72.

[135] B.N., Ms. fr. 17393, fols. 96–97, 108–110.

[136] *Ibid.*, fols. 193–196.

[137] B.N., Ms. fr. 18977, fols. 169–171.

[138] B.N., Ms. fr. 17393, fols. 203–204.

[139] A.A.E., 1716, fol. 25; B.M., Harleian 4575, fols. 104–104v.

[140] A.A.E., 1716, fols. 16–18, 90–91, 100–101, 131–132.

The sword nobility's traditional hostility to the robe surfaced, and the parlementaires had trouble enticing sword nobles to join them, a difficulty that the governor did not share. In general, the sword nobles of Provence supported Alais and the communities supported the Parlement. Jacques de Cambis, baron d'Alès, wrote that the sword nobility of the Rhone valley were angered by the temerity of the Aix parlementaires, whom they considered upstarts, and flocked in droves to fight the rebels, regarding the war as a crusade.[141] Several mazarinades of 1649 expressed this sword-robe hostility; for instance, *Les plaintes de la noblesse de Provence contre l'oppression du Parlement, Remontrance au peuple de Provence*, and *Remontrances de ceux du pays de Provence au Roy, principalement contre le Parlement de Provence.*[142]

The parlementaires sent a flood of protest letters to Paris in June—Alais had the baron d'Alès levy three hundred horsemen in Languedoc and bring the Perault infantry regiment and a hundred riflemen to the châteaus of Tarascon and Orgon. As a lieutenant colonel in the light cavalry, Alais diverted the cavalry regiments Saint André Montbrun and Saint Auney from Dauphiné to the citadel of Sisteron. He placed these troops under the command of his brother-in-law Villefranche, and they lived off the countryside. The baron d'Hugues levied troops for Alais in Haute-Provence and Dauphiné.[143] The governor issued commissions to the chevalier Du Vins and others to levy troops in Basse-Provence. He diverted troops meant for the Catalonian and Italian cam-

---

[141] B.M., *Parlement de Bordeaux*, fol. 55, *Les plaintes de la noblesse de Provence* (1650); A.A.E., 1715, fols. 273–279, *Les doléances de la noblesse de Provence*; B. Méjanes 794, fols. 304–313, Alais's supporters among Provençal nobility and clergy; B.N., Ms. fr. 18977, fols. 322–326, the Parlement's supporters among provincial nobility; Pillorget, *Les mouvements insurrectionnels*, pp. 619–629; Grimaldi and Gaufridy, *Mémoires*, p. 37; J. de Romefort, "Au temps de la Fronde: Lettres de guerre de Jacques de Cambis, baron d'Alès, maréchal du camp des armées du Roi (1645–1653)," *Mémoires de l'institut historique de Provence*, 7 (1930), 83–89.

[142] B. Marseille 1792, also B.M., *Parlement de Bordeaux* (1650); B.N., Dupuy 754; B.N., Ms. fr. 18977.

[143] B.M., Harleian 4575, fol. 122v; Delib. Parl., B. Méjanes 953, fol. 239; B.N., Ms. fr. 18977, fols. 186–189; B.N., Dupuy 754, fol. 224; B.N., Clairambault 422, fols. 88–89, 122–123, 165–166; A.A.E., 1716, fols. 22–24, 39, 63–64.

paigns, and he circulated an ordinance forbidding the provincial nobility and communities to aid the parlementaires.[144] Councilor Cauvet de Bormes gave money to his nephew, the new marquis de Marignane, to raise a company of light cavalry for Alais.[145] The governor's troops in June included the Alès, Montpezat, Perault, Saint André, and Saint Auney regiments, the Monaco gendarmes company, the new provincial regiment, the Antibes and Toulon garrisons, provincial nobles, and unemployed soldiers from the royal galleys regiment and disbanded provincial regiment.[146] It was a formidable force.

On June 14, 1649, eight hours from Aix on the plain of Val near Brignoles, the parlementaires attacked the Saint André cavalry regiment. Led by Louis Decormis and the comte de Carcès, the parlementaires' force of five hundred cavalry and twelve hundred infantry were defeated by half their number: the parlementaires' troops were inexperienced and ran in panic when the cavalry charged. The comte de Carcès, Oppède, and Escalis de Bras had brought troops from the Comtat Venaissin to fight at the Val.[147] After their defeat, Escalis de Bras went to Pertuis, Glandèves to Hyères, and Régusse to La Ciotat to raise more troops; Régusse levied one regiment of infantry and one company of cavalry at his own expense.[148] Parlementaires Aymar d'Albi, Forbin de La Roque, and Valbelle were recruiting at their châteaux, as was Forbin de La Barben.[149]

Emboldened by his success, Alais encircled and besieged Aix in July, billeting troops in nearby villages and making his camp at Pelissane, then at Rognes. Living off the countryside around Aix,

[144] Delib. Parl., B. Méjanes 953, fol. 239; B.N., Dupuy 754, fols. 220, 225; B. Marseille 1790, *Arrêt de la cour du Parlement de Provence . . . 23 juin 1649*; A.A.E., 1716, fols. 22–24, 39.

[145] B.M., Harleian 4574, fol. 126v.

[146] *Ibid.*, fol. 123v.

[147] *Ibid.*, fols. 77, 78, 106v–109v, 112; A.A.E., 1715, fols. 273–279; Grimaldi and Gaufridy, *Mémoires*, p. 38; B.N., Ms. fr. 18977, fols. 186–189; B. Marseille 1794, *Relation véritable de ce qui s'est passée en la défaite des troupes de Provence par le regiment de cavalerie de S. André-Monbrun; Relation véritable de tout ce qui s'est fait et passée en la bataille du Val en Provence.*

[148] Grimaldi and Gaufridy, *Mémoires*, pp. 39–40.

[149] B.M., Harleian 4575, fols. 143v–144.

the troops were destructive. Nobles from Languedoc drove live-stock across the Rhone worth 150,000 livres. Alais destroyed the bastides and occupied the châteaux of parlementaires Forbin de La Roque, Valbelle, Aymar d'Albi, and Cour des Comptes president Séguiran.[150] The parlementaires hired the chevalier de Maugiron to serve with Carcès as army lieutenant general. Régusse, Oppède, Escalis de Bras father and son, Decormis, and Glandèves became camp masters.[151]

The parlementaires were hampered by an inability to tax. Their financial resources were limited to their purses, which were inade-quate for paying, provisioning, and equipping a fighting force. They borrowed repeatedly, but the company was chronically in debt, and they were unable to borrow enough. The cathedral chap-ter gave them 6,000 livres, the university 4,000 livres, a municipal merchant and artisan organization 10,000 livres, and the General Assembly 30,000 livres. On July 3, they voted to use the épices from the common purse for the defense of Aix, and they each gave 1,000 livres in cash. On July 9, they confiscated and sold the property of Semester councilors and Alais's supporters. On July 23, they ordered absent parlementaires to appear, then garnished their gages as a penalty, and they levied a general tax on all parle-mentaires in the city. The women of Aix donated their jewels to the cause. But by August, the parlementaires had exhausted their financial resources.[152] On July 15, the parlementaires had asked the procureurs du pays to impose a tax of 100 livres per feu, which was approved by the Cour des Comptes. But with Alais besieging the city and intimidating the surrounding communities, there was no way of collecting the tax.[153] By an ordinance on June 20, Alais forbade provincial treasurer Gaillard and all consuls of Provençal communities to deliver tax money to Aix. As an addi-

[150] B.N., Ms. fr. 20473, fols. 15–17; B.N., Dupuy 754, fols. 308–314; Haitze, *Histoire*, V, 135–136; B.M., Harleian 4575, fols. 126v, 143v–144; "Recueil de mémoires et pièces sur la Provence," B. Méjanes R.A. 9, fols. 151–155, "Brième relation du siège du château de Meyrargues (de Léon de Valbelle) au mois d'août, 1649 par M. Thus, prêtre du lieu de Jouques."

[151] B.M., Harleian 4575, fols. 121–122, 125v.

[152] B.N., Dupuy 754, fol. 235; Delib. Parl., B. Méjanes 953, fols. 237–248; B.N., Ms. fr. 18977, fols. 199, 250.

[153] B.N., Ms. fr. 18977, fol. 201. The tax was later levied to pay Alais's military expenses and became a voluntary gift to the crown; cf. Lublinskaya, *Vnutrenniaia*, pp. 331–333; B.N., Dupuy 754, fols. 312–314.

tional precaution, he moved the general receipts bureau to Toulon.[154]

Mazarin announced in June that he was sending Jean d'Estampes, sieur de Valençay, to Provence to mediate a truce and enforce the Bichi Treaty, which had been blatantly ignored by both sides. Valençay made a leisurely journey to Provence, which allowed Alais to encircle the city. Leaving Paris in the previous month, Valençay arrived in Lyon on July 13 and Avignon a week later, when he met deputies from the Parlement. On July 23, he rode up before Alais's tent, which was flying the fleurs de lys, in the Pelissane camp. Alais, Sève, and the archbishop of Arles listened to Valençay complain about the heat and dust of a Provençal summer. Alais was cold and hostile. He told the royal mediator that his agreement to the Bichi Treaty had been extorted "with a knife at this throat," and he had no intention of honoring it. Valençay spent July 24–25 in a futile attempt to convince the governor to compromise. Deputies with letters from the Estates of Languedoc and the Parlement of Toulouse voluntarily acting as mediators had no effect in persuading either side to temporize.[155]

On July 29, Valençay entered Aix. The streets and windows were full of Aixois shouting, "Vive le Roy!" Frightened by the siege, they regarded Valençay as a savior and hoped that he could force Alais to withdraw. He was received with full honors, as if he were a royal minister; deputies from the royal courts, municipal government, and cathedral chapter made complimentary speeches. Valençay was flattered and pleased by his reception. On July 30, he sent to Paris a moderate version of Alais's demands for withdrawal.[156] Then he went to Carpentras to visit Cardinal Bichi. Sève commented that Valençay refused to work with him and the archbishop of Arles, fearing their prejudice against the parlementaires and not wanting to share the credit for a successful reconciliation. Sève thought him incompetent.[157]

---

[154] *Ordonnance de Monseigneur Louis de Valois, comte d'Alais, colonel-général de la cavalerie légère de France*, B. Marseille 1794.

[155] Delib. Parl., B. Méjanes 953, fol. 240v, June, 1649; B.M., Harleian 4575, fol. 115v.

[156] Lublinskaya, *Vnutrenniaia*, pp. 331–336; A.A.E., 1716, fols. 17, 19, 171; Mousnier, *Lettres*, II, 1022–1023; Haitze, *Histoire*, V, 124–125; B.N., Dupuy 754, fols. 236–241.

[157] B.M., Harleian 4575, fols. 133v–134.

Valençay had not persuaded Alais to withdraw; his reports emphasized the governor's obstinacy, vindictiveness, and hostility. Three weeks later François de Beauvillier, duc de Saint Aignan and maréchal du camp, arrived in Provence with a thirteen-article peace treaty issued in August. As an alternative, he carried in his saddlebags eighty blank commissions to levy troops. Estampes de Valençay estimated that the commissions could be used to levy two thousand men in four cavalry regiments, who could force Alais to make peace. Saint Aignan also carried lettres de cachet for Alais, Carcès, the opposition leaders, and the consuls of Aix.

The commissions posed a serious problem for Alais. He had promised brevets as camp marshals and camp masters to nobles such as Montmeyan, Villefranches, and the baron d'Hugues. They were angry when he was unable to deliver: Alais could issue his own letters, but he could not obtain royal letters. The baron d'Alès left for Catalonia when Alais could not provide the commission and money for a cavalry company, as he had promised.

Alais ordered his troops to live off the countryside, and he taxed illegally to pay them. But this was not enough, and in July, as a condition of peace, he demanded that the parlementaires pay his military expenses. Alais was finally forced to sell his library in 1652 to pay his debts.[158] Sève remarked that "the confusion with which this prince was acting and his economies in levying troops presented more danger of shame than hope of honor."[159]

Alais was forced to accept the August Treaty. The parlementaires released lieutenant Artaud on August 22, disbanded their troops, and published the treaty on August 25. Alais grudgingly and unwillingly signed the treaty. He received Carcès, Maugiron, Forbin de La Roque, and Oppède in the Place des Prêcheurs, his troops behind him in battle order, then withdrew.[160] The Aixois watched the dust of his retreating troops with relief. A victory for the parlementaires, the August Treaty was a confirmation of the Bichi Treaty. But the hostilities did not end. Alais was stubborn. He withdrew to Toulon determined to win, and Provence slid into civil war.

---

[158] *Ibid.*, fols. 105v, 126–127, 134, 142; Joseph Billioud, *Le livre en Provence du XVI^e au XVIII^e siècle* (Marseille, 1962), p. 139; Romefort, "Au temps de la Fronde," 83–89.

[159] B.M., Harleian 4575, fol. 127v.

[160] *Ibid.*, fols. 138v, 149.

There was almost unanimous agreement that the Fronde was caused by Alais's unwillingness to compromise after the Aix revolt. This was the opinion of intendant Sève and the royal mediators. The parlementaires were hardly a model of restraint—they incited the 1649 revolt; they recruited troops in 1648 and 1649; they attacked the governor's troops on the plain of Val. But the greater responsibility belongs to Alais, who sought revenge at whatever cost. As Ernst Kossmann has noted, "The facts demonstrated that civil war appeared only in provinces where a governor and a parlement confronted each other. . . . We shall try to show that, in the provinces, the Fronde was a Fronde of provincial governors. They had caused it by their pretensions which became exorbitant in proportion to the weakening of royal power."[161] The origins of the Provençal Fronde lay in a power struggle between the governor and the Parlement of Aix.

The civil war in Provence from 1650 to 1653 has been described elsewhere.[162] We are interested in the activities and motivations of the parlementaires who participated in the Provençal Fronde. The Parlement of Aix withdrew to Salon in March to avoid an outbreak of plague in the capital, although the October rentrée was held at Aix, as usual.[163] Many parlementaires retired early to their country estates in the summer of 1650 to avoid the risk of disease and the expense and discomfort of lodging in a strange town. The governor's recall to Paris in August and his departure in December 1650 encouraged the parlementaires' vacation.[164]

The opposition party dispersed in 1650. Thereafter, only a few parlementaires actively participated in the Fronde. The Sabreurs, or Sabers, were the party of Provençal nobles supporting the Princes. They took their name from their leader, Jean-Henri de

[161] Kossmann, *La Fronde*, p. 18.

[162] Pillorget, *Les mouvements insurrectionnels*, pp. 603–705; EDB, III, 77–91; Haitze, *Histoire*, V, 182–292; Adolphe Crémieux, *Marseille et la royauté pendant la minorité de Louis XIV*, 2 vols. (Paris, 1917), I, 266–423; Bouche, *La chorographie*, I, 950–987.

[163] Bouche, *La chorographie*, II, 952; Haitze gives the month as February, cf. *Histoire*, V, 182–183; and Guidy gives it as April, cf. "Histoire du Parlement," B. Méjanes R.A. 54, fol. 290.

[164] A.A.E., 1716, fol. 406, Régusse to Mazarin, December 13, 1650, fols. 407–408, Aiguebonne to Mazarin, same date; Pillorget, *Les mouvements insurrectionnels*, p. 652.

Puget, baron de Saint Marc, who carried a heavy saber and threatened his enemies with, "I'll take my saber to you, and that will bring you to your senses!" Robe Sabreurs included president Oppède and his brother the abbé Louis, their cousin president Forbin de La Roque and their brother-in-law councilor Boyer, councilor Pierre de Laurens (whose grandson married Oppède's daughter), president of the Enquêtes Jacques de Gallifet, councilor Saint Marc, councilor Glandèves, and his brother-in-law the baron de Bras. There was also Oppède's cousin Forbin de La Barben, Jean-Baptiste de Puget, who was seigneur de Barbentane and kinsman of the baron de Saint Marc, Reynaud de Séguiran, sieur de Bouc and first president en survivance of the Cour des Comptes (his uncle by marriage was Laurens), Galaup-Chasteuil, who was procureur-général of the Cour des Comptes, and councilor Antoine of the same court. Three president and five councilors of the Parlement, one president, one royal attorney, and one councilor of the Cour des Comptes were Sabreurs. Their chiefs were the baron de Saint Marc and the baron d'Oppède.[165]

The Canivets, or Penknives, supported Mazarin, and were also known as the Mazarinistes. Their name alluded to the tag that the pen is mightier than the sword, since penknives were used to sharpen writing quills. Their enemies claimed they were incapable of wielding any weapon except a penknife. Among the Mazarinistes in the Parlement were presidents Régusse, Decormis, Foresta de La Roquette, councilors Villeneuve and his brother-in-law Mazargues, Bonfils, Rascas Du Canet, Antelmi, Tressemanes-Chasteuil, Guérin, Gautier, Fabri de Rians, Honorat de Pourcieux, Barrême, Agut, Signier, Estienne, Raffelis, and Leidet-Sigoyer. Other Mazarinistes included the older Séguiran of the Cour des Comptes, ex-parlementaire Venel, and the comte de Carcès. Mazarinistes in the Parlement included three presidents, one royal attorney, and fifteen councilors. They were more numerous than

---

[165] Grimaldi and Gaufridy, *Mémoires*, pp. 41–42; Delib. Parl., B. Méjanes 953, fols. 449–451; Haitze, *Histoire*, V, 202–203, 207–209, 212, 214, 236; Savine, *Relation des troubles*, p. 147; B. Marseille 1792, *Le courrier provençal sur l'arrivée du duc de Mercoeur* (Paris, 1652), p. 6; Pillorget, *Les mouvements insurrectionnels*, p. 670. Councilor Louis de Saint Marc was a Sabreur who may later have become a Mazariniste; cf. Guidy, "Histoire du Parlement," B. Méjanes R.A. 54, fol. 305.

the Sabreurs, but a minority of the Parlement.[166] The majority of the Aix parlementaires were politically inactive after 1649.

The Semesters were former members of the Semester, fighting for the reestablishment of their court and the return of Alais as governor of Provence. Their leader was a brother-in-law of Oppède, Parlement councilor Cauvet de Bormes, who became head of the party of provincial nobles supporting Alais in 1647 after his brother's death. He was the only one of the anciens officiers to support Alais, but most of the provincial nobility supported the governor.[167]

The goal of the Sabreurs was to rid Provence of Alais, and they turned to the Paris princes for help, especially after Alais lost the support of Condé. The Sabreurs enjoyed power and prestige at Aix in the years when Mazarin's fortunes were at low ebb. They intrigued successfully for the election of the baron de Saint Marc as first consul in September 1650, and the election of Oppède's cousin, Laurent de Forbin-Janson, as first consul in September 1651, defeating Mazariniste candidate Rascas Du Canet.[168] Régusse noted that most of the consulaires and noble cadets of Aix supported Forbin-Janson.[169]

Oppède and the baron de Saint Marc decided that the way to stop the return of Alais to Provence was to ask his cousin and patron, the prince de Condé, to appoint his own brother, the prince de Conti, as governor.[170] Régusse alleged that Oppède hoped to profit personally from the support of Condé, who promised to secure for him the office of Parlement first president.[171] The baron de Saint Marc also sought the patronage of Condé. His family

---

[166] Grimaldi and Gaufridy, *Mémoires*, pp. 43–44; Delib. Parl., B. Méjanes 953, fols. 431–432v, 449–451; Haitze, *Histoire*, V, 198–200, 231–233, 239–240, 251; ADBR, Aix, Moissac, "Histoire du Parlement," II, fol. 175; B. Marseille 1792, *Le courrier provençal sur l'arrivée du duc de Mercoeur* (Paris, 1652), p. 4.

[167] B.M., Harleian 4575, fol. 115; B.N., Ms. fr. 18977, fols. 322–326.

[168] Haitze, *Histoire*, V, 195, 197; Grimaldi and Gaufridy, *Mémoires*, pp. 42–44.

[169] Pitton, *Histoire de la ville d'Aix*, p. 454; Grimaldi and Gaufridy, *Mémoires*, p. 44.

[170] A.A.E., 1717, fol. 235; B.N., Clairambault 434, fols. 330–331; Haitze, *Histoire*, V, 197; B. Méjanes 929, fols. 803–804; Crémieux, *Marseille sous la royauté*, I, 384–386.

[171] Grimaldi and Gaufridy, *Mémoires*, p. 43.

belonged to the sword nobility of Provence and held several important fiefs, but they had more glory than wealth. Condé's patronage would have helped the family fortunes.[172] The consuls of Aix, Marseille, and Arles, as well as the Cour des Comptes and Trésoriers Généraux de France wrote letters to Paris expressing dread at the possibility of Alais's return—although they did not request Conti's appointment as governor—and the Parlement sent Jacques de Gallifet as its deputy to court to request a new governor. Gallifet, "young, audacious, and ambitious," delivered an impassioned attack on Alais.[173] Parlement councilor Jean-François de Glandèves-Rousset went to inform Condé unofficially that the Sabreurs wanted his brother Conti as governor. Mazarin opposed the appointment, convincing the queen regent to refuse it in 1651. He feared Condé's control over a province so close to Italy and Spain.[174]

Régusse in 1652 reported that he and Decormis had received poisoned letters "of a dirty yellow color and foul-smelling" in the handwriting of Gallifet, whom he described as "unstable and ambitious."[175] The Gallifets father and son had been clients of Condé for several years. Condé may have promised the younger Gallifet the office of first president.[176] Condé sent to Provence his brother Conti, his guard captain Du Mesnil, and Jean-Baptiste de Puget, seigneur de Barbentane, with letters of créance to recruit supporters for him.[177] Jacques de Gallifet was arrested in 1653 for his ties with Condé and sent to the citadel of Sisteron, from which he was released in 1654 through the intercession of Conti. A

[172] *Ibid.*, pp. 42–43; EDB, IV–2, 393; Edouard Baratier et al., *Atlas historique, Provence, Comtat Venaissin, Principauté de Monaco, Principauté d'Orange, Comté de Nice* (Paris, 1969), pp. 139–140.

[173] B.N., Clairambault 434, fols. 366–367; 435, fols. 14, 16, 20–21, 24–25, 84–85, 107; A.C., Aix, BB 102, fol. 208; B. Marseille 1792, *Remontrance faite au roy et à la reine regente par M. le président de Gallifet, député du Parlement de Provence, pour le changement du gouverneur* (Paris, 1651); Grimaldi and Gaufridy, *Mémoires*, p. 42; Guidy, "Histoire du Parlement," B. Méjanes R.A. 54, fols. 291, 305.

[174] Pillorget, *Les mouvements insurrectionnels*, p. 666; Chéruel and Avenel, *Lettres de Mazarin*, IV, 254–255, Mazarin to Lionne, June 9, 1651, 262 and n. 2; A.A.E., 1719, fol. 29.

[175] Grimaldi and Gaufridy, *Mémoires*, pp. 42, 52; EDB, III, 85.

[176] EDB, III, 86.

[177] Grimaldi and Gaufridy, *Mémoires*, p. 43.

search of his house had revealed incriminating letters from the princes and copies of Bordeaux mazarinades.[178]

Competition for the office of Parlement first president influenced the Fronde at Aix after 1650. First president Mesgrigny had been called to Paris in May 1650 with the comte de Carcès to explain his participation in the Aix revolt.[179] Disgraced by the revolt, Mesgrigny quietly and unofficially retired from office. It was well known that he wanted to resign, although he was not replaced until 1655.[180] Presidents Régusse and Oppède, chiefs of the Mazarinistes and Sabreurs, competed to replace him.

The most likely candidate was third president Charles de Grimaldi, granted the titles baron de Roumoules and marquis de Régusse by Mazarin in November 1649.[181] A friend of Mazarin's brother, the archbishop of Aix, Régusse had attracted the attention of the cardinal himself, as we learn from a letter of December 3, 1653, when Mazarin's nieces were visiting Aix.[182] Régusse had sent a messenger in 1649 to ask the cardinal's plans for Provence. Mazarin answered that he wanted the differences between the governor and Parlement resolved, and to this end Régusse met secretly with intendant Sève and Alais's secretary at an inn on the road to Roquevaire. Régusse was accompanied by his son-in-law, Grimaldi-Antibes, marquis de Courbons. Régusse emphasized his crédit within the Parlement and city of Aix, dwelling on his friendship with Escalis de Bras, connections with the Grimaldi-Monaco through his son-in-law, ties with the young nobles and parlementaires. Sève was dubious. He thought Régusse was exaggerating, and the municipal elections of 1651 proved him correct. The meeting ended because Régusse refused to withdraw from the Parlement and establish a rival court in another city.[183]

---

[178] Haitze, *Histoire*, V, 263–266, 281. Mazarin ordered Mercoeur to free Gallifet on June 22, 1654; cf. Chéruel and Avenel, *Lettres de Mazarin*, VI, 572.

[179] ADBR, Aix, B 3367, Mesgrigny's name does not appear in the attendance records for 1649.

[180] A.A.E., 1716, fols. 155, 201–202, 289–290.

[181] ADBR, Aix, B 3357, fol. 8.

[182] Grimaldi and Gaufridy, *Mémoires*, pp. 22, 25; Chéruel and Avenel, *Lettres de Mazarin*, III, 1063, Mazarin to Régusse, October 7, 1648; VI, 536, nieces to Mazarin, December 3, 1653.

[183] Grimaldi and Gaufridy, *Mémoires*, pp. 37, 40; B.M., Harleian 4575, fols. 127v–131.

Régusse became chief of the Mazarinistes in 1650, an honor he shared with ex-parlementaire Gaspard de Venel, husband of the governess to Mazarin's nieces.[184] Régusse expected to be rewarded for his loyalty with the office of Parlement first president. He was acting first president while the Parlement was at Salon—the first and second presidents were at Paris.[185] Later, he alternated in this position on a weekly basis with fourth president Henri de Forbin-Maynier, baron d'Oppède.[186] Régusse complained to Sève that he did not like serving under a younger man with a lower rank in the Parlement.[187] Governor Mercoeur was warned when he first came to Provence that Oppède through his crédit and personal fortune was a dangerous member of the Sabreurs.[188] Oppède's great political asset was his kinship with the Forbins, who provided him with an extensive clientele in Provence: Oppède had the crédit that Régusse claimed to have.[189]

The competition between the two presidents developed into a personal feud and split the Parlement into warring factions. By the summer of 1651, a strong parlementaire party had coalesced around Régusse, supporting Mazarin and favoring reconciliation. Mazarin sent letters announcing his return to France to the first presidents of the parlements of Aix, Grenoble, and Toulouse on December 31, 1651, because of their special friendship for him.[190] After Alais left Provence, there was less fear of the Semester, and the natural conservatism of the parlementaires began to reassert itself about the time that Mazarin's fortunes began to improve. The Mazarinistes flourished as the cardinal's prospects brightened and those of his opponents dimmed. This trend resulted in the expulsion of Oppède and the Sabreurs from Aix in the autumn of 1651. The two factions fought for control of the city, and the Mazarinistes won.

[184] Haitze, *Histoire*, V, 196; Grimaldi and Gaufridy, *Mémoires*, pp. 24–25, 43–44.

[185] Grimaldi and Gaufridy, *Mémoires*, p. 41; A.A.E., 1716, fols. 297–298, 412–413.

[186] Haitze, *Histoire*, V, 194.

[187] B.M., Harleian 4575, fols. 127v–128.

[188] A.A.E., 1718, fol. 141.

[189] The author discusses Oppède's crédit and clientèle in a forthcoming article.

[190] Grimaldi and Gaufridy, *Mémoires*, p. 42; A.A.E., 1716, fols. 423–424; 1719, fol. 29; Chéruel and Avenel, *Lettres de Mazarin*, VI, 779.

A quarrel between one of the brothers of Mazariniste Decormis and Sabreur chief Saint Marc on the afternoon of October 3, 1651, led to street fighting in the Place des Prêcheurs. Two large groups of men assembled, and Saint Marc and his supporters withdrew to the town hall, where the municipal arsenal was located. Perhaps they intended to issue a call to arms: Saint Marc had recently been first consul. Despite the objections of Oppède and his cousin Forbin de La Roque, the Parlement went to calm the excited men. Oppède on his own initiative went to the town hall to talk to Saint Marc. Councilor Tressemanes-Chasteuil, easily excitable, suspected a conspiracy, threw off his judicial robe, grabbed a sword, and ran to warn the city.

A large, hostile crowd of Aixois gathered around the town hall. Régusse and Foresta de La Roquette, representing the Parlement, pushed past two guards at the entrance to confront about fifty to sixty young men, including the brothers of Oppède and the son of Laurens. They asked Oppède and the baron de Saint Marc to leave Aix, indicating the intention of the Parlement to issue an arrêt to this effect. The archbishop of Arles advised that they leave. Oppède courageously returned to the palace of justice on foot through the hostile crowd in an attempt to explain his actions to the Parlement. But he left Aix a few days later, accompanied by Forbin de La Roque and the younger Séguiran, and was soon raising men on his nearby estates at La Fare and Vitrolles. Saint Marc was escorted to the city gates by Régusse, Guérin, and Antelmi. The brothers of Oppède went home. Régusse invited three officers and a hundred fifty men of the Vendôme regiment, billeted in the neighborhood, into the city of Aix to secure it for the Mazarinistes.[191]

Laurens d'Urre, marquis d'Aiguebonne, was given the power to command in Provence in the absence of Alais by royal letters dated September 21, 1650, and published by the Parlement on December 19 after the governor's departure.[192] Aiguebonne was received at Aix with full honors as acting governor in the absence of the lieutenant general, the comte de Carcès, on December 21, 1650, and established a permanent residence at the château of La Tour

[191] Grimaldi and Gaufridy, *Mémoires*, pp. 45–47; A.C., Aix, BB 102, fol. 222v; A.A.E., 1717, fol. 317.
[192] ADBR, Aix, B 3357, fols. 227v–232.

d'Aigues north of Aix.[193] From an undistinguished noble family of Dauphiné, Aiguebonne was an aging military man without much political sense. Régusse described him as "more properly the commander of a garrison than a province, slow to make decisions and cold in negotiations."[194] Aiguebonne and the Parlement soon quarreled over authority.[195]

Jean de Pontevès, third comte de Carcès (1599–1656), became Grand Seneschal of Provence at his father's death in 1610 and lieutenant general of Provence by royal letters in August 1635.[196] The offices of Grand Seneschal and lieutenant general had been held jointly by the Pontevès de Carcès since the mid-sixteenth century. The Pontevès de Carcès were among the most illustrious, wealthy families of the Provençal sword nobility. Their estate at Carcès in the Var near Brignoles brought 6,500 livres a year in 1668; the annual income from their other fiefs in Provence was at least 35,000 livres.[197] The family had a tradition of military and royal service that gave them enormous crédit in Provence. The grandfather, Jean de Pontevès, first comte de Carcès (1512–1582), was chief of the Catholic party in Provence, and his nephew Hubert de Garde, seigneur de Vins, was his second in command.[198] The first comte de Carcès became grand seneschal in 1566 and lieutenant general in 1572. He was succeeded in office by his son Gaspard de Pontevès, second comte de Carcès (1567–1610), who joined Garde de Vins as chief of the League in Provence. In 1591, Gaspard married Eléonore de Montpezat, daughter of the wife of the duc de Mayenne. The duc de Mayenne declared Gaspard governor of Provence in 1592, an office he held until 1594, when he voluntarily accepted Charles de Lorraine, duc de Guise, the choice

---

[193] Bouche, *La chorographie*, II, 967; A.A.E., 1716, 1717.

[194] Grimaldi and Gaufridy, *Mémoires*, p. 44; A.A.E., 1719, fol. 31.

[195] A.A.E., 1716, fols. 156, 423–424; 1717, fols. 203–204; B.N., Clairambault 434, fol. 167.

[196] ADBR, Aix, B 3350, fols. 503–509; EDB, III, 658–660.

[197] B. Méjanes 630, "Etat du florinage contenant le revenu noble de tous les fiefs et arrière-fiefs de Provence avec les noms du possesseurs fait par Maynier d'Oppède en 1668."

[198] B.N., Pièces originales 2335; B. Méjanes, three copies available, 632, 802, or R.A. 6, "Vie des seigneurs Jean et Gaspard de Pontevès, comtes de Carcès"; EDB, III, 37–62; Edouard Baratier, ed., *Histoire de la Provence* (Toulouse, 1969), pp. 258–261.

of the king, Henry IV, as governor of Provence.[199] Jean de Pontevès, third comte de Carcès, followed the example of his father
and grandfather in a military career highlighted by expelling the
Spanish from Provence in 1637.[200]

Pontevès de Carcès joined the rebel parlementaires in 1649. He
had long-standing family ties with members of the court,[201] and he
hoped for a greater role in the provincial government. As long as
Alais was governor, Pontevès de Carcès had only titular authority
and a shadow role. The parlementaires requested a more substantial role for him in their demands after the revolt, and a 1650
mazarinade accused him of excessive ambition.[202] Carcès's es-
pousal of the parlementaires' cause in 1649 helped to secure the
support of the cadets of Aix as Régusse noted. Carcès's name
appears first on the somewhat attenuated list of provincial nobles
supporting the parlementaires in 1649, followed by his relatives
the marquis de Gordes, the marquis de Vins, the comte de
Grignan, the seigneurs de Sillans, Beauden, Cadanet, Buoux, and
Du Castellar.[203] In April 1649, Carcès had appeared with three
hundred of his supporters at the Marseille General Assembly of
the Nobility called by governor Alais. These men fought under the

[199] *Ibid.*; Maurice Wilkinson, *The Last Days of the League in Provence,
1588–1598* (London, 1909); Balteau, *Dictionnaire*, VII (1956), 1117–1118;
Honoré Louis de Castellane, sieur de Besaudun, *Mémoires pour servir à
l'histoire de la Ligue en Provence* (Aix, 1866, from manuscript at B. Méjanes), and *Manifeste et declaration de la noblesse de Provence contenant
les causes qui l'ont mue de prendre les armes contre le sieur d'Espernon*
(1595), available at B.N. The definitive history of the League in Provence
is yet to be written.

[200] Balteau, *Dictionnaire*, VII, 1118–1119; B.M., Harleian 4468, fols.
138–166, "Relation que je fais à Monseigneur de toutes les choses que se
sont passées dans l'armée commandée par Monsieur le comte d'Harcourt
et Monsieur le maréchal de Vitry jusqu' après la prise des Iles Sainte Marguerite et Saint Honorat"; ADBR, Aix, B 3348, fol. 199, May 1629, royal
letters for Pontevès de Carcès to levy an infantry regiment of ten companies
for use in Italy; Grimaldi and Gaufridy, *Mémoires*, pp. 41, 48.

[201] Fleury Vindry, *Les parlementaires français au XVIe siècle*, 3 vols.
(Paris, 1909–1912), I, 7, 11, 13, 22, 39, 63, 82–83; Auguste Du Roure,
*Généalogie de la maison de Forbin* (Paris, 1906), pp. 18, 51.

[202] *Les plaintes de la noblesse de Provence*, B.M., *Parlement de Bordeaux*
(1650), fol. 55.

[203] B.N., Ms. fr. 18977, fols. 322–326; B.M., Harleian 4575, fol. 115;
Grimaldi and Gaufridy, *Mémoires*, p. 38.

command of Carcès in June 1649 when he led the parlementaire forces against the governor's troops at the disastrous battle of Val.[204] However, the bulk of the Provençal nobility, including the old and famous names, joined the governor. Carcès's crédit was not great enough to overcome the robe stigma of the rebels and offset the éclat of Alais, who was the last of the Valois. Carcès was summoned to Paris in the spring of 1650 for explanations, and his functions as lieutenant general were suspended. He returned to Provence without permission in 1651 to receive a warm welcome at Aix. He supported Régusse and the Mazarinistes.[205]

The presence of Carcès at Aix disturbed Aiguebonne, who as acting governor considered him a rival for authority in Provence. Aiguebonne decided to confront Carcès at Aix. He forced the issue by making a formal entry, requiring the Parlement and Carcès to recognize his authority in the city. On the afternoon of November 8, 1651, he stopped outside the walls in the Faubourg des Cordeliers and announced to Régusse and the Parlement his intention of making an entrance the next morning. Although warned there might be rioting, he persisted, and with a large party of men, he rode into Aix. As he came through the city gate, shots were fired, and a crowd of Aixois moved menacingly to engulf him. Several youths began to shut the gate separating him from the rest of his entourage, and Aiguebonne turned and rode from Aix in haste. Régusse and the Mazarinistes of the Parlement remained masters of the city. Aiguebonne blamed them for denying him entrance.[206]

Called again to court to explain his role in the events at Aix, Carcès did not answer and withdrew to his estates in the comtat.[207] He supported the duc de Guise as a candidate for governor in 1652.[208] Forced into retirement, Carcès died in the

[204] B.M., Harleian 4575, fols. 77, 106v; B. Marseille 1792, *Relation véritable de ce qui s'est passée en la défaite des troupes de Provence* (1649); *Relation véritable de tout de ce qui s'est fait et passée en la bataille du Val en Provence* (1649); A.A.E., 1717, fol. 317.

[205] Grimaldi and Gaufridy, *Mémoires*, pp. 47–48; Jean-Pierre Papon, *Histoire générale de Provence*, 4 vols. (Paris, 1777–1786), IV, 539.

[206] *Ibid.*, pp. 49–50; Delib. Parl., B. Méjanes 953, fol. 432v; Haitze, *Histoire*, V, 202–203.

[207] Grimaldi and Gaufridy, *Mémoires*, p. 51.

[208] B. Marseille 1792, *Lettre des Trois Etats de Provence à Monsieur le duc de Guise par laquelle il est prié d'accepter the gouvernement de Provence* (1652).

arms of his friend, Oppède, in August 1656. Oppède may have helped to convince him to support the rebel parlementaires.[209] Oppède in 1637 had married Marie-Thérèse de Pontevès, daughter of Jean-André, écuyer of Cadanet, from a cadet branch of the Pontevès family.[210] The comte de Carcès died childless in 1656 and was succeeded as grand seneschal and lieutenant general of Provence by his nephew, François de Simiane, marquis de Gordes, who also inherited his title of comte.[211] Obscured by time, Carcès's personality is somewhat of a mystery. He was unkindly described by a contemporary historian, Pierre-Joseph de Haitze (1656–1737) as "little regretted never having been truly a friend or enemy of anyone; dissatisfied with what he had and desirous of what he had not; outspoken for peace although the first to take up arms; passionate about women which shortened his days."[212]

Hoping to regain control of the city of Aix, Aiguebonne in 1651 joined the Sabreurs.[213] This discredited him in the eyes of the province and Paris, and he was recalled.[214] In January 1652, the Sabreurs affiliated with the Semesters against their mutual enemies, Mazarin and the parlementaires. Toulon became their headquarters.[215] Toulon had been Alais's stronghold. The duc de Mercoeur was named acting governor by royal letters on April 18, 1652, and was in Provence by May.[216] The Sabreurs and Semesters circulated mazarinades against Mercoeur. Since Conti was not to be appointed governor, they sought the appointment of Alais's son-in-law, Louis de Lorraine, duc de Joyeuse, son of governor Guise.[217]

---

[209] B.M., Harleian 4490, fols. 2–3, August 14, 1656; Pillorget, *Les mouvements insurrectionnels*, p. 638.

[210] Du Roure, *Généalogie de la maison de Forbin*, p. 51.

[211] EDB, III, 658–660; ADBR, Aix, B 3358, fols. 1033–1039.

[212] EDB, IV-2, 119–120.

[213] Grimaldi and Gaufridy, *Mémoires*, p. 51; Haitze, *Histoire*, V, 199.

[214] One of Aiguebonne's last letters from Provence was dated March 19, 1652, La Tour d'Aigues; cf. A.A.E., 1719, fol. 29.

[215] A.A.E., 1718, fol. 21; Haitze, *Histoire*, V, 210–214. Maynier d'Oppède for the Sabreurs had first approached the Semesters in December 1651, possibly because his brother-in-law was their leader; cf. A.A.E., 1717, fol. 316.

[216] A.A.E., 1718, fol. 59; Félix Tavernier, *Marseille et la Provence sous la royauté, 1481–1789* (Aix, n.d.), p. 61, text of letter announcing Mercoeur's arrival in Provence.

[217] M.A. 336, *Entretien d'un gentilhomme, d'un avocat et d'un marchand sur les troubles de Provence* (1652); B. Marseille 1792, *Le courrier proven-*

Mercoeur was supported by the Parlement and city of Aix, where he convoked the provincial militia. His Vendôme regiment was already in Provence, and he obtained the loyalty of the provincial regiment by promising to pay their salaries, which were in arrears. He assumed command of two infantry regiments in transit through Provence and a naval squadron on its way to Barcelona. With these troops, he intimidated Sisteron and Tarascon into opening their gates to him, then established a blockade by land and sea of Toulon. It was the time of the vendanges, the grape harvest, and the Toulonnais, fearing destruction of their vines and facing a superior military force, opened their gates to Mercoeur on September 15, 1652.[218] A few days later a general amnesty was presented to the Parlement for registration. Peace was declared in October.[219]

Mercoeur's prompt military action averted bloodshed and brought peace to Provence in 1652. One of the secrets of Mercocur's success was his ability to attract rebels as supporters and clients. When Sabreur chiefs the baron d'Oppède and the baron de Saint Marc joined Mercoeur in the summer of 1652, they started a scramble to join the winning side. Saint Marc became captain of Mercoeur's guards, and Oppède was appointed first president of the Parlement by royal letters on September 19, 1655.[220]

A small group of political activists in the Parlement participated in the Fronde for the same motives that lay behind their participation in the revolts of 1630 and 1649—clientage ties, judicial politics, private feuds, and political opinion. Many Sabreurs were relatives, friends, and clients of Henri de Forbin-Maynier d'Oppède, while the competition between Oppède and Régusse for the office of first president developed into a personal feud dividing the Parlement after 1650. This was not the only instance of a feud

---

çal sur l'arrivée du duc de Mercoeur (1652); *Relation du soulèvement de Provence contre le duc de Mercoeur* (1652); *Lettre des Trois Etats de Provence à Monsieur le duc de Guise* (1652); Grimaldi and Gaufridy, *Mémoires*, p. 53.

[218] Grimaldi and Gaufridy, *Mémoires*, pp. 53-55; Pillorget, *Les mouvements insurrectionnels*, pp. 676–680, 687–693.

[219] Haitze, *Histoire*, V, 244; Tavernier, *Marseille et la Provence*, pp. 62–63, text of amnesty reproduced.

[220] Grimaldi and Gaufridy, *Mémoires*, p. 67.

determining political affiliation. Sextius d'Escalis-Sabran, baron de Bras, quarreled with Mazarinistes Decormis and Venel, and although the baron died in 1650 during the plague at Aix, his son Henri, a councilor in the Parlement, and Henri's brother-in-law Glandèves-Rousset, also a councilor, joined the Sabreurs because of this quarrel.[221] Moreover, opposing parlementaire factions supported Alais, Conti, Joyeuse, and Mercoeur as governor of Provence. The internal divisions and alliances of the parlementaires motivated their participation in the Fronde. The hostilities generated during the Fronde at Aix were not dissipated until the revolt of 1659.

[221] *Ibid.*, p. 41.

# Chapter Nine

# THE SAINT VALENTINE'S DAY REVOLT
## OF 1659

After Lyon, the air route to Marseille follows the Rhone valley until the crevices and peaks of the Lubéron appear, pale gold in the setting sun. The Lubéron is a range of limestone mountains east of Avignon in the Comtat Venaissin. The double town of Oppède-le-Vieux perches on one of its rocky spurs, hôtels on the summit restored as summer homes, farming village sheltered in the valley below. This was the ancestral home of Sabreur chief Henri de Forbin-Maynier, baron d'Oppède, the most controversial man in Provence for a decade. His rise to power in 1655 provoked resentment among his old comrades-at-arms in the Parlement and threatened his political rivals in the provincial government. Oppède was attacked during the 1659 revolt at Aix by a mob encouraged by parlementaires, hoping to force his voluntary resignation or recall by Mazarin.

Oppède was appointed first president of the Parlement of Aix on September 19, 1655.[1] The favored candidate, Régusse, lost the appointment because he had less crédit than Oppède. Régusse failed to obtain the approval of the Manosque General Assembly for tax demands he presented as a royal commissioner in August 1653. The assembly granted only 140,000 of the 800,000 livres extraordinary tax demanded.[2] Régusse was opposed at the assembly by a former friend, Rascas Du Canet, whose election as first consul of Aix he had secured in September 1652. Régusse wrote in his memoirs that he quarreled with Rascas Du Canet, who detested the new governor.[3] Rascas Du Canet as first procureur du pays led the assembly's opposition to the crown's tax demands presented

[1] ADBR, Aix, B 3358, fol. 528.

[2] ADBR, Marseille, C 33, fol. 181; C 988, September 25, 1653; A.A.E., 1718, fol. 174; 1719, fols. 285–288.

[3] Charles de Grimaldi and Jacques Gaufridy, *Mémoires pour servir à l'histoire de la Fronde* (Aix, 1870), p. 61.

by Régusse and the governor. Oppède's candidates had been elected to municipal office at Aix in 1650 and 1651. Now, when one of Régusse's friends obtained office, he proved unreliable. The incident convinced Mazarin that Régusse lacked the crédit and clients to represent the crown successfully in Provence. This opinion was strengthened by the bishop of Orange's extraction of the same demands from the Brignoles assembly five months later.[4]

Oppède at court profited from Régusse's failure by convincing Mazarin that, owing to his clients and crédit in Provence, he could successfully manage the General Assemblies and procureurs du pays.[5] Régusse protested without effect that Oppède did not have the crédit he claimed.[6] But Oppède's activities as Sabreur chief were remembered, and his cousins had been first consuls of Aix in 1651, 1653, and 1654. In fact, seven of the first consuls of Aix in thirty years were relatives of Oppède.[7] Moreover, troops were quickly raised for his support in the Comtat Venaissin in August 1648 and February 1659.[8] Cardinal Mazarin expressed surprise on April 9, 1655, that the governor through his friends and those of president Oppède had not yet obtained cooperation from the General Assembly sitting at La Valette since February.[9] A short while later, after the assembly had voted a large sum of money to the crown, Mazarin wrote to Mercoeur and the bishop of Orange, "You will both admit that the friends of president d'Oppède were a marvelous help."[10] On October 25, 1658, Oppède wrote to Mazarin that Provence had been well rid of the Estates for twenty years, adding: "I dare even to say without vanity that

---

[4] *Ibid.*, pp. 61–64; ADBR, Marseille, C 32, fols. 169–220, 239–292; C 33, fol. 181; C 988, September 25, 1653; B.N., Ms. fr. 29655, fols. 79–84; Pierre-Joseph de Haitze, *Histoire de la ville d'Aix*, 6 vols. (Aix, 1880–1892), V, 244–245; A.A.E., 1718, fol. 174; 1719, fol. 285; René Pillorget, *Les mouvements insurrectionnels de Provence entre 1596 et 1715* (Paris, 1975), pp. 725–726.

[5] Adolphe Crémieux, *Marseille et la royauté pendant la minorité de Louis XIV*, 2 vols. (Paris, 1917), II, 464–470; Pierre Daverdi, *Oraison funèbre de Henri de Forbin d'Oppède*, notes by A.-J. Rance Bourrey (Marseille, 1889), p. 47.

[6] Grimaldi and Gaufridy, *Mémoires*, p. 63.

[7] *Ibid.*, p. 62; see Appendix II, 1629, 1637, 1640, 1651, 1653, 1654, 1657.

[8] A.A.E., 1723, fols. 340-345; B.N., Ms. fr. 18976, fols. 83–85, 87–99; B.N., Ms. fr. 24166, fol. 343.

[9] AA.E., 1718, fol. 298; Grimaldi and Gaufridy, *Mémoires*, p. 63.

[10] A.A.E., 895, fol. 64.

the Estates (if convoked) would be my forte, and I would dispose of all sentiment in regulating the power of the assemblies."[11] Finally, he had a large personal fortune that he was willing to use in Mazarin's interests. On August 27, 1658, Oppède wrote to Mazarin that he could not supply money to the royal galleys because he was low on cash, Colbert not having yet reimbursed him for the sums he had previously advanced. Oppède had lent Mazarin 6,000 livres in September, 1656.[12]

Expecting to obtain the office as a long-time supporter of Mazarin, Régusse was too complacent in allowing Oppède to spend more time and money in soliciting it.[13] In 1653, Régusse and Oppède negotiated with Mesgrigny at Aix for the office. Régusse offered 55,000 écus (165,000 livres), but Mesgrigny wanted 60,000 écus (180,000 livres). Oppède offered the full price.[14] It was an exorbitant sum, since his father had bought the office for 105,000 livres in 1621 and sold it for 100,000 livres in 1631.[15] The office was only selling for 130,000 livres at the end of the century.[16] Mesgrigny secretly signed a bill of sale for the full price with Oppède, who then went to court to solicit Mazarin's approval. Régusse went to Paris at the same time, ostensibly to secure repayment of 60,000 livres he had lent Mazarin's brother in 1648. Colbert repaid him the money, and Régusse returned to Provence a month later to serve as royal representative at the disastrous Manosque assembly. Oppède remained in Paris until the autumn of 1655.[17]

[11] A.A.E., 1723, fols. 234–235.

[12] *Ibid.*, fol. 151; 1720, fol. 56; 1721, fol. 33.

[13] Grimaldi and Gaufridy, *Mémoires*, p. 58.

[14] *Ibid.*, pp. 58–59; private communication from Richard Holbrook based on his doctoral dissertation, "Baron d'Oppède and Cardinal Mazarin: The Politics of Provence from 1641 to 1660" (University of Illinois at Chicago Circle, 1976). The figure of 180,000 livres is confirmed by Oppède's livre de raison, fols. 122v–124, conserved in the family archives, Château Saint Marcel, Marseille, and by Philippe de Commines, "Les luttes du président de Forbin d'Oppède et du marquis de Grimaldi-Régusse pour la première présidence du Parlement de Provence," Lourmarin Conference, 1972.

[15] ADBR, Aix, Fonds Lombard 309E, 1069, fol. 507 (1621); 1074, fol. 758 (1631); B. Inguimbertine 1841, fol. 441v.

[16] Louis Wolff, *Le Parlement de Provence au XVIII<sup>e</sup> siècle* (Aix, 1920), p. 57.

[17] Grimaldi and Gaufridy, *Mémoires*, pp. 59–62, 65–66; Haitze, *Histoire*, V, 287.

Oppède was rumored to have offered the bishop of Fréjus, one of Mazarin's secretaries, 30,000 livres for assistance in obtaining the office.[18] And he made other money gifts. Régusse wrote that Oppède secured the appointment after pursuing it for three years and "offering many generous presents."[19] Mercoeur and his wife Laura Mancini, the niece of Mazarin, preferred Régusse. But their attitude changed when Mercoeur's father, César, duc de Vendôme, visited Aix in 1655. Recently appointed Controller General of Commerce and Navigation, Vendôme stopped to receive his oath of office from the Parlement of Aix on his way to Catalonia.[20] He attempted unsuccessfully to borrow money from Régusse, who had lent Mercoeur considerable sums that had not been repaid. Oppède obligingly offered the duc de Vendôme 30,000 livres.[21] Oppède regularly visited the duchesse de Mercoeur at court, allowing her to win considerable sums at cards.[22] Mercoeur soon withdrew his support for Régusse, whom he had never really liked. But Oppède did not receive the governor's full support until his return to Aix as first president in November 1655: Mercoeur was won over by Oppède's deference, attentiveness, and willingness to work.[23] Mercoeur also realized the value of the first president's extensive crédit and generous purse.

Oppède had personal charm. His portrait shows a round, chubby face with large, brown eyes gazing directly at the viewer. Clean-shaven except for a small mustache, short brown hair curling disarmingly above the ermine collar of his president's robe, he appears candid, direct, honest.[24] A contemporary historian wrote, "First president d'Oppède was of medium height, well-proportioned, with a round face and laughing air, an agreeable appearance, engaging and generous manners, always ready to please,

[18] ADBR, Aix, J.L.H. Hesmivy de Moissac, "Histoire du Parlement de Provence, 1501–1715," 2 vols., II, 185.

[19] Grimaldi and Gaufridy, *Mémoires*, p. 66.

[20] ADBR, Aix, B 3358, fol. 375, December 7, 1654.

[21] Haitze, *Histoire*, V, 318, 328–332; Grimaldi and Gaufridy, *Mémoires*, pp. 36, 58, 60.

[22] ADBR, Aix, Moissac, "Histoire du Parlement," II, 185.

[23] Grimaldi and Gaufridy, *Mémoires*, p. 66.

[24] EDB, III, pl. XIX; Jacques Cundier, *Portraits des premiers présidents du Parlement de Provence* (Aix, 1724), B. Méjanes 963, p. 51; Daverdi and Rance-Bourrey, *Oraison funèbre*, frontispiece.

always a warm friend."[25] His enemy Régusse noted his "agreeable manner, political skill, and boundless ambition."[26] Oppède's motives remain, as the man does beneath a veneer of Provençal charm, somewhat of an enigma. He had rank, title, office, and wealth. He sought the position of first president, acting intendant, and acting governor because he enjoyed the exercise of power, although he betrayed the parlementary cause for which he had fought in 1649. He was ambitious; he may have been arrogant. He was certainly an able administrator and invaluable royal servant.

The appointment of a former Sabreur chief to the office of first president left Régusse resentful and aggrieved. He felt cheated. He continued to dislike and distrust Oppède, and their wives quarreled. Régusse relieved his emotions by encouraging a group of magistrates and provincial officials to block Oppède's political ambitions, particularly after he became acting intendant and acting governor in 1657.[27] Most of the conspirators were former Frondeurs. The power struggle between Régusse and Oppède developed into a power struggle within the provincial administration.

In August 1656, Oppède accused Régusse of fomenting sedition at Draguignan, where he had gone as presiding judge of the Vacations to investigate a riot. On August 15, he criticized Régusse's conduct of a criminal case, accusing him of encouraging intrigues within the company.[28] In letters to Mazarin in January 1658, Oppède accused Régusse of contributing to the Parlement's internal divisions and issuing unauthorized arrêts. Mercoeur wrote that Régusse was conspiring with Oppède's enemies.[29] On February 27, Mercoeur wrote that Régusse had incited a riot at Aix and demanded a lettre de cachet exiling him from the city.[30] Oppède on March 12 accused Régusse of political conspiracy, and on March 19 he requested a lettre de cachet for Régusse.[31] Régusse made a formal farewell to the Parlement on April 8, 1658, inform-

---

[25] Cundier, *Portraits*, p. 51; Pierre-Joseph de Haitze was the author of the text. Also see Haitze, *Portraits ou éloges historiques des premiers présidents du Parlement de Provence* (Avignon, 1727), p. 123.

[26] Grimaldi and Gaufridy, *Mémoires*, p. 54.

[27] *Ibid.*, pp. 66–68.

[28] B.M., Harleian 4489, fols. 164–165, Oppède to Séguier, August, 1656, fols. 188–190, the same, August 15, 1656.

[29] A.A.E., 1721, fols. 324–329, 342–346, 348–351.

[30] *Ibid.*, fols. 416–422, 425.      [31] *Ibid.*, fols. 441–444, 449–453.

ing his colleagues that he had received two lettres de cachet. On his way to Paris he was detained by royal letters for a year at Issoudun, southeast of Tours. He only returned to his home at La Ciotat a few days before the 1659 revolt, in which he did not participate.[32] But his friends and Oppède's enemies continued to intrigue in his absence. They led the 1659 revolt.

Gaspard de Venel had resigned his office of councilor in the Parlement to his brother-in-law Gaillard-Longjumeau in 1648. Active in the events of 1648–1649, he became a Mazariniste chief in 1650. By 1652, he was a bitter enemy of Oppède, and their hostility persisted after the Fronde.[33] Venel conspired with Régusse. On May 8, 1657, Oppède wrote to Mazarin that he was being slandered at court by Madame de Venel, governess to Mazarin's nieces.[34] Later that month the governor's secretary complained that he, Oppède, and the bishop of Orange had been persistently slandered by the Venels for three years.[35] On September 4, 1657, Venel complained to Mazarin that Mercoeur had threatened him with loss of his pension.[36] On March 12, 1658, after the riot at Aix, Oppède wrote that Régusse and Venel, among others, were conspiring against him in secret daily conferences of three to four hours.[37] Although Venel protested his innocence to Mazarin in a letter on April 2, he was implicated in the riot and forced to a humiliating public apology.[38] Venel did not participate in the 1659 revolt, but he had lost Mazarin's favor: he was sharply reprimanded on September 23, 1659, after Mercoeur reported that he had insulted the baron de Saint Marc, the former Sabreur chief who was captain of Mercoeur's guards.[39]

Oppède also wrote several letters to Mazarin on the conduct of president Henri d'Escalis-Sabran, baron de Bras, a former Sabreur who had purchased Oppède's office of president in December 1654

[32] *Ibid.*, fols. 493–494; Delib. Parl., B. Méjanes 954, fols. 158v–159; Haitze, *Histoire*, V, 415; Pierre-Adolphe Chéruel and Georges d'Avenel, *Lettres du cardinal Mazarin pendant son ministère*, 9 vols. (Paris, 1872–1906), VIII, 708, Mazarin to Régusse, May 7, 1658.

[33] Grimaldi and Gaufridy, *Mémoires*, p. 43; A.A.E., 1721, fols. 511–512, Venel to Mazarin, April 23, 1658.

[34] A.A.E., 1721, fols. 125–128.

[35] *Ibid.*, fols. 129–131.     [36] *Ibid.*, fols. 191–192.

[37] *Ibid.*, fols. 441–444, 484–485.     [38] *Ibid.*, fols. 513–518.

[39] A.A.E., 1724, fols. 220–221; Chéruel and Avenel, *Lettres de Mazarin*, IX, 856, 857.

for 144,000 livres, a high price.[40] Oppède wrote on June 17, October 8, and November 8, 1658 that Escalis de Bras was politically unreliable, having joined the conspirators.[41] On December 10, he accused Escalis de Bras of distributing fifty pistoles among vagrants and idlers in the cabarets and wine shops of Aix to stir up trouble.[42]

On December 19, Oppède accused president Louis Decormis and his brother of assembling men on their nearby estate at Beaurecueil to bring into Aix to cause trouble.[43] Decormis brought men into Aix during the 1649 revolt, as he did in 1659. A leader of the 1649 revolt, he had fought at the battle of the Val and later became a Mazariniste. Régusse described him as "a violent man." In fact, Régusse preferred the election of Sabreur chief Saint Marc as first consul of Aix in September 1650 to Decormis, whose violent temper he distrusted. In the letter of December 19, Oppède described Decormis as disobedient and disloyal, a member of a group of "seditious" parlementaires including Escalis de Bras, avocat-général Galaup-Chasteuil, councilor Leidet-Sigoyer, and his son.[44] These parlementaires led the 1659 revolt. Galaup-Chasteuil had been a Sabreur, Leidet-Sigoyer a Mazariniste.

A quarrel at mass in 1657 between Mesdames Rascas Du Canet and Maynier d'Oppède reflected the hostility between their husbands.[45] Rascas Du Canet resigned his office of councilor in the Parlement in 1656. He later mended his friendship with Régusse. A former Mazariniste and enemy of Mercoeur, he disliked Oppède, who considered him politically unreliable. On September 3, 1658, Oppède wrote to Mazarin that a lettre de cachet might be necessary to prevent Rascas Du Canet's election as first consul of Aix.[46]

In a letter to Mazarin on October 2, 1657, Oppède accused ex-councilor Glandèves-Rousset, brother-in-law of Escalis de Bras and a former Sabreur, and his friend seigneur de Barbentane "of an intrigue so insolent and so extraordinary to fill these [Aix municipal] offices with persons so badly intentioned for the royal

---

[40] Private communication from Richard Holbrook based on Oppède's *livre de raison*, fol. 130; ADBR, Aix, B 3358, fol. 531v.

[41] A.A.E., 1723, fols. 40–41, 212–214, 244.

[42] *Ibid.*, fol. 258.          [43] *Ibid.*, fols. 273–276.

[44] *Ibid.*; ADBR, Aix, B 3357, fol. 90v; Grimaldi and Gaufridy, *Mémoires*, p. 42.

[45] Grimaldi and Gaufridy, *Mémoires*, p. 70.

[46] A.A.E., 1723, fol. 179.

service that it was necessary to oppose them with full authority."[47]
The first president added that Glandèves had been forced to sell
his parlementary office in the previous year to pay his debts.[48] Mercoeur and Oppède unofficially intervened in the Aix municipal
election of September 1657 to block Glandèves's election as first
consul. They substituted Oppède's cousin, Jacques de Forbin de
La Barben, who was expected to help them in controlling the procureurs du pays. La Barben, son of the 1629 first consul, had supported the 1649 rebel parlementaires. They had unsuccessfully
requested a place for him in the provincial government. He later
became a Sabreur and in 1656 a syndic of the provincial nobility.[49]
The estate of seigneur de Barbentane in the Comtat Venaissin
southeast of Avignon had served as a recruiting center for the rebel
parlementaires in 1648, and he had carried messages to Paris as
their deputy in 1649. He also became a Sabreur.[50]

The parlementaires' hostility to Oppède intensified in 1658. In
January 1658, the procureurs du pays refused to approve a new
tax levy requested by Mercoeur and Oppède.[51] As a result, first
consul Forbin de La Barben, General Assembly secretary Meyronnet, and his clerk Revest (whose attache was necessary to enforce
the governor's tax ordinance) received lettres de cachet in February summoning them to Paris for explanations.[52] Barbentane
left Aix to avoid receiving a letter. Glandèves stubbornly refused
to leave. Mazarin wrote on February 8 that orders had been sent
for his arrest. Glandèves was arrested on February 25 in the Place
des Prêcheurs while taking an afternoon promenade with first consul La Barben and ten or twelve gentlemen. He was put into a
waiting carriage by Mercoeur's guard captain, the baron de Saint
Marc, a former Sabreur colleague, and taken to the royal fortress
Tour de Bouc, then transferred to the citadel of Saint Tropez.[53]
Glandèves was released only a few days before the 1659 revolt,
in which he did not participate.

News of Glandèves's arrest spread swiftly through Aix. Thirty

---

[47] A.A.E., 1721, fols. 227–230.     [48] *Ibid.*; see Chapter Seven.
[49] Haitze, *Histoire*, V, 392–394; A.A.E., 1714, fols. 84, 101–102; 1721,
fols. 232–235.
[50] A.A.E., 1714, fols. 35–36, 84, 151, 265.
[51] See Chapter Three.
[52] A.C., Aix, BB 103, fol. 59; A.A.E., 1721, fols. 274–275, 426.
[53] Grimaldi and Gaufridy, *Mémoires*, p. 70; A.A.E., 1721, fols. 393–407.

minutes later a hundred angry men, many of whom were soldiers demanding their back pay, gathered before the palace of justice. Oppède and Mercoeur called an emergency meeting of the Parlement, but three presidents and six councilors sent to calm the protesters were unable to leave the palace. The men at the foot of the grand staircase refused to make way and demanded an explanation from Mercoeur. Oppède summoned first consul La Barben to speak to the crowd, but La Barben refused to come. Rumors had swept Aix that he would be imprisoned, and he had taken refuge with archbishop Grimaldi of Aix. A president and two councilors went to his empty hôtel; the other consuls of Aix went to the archbishop's palace. Milling aimlessly before the palace of justice and the empty hôtels of Glandèves and La Barben until evening, the crowd finally dispersed.[54]

La Barben wrote to Paris on March 5 that he would observe his lettre de cachet, and he left Aix in mid-April.[55] He was arrested at court on June 19, the morning after he had fought near Dunkerque in the Battle of the Dunes. He was imprisoned in the citadel of Calais.[56] A procès-verbal sent by the Parlement under Oppède's direction accused La Barben of provoking the February riot and Régusse of being his accomplice, since the president had been absent from the palace of justice until the riot ended.[57] In a memoir on February 27, Mercoeur wrote that the procureurs du pays' stubborn refusal to approve his tax ordinance—encouraged by La Barben and Régusse among others—had provoked the riot.[58] On February 26, the Parlement sent the prévôt's lieutenant and three councilors to arrest Rogery (municipal guard captain), Fortis, and ex-consul Vaucluse for their participation in the riot.[59] The Aix municipal elections were held in September 1658 as scheduled, although Oppède wanted their suspension. Roquemartine, a relative of La Barben, was elected first consul after letters endorsing

---

[54] A.A.E., 1721, fols. 393–407; Delib. Parl., B. Méjanes 954, fols. 151–153.

[55] A.A.E., 1721, fols. 435–436.

[56] A.A.E., 1722, fol. 139; Delib. Parl., B. Méjanes 954, fol. 169; Grimaldi and Gaufridy, *Mémoires*, p. 70; Haitze, *Histoire*, V, 418–419.

[57] A.A.E., 1721, fols. 393–407, 431–434.

[58] *Ibid.*, fols. 416–422. Mercoeur also accused Gordes and Glandèves.

[59] A.A.E., 1721, fols. 393–396; Delib. Parl., B. Méjanes 954, fols. 151–153. Vaucluse had been sent home from Paris on twenty-four hours' notice on October 27, 1657, for rash speech; cf. A.A.E., 1721, fols. 243–244.

his candidacy were read from La Barben, Glandèves, and Escalis de Bras.[60] Oppède on July 30 and September 3, 1658, advised against freeing La Barben, Glandèves, or Régusse. Mazarin wrote the procureurs du pays a letter to this effect on September 13.[61] Glandèves's brother and his brother-in-law Escalis de Bras had interviews with Mazarin at Amiens in May and Calais in June to request his release, without result.[62]

There was a political conspiracy at Aix in 1658 whose object was Oppéde. Its members included Régusse, Decormis, Escalis de Bras, Galaup-Chasteuil, Leidet-Sigoyer father and son, Venel, Glandèves, Rascas Du Canet, and Barbentane. All except Galaup-Chasteuil had participated in the events of 1648–1649. All were Frondeurs. Former friends and enemies of Oppède, they belonged to the small group of political activists who had been resisting the crown for nearly three decades. They distrusted the political ambitions of the first president, whose resignation or recall they wanted. However, the most powerful enemies of Oppède were not parlementaires. They were his political rivals within the provincial government, Jerôme de Grimaldi, archbishop of Aix, and François de Simiane, marquis de Gordes and lieutenant general of Provence.

Grimaldi was in Rome on August 17, 1655, when he learned that his candidacy for the archbishopric of Aix—which had been vacant since 1648 in a dispute between king and pope over nomination—had been approved.[63] Scion of a famous noble family of Genoa, Grimaldi was sixty years old. Former papal nuncio extraordinary to France and Germany, Grimaldi had aided Mazarin while governor of Rome and thus became cardinal Saint Eusebius in 1643. In 1645, he helped secure the Aix archbishopric for Michel Mazarin.[64] Régusse and Grimaldi became friends, possibly because of a mutual dislike of Oppède.[65] Grimaldi was a cultured man with a fine library, which he left upon his death to the

---

[60] A.A.E., 1723, fols. 203–208, Oppède to Mazarin, October 20, 1658. A letter was also read from Gordes.

[61] *Ibid.*, fols. 87, 179; ADBR, Marseille, C 988.

[62] A.A.E., 1722, fols. 132v, 139.

[63] Chéruel and Avenel, *Lettres de Mazarin*, VII, 563.

[64] Commines, "Les luttes du Président de Forbin d'Oppède," p. 13; Grimaldi and Gaufridy, *Mémoires*, pp. 24, 199–200; Chéruel and Avenel, *Lettres de Mazarin*, II, 157–163, 181–184, 204–205.

[65] Grimaldi and Gaufridy, *Mémoires*, p. 67.

Aix seminary he had founded. An effective archbishop, he acquired the sobriquet *tête de fer* for his determination.[66]

Grimaldi and Oppède quarreled immediately over authority and precedence. Such quarrels were frequent between the archbishop of Aix and Parlement first president.[67] An energetic proselytizer, Grimaldi had founded the society for the Propagation of the Faith at Aix in 1656. In the same year, he quarreled with the Parlement over publication of a book entitled *Préadamites* by Isaac de La Pereye, who maintained that men existed before Adam. Grimaldi condemned the book. The Parlement issued an arrêt prohibiting its sale and ordering its seizure and destruction. Grimaldi then protested that his ecclesiastical authority had been usurped, but Mazarin reminded him in July 1656 that only secular authority could assign temporal punishment. On November 21, Oppède protested that Grimaldi had executed an indult, a papal privilege, without having it registered by the Grand'Chambre—a unique privilege of the Aix Parlement that the archbishop had frequently ignored.[68]

Grimaldi and Oppède quarreled publicly in May 1657 over their marching positions in the Fête Dieu procession. Both claimed the right to march directly behind the sacrament. A furious Grimaldi cancelled the procession, locked up the communion host, which was to be paraded around the city, pocketed the key, and went home. The Parlement seized his revenues and sent a remonstrance to Paris. The dispute continued until Saint Sebastian's Day 1658, when a conciliar decree upheld a compromise suggested by Mercoeur. Oppède marched first, and Grimaldi followed with four attendants. The two antagonists were ordered to participate

[66] EDB, IV–2, 254; Jacques Billioud, *Le livre en Provence du XVIe au XVIIIe siècle* (Marseille, 1962), pp. 135–136; J.-H. Albanès, *Gallia Christiana Novissima*, 7 vols. (Valence, 1899–1920), I, 142–144.

[67] Maximin Deloche, *Un frère de Richelieu inconnu: chartreux, primat des Gaules, cardinal, ambassadeur* (Paris, 1935), pp. 114–132; ADBR, Aix, Moissac, "Histoire du Parlement," I, 428–433; Jules de Cosnac, ed., *Mémoires de Daniel de Cosnac*, 2 vols. (Paris, 1852, reprinted 1968), II, 369–373.

[68] Victor-Louis Bourrilly, *Les protestants de Provence au XVIIe et XVIIIe siècles* (Gap, 1956), p. 31; Chéruel and Avenel, *Lettres de Mazarin*, VII, 650; B.M., Harleian 4489, fols. 115–117; 4490, fols. 53–54; A.A.E., 1721, fols. 46–48.

by lettre de cachet.[69] Grimaldi marched with anger and revenge in his heart.

The archbishop used his office of first procureur du pays to block Oppède's efforts as acting intendant to obtain the new tax levy. Grimaldi sent a letter to Mazarin in January 1658 protesting the economic misery of Provence and its inability to pay higher taxes; he advised that the tax request be withdrawn.[70] He encouraged the other procureurs du pays to stand firm in their refusal to approve the tax increase. Oppède wrote that Grimaldi was inciting riot at Aix and encouraging provincial lieutenant general Gordes and vicar general Mimata in disobedience.[71] On February 12, Mercoeur wrote that Grimaldi and first consul La Barben had delivered inflammatory speeches against the tax increase at a municipal council meeting.[72] La Barben took refuge with Grimaldi during the riot on February 25, after the archbishop warned Barbentane and Glandèves to leave Aix.[73] On January 4 and 11 and February 1, Mazarin ordered Grimaldi to stop his obstructions. On May 4, the archbishop of Aix was informed that his nephew would not be nominated to office because of his obstructions.[74] In June and July, Mazarin warned Grimaldi that his stubbornness was disrupting the provincial government.[75] On September 13, 1658, he was threatened with a lettre de cachet.[76] Protected by his archbishop's robes and cardinal's hat, Grimaldi never went to Paris. But he was temporarily exiled from Provence after the revolt.

Oppède also quarreled over precedence with François de Simiane, marquis de Gordes and provincial lieutenant general. Their quarrel masked a dispute over authority. Oppède engineered the quarrel, then used it to remove Gordes from office. Gordes was the nephew of Jean de Pontevès, comte de Carcès, who had died childless in 1656. The Pontevès de Carcès and Simiane de Gordes were among the oldest families of the Provençal sword

[69] A.A.E., 1720, fol. 171; 1721, fols. 139–148, 165–166, 354–355; Delib. Parl., B. Méjanes 954, fol. 150; B.M., Harleian 4490, fols. 240–243.

[70] A.A.E., 1721, fols. 167, 324–329, 356.

[71] *Ibid.*, fols. 330–335.      [72] *Ibid.*, fols. 371–373.

[73] *Ibid.*, fols. 393–396.

[74] Chéruel and Avenel, *Lettres de Mazarin*, VIII, 663, 666, 675, 703.

[75] *Ibid.*, pp. 724, 755.

[76] *Ibid.*, IX, 773. Oppède had written to Mazarin on September 8 that Grimaldi was encouraging troublemakers at Aix; cf. *ibid.*, p. 716.

nobility, and Gordes probably felt superior in rank to Oppède. The two men were rivals about the same age. The Parlement acted as governor from Carcès's death in August until October 1656 because Mercoeur was absent from Provence.[77] Oppède may have found his power as presiding magistrate intoxicating.

Gordes received his provision letters as the new lieutenant general in October 1656.[78] In November, Oppède told him not to attend the Parlement joint meeting to register his letters because they would not be accepted. He asserted they contained extralegal clauses not in the letters of his predecessor, although a comparison shows they were identical.[79] Gordes was furious. Six months later he was refused reception into his new office on the grounds that he had not paid a ceremonial visit to the first president before swearing his oath of loyalty. Oppède wrote Mazarin on June 12, 1657, that Gordes had declared the first president should visit him, then had visited the lowest ranking parlementaire.[80] On May 26, Gordes went to the palace of justice to swear his oath accompanied by a large retinue of nobles, although he had been warned there would be no reception without an honorary visit. He was kept waiting on the grand staircase, then told that he would be received alone in a private room. Gordes left the palace in a fury and appealed to Paris. He claimed that his uncle had been received with an entourage, and he demanded the same honor. Oppède sent to Paris extracts from the Parlement's registers describing earlier receptions, which contain no mention of whether they were public or private.[81] Mazarin wrote to Gordes on August 17 suggesting that Mercoeur mediate.[82] Gordes was received into office with full honors in November 1657, after Mercoeur tactfully went to Paris for three weeks so he could be received as acting governor.[83]

Oppède had provoked the quarrel. Having received authority from Mazarin in February and April 1657 to act as governor in Mercoeur's absence, he had no intention of losing this authority.[84]

---

[77] B.M., Harleian 4490, fols. 2–3.

[78] ADBR, Aix, B 3358, fol. 1033.

[79] A.A.E., 1720, fol. 111; 1721, fols. 46–48; ADBR, Aix, 3350, fols. 503–508; B 3358, fols. 1033–1037.

[80] A.A.E., 1721, fols. 149–150.

[81] *Ibid.*, fols. 149–155, 158–159; Haitze, *Histoire*, V, 385–386.

[82] Chéruel and Avenel, *Lettres de Mazarin*, VIII, 612.

[83] A.A.E., 1721, fols. 268–273.

[84] A.A.E., 1720, fols. 123, 153; B.M., Harleian 4490, fols. 240–243.

He did not want a lieutenant general replacing him as acting governor. By obstructing registration of Gordes's letters and his reception into office, Oppède could continue to act as governor until the autumn of 1657, when he began a campaign of slander to have Gordes removed from office.[85] On January 29, 1658, Mercoeur wrote that Gordes, Grimaldi, Glandèves, Barbentane, and Régusse were members of a conspiracy against the first president.[86] Oppède wrote in January that Grimaldi was encouraging Gordes's disobedience and sympathized with Glandèves and Barbentane.[87] Oppède wrote letters on February 6 and 27, and March 12 and 26, accusing Gordes of helping to provoke the riot at Aix and requesting a lettre de cachet.[88] Mercoeur wrote a similar memoir in February.[89]

Gordes received a letter from Mazarin on February 14 requesting an explanation. A lettre de cachet on April 2 called him to court to explain his behavior.[90] He was imprisoned on June 19 in the citadel of Calais with La Barben, released in August, but detained in the north for the rest of the year.[91] He did not participate in the 1659 revolt. On March 29 and June 20, 1658, Oppède received full written authority to act as governor.[92] Gordes's protestations of innocence were futile, since Mercoeur went to Paris on March 10 to deny them.[93] Gordes was never reinstated. On October 19, 1659, François de Moutiers, comte de Mérinville, was sent to Provence to command in the absence of Mercoeur.[94] Significantly, Oppède was not given this authority, indicating the provocative nature of his recent service. Mérinville was nominated lieutenant general by letters patent on February 25, 1660, and appointed upon the resignation of Gordes in April 1662.[95]

[85] ADBR, Marseille, C 37, fols. 20, 176. In February, Mercoeur was in Paris, and from April until the end of summer he was on campaign.

[86] A.A.E., 1721, fols. 348–351.

[87] *Ibid.*, fols. 324–329, 330–335.

[88] *Ibid.*, fols. 365–366, 422–423, 441–444, 467–470.

[89] *Ibid.*, fols. 416–422.

[90] *Ibid.*, fols. 380–381, 467–477; 1722, fol. 98.

[91] A.A.E., 1722, fol. 139; Chéruel and Avenel, *Lettres de Mazarin*, VIII, 738, 739; IX, 794.

[92] A.A.E., 1722, fol. 100; Chéruel and Avenel, *Lettres de Mazarin*, VIII, 739.

[93] Delib. Parl., B. Méjanes 954, fol. 154v.

[94] ADBR, Aix, B 3359, fol. 464.

[95] ADBR, Marseille, C 988; Aix, B 3360, fol. 845v.

There were several incidents of protest in the Parlement before the 1659 revolt. Régusse and councilors Leidet-Calissane and Agut, former Mazarinistes, were cited to Paris by lettres de cachet on December 28, 1656, for opposing registration of a royal edict on domaine lands.[96] The Parlement proved unruly and uncooperative despite Oppède's efforts, and it refused to register the edict. Six magistrates of the Cour des Comptes were cited in lettres de cachet in June 1657 for their opposition.[97] On June 25, the edict was sent to the Trésoriers Généraux de France for enforcement without registration by either sovereign court.[98]

On May 31 and June 1, 1658, joint meetings of the Parlement prohibited enforcement of the tax ordinance Oppède had recently issued as acting governor; he was attempting to circumvent the procureurs du pays, who still refused their approval. Oppède himself chaired the meeting on May 31, attended by forty-one parlementaires. Significantly, Decormis chaired the meeting on the next day, attended by twenty-eight parlementaires.[99] The controversy caused some parlementaires to avoid the palace of justice. Those who remained included political opponents of the first president. In a secret memoir for Colbert in 1663, Oppède described avocat-général Gautier as "unreliable in important matters" and councilor Raffelis as "one of the strongest men in the Parlement but never the friend of the first president." Barrême, the only clerical councilor, was "unreliable and secretive."[100] The three were former Mazarinistes and friends of Régusse. Avocats-généraux Gautier and Gallaup-Chasteuil called the joint meeting on February 14, 1659, which provoked the crowd into attacking the palace of justice in its search for Oppède. The brother of Galaup-Chasteuil

---

[96] A.A.E., 1720, fol. 98.

[97] Haitze, *Histoire*, V, 418.  [98] A.A.E., 1720, fol. 359.

[99] ADBR, Aix, B 3368, May 31 and June 1, 1658.

[100] B.N., Mélanges de Colbert 7, fols. 49–55; G. B. Depping, *Correspondance administrative sous le règne de Louis XIV*, 4 vols. (Paris, 1851), II, 94–96. Pierre de Barrême, born in 1602, was tonsured in 1611 and became a clerical councilor in the Parlement of Aix in 1640. Senile by 1676, he died of disappointment following the loss of a lawsuit against his fellow councilor Benault de Lubières before the Parlement of Toulouse; cf. Auguste Du Roure, *Généalogie de la maison de Barrême* (Paris, 1906), p. 24; *Inventaire analytique de titres et documents originaux tirés des archives du Château de Barbegal* (Paris, 1903), p. 59.

had participated in the duel that provoked the crowd to assemble. All three Galaup brothers were rebels in 1659. Councilors Agut and Raffelis were sent to disperse the crowd because their opposition to Oppède was well known. The Parlement's opposition had revived and was functioning again by 1658.

Mazarin was able once more to pursue his pre-Fonde program of bringing the frontier provinces under central control, and in December 1656 he sent Orgeval to Provence as intendant. Orgeval was not accepted. Mazarin instead used the Parlement first president as acting intendant, since he had successfully been performing the office for a year. Oppède became the new instrument of centralization in Provence. A year later he was appointed acting governor and proceeded to exclude the Grand'Chambre from decision making. He acted as intendant without royal letters of commission registered by the Parlement. In 1657, he permitted the enforcement of an edict without registration. In 1658, he bullied, intimidated, and arrested political opponents such as the procureurs du pays, then billeted troops on Aix without their approval. At the same time, he attempted to tax illegally by ordinance without approval, and he interfered in municipal elections at Aix and Marseille.[101]

The parlementaires who had fought beside Oppède in the 1649 revolt and the Fronde bitterly resented his emergence as a créature of Mazarin. They thought his boundless ambition had led him to betray the interests of the company he now headed. It was galling to former Mazarinistes to see the spectacular rise of a Sabreur chief. Oppède acquired more enemies by encroaching upon the authority of rival officials in the provincial government. By 1658, he was the most powerful and unpopular man at Aix. What began in 1650 as a Parlement power struggle over the office of first president developed after 1655 into a power struggle within the provincial administration at Aix. Although a shadow of its former self, enjoying only a remnant of its former power and prestige, the parlementaire opposition actively fought Oppède's acquisition

---

[101] For an account of events at Marseille from 1657 to 1659, consult Pillorget, *Les mouvements insurrectionnels*, pp. 767–781, 812–823; Crémieux, *Marseille et la royauté*, II, 513–667; Raoul Busquet, *Histoire de Marseille* (Paris, 1945), pp. 251–271; EDB, XIV, 196–238; Mireille Zarb, *Les privilèges de la ville de Marseille* (Paris, 1961), pp. 128–130.

of power. Most of his enemies were former Mazarinistes; many of his supporters were former Sabreurs. Thus the politics of a decade earlier influenced political behavior at Aix in 1659.

There was a network of family and political ties among the 1658–1659 rebels, centering around Leidet-Sigoyer and Régusse. Many of the members were related to Jean de Leidet-Sigoyer, a participant in all three revolts. They included his son Pierre, who held office en survivance, his brother Pierre de Leidet-Calissane, his brother-in-law Louis Decormis, his son-in-law Rascas Du Canet, his maternal cousin Régusse, and Raffelis-Roquesante, who was a close friend of Régusse. They had all been Mazarinistes, as had Agut, Gautier, and Barrême. Régusse was allied to the Valbelle faction of Marseille opposing Oppède. The Marseille rebel Glandèves-Niozelles belonged to this faction and was the first cousin of ex-councilor Glandèves, whose brother-in-law was Escalis de Bras. The mother-in-law of Escalis de Bras was a Simiane de Gordes of the lieutenant general's family. Glandèves and Barbentane were old friends, having fought together as Sabreurs with Escalis de Bras and Forbin de La Barben. Simiane de Gordes and Régusse were friendly with Jerôme de Grimaldi, who may have been in touch with Glandèves-Niozelles.[102]

Oppède also had clients in the Parlement. They included his cousins Forbin de La Roque, Thomassin, and the two Valbelles, as well as Forbin de La Roque's brother-in-law Coriolis, Oppède's own brother-in-law Boyer, who died in May 1659, and his Sabreur friends Gallifet and Saint Marc. Pierre de Laurens had been a Sabreur, and his son Henri, who inherited his office of councilor in 1654, continued to support Oppède. Henri's son, Pierre-Joseph, married Oppède's daughter in 1665, and inherited his father's office in 1674. Forbin de La Roque, Thomassin, the two Valbelles, Laurens, Saint Marc, and Gallifet were among the parlementaires who assembled at Lambesc in support of Oppède on February 21, 1659. Others included the two Maurels, Benault de Lubières, and

---

[102] Réne Pillorget, "Destin de la ville d'ancien régime," in *Histoire de Marseille*, ed. Edouard Baratier (Toulouse, 1973), pp. 178–179; A.A.E., 1723, fols. 112–116, Oppède to Mazarin, August 13, 1658; he wrote that Mme de Cabriès, sister of Glandèves-Niozelles, acted as emissary between him and the archbishop; Grimaldi and Gaufridy, *Mémoires*, p. 16; Balthasar de Clapiers-Collongues and marquis de Boisgelin, *Chronologie des officiers des cours souveraines* (Aix, 1909–1912), p. 22.

Foresta de La Roquette. Benault de Lubières was the brother-in-law of Laurens; the Maurels were his kinsmen and clients. Oppède's other brother-in-law in the Parlement, Cauvet de Bormes, had resigned his office in 1655. The Maurels, Foresta de La Roquette, Forbin de La Roque, Laurens, Coriolis, and Saint Marc were members of the Grands Jours court sent to Marseille in January 1660 to try the rebels of that city.[103]

The strength of family ties must not be exaggerated. Dean Gautier supported Oppède in 1659; the avocat-général, his son, favored the rebels. Oppède's cousin Forbin de La Barben became his political enemy. His other cousins, Léon and Jean-Baptiste de Valbelle, went unsuccessfully to Marseille in 1658 to pacify their relatives, who were enemies of Oppède.[104] Political opinions were as important as clientage ties in determining political behavior at Aix in 1659. But the interaction of political groups with kinship networks at their center should be recognized.

On Saint Valentine's Day 1659, Aix cadets Saint Jean and Moriès were returning from an early-morning duel with one of the younger Galaup brothers. They encountered Jean-Louis Barate, the prévôt's lieutenant, on the Marseille road. Saint Jean supported Oppède, while Barate opposed him. Intoxicated by the duel, Saint Jean reined in and challenged the lieutenant, daring him to dismount and fight. Two shots were fired, and Barate fell, seriously wounded. Saint Jean later blamed the shots on his valet. Brash young servants precipitated quarrels for their masters by boasts and provocative actions. But they also made convenient scapegoats.

Rumors circulated in Aix that Oppède had ordered the shoot-

---

[103] A.A.E., 1723, fols. 364–367; 1724, fol. 249; 1725, fols. 191, 202, 208v, 220, 238; Auguste Du Roure, *Généalogie de la maison de Benault de Lubières* (Paris, 1906), p. 13; Emile Périer, *L'hôtel et le château d'un financier aixois* (Valence, 1902), p. 239; marquis de Boisgelin, *Maurel de Villeneuve de Mons* (Digne, 1904), p. 29; Roure, *Généalogie de la maison de Forbin* (Paris, 1906), pp. 49–51; Clapiers-Collongues, *Chronologie*, pp. 81, 97, 105. A delegation from the Parlement sent to Avignon in 1663 included Oppède, Forbin de La Roque, Gautier, Villeneuve, Lombard, Thomassin, Signier, and Saint Marc, all members of the first president's network; cf. Jean-Pierre Papon, *Histoire générale de Provence*, 4 vols. (Paris, 1777–1786), IV, 600.

[104] A.A.E., 1723, fols. 261–264.

ing of Barate. A crowd of nobles and gentlemen armed with swords and pistols gathered in the early afternoon at two unidentified hôtels. There were twenty or twenty-five cadets. They were joined by a crowd of Aixois, some waving halberds. The cry, "Farre boutique, Farre boutique" (Close the shops), echoed through the city. About one hundred protesters marched to the Place des Prêcheurs and entered the palace of justice, shouting "Vive le Roy! Nous voulons la justice!" (Long live the King! We want justice!) and "Lou ave! Lou ave! Mouru lou confeso!" (Get him! Get him! Death to the guilty one!). The crowd demanded the arrest of Saint Jean and Oppède for the murder of Barate, who had only been wounded. They marched up the grand staircase to the doors of the salle dorée, held by bailiffs. The Parlement was sitting in an emergency session called by avocats-généraux Hubert de Galaup-Chasteuil and Jean-Baptiste de Gautier. The crowd remained at the doors, calling for Oppède and shouting threats for the rest of the afternoon. President Escalis de Bras, avocat-général Galaup-Chasteuil, and councilors Leidet-Sigoyer, Raffelis, and Agut, known for their opposition to Oppède, were sent to disperse the crowd. They tried twice, unsuccessfully.

A crowd milled below in the Place des Prêcheurs crying, "Justice, Justice for Barate," and waving pistols, swords, and muskets. They tore up paving stones and began throwing them. Faint shots were heard from the hôtel Maynier d'Oppède, where another crowd had gathered. The municipal clocktower rang the tocsin. Oppède forced his carriage through the crowds, then elbowed his way through the protesters to reach the salle dorée, displaying his habitual courage. The men fell back and let him pass, but their mood changed. By late afternoon, they were threatening to break down the doors and take Oppède or throw him from a window if justice were not done by the Parlement. They shouted, "Long live the King and Cardinal Grimaldi!"[105] Oppède refused to escape through a back door to the governor's apartments, adding somewhat melodramatically: "I prefer to die on the fleurs de lys in serving the King and fulfilling the functions of my office than in cowardly saving my life." This attitude saved his

---

[105] B.N., Ms. fr. 20473, "Relation des mouvements de Provence, 1659," fols. 13–16; "Recueil de pièces sur le Parlement," B. Méjanes 1155, Parlement's interrogations in March, 1659, on revolt; Delib. Parl., B. Méjanes 954, fols. 193v–195v; Haitze, *Histoire*, V, 436.

life because there were men waiting to kill him in the passage leading to the governor's apartments.[106]

The parlementaires were unable to leave the salle dorée. Councilor Honorat de Pourcieux was attacked on the staircase as he attempted to leave; he was only saved by the arrival of first consul Roquemartine.[107] The consuls of Aix were unable to disperse the crowd. The consuls reported that the prévôt and the five captains of the municipal guard were absent from Aix. This was rejected as unlikely. The consuls were later removed from office by royal letters for complicity in the revolt.[108]

About seven o'clock in the evening, after four hours of noisy threats, Ballon and Mazargues were sent to request the aid of Grimaldi. The archbishop of Aix arrived at the palace around eight o'clock. He escorted Oppède to the safety of his carriage under the protection of his cloak. President Escalis de Bras walked on one side; councilor Thomassin walked ahead with drawn pistol and sword to clear the way. After the archbishop and first president had entered the carriage, president Escalis de Bras and sieur Mathieu, the secretary of the cathedral chapter of Saint Sauveur, mounted the carriage steps on Oppède's side. Saint Sauveur canons Du Chaine and Arnaud mounted the steps on the other side. Du Chaine had saved the consuls from the crowd in 1649. In the flickering torchlight, men on the stairs shouted insults and threatened to kill Oppède. For a moment it appeared they would rush the carriage, but it rolled away safely, although someone ran a sword through Oppède's side of the vehicle.[109]

The city council and the Parlement by arrêt created an emergency bourgeois guard commanded by parlementaires to calm the city. Guards were posted at the doors of the archbishop's private apartments, where Oppède had taken refuge. There were also guards at the doors of the archbishop's palace, at the palace of justice, at the city gates, and guards patrolled the streets in

---

[106] Crémieux, *Marseille et la royauté*, II, 683; ADBR, Aix, Moissac, "Histoire du Parlement," II, 233.

[107] Delib. Parl., B. Méjanes 954, fol. 194; "Recueil de pièces," B. Méjanes 1155.

[108] A.A.E., 1723, fol. 384v; A.C., Aix, BB 103, fols. 105–106, 112–118; AA 6, fols. 14–15v.

[109] Delib. Parl., B. Méjanes 954, fols. 194–195v; ADBR, Aix, Moissac, "Histoire du Parlement," II, 233–234; "Recueil de pièces," B. Méjanes 1155.

pairs.[110] Oppède reported in his procès-verbal that he was held prisoner for ten days in the archbishop's private apartments despite his word of honor not to escape. His guards included the brother of avocat-général Galaup-Chasteuil, a captain in the provincial regiment, a municipal guard captain named Minchon, a lieutenant in the royal guards' regiment named Morel, and several cadets of Aix.[111]

A crowd disrupted a meeting in the courtyard of the archbishop's palace the next day, February 15. The parlementaires and municipal councilors were discussing methods of restoring peace. The meeting began two hours late from the unexplained tardiness of president Escalis de Bras, avocat-général Galaup-Chasteuil, and consuls Roquemartine and Michaelis. It was disrupted immediately after their arrival by fifteen or twenty men who chased the first president into the sacristy. They intended to kill him. They shouted, "Lou fau foua! Lou voleur! Vive lou res! Fouere voleurs!" (Beat the thief! Long live the King! Down with thieves!) Among them, Oppède recognized the younger Galaup brothers and Menouillon, captain of the guard at the Saint Jean gate. Menouillon was also recognized at the hôtel of president Escalis de Bras. The men in the courtyard fetched axes and a battering ram, trying unsuccessfully to break down the sacristy's heavy doors. After milling around for awhile and visiting the archbishop's private apartments, they left. Oppède remained in the sacristy. That evening in a joint meeting at the palace of justice, the parlementaires vetoed the request of president Melchior Forbin de La Roque to release the first president and escort him from the city.[112]

On February 16, the tocsin rang again. There had been political speeches in the marketplace. Events at Aix attracted rebels from Marseille and La Ciotat, perhaps as many as two hundred men. A crowd gathered and attempted to storm the hôtel Maynier d'Oppède with the intention of sacking it. They cried, "Death to the first president!" But they had to be content with destroying his property. The first president's servants defended the hôtel, firing from the windows and killing several men, including the chev-

---

[110] A.A.E., 1723, fols. 306–340; Delib. Parl., B. Méjanes 954, fol. 199v.
[111] A.A.E., 1723, fols. 306–340; Delib. Parl., B. Méjanes 954, fols. 193v–195v; "Recueil de pièces," B. Méjanes 1155.
[112] A.A.E., 1723, fols. 306–340; "Recueil de pièces," B. Méjanes 1155.

alier de La Coste, kinsman of the lieutenant general of Provence. The crowd began to chant, "Fau anar au palai" (Go to the palace), "Voleur de premier président, Lou fau tuar" (Thief of a first president, Kill him). They tried to storm the archbishop's palace, bringing a canon from the Place des Prêcheurs, which they trained, alternately, on the hôtel and the archbishop's palace. Councilor Paule of the Cour des Comptes and canon Decormis of Saint Sauveur stood in front of the gun all afternoon to prevent its being fired; it was returned, unused, to the Place des Prêcheurs the next day. The crowd had to content itself with erecting barricades around the hôtel and the palace.[113]

Councilors Mazargues and Guérin were sent as deputies to Mercoeur at the château of the baron de Saint Marc near Lambesc, ten miles northeast of Aix, on February 16. President Coriolis went on February 17. On February 18, Mercoeur ordered the Parlement to come as a body to Lambesc, leaving only a Vacations Chamber at Aix. He sent similar letters to the Cour des Comptes and Trésoriers Généraux.[114] There were sixteen parlementaires present at Lambesc on February 21: François Thomassin, Léon and Jean-Baptiste de Valbelle, André and François Maurel, Suffren, Forbin de La Roque, Foresta de La Roquette, Benault de Lubières, Antoine, Honorat, Saint Marc, Gallifet, Villeneuve, Antelmi, and Laurens.[115] Their number soon increased.

Some parlementaires did not answer the governor's summons— there were twenty-six parlementaires present in Aix at the joint meeting on February 20; twenty-eight on February 21; twenty-three on February 22; twenty-five on February 24; and twenty-one on February 27, the day Mercoeur entered the city.[116] At least ten of these magistrates were opponents of Oppède. They were Decormis, Escalis de Bras, Raffelis, Barrême, Leidet-Sigoyer father and son, Leidet-Calissane, Agut, Gautier son, and Galaup-Chasteuil. Also present in Aix during the revolt were Coriolis, Du Chaine, Ballon, Mazargues, Gautier father, Dedons, Foresta de La Roquette, Roux, Trichaud, Ollivier, André, Albert, Thoron,

---

[113] Delib. Parl., B. Méjanes 954, fols. 195–197; ADBR, Aix, Moissac, "Histoire du Parlement," II, 236; "Recueil de pièces," B. Méjanes 1155.

[114] A.A.E., 1723, fols. 306–340; Delib. Parl., B. Méjanes 954, fols. 195v, 197–198.

[115] A.A.E., 1723, fols. 364–365, 366–367.

[116] ADBR, Aix, B 3368.

and Cadenet. Some opposed Oppède. Some, such as Foresta de La Roquette, Gautier father, Du Chaine, and Coriolis, may have felt it their duty to remain and attempt to control the rebels.

Attendance at joint meetings fell by one-third after Mercoeur's letter reached Aix in February 19—there had been thirty-seven parlementaires present at the meeting on February 14; thirty-eight on February 15; thirty-six on February 16; thirty-three on February 17 and 18.[117] At least twenty-five parlementaires, nearly one-half of the company, never went to the palace of justice during the two weeks. A large number of parlementaires were repelled by the violence, fearing similar attacks on other magistrates. Using a mob to attack and imprison the first president was not a popular tactic with most parlementaires.

The membership of the Parlement had changed radically in the decade between 1649 and 1659. A number of 1649 rebels had died or resigned, for instance, Venel, Glandèves, Rascas Du Canet, Milan, Arbaud, and Bonfils; while the sons of Laurens, Espagnet, Guiran, Forbin de La Roque, and Antelmi had succeeded to office without inheriting their fathers' opposition politics. There were at least fifteen new members who did not participate in the events of 1658–1659.[118] Many of the 1649 rebels supported Oppède, for instance, François and Jean-Baptiste Thomassin, Léon and Jean-Baptiste de Valbelle, Saint Marc, Gallifet, and Du Chaine.

On February 19, president Escalis de Bras strengthened the guard around the archbishop's palace as a crowd of two thousand gathered at its doors. They had assembled at the news of Mercoeur's ordinance issued on February 16, convoking the *ban* and *milice* in Provence. Mercoeur requested five hundred cavalry, three thousand infantry, and cannon from the provincial nobility to assemble at Lambesc. The communities were requested to send one man per feu, to be assembled by the viguerie chiefs and marched to Lambesc.[119] By February 27, Mercoeur had assembled a thousand infantry, two hundred cavalry, eighty nobles, and two cannons, to which he added fifteen companies of the provincial infantry regiment and his own guard company. With these men,

---

[117] *Ibid.*

[118] B.N., Mélanges de Colbert 7, fols. 49–55; Clapiers-Collongues, *Chronologie*, pp. 93–99; ADBR, Aix, B 3357, B 3358, B 3359, *passim*.

[119] A.A.E., 1723, fols. 340–345. Mercoeur had returned to Provence from court on January 20, 1659; cf. Delib. Parl., B. Méjanes 954, fol. 191.

he marched on Aix to besiege the city and force the rebels to surrender.[120]

Madame Maynier d'Oppède visited her husband on February 19, forcing her way into the archbishop's palace, then leaving Aix with the members of her family to join the governor at Lambesc.[121] Presidents Escalis de Bras and Decormis appeared in the streets of Aix in their judicial robes carrying pistols on February 19. Decormis brought two hundred men into Aix through the Villeverte gate from his nearby estate at Beaurecueil. The men assembled at his hôtel; that night they toured Aix by torchlight, visiting Oppède.[122] President Escalis de Bras had gathered forty to sixty men at his hôtel, and they promenaded through the streets of Aix to the sound of a drum.[123] Oppède wrote in his procès-verbal that Decormis and Escalis de Bras, Galaup-Chasteuil, Barrême, and Leidet-Sigoyer father and son openly assumed leadership of the rebels on February 21. That night Escalis de Bras and the younger Leidet-Sigoyer insisted on sleeping in his room.[124] He was also visited by the bishop of Senez, who was the uncle of president Du Chaine, canons Du Chaine and Arnaud, who had protected his carriage, and first president Séguiran of the Cour des Comptes. They offered sympathy and support.[125]

On February 24, the parlementaires came to escort Oppède to the palace of justice. He refused to go with them. On February 25, they assembled at the archbishop's palace to request his pardon, intervention on their behalf with the governor, and procurement of a general amnesty. Oppède refused to make any concessions. Released the same day, he left immediately for Lambesc to join the governor. Decormis opposed his release.[126] The city council tardily sent first consul Roquemartine, assessor Peysonnel, General Assembly secretary Meyronnet, and eight consulaires to assure Mercoeur of the city's loyalty.[127] The bourgeois guard and the municipal guards at the city gates and public buildings were

[120] A.A.E., 1723, fols. 376–376v.

[121] B.N., Ms. fr. 20473, fol. 20, councilor de La Marc at Dijon to councilor Pianello at Lyon; B.N., Ms. fr. 18977, fols. 18–19, eyewitness account of Jean Bernet, soldier.

[122] "Recueil de pièces," B. Méjanes 1155; Haitze, *Histoire*, V, 449.

[123] "Recueil de pièces," B. Méjanes 1155.

[124] A.A.E., 1723, fols. 306–340.     [125] *Ibid.*

[126] *Ibid.*     [127] Haitze, *Histoire*, V, 456.

disbanded. On February 27, Mercoeur entered Aix unopposed. The city gates stood open awaiting his arrival. He was met by the consuls and Aix nobility. Oppède returned to Aix the next day, escorted by approximately thirty-five loyal parlementaires.[128] His opponents had fled. The revolt was crushed.

Oppède proved a dangerous enemy: he tried to destroy the parlementaires who had imprisoned and humiliated him. Oppède had already shown himself willing to exaggerate for effect in writing to Mazarin. On August 12, 1648, he wrote that Sève's reports of his recruiting in the Comtat Venaissin were based on rumors and false testimony.[129] But Sève had sent nine eyewitness reports to Paris.[130] Oppède wrote Mazarin on March 5, 1659, that the governor had assembled three thousand infantry and five hundred cavalry, although Mercoeur himself had written on February 27 that he had assembled half that number, a thousand infantry and two hundred cavalry.[131] On June 4, 1658, Oppède wrote that he had overcome all obstacles in the way of enforcing his May 30 ordinance.[132] In fact, the ordinance was never enforced. It was prohibited by the sovereign courts on May 31 and June 1, and Mazarin annulled it two days after the 1659 revolt began.[133] Oppède's willingness to exaggerate became dangerous when he sent a procès-verbal on the revolt to Paris.

Oppède vigorously pursued his enemies. On February 15, 1658, he wrote the papal vice-legate and governor of Orange not to shelter the rebels.[134] On February 27, he advised Mazarin to send Régusse and Forbin de La Barben, recently returned, back into exile. He demanded that Glandèves, Decormis, Escalis de Bras, Barrême, Galaup-Chasteuil, and Leidet-Sigoyer be prosecuted as rebels. Decormis, Escalis de Bras, and Galaup-Chasteuil were clearly

---

[128] *Ibid.*, 450, 457; A.A.E., 1723, fols. 340–345. This number may be high. For another account of the 1659 revolt, see Pillorget, *Les mouvements insurrectionnels*, pp. 784–799.

[129] B.N., Clairambault 417, fols. 290–291.

[130] B.N., Ms. fr. 18977, fols. 83–85, 87–99, 100–102; 17390, fols. 79–82.

[131] A.A.E., 1723, fols. 376, 388v.

[132] *Ibid.*, fol. 12.

[133] ADBR, Marseille, C 37, fols. 372v–375; ADBR, Aix, B 3368, May 31, June 1, 1658; A.C., Aix, AA 14, fol. 747.

[134] A.A.E., 1723, fol. 349v.

guilty from the March interrogations of the Parlement, but the only evidence against the others was Oppède's procès-verbal. The first president also demanded that Gordes be replaced as lieutenant general and Grimaldi be returned to Rome.[135] Mazarin granted most of his requests. Oppède was a valuable royal agent, and Mazarin had no patience with rebels: the cardinal had recommended exemplary punishment of the Marseille rebels in the previous summer.[136] On April 23, Oppède unsuccessfully requested that his brother, the abbé de Saint Floran, be made coadjutor of the archbishopric of Aix, and on April 29, Mercoeur wrote wistfully of rumors that Grimaldi had received a lettre de cachet sending him to Rome.[137] On June 3, Oppède demanded the death penalty for Escalis de Bras and Galaup-Chasteuil.[138]

On March 3, 1659, councilors Gautier, Ballon, Valbelle, and Villeneuve began the Parlement's interrogations on the revolt.[139] On March 27, the Parlement issued an arrêt condemning twenty-four men. Ten were to be hanged; eight were to be broken on the wheel and their houses razed; five were to be degraded from the nobility, fined 30,000 livres, and beheaded; Pierre Suque, saddlemaker from Grasse, was to attend the executions and serve ten years in the galleys. He attended eighteen executions in effigy at four o'clock on the afternoon of March 28—most of the rebels had fled to Marseille. Their houses were razed that afternoon.[140] Eighteen more rebels were held for trial by the intendants.[141]

Letters of commission were sent to Claude Bazin, seigneur de Bezons and an intendant in Languedoc, and Michel de Verthamont, master of requests in that province, to sit as a sovereign court to prosecute the Aix rebels. They were aided by six royal

---

[135] Ibid., fol. 384v. Oppède also advised Mazarin on July 30 and September 3, 1658, and March 4, 1659, against allowing La Barben, Glandèves, Gordes, or Régusse to return to Provence; cf. *ibid.*, fols. 87, 179, 399v. Oppède's procès-verbal is A.A.E., 1723, fols. 306–340.

[136] Chéruel and Avenel, *Lettres de Mazarin*, VIII, 548–549, August 19, 1658.

[137] A.A.E., 1723, fols. 496–498, 502v.

[138] *Ibid.*, fol. 536v; B.M., Harleian 4493, fols. 70–73.

[139] "Recueil de pièces," B. Méjanes 1155; B.N., Ms. fr. 18977, fol. 17.

[140] *Ibid.*, fols. 409–418, 431, 432v, 514–516.

[141] B.M., Harleian 4442, fols. 18–19, Verthamont to Séguier, May 6, 1659, fols. 42–45, extract from commissioners' judgment, June 4, 1659.

judges from the towns of Uzès, Sommières, Lunel, Villeneuve, Beaucaire, and Nîmes in Languedoc.[142] Claude de Bazin was made an honorary councilor in the Parlement of Aix by royal letters on January 22, 1660.[143] The two commissioners arrived in Aix on April 22 and began their investigations the next day.[144] The Parlement objected to their assumption of its authority, but the commissioners had a conciliar decree allowing them to evoke the case. The Parlement acquiesced when Oppède threatened the protesters with prison; it was clear that he could enforce his threat.[145] Royal commissioners had been used to prosecute the cascaveoux rebels and Estienne de Vaillac—special commissions to judge cases of treason were used as an instrument of centralization and deeply resented by the royal courts. Bazin and Verthamont issued warrants of arrest, and on May 19 they withdrew to Villeneuve-lès-Avignon in the Comtat for judgment. Mercoeur wanted the trial outside Provence for safety, and the Parlement of Toulouse forbade the use of cities in Languedoc.[146]

The trial began on May 29. The commissioners and Oppède felt that exemplary punishment was necessary. Sentences included hanging, breaking on the wheel, life servitude in the galleys, temporary and perpetual banishment, confiscation of property, and destruction of houses. Six parlementaires previously indicted by ordinance and lettres de cachet were sentenced. Galaup-Chasteuil was banished in perpetuity from France; his office and two-thirds of his property were confiscated. President Escalis de Bras was sentenced to five years exile from France and five from Provence, forced sale of his office, and a fine of 30,000 livres. President Decormis was exiled from Provence for ten years and fined 1,000 livres. He was given six weeks to dispose of his office, which he resigned to his son Pierre, who in turn resigned it to Auguste de Thomas. Barrême and the Liedets-Sigoyer were fined and tem-

---

[142] A.A.E., 1723, fol. 383; Haitze, *Histoire*, V, 466; B.M., Harleian 4442, fols. 10–11, Bezons to Séguier, April 22, 1659, fols. 12–13, Verthamont to Séguier, April 29, 1659.

[143] ADBR, Aix, B 3360, fol. 872v.

[144] A.A.E., 1723, fol. 492.

[145] *Ibid.*, fol. 494.

[146] *Ibid.*, fols. 520, 522, 530; B.M., Harleian 4442, fols. 30–31, Bezons to Séguier, May 13, 1659; fols. 34–35, the same, May 20, 1659; fols. 38–39, the same, May 28, 1659.

porarily suspended from office; they were serving again in 1663.[147]

Aix consuls Redortier and Michaelis and assessor Peysonnel were suspended from office and prohibited from becoming consulaires; first consul Roquemartine was appointed interim administrator. Consulaire Estienne and municipal guard captains Rogery, Minchon, and Beaumont were interrogated.[148] The Parlement by arrêt replaced Roquemartine, who refused to serve, with Jean de Séguiran, second consul in 1657. Séguiran was ordered into Aix from his country house by Mercoeur on July 29.[149] Municipal elections in September 1659 were suspended by royal letters, and new municipal officials were named by the crown.[150]

More than sixty Aixois were interrogated or prosecuted for participating in the 1659 revolt. Seventeen were officials. Another thirty or so were ordinary Aixois. At least seventeen were nobles.[151] The nobility had played an important role in all three revolts. There was a high percentage of nobles in Aix, and their

[147] Clapiers-Collongues, *Chronologie*, pp. 21, 22, 165; ADBR, Aix B 3360, fol. 560; A.A.E., 1723, fol. 534; Haitze, *Histoire*, V, 466; B.M., Harleian 4442, fols. 12–13, Verthamont to Séguier, April 1659; fols. 18–19, the same, May 6, 1659; fols. 20–21, Bezons to Séguier, May 6, 1659; fols. 42–45, extract from commissioners' judgment, June 4, 1659; B.N., Mélanges de Colbert 7, fols. 49–55. François de Honorat bought Galaup-Chasteuil's office in 1661, and Jean de Simiane de Lacépède bought Bras's office in 1662.

[148] A.A.E., 1637, fol. 370; B.M., Harleian 4442, fols. 67–78.

[149] A.C., Aix, BB 103, fols. 105–106; B.M., Harleian 4493, fols. 87–90, Oppède to Séguier, July 29, 1659.

[150] A.C., Aix, BB 103, fols. 112–118; AA 6, fols. 14v–15; B.M., Harleian 4493, fols. 113–114.

[151] Eight noble cadets were sentenced: Melan, Perrin, Riquet, Rougnac, Jujardy, Alphéran, Audifredi, Gilbert (or Gibert). Another four were interrogated and released. Officials sentenced included consuls Michaelis, Peysonnel, and Redortier; the sons of the latter two; consulaire Estienne (son of a seneschal councilor); captains Rogery, Minchon, Beaumont, Menouillon of the municipal guard; prévôt's lieutenant d'Anne (or his brother); several lawyers and officers of the provincial regiment. Other rebels included two valets of president Escalis de Bras, valets of Glandèves and d'Anne, an unnamed tailor, the innkeepers of the Cross of Lorraine and the Galleon, a butcher, the son of a bailiff, and eighteen others including Bernard nicknamed Touasse, Gerard (or Bernard) nicknamed Cantonnet, and Beau nicknamed Medaille. They were sentenced. Six more rebels were interrogated and released, cf., B. Méjanes 1155, fol. 229 and Pillorget's analysis in *Les Mouvements insurrectionnels*, pp. 835–836.

presence in the Parlement and municipal government contributed to the unruliness of these bodies. Many were young, hot-headed cadets, and their valets or male servants helped to provoke the revolts.

Mercoeur sent troops to arrest the parlementaires and escort them to the prisons of Pierre Scize fortress at Lyon. He wrote Mazarin on March 13 that Decormis had been arrested in church three days earlier. Decormis was later sent into exile in Normandy. His son and two brothers were temporarily forced to leave Aix; his son had been interrogated and released. Barrême was at mass in Saint Sauveur when the soldiers came to his house. Warned by a servant, he escaped through the sacristy, and the soldiers fruitlessly searched Saint Sauveur to the crypt. Barrême took refuge in Avignon. The Leidets-Sigoyer fled across the roofs and escaped to Marseille, where the three Galaup brothers were hiding. They later quietly returned to Provence, where Galaup-Chasteuil lived on his wife's dowry. Escalis de Bras and his brother-in-law Glandèves were variously reported in Marseille, Languedoc, Genoa, Paris, the Comtat Venaissin, and Besançon in the Franche-Comté.[152]

Gordes was replaced as lieutenant general by François de Moutiers, comte de Mérinville, in October 1659, and was sent to Reims.[153] Grimaldi, with precedence as cardinal, was told not to be in Aix when Mazarin visited the city in January 1660. Grimaldi retired to the Carthusians at Villeneuve-lès-Avignon, then went to Rome as extraordinary ambassador and did not return to Aix until 1662. He consecrated Oppède's brother as bishop of Toulon in 1664 and Mercoeur as cardinal in 1667. Grimaldi died in office in 1685.[154] Neither Gordes nor Grimaldi was present at the February 3 Te Deum mass in Saint Sauveur celebrating Louis XIV's visit to Aix.[155]

Richelieu had been distracted by his struggle with the queen mother in 1630. Mazarin in 1649 faced a revolt by the Parlement and city of Paris. But in 1659 Mazarin was firmly in control of the

[152] A.A.E., 1723, fols. 409–418, 444v, 479, 543, 549; Haitze, *Histoire*, V, 461; Grimaldi and Gaufridy, *Mémoires*, pp. 82, 92; EDB, IV, 185; B.M., Harleian 4442, fols. 18–19, 20–21; 4493, fols. 81–90.

[153] ADBR, Aix, B 3359, fol. 464.

[154] Commines, "Les luttes du Président de Forbin d'Oppède," p. 18; EDB, IV–2, 254; Albanès, *Gallia*, I, 144.

[155] Edouard Baratier, ed., *Documents de l'histoire de la Provence* (Toulouse, 1971), pp. 216–217.

Paris government and was served by a reliable governor in Provence, who quickly suppressed the revolt. In 1631, about forty Aixois had been indicted, but only three sentences were executed, and few parlementaires were punished. In 1649, there was a general amnesty. In 1659, more than sixty rebels were sentenced, although not all sentences were carried out. The parlementaires were harshly punished. Meant to discourage future protest, the severity was effective: the Aix parlementaires did not rebel again. Nothing remained of the 1649 victory. The opposition was crushed, its members in disarray, and Oppède never permitted them to regroup or rise above a powerless faction. He could assure Séguier on November 4 that the city and the Parlement were calm.[156]

René Pillorget views the 1657–1658 revolt at Marseille and the fiscal problems of Provence as the main causes of the 1659 protest at Aix.[157] He neglects the opposition politics of the Parlement as a cause. In fact, he minimizes the continuity between the 1649 and 1659 revolts and ignores the significance of the parlementaires' participation in 1659.[158] Searching for common patterns and characteristics in order to construct general models of seventeenth-century revolts, Pillorget is preoccupied by classification. He is interested in the structures of all the revolts. We are interested in particular revolts and individual participants: the three revolts at Aix, the role of the Parlement in these revolts, and the participation of individual parlementaires. If we look at the provincial government as a living political organism, and for several decades we study the behavior of a member institution, the Parlement, in relation to the whole, we achieve a different perspective on the revolts, which we see against a background of provincial and judicial politics. The revolts become a vehicle for studying the internal politics of the Parlement, and the role of individuals becomes important. Pillorget does not view the Aix revolts through the interaction of local governing institutions and their members. As a result, we believe that he underestimates the role of the parlementaires in the revolts. Focusing on the participants rather than the events changes our perception of the Aix revolts.

---

[156] B.M., Harleian 4493, fols. 133–134. There had been a hundred soldiers in Aix throughout the summer to assure peace; cf. *ibid.*, fols. 87–90.

[157] Pillorget, *Les mouvements insurrectionnels*, pp. 783–784, 788–791.

[158] *Ibid.*, p. 795.

An opposition party developed in the Parlement after 1631 from a core of discontented former cascaveoux. Members of this party led the 1649 revolt. Dispersing in 1650, they participated on an individual basis in the Fronde, but they regrouped in 1656 and led the 1659 revolt, when they were permanently scattered. We see the 1659 revolt at Aix as the denouement of three decades of parlementaire protest stretching back to the 1630 cascaveoux revolt. The parlementaire Fronde at Aix in 1649 must be understood in this context. Parlementaire leadership gave continuity to the revolts at Aix. Pillorget's concept of community is important as a principle of classification because it emphasizes the role of local political factionalism in causing revolts. We have emphasized local politics as a cause of the Aix revolts. Investigating the local politics of other rebellious elites may increase our general understanding of seventeenth-century revolts.

# CONCLUSION

On February 28, 1659, Oppède made his triumphal return to Aix "to take his rightful place on the fleurs de lys." Escorted on horseback from Lambesc by the loyal parlementaires in red robes, he entered Aix through the southeastern city gate, where he was greeted by Mercoeur and the assembled nobility. The governor's troops were ranged in battle order on the Place des Prêcheurs, at the city gates, and on the Place d'Orbitel in the Mazarin quarter. Riding toward his hôtel, Oppède stopped at the house of the Augustinian canons to be greeted by the city consuls. He may have accepted an honorary escort of guards in yellow and a trumpeter in red to announce his progress. The Saint Jean gate should have been decorated with flowers and greenery, his arms, and those of the city, the streets lined with floral arches. But he did not receive these honors. There were no cheering crowds; the streets were offensively silent and empty. Oppède was escorted to his hôtel, where he received representatives from the royal courts. Later, he was escorted to the palace of justice, where he was formally reinstated as the Parlement's first president.[1] Our story ends where it began—at the hôtel Maynier d'Oppède on the Place Saint Sauveur opposite the cathedral.

It was here Oppède drafted his memoir on the Aix parlementaires that he sent to Colbert in 1663.[2] Perhaps he dictated it from an armchair overlooking the cathedral where he could hear the bells chime the passing hours; the hôtel's thick walls muffled the noise from the inner courtyard. The memoir was a collection of terse marginal comments: the occasional silences and one-word

---

[1] A.A.E., 1723, fols. 340–345, 382–383, 388v. Also see Louis Wolff, *Le Parlement de Provence au XVIIIᵉ siècle* (Aix, 1920), pp. 183–188, description of municipal reception of a new first president; Maximin Deloche, *Un frère de Richelieu inconnu* (Paris, 1935), pp. 102–105, description of reception of a new archbishop; Maurice Wilkinson, *The Last Phase of the League in Provence, 1588–1598* (London, 1909), pp. 79–80, description of reception of a new governor.

[2] B.N., Mélanges de Colbert 7, fols. 49–55, published by G. B. Depping, ed. *Correspondance administrative sous le règne de Louis XIV*, 4 vols. (Paris, 1851), II, 94–96.

dismissals eloquently express the writer's estimation of his colleagues' abilities. Such a memoir would not have been sent in 1629, when Oppède's father was first president. Its existence in 1663 underscores the major changes which had occurred: the Parlement had come firmly under the first president's grip; the opposition was crushed; his political enemies were destroyed. The Aix parlementaires were transformed from a disorderly company of rebels into obedient, if sullen, servants of the king.

Why were the Aix parlementaires able to resist the crown for three decades, and why were they defeated? They were able to resist effectively when they could organize into an opposition party with political unity and a common purpose. Their success was temporary because they could not achieve permanent unity, a broad reform program, or widespread provincial support.

The 1649 victory of the Aix parlementaires can be attributed in part to their organization into an opposition party after the 1630 revolt. The opposition developed gradually from a small nucleus of discontented parlementaires who had made use of a popular revolt in 1630. It grew to approximately half the company's membership in 1649, the apogee of its power and influence. This growth has been described in terms of the issues that produced it. Voting together as a bloc in joint meetings to reject registrations, draft remonstrances, and issue regulatory arrêts, the opposition achieved temporary unity on certain political issues such as disciplinary citations and forced registrations of unpopular creations, abolition of the Chambre des Requêtes, the Semester, and the intendants of justice. It advertised its resistance inside and outside the Parlement, attacking those who ignored its warnings. Revolt was the ultimate weapon. Intent on forcing changes in royal policy, the opposition was capable of coordinated political activity, and it had continuity of membership, goals, and tactics.

The opposition was really a cluster or movement within the Parlement: there were no neat, clear-cut political parties in the modern sense. It had fluid membership and informal organization without real discipline or public recognition. A small core of dedicated opposition members provided the goals, tactics, and esprit de corps that made it effective. A complex network of family alliances and personal feuds helped to determine its membership, as did rank, age, and chamber of service. But political opinion was the most important determinant. Success for the opposition depended upon attracting the support of the politically uncommitted majority, a large, floating group of parlementaires without political ties. The royalists were a small group without coherence or organization. The crown granted honors, pensions, and appointments to secure support, concentrating its efforts on opposition leaders, while creating a new chamber and a Semester filled with magistrates intent on protecting their new offices. Motivated more by personal interest than by political opinion, fewer in number than the opposition parlementaires, the royalists never had the same unity, esprit de corps, or capability for coordinated action.

By 1659, the opposition had become a disorganized faction with unclear goals and unpopular tactics. It lost credibility by attacking the first president in February 1659. Most parlementaires feared mob violence, particularly against members of their own company, and they refused to support the 1659 revolt. Served by a loyal, competent governor in Provence, the crown was stronger than it had been during the Fronde. Mazarin used the 1659 revolt at Aix as a pretext to crush the parlementaire opposition. He had already repudiated the concessions in the Bichi Treaty and obliterated the 1649 victory; now he silenced and dispersed the parlementaire opposition.

The parlementaires were self-avowed royalists, cautious and conservative members of a high judicial court sworn to interpret and enforce royal law. Their participation in the revolts at Aix was as unexpected as would be the appearance of state supreme court judges in the streets of Albany or Sacramento, wearing red arm bands over their black robes and distributing Marxist literature. The parlementaires were not true revolutionaries. They did not launch a sweeping attack on the monarchy or develop a comprehensive program of political reform offering a viable alternative to the monarchy. They did not attempt to overthrow the royal government, act in its place, or form an alternate government. Whatever they might claim regarding the customary constitution of Provence, they were primarily interested in protecting their own privileges and interests. The particularism of their outlook is affirmed by their actions and by their words: the parlementaires meant to force the elimination of abuses affecting them as an elite group. Their political thinking was evasive and conservative. They never defined the boundaries of royal authority or their own role in local government. They never clarified or defined the customary constitution. They never discussed practical, effective reform of royal or provincial government. As Ernst Kossmann has suggested, the parlementaires were too conservative and too committed to divine-right monarchy to challenge basic principles. They avoided the main issues, and by doing so, they tacitly accepted royal absolutism. The parlementaires' grievances were narrow and personal. Their misfortune was that protest in the streets of Aix was insufficient to force permanent changes in royal policy without attacks on basic principles and comprehensive reform attracting wide provincial support.[3]

Nor could the parlementaires and other magistrates of Aix overcome their chronic strife to combat the crown's attacks on their authority. Ancient enmities and hostilities proved stronger than the desire to combat the crown. There was no reciprocity or mutual aid among the royal courts of Aix. They never united in a Chambre Saint Louis, as the Paris courts did. The Parlements of Aix and Paris never united because of their narrow interpretations of judicial reform, an obstacle to unity among all French parlements. Government by a centralizing monarchy was not necessarily worse than government by a group of quarreling, self-serving provincial officials. Parochial self-interest too often characterized the behavior and attitudes of provincial officials.

The dissension among officials at Aix contributed to the causes of revolt. The parlementaires' internal divisions lengthened the cascaveoux protest. The animosity between individuals and factions became so great in the autumn of 1630 that it spilled outside the Parlement into the streets of Aix. A disgruntled minority made use of a spontaneous popular revolt to revenge themselves on their enemies within the Parlement: a faction of discontented parlementaires led the 1630 revolt as an outgrowth of a power struggle between two chambers created in the previous year when the court left Aix because of the plague. A similar incident occurred three decades later in 1659, when a faction of presidents and councilors used a revolt begun by nobles and gentlemen to attack the first president. Resenting the first president's newly aggrandized authority as acting intendant and acting governor, they hoped to force his resignation or recall. Most of these parle-

---

[3] Theme of a paper presented at the French Historical Society's annual conference at the University of California, Berkeley, in April 1977.

mentaires had participated in the 1649 revolt and fought in the Provençal Fronde. They regrouped and led the 1659 revolt.

The parlementaires' disputes with other provincial officials also helped to cause the revolts. The 1630 revolt was exacerbated by the actions of governor Guise, who revenged himself on the Parlement for a long-standing feud by refusing to suppress the revolt at Aix. The abrasive personalities and arbitrary actions of governors Vitry and Alais contributed to causing the 1649 revolt, while the belligerence of Alais after the revolt caused the Provençal Fronde. In 1658, the parlementaires joined a provincial opposition that had developed from the first president's power struggles with the archbishop of Aix, the lieutenant general of Provence, and the procureurs du pays. Precedence disputes and personality clashes often masked power struggles. Hostilities generated by the parlementaires' internal and provincial quarrels intensified their anger and became entangled in their struggles with the crown, obscuring deeper political issues.

The dissension among officials at Aix was an inherent political and administrative problem, heightened by the stress of the Habsburg War. The basic structural problem was venality, the network of private interests in office-holding threatened by the crown's attempts to centralize the provincial administration and increase revenues. The men in Paris attempting administrative reform alienated officials at the provincial level whose loyalty and support were necessary for successful reform. A related structural problem, as serious but hitherto unrecognized, was the strife between overlapping provincial authorities and the competition between officials inside and outside the Parlement of Aix. Fragmented powers, conflicting loyalties, and administrative strife were a medieval legacy, which the crown in fiscal desperation intensified by creating and selling new offices without abolishing old ones. Power struggles among officials in the provincial administration, heightened by the crown's venal policies, were an important cause of the Aix revolts.

The crown used the dissension to increase its control over provincial institutions in a policy of divide and rule hardly needed with the chronic strife. Royal agents worked to draw provincial institutions closer to the throne. Besides exploiting internal divisions and provincial disputes, the crown used intimidation as a technique of control. From 1631 to 1659, eighty-three citations to Paris and temporary suspensions from office were issued for parlementaires of Aix in disciplinary arrêts du conseil and lettres de cachet. Approximately 45 percent of the Parlement were cited at least once by 1649; a minority of 25 percent were cited more than once. They were the opposition members. The Parlement as an institution was threatened with permanent transfer from Aix, refused adjournment for the summer recess, and prohibited adjudication of cases until edicts were registered. In 1641, an unwanted new chamber was added. In 1647, a new Semester was created to replace the Parlement for six months a year. The crown also sought alternate registration by the Cour des Comptes. The harshness of these techniques deserves the term intimidation: to force obedience, the crown systematically attacked the liberty and property of individuals and the functioning of the court as a whole. Disciplinary legislation was a powerful form of coercion, more effective than threats to revoke the Paulette. But the crown's policy of intimidation had unforeseen results at Aix. It stiffened the parlementaires' resistance and helped to create an opposition party, which led a successful revolt in 1649. After 1641, the crown was not able to disperse the opposition with bribes, threats to revoke the Paulette, or disciplinary legislation.

Although bribery and patronage gained some notable supporters for the crown, favors were not available in large enough numbers to be a significant means of control at Aix. The crown was not entirely successful in pursuing a policy of divide and rule, using bribery and intimidation, to control the Parlement. Overshadowed by its final victory, the crown's difficulty in subduing the Aix parlementaires has not been fully recognized. As A. Lloyd Moote has suggested, the duration and intensity of the parlementaires' resistance has been underestimated. Our assessment of the royal tactic of divide and rule, as described by Roland Mousnier, needs reexamination.[4]

Moote notes that the parlementaires' chief weakness was their internal disunity, encouraged and exploited by the crown. He argues rightly that while the parlementaires never fully united, they

[4] A. Lloyd Moote, "The French Crown versus its Judicial and Financial Officials, 1615–1683," *Journal of Modern History*, No. 34 (1962), pp. 146–160; *The Revolt of the Judges: The Parlement of Paris and the Fonde, 1643–1652* (Princeton, 1971), pp. 35, n. 52; 52–53; 368–376.

achieved enough cohesion to lead serious revolts and frighten the central government.[5] But his argument is weakened by his failure to explain exactly how the parlementaires of Paris overcame their internal strife to resist the crown. We agree that the parlements were riddled by feuds and factions, a serious handicap that helped to cause the Aix revolts. But we have demonstrated how a party of parlementaires was able to achieve enough unity on three separate occasions to resist the crown effectively. In describing how this was done—the tactics and methods used—we have explained the seeming paradox that internal disunity could lead to serious revolt.

The opposition at Aix suffered from sporadic disorganization, limited goals, and fluctuating membership. No more than a faction in 1630 and 1659, it was as much the result of clientage ties within the Parlement as political opinion. It was never a political party in the modern sense. Yet it existed tenaciously in one form or another for three decades, and its leadership gave some continuity to the revolts at Aix. We must not overlook this thread of continuity, the similarities in attitudes and goals of the rebel parlementaires, in studying the feuds and factions that produced the revolts. Although there were defections, members of fifteen parlementaire families participated in two or three of the revolts. The parlementary Fronde at Aix was one episode in a three decade struggle by the Aix magistrates against the crown. The 1630 revolt was the introduction, the 1649 revolt the climax, and the 1659 revolt the denouement.

The crown eventually won because it had a comprehensive program of long-range goals and an offensive strategy, although its attempts to control the parlementaires have an ad hoc, unplanned quality. Richelieu and Mazarin stumbled along a path lined with semifailures, near-defeats, and compromises pleasing no one. But they won. The crown had begun to achieve its goal of bureaucratic centralization in Provence by 1661. There were fewer revolts in Provence after this year; the Aix parlementaires were more obedient; and the crown exercised greater control over Provençal institutions. The crown could go after its goals repeatedly, from new angles with new projects, while the parlementaires and other provincial officials fought the difficult defensive strategy of trying

[5] Moote, *Revolt of the Judges,* p. 13.

to maintain the status quo against repeated assaults. Time favored the crown, which could renew its offensive again and again in a war of attrition, while the opposition had to maintain itself in perpetual fighting trim. When the parlementaires relaxed and dispersed, the crown struck. With no comprehensive program of political reform, no offensive strategy, no popular or provincial support, no unity with other institutions, and only sporadic internal unity, the parlementaires' defeat was inevitable.

The crown's success was enduring: France is a highly centralized nation today. But it is a mistake to exaggerate the Paris government's efficiency in the seventeenth century or to credit it with creating the first modern bureaucracy. If royal agents acquired more control over provincial institutions and municipalities, the average Provençal could still live almost entirely outside the government's interference, particularly in the countryside. The autonomy of Provençal life is demonstrated by the number of parlementaires and municipal officials who did not obey summonses to appear in Paris. Pleading the distance and weather, their health and family problems, they did not go, and the crown did not force them. The remoteness of Provence limited the amount of royal control. The crown interfered more often and emphatically after 1661, but it did not control Provençal life.

# COMPOSITION OF THE AIX PARLEMENT, 1641–1649

There were 45 councilors in the Aix Parlement in 1642, 3 presidents of the Enquêtes, 5 presidents à mortier with 2 offices vacant, and 4 royal attorneys, for a total of 59 offices. The Chambre des Requêtes added 14 new offices in 1641, which the Semester increased by 8 to 22 in 1648, all abolished in 1649. There were 7 new offices created in 1650, 1 president à mortier and 6 councilors, for a total of 66. The councilors of the Grand'Chambre rotated annually with those of the Tournelle. The 1642 composition is given here. Opposition members appear in italics and royalists in capitals.

### Grand'Chambre

2d president *Jean-Baptiste de Forbin de La Roque,* acting first president until *Jean de Mesgrigny-Vandeuve* assumed office in 1644

4th president Louis de Paule, who died in 1644; Honoré de Coriolis-Corbières received in this office as 5th president in January 1646, followed by his son Pierre de Coriolis-Villeneuve in 1651

5th president *Charles de Grimaldi-Régusse,* received in 1643; became 4th president in 1644

6th president *Henri de Forbin-Maynier d'Oppède* received in vacant office in February 1646; *Henri d'Escalis de Bras* assumed this office in 1655, when Maynier d'Oppède became first president

7th president Lazare Du Chaine, received in vacant office in June 1646

8th president *Louis Decormis-Beaurecueil,* received in 1650

dean *Jean-Baptiste de Boyer-Eguilles,* who died in 1648; son *Vincent* received reversion letters in 1638

337

councilors *Alexandre Thomassin-Ainac,* who died in 1644; son
   *Jean-Baptiste* received reversion letters in 1634
*Louis d'Arnaud* died in 1644
Armand Bermond-Pennafort
François-Louis de Leidet-Fombeton
Jacques de Boniface de La Mole
Scipion de Foresta-Collongues
*Pierre de Laurens-Saint Martin de Pallières*
*Louis d'Antelmi*
*Gaspard de Villeneuve-Mons*
*Raymond d'Espagnet*
*Charles de Guérin Du Castelet*
*Léon de Valbelle-Meyrargues*
Scipion de Chailan-Mouriès

### Chambre de La Tournelle

3d president Jean-Augustin de Foresta de La Roquette; re-
placed by 2d president Forbin de La Roque in 1644
councilors Louis-Hugues Dedons-Pierrefeu
   André de Ballon
   Antoine de Gautier-Mimet, implicated in 1630; inactive in 1649,
      because son a member of Requêtes; dean and loyalist in
      1659
   Melchior de Mazargues-Malijai
   *Jean de Leidet-Sigoyer;* son *Pierre* received reversion letters in
      1649
   François de Trichaud-Saint Martin
   Jean de Roux-Gaubert
   *Honoré de Rascas Du Canet*
   *Jean-Barthélemy d'Agut;* son *Pierre* received in this office in
      1650
   Claude de Fabri-Rians
   *Charles de Lombard-Montauraux, Gourdon*
   *Marc-Antoine d'Albert-Roquevaux*
   *Gaspard de Venel-Ventabren;* brother-in-law César de Gaillard-
      Longjumeau received in this office in 1649.

338

## CHAMBRE DES ENQUÊTES

1st president *Jean de Guiran de La Brillane,* resigned in favor of François Thomassin in 1648

2d president *Alexandre de Gallifet-Tholonet*; son *Jacques* received reversion letters in 1647

3d president *Charles de Tabaret-Volonne*

councilors *Jean d'Arbaud-Bargemon*

*François Thomassin-Saint Paul*

François de Périer-Clumanc, father *Julien,* dean, who died in 1639; son cited in 1641 and 1645, inactive thereafter

*Jean-Pierre Signier*

*Jean-François de Glandèves-Rousset*

*Jean-François Aymar d'Albi-Châteaurenard*

*Jean-Baptiste de Valbelle-Saint Symphorien*

*Louis de Saint Marc*

GASPARD DE CAUVET-BORMES

*Pierre de Barrême*

*César de Milan-Cornillon*

*Pierre de Raffelis-Roquesante*

*Jacques d'André*

Gaspard d'Honorat-Pourcieux

Amand de Monier-Châteaudeuil

*Jean-Antoine de Bonfils-Villeverte*

## ROYAL ATTORNEYS

*Pierre Decormis-Beaurecueil,* first avocat-général; son *Louis* received reversion letters in 1635 and assumed office in 1646, at his father's death

François Maurel-Volonne was received in this office in 1653, followed by *Jean-Baptiste Gautier de La Molle* in 1655

LOUIS-FRANÇOIS DE RABASSE-VERGONS, first procureur-général; son GUILLAUME received reversion letters in 1639, assumed office in 1647 (?)

PIERRE DE PORCELLET-UBAYE, second avocat-général; Christophe Fauris was received into this office in 1645, followed by *Hubert de Galaup-Chasteuil* in 1655

FRANÇOIS DE GANTÈS-VALBONNETTE, second procureur-général

## CHAMBRE DES REQUÊTES

presidents JACQUES DE GAUFRIDY and

*Pierre de Leidet-Calissane,* received into new office of councilor in 1650

councilor Melchoir de Forbin de Saint André, received reversion letters for father's office of president à mortier in 1644

Julien de Gautier-Gardanne, received into father's office of councilor in 1653

François Thomassin de La Garde

FRANÇOIS DE BEAUMONT-SUAVIS

ANTOINE DE SUFFREN

CHARLES DE TRESSEMANES-CHASTEUIL, received into Enquêtes in 1646; did not sell office until 1648, after Semester established

Alexandre de Coriolis de La Bastide

BALTHAZAR DE RABASSE-VERGONS

JEAN DEDONS DU LYS

LÉON DE TRIMOND

François de Clapiers-Puget, received into Tournelle in 1643; replaced by André de Bernard

*Charles de Laugier-Montblanc*

Gaspard de Ballon-Saint Julien, received into father's office of councilor in 1660

## SEMESTER

former Requêtes members Gaufridy, Gautier, Thomassin, Beaumont, Suffren, Coriolis, Rabasse, Dedons, Bernard, Laugier, Ballon, Trimond

new purchasers: president FRANÇOIS DE GRASSE-SAINT CÉSAIRE

councillors CHARLES-HONORÉ DE RAPHAELIS D'AGOULT-CANAUX

    LOUIS FLOTTE DE MEAUX

    ANDRÉ MARIN DE SAINT MICHEL

    ANTOINE HENRICI

    CHARLES DE TRETS

    HONORÉ DE GASQUET, questionable

    LA MOLLE, questionable

Grasse, Raphaelis d'Agoult, and Flotte were from old families of the Provençal sword nobility. Gasquet may have been lieutenant of the Arles seneschal court and La Molle from the municipal government of Grasse. This is an incomplete list. There are several members of the Semester whose names are unknown. The total number of members was twenty-two.

### SOURCES

ADBR, Aix, B 3346–3356, royal letters of provision to office.

Balthazar de Clapiers-Collongues, *Chronologie des officiers des Cours souveraines de Provence, 1501–1790* (Aix, 1909).

B.N., Dupuy 754, fols. 221, 244; Ms. fr. 18976, fol. 173; Ms. fr. 18977, fols. 37–39, 322–323; Ms. fr. 17389, fols. 300–301; Ms. fr. 24166, fol. 245.

Delib. Parl., B. Méjanes 952, 953; ADBR, Aix, B 3366, 3367.

"Recueil de pieces relatives au Parlement de Provence," B. Méjanes 943, fol. 3.

Pierre de Louvet, "Histoire du Parlement de Provence," B. Méjanes R.A. 53, fols. 400–401.

ADBR, Aix, J.L.H. Hesmivy de Moissac, "Histoire du Parlement de Provence," II, fols. 73, 76.

## MUNICIPAL BUDGET OF AIX

*Municipal Expenditures, 1653*

| | |
|---|---:|
| university, streets, fountains | 65,000 livres |
| taille | 30,520 livres |
| taillon | 770 livres |
| Estates expenses | 2,300 livres |
| payments on debts | 40,000 livres |
| miscellaneous | 25,000 livres |
| Total | 103,520 livres |

*Municipal Revenues, 1653*

| | |
|---|---:|
| meat rêve | 5,000 livres |
| fish rêve | 15,500 livres |
| wine rêve | 18,000 livres |
| wine-sellers' licenses | 500 livres |
| public baths | 200 livres |
| beef tongue rêve | 100 livres |
| flour rêve | 2,700 livres |
| public hospital | 1,200 livres |
| cabriderie | 700 livres |
| Total | 65,950 livres |

These figures were taken from A.C., Aix, AA 14, fol. 322. They are not entirely accurate (see below), since they were used to support the municipal government's petition for a tax increase. Municipal rêves were collected by tax farmers on a contractual basis. There were eight tax farmers listed in the 1695 capitation; cf. Jean-Paul Coste, *La ville d'Aix en 1695. Structure urbaine et société*, 3 vols. (Aix, 1970), II, 813–814.

## Municipal Taxes in 1638

| | |
|---|---:|
| La rêve de la boucherie | 40,500 livres |
| La rêve de cinq sols pour quintal de farine | 29,250 livres |
| La rêve sur le poisson | 14,300 livres |
| La rêve du vin sur les hôtes | 9,000 livres |
| La rêve sur les boulangers | 29,000 livres |
| Les quatre tables de Cabriderie | 480 livres |
| Les langues de boeufs | 100 livres |
| L'infirmerie | 500 livres |
| Les bains | 200 livres |
| Licenses | 350 livres |
| Les degres de la place | 135 livres |
| Total | 97,815 livres |

These figures were taken from "Rêves et routes que la ville d'Aix a eues en l'an 1638 que j'ai retiré en charge d'assesseur, Jacques Gaufridy," B. Méjanes 799, "Recueil de pièces concernant la Provence," published in *Mémoires pour servir à l'histoire de la Fronde en Provence* (Aix, 1870), pp. 195–198.

# THE CONSULS AND ASSESSORS OF AIX, 1629–1659

Consuls appear in the following order: first consul, assessor, second consul, and third consul. The source is the Red Book, printed in 1694 at Aix and based on the deliberations of the city council. It is available in "Administration du pays de Provence," B. Méjanes 608, fols. 94–122; A.C., Aix, BB 129; B.N., *Catalogue des consuls et assesseurs de la ville d'Aix*, Aix, 1699.

1629: Gaspard de Forbin, sieur de La Barben; Joseph Martelli; Balthazar de Veteris Du Revest, écuyer; François Bourilly, écuyer

1630: Sextius d'Escalis, baron d'Ansouis et de Bras; Henri des Rollands de Réauville, sieur de Cabanès; Ardoin de Boniparis, écuyer; Jean Anglès, bourgeois

1631: Alphonse d'Oraison, comte de Boulbon; Jean de Montaud; François de Beaumont, écuyer; Esprit Delapalud

1632: Rolland de Castellane, sieur de Montmeyan; Jacques Viani; Charles de Raphaëlis, sieur de Saint Martin; Blaise Cabassol, bourgeois

1633: Scipion de Villeneuve, baron de Vence; Claude Augeri; Gaspard Audibert, écuyer; Jean-Baptiste Arnaud, écuyer

1634: François de Rascas, sieur Du Muy; Hercule de Pontèves; Pierre de Pelicot de Saint Paul; Mathieu Brun, bourgeois

1635: Claude d'Autric de Vintimille, sieur des Baumettes; Gaspard de Julianis; Antoine de Matheron, sieur de Salignac; Balthazar de Bouche, bourgeois

1636: by royal letters the above-named continued in office

1637: Gaspard de Forbin, marquis de Janson; Scipion Du Périer; François Audibert, écuyer; Joseph Templeri, écuyer

1638: François de Villeneuve, sieur d'Espinouse; Jacques Gaufridy; Melchion de Bompar, écuyer; Roullet Biolles, bourgeois

1639: François de Vintimille, sieur Du Luc (des comtes de Marseille); Antoine Decormis; Charles de Tressemanes, sieur de Chasteuil; Philippe Moricaud, bourgeois

1640: Jean-Baptiste de Castellane, sieur de La Verdière; Joseph Garidel; Jean-Baptiste d'Arcutia, sieur Du Revest; Jean Perrin, écuyer

1641: Henri de Cauvet, baron de Marignane; Jacques Mourgues; Jean de Séguiran; Gaspard Simon

1642: Charles de Grasse, comte Du Bar; Reynaud Du Fort; Melchion de Veteris, sieur Du Revest; Honoré Blegier, écuyer

1643: Armand de Romans, sieur de Serenon; Jean-Joseph Chabert; François de Boisson, écuyer; Honoré Fabre, bourgeois

1644: Jean d'Escalis, sieur de Saint Martin; Jean-Louis de Matheron, sieur de Salignac; Melchion de Bompar, écuyer; Jean-Baptiste d'Isnard, écuyer

1645: Alphonse d'Oraison, comte de Boulbon; Jean Blegier; Gaspard de Garnier de Ruffan, sieur de Rousset; Barthélemy Laget, bourgeois

1646: François de Rascas, sieur Du Muy; Jean d'Antelmi; Gaspard de Séguiran, sieur d'Auribeau; Jean Perrin, écuyer

1647: Sextius d'Escalis, baron de Bras et Ansouis; Guillaume de Séguiran; Louis Fortis, sieur de Claps; Barthélemy Bouche, bourgeois

1648: François de Villeneuve, sieur d'Espinouse; Jacques Viani; François de Beaumont, écuyer; Balthazar Rostolan, bourgeois

1649: by arrêt of the Parlement on January 21, and royal letters verified on March 27, it was ordered that second and third consuls be elected to serve with Sextius Escalis de Bras as first consul and Guillaume de Séguiran as assessor. On April 17 François de Durant, sieur de Montplaisant, and François Barthélemy, écuyer, were elected. By the treaty of August 8, the city was ordered to elect new consuls: Honoré de Brancas de Forcalquier, baron de Villeneuve; Antoine de Croze, sieur de Lincel; Pierre de Pelicot, sieur de Saint Paul; François Alphéran, écuyer.

1650: Jean-Henri de Puget, baron de Saint Marc; André Mathieu, sieur Du Fuveau; Marc-Antoine de Durant, écuyer; Melchion Delphin Hupays, écuyer

1651: Laurens de Forbin, marquis de Janson; Guillaume Blanc; François d'Honorat, sieur de Pourcils; Esprit Anglès, bourgeois

1652: Henri de Rascas, sieur Du Canet; Noel Gaillard; Pierre Thomassin, sieur Du Loubet; Joseph Cabassol, écuyer

1653: André d'Oraison, marquis d'Oraison et de Cadenet; Jean-Antoine de Michaelis, sieur Du Sueilh; Blaise de Thomas, sieur de Pierre-feu; Jean Bardon, bourgeois

1654: Jean-Baptiste de Castellane, sieur de La Verdière; Melchion Simon; Amant de Villeneuve, sieur de Vaucluse; Gaspard Dille, bourgeois

1655: François de Brancas de Forcalquier, baron de Vitrolles; Jean de Montaud; Joseph Dedons; Henri Colla, notaire

1656: M. de Castellane, sieur de Montmeyan; Joseph de Mimata; Joseph de Robert, sieur de Saint Césaire; Louis Cameron, bourgeois

1657: Jacques de Forbin, sieur de La Barben; Jacques Bounaud; Jean de Séguiran, écuyer; Antoine Estienne, écuyer

1658: André d'Aube, sieur de Roquemartine; Jean Peyssonel; Alexandre de Michaelis, écuyer; Joseph Redortier. By arrêt of the Vacations Chamber of the Parlement on July 22, Jean de Séguiran, second consul in 1657, was ordered to act as interim authority.

1659: Royal letters of August, verified on October 4, named François de Vintimille, sieur Du Luc (des comtes de Marseille); François d'Aymar; Christophe de Meynier, sieur de Lambert; Antoine Bonneau, bourgeois

# BIBLIOGRAPHY

Only primary sources have been listed in the bibliography. The footnotes are complete, and references to secondary works on specific subjects can be found there.

## MANUSCRIPTS

*Archives du Ministère des Affaires Etrangères*, Paris, Fonds France
Affaires intérieures, Provence, 794, 795 bis, 796, 797, 798, 800, 809, 858, 890, 895.
Provence, XVII<sup>e</sup> siècle, 1700, 1701, 1702, 1703, 1704, 1705, 1706, 1707, 1708, 1709, 1710, 1711, 1712, 1713, 1714, 1715, 1716, 1717, 1718, 1719, 1720, 1721, 1722, 1723, 1724, 1725.

*Archives départementales des Bouches-du-Rhône*, Marseille
Délibérations des Etats et des Assemblées générales des communautés, C 15, 16, 17, 19, 20, 22, 23, 25, 26, 27, 29, 30, 32, 33, 35, 37, 39.
Droits des amortissements, nouveaux acquêts, francs-fiefs, C 166.
Correspondance royale, C 986, 987, 988.
Privilèges du pays de Provence, C 2045, 2046, 2047, 2048, 2049, 2050, 2053, 2056, 2057, 2058, 2059.
Cahiers des remontrances des Trois Etats, C 2069, 2070.
Amirauté de Marseille, IX B2, IX B3.
Will of Charles III of Anjou, last comte de Provence, B 704.

*Archives départementales des Bouches-du-Rhône*, Aix-en-Provence
Fonds des notaires, Berlie, 301E, 217, 227E, 228, 232, 233, 234, 235; Lombard, 309E, 1067, 1070, 1071, 1072, 1074, 1077.
Lettres royaux, B 3347, 3348, 3349, 3350, 3351, 3352, 3353, 3354, 3355, 3356, 3357, 3358, 3359, 3360.
Procès de préséances, B 3588.
Taille des officiers du Parlement et de la Cour des Comptes, B 3598.
Délibérations et remontrances du Parlement, XVII<sup>e</sup> siècle, B 3663, 3664, 3665, 3666, 3667, 3668, 3684.

Bureau de police, B 3716, 3718, 3719, 3720.

"Recueil d'édits, déclarations, ordonnances, et arrêts, 1501-1789."

J.L.H. Hesmivy de Moissac, "Histoire du Parlement de Provence, 1501–1715," 2 volumes.

*Archives municipales, Aix-en-Provence,* Fonds anciens

Actes constitutifs et politiques, AA 1, AA 5, AA 6, AA 14, AA 21.

Délibérations des assemblées de la maison commune, BB 99, 100, 101, 102, 103, 104, 105.

Cartes et imprimés, F 24.

*Archives Nationales,* Paris

Arrêts du Conseil d'Etat, E 106A, 119A, 122D, 124B, 130B, 131A, 142A, 146A, 147A, 149A, 151C, 151D, 152B, 170B, 181A, 220A, 228A, 1684, 1689.

Registres du Conseil secret du Parlement de Paris, U28, U29.

*British Museum,* London

4421, "Les plans . . . des forteresses maritimes de Provence, F. Blondel, 1621."

4442, "Lettres de divers officiers au chancelier Séguier, 1659–1661."

4468, "Relation de toutes les choses se sont passées dans l'armée commandée par Monsieur le comte d'Harcourt et Monsieur le maréchal de Vitry, 1636."

4489, "Copies des lettres écrites par Mgr. le chancelier et lettres originales audit seigneur, 1656."

4490, "Lettres, missives originales écrites à Mgr. le chancelier par Mssrs. des Parlements de Provence, Rouen, Toulouse, Grenoble, 1656–1657."

4493, "Lettres des officiers des provinces à Mgr., 1658–1662."

4496, "From the Séguier collection: Various tracts printed and written on the subjects of coinage in France."

4575, "Semestre de Provence par M. de Sève, conseiller d'Etat."

4588, "Mémoires de M. le maréchal de Bassompierre," volume III.

*Bibliothèque Municipale,* Apt

"Collection sur la Provence," pièce 30, "Relation de ce qui s'est passé au Parlement de Provence sur la présentation de l'édit de la Chambre des Requêtes au mois de mars 1641."

*Bibliothèque Inguimbertine*, Carpentras
1841, "Actes et mémoires pour l'histoire de Provence depuis l'an 1590 jusques à 1637," fols. 346–370.

*Bibliothèque Mazarine*, Paris
2698, "Conseil secret de Parlement de Paris, copie des registres, 1648–1650," fols. 26–27, 39v–41.

*Bibliothèque Méjanes*, Aix-en-Provence
The first number is the item number in the *Catalogue général des manuscrits des bibliothèques publiques de France*, volume XV (Paris, 1894) by the abbé Albanès, for which there are two supplements. The second number in parentheses is the call number at the Méjanes. Short titles are used. Item and call numbers of additional copies of the manuscript also appear.

714 (792), "Mémoire du pays de Provence par Le Bret, intendant."
715 (259), "Mémoires concernants la Provence rédigés par M. Le Bret, intendant."
721–725 (608–612), "Administration du pays de Provence," 5 volumes.
726–732 (822–828), "Recueil de pièces sur la Provence," 7 volumes.
733–737 (829–833), "Recueil de pièces sur la Provence," 5 volumes.
739 (868), "Table des délibérations des Etats de Provence."
740–746 (613–619), "Table des délibérations des Assemblées générales des communautés."
776 (R.A. 8), "Recueil de mémoires et pièces relatifs à l'histoire de Provence et de la ville d'Aix," fols. 208–216, "Relation de la peste de 1629–1630 par Jean-Nicolas de Mimata, chanoine de l'église d'Aix, extrait du registre des délibérations du chapitre d'Aix de 1629 à 1639."
777 (R.A. 9), "Recueil de mémoires et pièces sur la Provence et la ville d'Aix," fol. 116, "Les grandes mémoires de Jacques de Gaufridi, 1622–1666."
781–782 (793–794), "Mémoires pour l'histoire de Provence," 2 volumes.
789 (R.A. 7), "Mémoires de Honoré d'Agut (1565–1643) et autres pièces relatives à l'histoire de Provence."
790 (625), "Histoire de Provence sous le règne de Louis XIII, par Jacques Gaufridy."

791 (799), "Recueil de pièces et histoire concernant Provence."

792 (800), "Recueil sur la Provence."

793 (R.A. 26), "Mémoires de Jacques de Gaufridy."

794 (R.A. 39), also 795 (736) and 796 (R.A. 39), "Histoire de Provence sous le fameux gouvernement du comte d'Alais par le sieur Pierre-Joseph de Haitze."

798 (R.A. 73), "Mémoires de Charles de Grimaldi, marquis de Régusse."

799 (1054), "Recueil de pièces sur la Provence par Mssrs. de Saint-Vincens."

800 (389), "Mémoires de Jean Robert de Brianson aixois (1633–1696)."

812 (836), "Histoire des troubles de Marseille sous la Fronde" appearing in "Recueil A, Provence," sections 2 and 3.

823 (776), "Recueil G: Pièces historiques," No. 5, "Remontrances au Roy sur la commission de Valence par la Cour des Aides."

856 (R.A. 10), "Aix ancienne et moderne, ou la topographie de la ville d'Aix par Pierre-Joseph de Haitze, 1715."

858–860 (1012–1014), "Notes et recherches sur la ville d'Aix, par M. de Saint-Vincens," 3 volumes.

864 (R.A. 40), "Recueil des pièces concernant l'agrandissement de la ville d'Aix en 1646–1650."

927 (R.A. 3), "Mémoires de M. Antoine de Valbelle, dressées en 1682 par maître Jean Russel, avocat en la cour."

929 (R.A. 25), "Mémoires d'Antoine de Felix, mort en 1675."

936 (903), "Histoire du Parlement de Provence par Honoré d'Agut."

937 (906), "Discours de l'institution du Parlement de Provence par Honoré d'Agut."

938 (R.A. 54), also 939 (904), 940 (905), 941 (1113), and 942 (944), "Histoire du Parlement de Provence (1501–1671) par Dominique Guidy."

946 (R.A. 53), "Histoire du Parlement de Provence (1501–1660) par Pierre Louvet."

947 (902), also 948–949 (R.A. 43), "Histoire du Parlement de Provence (1501–1715) par Jean-Louis Hyacinthe Hesmivy de Moissac," 2 volumes.

950 (634), "Notice du Parlement de Provence, 1788, Père Bicais."

350

953 (943), "Recueil de pièces relatives au Parlement de Provence."

954–956 (929–931), "Actes, pièces et mémoires concernants le Parlement de Provence, par M. de Saint-Vincens," 3 volumes.

957 (899), "Cérémonial du Parlement de Provence par Jean-Louis Hyacinthe Hesmivy de Moissac."

958 (900), "Mercuriales (1535–1686) et remontrances (1554–1761) du Parlement de Provence par M. de Saint-Vincens."

961–962 (936–937), also 963 (R.A. 52), "Difficultés entre le Parlement et les diverses autorités, par J.L.H. Hesmivy de Moissac," 2 volumes.

964–967 (939–942) "Extraits des délibérations du Parlement de Provence, mercuriales et histoire," 4 volumes.

968–982 (947–961), "Délibérations du Parlement de Provence," 15 volumes.

984–993 (869–878), "Table des délibérations du Parlement de Provence."

995–996 (R.A. 51), "Mémoires des délibérations et procédures sur la suspension de la cour du Parlement de Provence," 2 volumes.

1005–1012 (891–898), "Table et analyse des registres des lettres royaux du Parlement de Provence," 8 volumes.

1013–1020 (860–867), "Table des lettres royaux enregistrées au Parlement de Provence," 8 volumes.

1023 (R.A. 57), "Registre des délibérations de la Cour des Comptes, 1649–1671."

1024 (1114), "Règlements, concordats, arrêts du Conseil, touchant les rangs, séances, jurisdictions et autorités des officiers de cette province."

1142 (R.A. 47), "Abrégé des délibérations du corps de la noblesse de Provence." 1142 (630), "Etat du florinage contenant le revenu noble de tous les fiefs et arrière-fiefs de Provence avec les noms des possesseurs fait par Maynier d'Oppède en 1668."

1182 (377), "Mémoire abrégé sur la vie de Magdeleine de Gaillard-Longjumeau."

1184 (632), also 1185 (802) and 1186 (R.A. 6), "Vie de seigneurs Jean et Gaspard de Pontevès, comtes de Carcès."

1258 (1140), "Livre de raison par Léon de Trimond, conseiller au Semestre."

1273 (1155), "Recueil de pièces sur le Parlement de Provence."

1421 (1286), "Recueil d'actes notariés et pièces diverses relatives à l'histoire de Provence et du comté de Nice."

1574 (1439), "Livre de raison de François-Boniface Laydet, seigneur de Fombeton (1675–1756)."

1626 (1491), "Recueil de pièces originales ou copies relatives à la famille d'Espagnet."

*Bibliothèque Nationale*, Paris

Cabinet des Titres, Pièces originales and Dossiers bleus.

Fonds Clairambault, 380, 388, 389, 390, 391, 392, 393, 394, 395, 396, 397, 398, 399, 400, 401, 403, 405, 408, 409, 410, 414, 416, 419, 420, 422, 434, 435, 657, letters of the comte de Brienne, secretary of state for Provence, 1643–1647.

Fonds Dupuy 154, 498, 659, 672, 754, mémoires, speeches, tracts on the Parlement.

Manuscrits français 16518, "Parlement et Etats de Provence, remontrances"; 17367–17397, "Correspondance de Pierre Séguier"; 18975–18977, "Recueil de pièces et manuscrits concernant la Provence et particulièrement le Parlement de Provence, composés de papiers du chancelier Séguier"; 24166. "Mémoire touchant le Parlement de Provence"; 24169, "Procès-verbal contenant l'état véritable de la côte maritime de Provence par Henri Ségurian de Bouc"; 20655-20656, "Papiers de Henri-Auguste de Loménie, comte de Brienne, 1640-1664."

Manuscrits français nouvelles acquisitions 173, fols. 382–489, "Recettes et dépenses pour les généralités de Toulouse, Bourgogne, Provence, Dauphiné en 1647"; 199, "Brevets de la taille en 1634, 1637, 1639, 1643, 1663, 1665, 1672."

Mélanges de Colbert 7, fols. 49–53, "Mémoire sur le Parlement de Provence, 1663," fols. 41v–43v, "Pensions des officiers du Parlement et de la Chambre des Comptes, Cour des Aides de Provence, 1606–1656"; 288 "Précis ou Abrégés des Etats de Provence, 1620–1664."

*Musée d'Arbaud*, Aix-en-Provence

"Plan géométrique de la ville d'Aix, capitale de la Provence, Jacques Cundier, 1640, 1683."

"Plan géométrat de la ville et ses dehors d'Aix, capitale de Provence divisée en ses cinq quartiers, Esprit Devoux." (Also B.N., Ms. fr. n.a. 677) "Comte de gouvernment de Provence avec les pays circonvoisins, Sanson d'Abbeville, 1690."

352

"Carte de Provence et des terres adjacentes, Guillaume Delisle, 1715."
The following cartons contain printed copies of seventeenth and eighteenth-century arrêts of the Parlement and Cour des Comptes, ordinances of the governors and intendants, lettres royaux, and arrêts du Conseil d'Etat: Provence 332, "Gouverneurs et intendants"; 348–349, "Parlement de Provence"; 352, "Divers institutions judiciaires, Intendants de Provence"; 353, "Famille de Forbin"; 355, "Conflits entre le Parlement de Provence et la Cour des Comptes"; 426–427, "La Noblesse"; Bouches-du-Rhône, Aix, 468, "Fronde et Ligue."

## PUBLISHED

Alliot, Gervais, and Langlois, Jacques. *Journal du Parlement de Paris*. Paris, 1648.

———. *Suite du Journal contenant ce qui s'est passé depuis le premier janvier*. Paris, 1649. (Bibliothèque Mazarine, Paris).

Baratier, Edouard, ed. *Documents de l'histoire de la Provence*. Toulouse, 1971.

Bomy, Jean de. *Recueil de quelques statuts et coutumes non encore imprimés jusques à present*. Aix, 1620.

———. *Statuts et coutumes du pays de Provence, avec les glosses de M. L. Masse*. Aix, 1620.

Boniface, Hyacinthe. *Arrêts notables de la cour du Parlement de Provence, Cour des Comptes, aides et finances du meme pays*. Aix, 1750, 9 volumes.

———. *Suite des arrêts notables de la cour du Parlement de Provence*. Lyon, 1689, 3 volumes.

[Bouchard]. *Les confessions de Jean-Jacques Bouchard, parisien, suivies de son voyage de Paris à Rome en 1630, publiées pour la première fois sur les manuscrits de l'auteur*. Paris, 1881.

Bouche, Honoré. *La chorographie ou description de Provence et l'histoire chronologique du même pays depuis l'établissement de son comté jusques aujourd'hui*. Aix, 1664, 2 volumes.

Brosses, Charles de. *Lettres familières sur l'Italie*. Paris, 1869.

Chouppes, Aymar de, Marquis. *Abrégés des délibérations de l'Assemblée générale des communautés de Provence, 1612–1689*.

———. *Mémoires du marquis de Chouppes (1612–1673), lieutenant général des armées du roi*, ed. C. Moreau. Paris, 1861.

Clapiers-Collongues, Balthasar de. *Chronologie des officiers des cours souveraines, publiée, annotée et augmentée par le marquis de Boisgelin*. Aix, 1909–1912.

Cundier, Jacques. *Portraits des premiers présidents du Parlement de Provence*. Aix, 1724. (Bibliothèque Méjanes 951 [963]).

Debezieux, Balthasar. *Arrêts notables de la cour du Parlement de Provence*. Paris, 1750.

Depping, G. P., ed. *Correspondance administrative sous le règne de Louis XIV*. Paris, 1850–1855, 4 volumes.

Grégoire, Paul abbé. *Explication des cérémonies de la Fête-Dieu d'Aix*, Aix 1777.

Grimaldi, Charles de, marquis de Régusse; and Gaufridy, Jacques. *Mémoires pour servir à l'histoire de la Fronde en Provence*. Aix, 1870.

Haitze, Pierre-Joseph de. *Les curiosités les plus remarquables de la ville d'Aix*. Aix, 1679.

———. *Histoire de la ville d'Aix, capitale de la Provence*. Aix, 1880–1892, 6 volumes.

———. *Portraits ou éloges historiques des premiers présidents du Parlement de Provence*. Avignon, 1727.

Isambert, François-André, ed. *Recueil général des anciennes lois françaises depuis l'an 420 jusqu'à la Révolution de 1789*. Paris, 1821–1833, 29 volumes.

Julien, Jean-Joseph. *Nouveau commentaire sur les statuts de Provence*. Aix, 1778, 2 volumes.

Lublinskaya, Alexksandra Dmitrievna, ed. *Vnutrenniaia politika frantsuzskogo absoliutizma, 1633–1649* [The Internal Politics of French Absolutism]. Leningrad, 1966.

Mazarin, Jules. *Lettres du cardinal Mazarin pendant son ministère*, Pierre-Adolphe Chéruel and Georges d'Avenel ed. Paris, 1872–1906, 9 volumes.

Mildmay, William, "An Account of the Southern Maritime Provinces of France," in *Political Treatises*. London, 1766.

Morgues, Jacques. *Les statuts et coutumes du pays de Provence*. Aix, 1635.

Mousnier, Roland, ed. *Lettres et mémoires adressés au chancelier Séguier (1633–1649)*. Paris, 1964, 2 volumes.

Nostradamus, César de. *L'histoire et chronique de Provence*. Lyon, 1624.

Peiresc, Nicolas Claude Fabri de. *Lettres aux frères Dupuy*, ed. Philippe Tamizey de Larroque. Paris, 1888–1898, 7 volumes.

Pitton, Jean-Scholastique. *Histoire de la ville d'Aix, capitale de la Provence, contenante toute de qui s'est passée de memorable dans son état politique jusqu'à l'année 1665*. Aix, 1666.

[Platter]. *Félix et Thomas Platter à Montpellier, 1552–1559, 1595–1599: notes de voyage de deux étudiants bâlois*. Montpellier, 1892.

Retz, Paul de Gondi, cardinal de. *Mémoires du cardinal de Retz, et Guy Joli, et de la duchesse de Nemours*. Paris, 1820, 6 volumes.

Richelieu, Armand Jean de Plessis, cardinal, duc de. *Lettres, instructions diplomatiques et papiers d'état du cardinal de Richelieu*, ed. Georges d'Avenel. Paris, 1853–1877, 8 volumes.

———. *Mémoires du cardinal de Richelieu*, ed. P. Lacour-Gayet and R. Lavolée. Paris, 1907–1931, 10 volumes. Two previous editions by Petitot in 1823 and by Michaud and Poujoulat in 1837–1838.

Ruffi, Antoine de. *Histoire de la ville de Marseille*. Marseille, 1696. Sapey, Charles-Alexandre. *Etudes biographiques pour servir à l'histoire de l'ancienne magistrature française: Guillaume Du Vair, Antoine Le Maistre*. Paris, 1858: 337–488, letters of Du Vair, 1597 to 1608.

Savine, Albert. *Relation des troubles occasionnés en Provence par l'établissement d'une Chambre-Semestre et du mouvement dit le Sabre*. Aix, 1881.

[Sévigné]. Monmerqué, Louis, ed. *Lettres de Madame de Sévigné*. Paris, 1862–1866, 14 volumes.

Sourdis, Henri d'Escoubleau, archbishop of Bordeaux. *Correspondance, 1636–1642*. Paris, 1839, 3 volumes.

Tavernier, Félix. *Marseille et la Provence sous la royauté, 1481–1789: textes pour l'enseignement de l'histoire*. Marseille, n.d.

Tholosan, J. *Privilèges, franchises et immunités concédés par les rois et comtes de Provence à la ville d'Aix*. Aix, 1620.

Young, Arthur. *Travels during the Years 1787, 1788, and 1789, Undertaken More Particularly with a View of Ascertaining the Cultivation, Wealth, Resources, and National Prosperity of the Kingdom of France*. 2d ed., London, 1794, 2 volumes.

**355**

MAZARINADES

*Bibliothèque municipale*, Marseille

1792, *Recueil de divers pièces sur les troubles de Provence*

*Relation véritable de ce qui s'est fait et passée dans la ville d'Aix* (1649), also M. Arbaud 468.

*Lettre d'un gentilhomme sur la ville d'Aix* (1649), also M. Arbaud 468.

*Lettre de Pierre de Provence à la reine* (1649).

*Relation véritable de ce qui s'est passée en la défaite* (1649).

*Relation véritable de toute ce qui s'est faite et passée en la bataille du Val* (1649).

*Ordonnance de Monseigneur Louis de Valois, comte d'Alais* (1649), also 1795.

*Arrêt de la cour du Parlement de Provence contre les perturbateurs du repos et tranquilité publique* (1649), also B.N., Dupuy 754.

*Très humble remontrance du Parlement de Provence au roy sur le gouvernement de Monsieur le Comte d'Alais* (1649), also 1794 and 1102.

*La voix du peuple de Provence* (1649), also 1796 and B.N., Ms. fr. 18977, fol. 264.

*Cahiers des remontrances faites au roy* (n.d., 1649?).

*Lettre du roy écrite à la cour du Parlement de Provence* (n.d., 1649?).

*Réponse d'Ariste à Clytophon* (1649).

*Très humbles remontrances du Parlement de Provence au semestre de janvier* (n.d., 1649?).

*Harangue faite par M. Theroult, conseiller député du Parlement de Provence à la Chambre des Vacations du Parlement de Paris, 20 octobre 1649.*

*Arrêt du Parlement de Provence sur les nouveaux troubles dans la ville de Marseille* (1650).

*Les plaintes de la noblesse de Provence contre l'oppression du Parlement* (n.d., 1650?), also British Museum, *Parlement de Bordeaux* (1650).

*Lettres de la noblesse de Provence à son altesse royale* (1650).

*Les bons sentiments de la véritable noblesse de Provence* (1650).

*Les pensées du provençal solitaire* (1650), also British Museum, *Parlement Bordeaux* (1650).

*Réponse du fidèle Provençal au calomniateur* (n.d., 1650?).

*Très humble supplication faite à Monseigneur le Garde des Sceaux* (n.d., 1650?).

*Arrêt du Parlement de Provence contre le cardinal Mazarin* (1651); Moreau condemns as false.

*Relation extraordinaire de ce qui s'est passée en Provence en faveur de Messieurs les princes* (1651).

*Remontrance faite au roy et à la reine regente par Monsieur le président de Gallifet* (1651), also 1798.

*Harangue faite au roy et à la reine regente par le sieur Girau (d?)* (1651).

*Relation envoyée par un gentilhomme de Provence* (1651), also M. Arbaud 468.

*Harangue faite à l'ouverture du Parlement de Provence par Monsieur le baron de La Roquette* (1651).

*Lettre du roy écrite au Parlement de Provence* (1651).

*Le courrier provençal sur l'arrivée du duc de Mercoeur* (1652).

*Relation du soulèvement de Provence contre le duc de Mercoeur* (1652).

*Lettres des Trois Etats de Provence à Monsieur le Guise* (1652).

*Lettre circulaire des Messieurs du Parlement de Provence* (1652).

1103, *Arrêt du Conseil d'Etat portant règlement entre la Cour de Parlement de Provence et Monsieur le maréchal de Vitry, gouverneur* (1649).

1790, *Arrêt de la cour de Parlement de Provence, 23 juin 1649.*

1791, *Discours fait par les députés du Parlement de Provence dans le Parlement de Paris, 15 et 28 janvier 1649.*

1797, *Arrêt du Conseil d'Etat sur les évocations accordées à ceux qui ont suivis et servis M. le comte d'Alais en ces derniers mouvements* (1650).

1799, *Arrêt de la Cour de Parlement tenant la Chambre des Vacations concernant règlement sur le fait de la peste du 17 juillet 1629.*

6039. *Remontrance faite à M. le prince dans la ville d'Avignon par Mssrs. les députés de la Cour de Parlement de Provence prononcée par M. le président de Monier, 13 fevrier 1631* (Aix, 1631).

*Bibliothèque Nationale*

Fonds Dupuy 754, *Remontrance au peuple de Provence* (1649).
  *Lettre de R. P. Archange, carme déchaussée* (n.d., 1649?).
  *Relation de ce qui s'est passée en la ville de Marseille* (1650).
  *Marseille delivrée de la tyrannie de Monsieur le comte d'Alais* (1650).
  Manuscrits francais 18977, *Remontrances de ceux du pays de Provence au roy, principalement contre le Parlement* (1649).
  *La justice persecutée par les armes du comte d'Alais* (n.d., 1649?), also Fonds Dupuy 754, fols. 270–278.
  *Manifeste de la ville d'Aix* (n.d., 1649?), also M. Arbaud 468.
  *Manifeste de Monsieur le comte d'Alais* (1649).
  *Justification des armes de Monsieur le comte d'Alais* (1649).
  *Réponse à la fausse relation du Parlement de Provence* (n.d., 1649?)
  *Articles donnés par Monsieur le comte d'Alais aux Messieurs les députés des Etats de Languedoc* (1649), *Avec réponse.*
  *Justification du comte d'Alais contre les calomnies du Parlement de Provence* (n.d., 1649?).
  *Factum servant au procès* (Marseille, n.d., 1650?).
  *Factum pour Jean-Baptiste Coquillat* (Marseille, n.d., 1650–1651?).

*Musée Arbaud*, Aix

468. "Fronde et ligue," *Déclaration de la volonté du roy et de la reine regente* (August, 1649).
  *Déclaration des volontés du roy* (August, 1649).
  *Relation de la défaite d'une compagnie de chevaux legers* (n.d., 1649?).

*Harvard Libraries*

*Relation de ce qui s'est passée à Marseille dans le voyage de Monsieur le comte d'Alais* (1650).

*Archives des Affaires Etrangères*, Paris

Fonds France 1714, fols. 273–279, *Les doléances de la noblesse de Provence* (1650).

*Bibliothèque Méjanes*, Aix

The Méjanes has a general collection of 4,000 to 5,000 mazarinades in 82 *recueils*. The most important, containing Provençal mazarinades, are 27136 and 27119. The titles have not been separately listed because they are mostly duplicates of those already listed.

Published sources on mazarinades include

Lindsay, Robert, and Neu, John. *Mazarinades: A Checklist of Copies in Major Collections in the United States.* Metuchen, New Jersey, 1972.

Moreau, Célestin. *Bibliographie de mazarinades.* Paris, 1850–1851, 3 volumes.

———. *Choix de mazarinades.* Paris, 1853, 2 volumes.

# INDEX OF SUBJECTS

# INDEX OF NAMES

Names of individuals appear as they are most frequently cited in the text.

LIBRARY OF CONGRESS CATALOGING IN PUBLICATION DATA

Kettering, Sharon, 1942–
    Judicial politics and urban revolt in seven-
teenth-century France.

    Bibliography: p.
    Includes index.
    1.  Aix, France—Politics and government.
2.  Judges—France—Aix.      3.  France—Parliament
(Aix)      4.  France—Politics and government—17th
century.      I.  Title.
DC801.A325K47          320.9′44′91032          77–85543
ISBN 0–691–05267–0